SAMS
Teach Yourself

Java 2

Rogers Cadenhead

in 24 Hours

THIRD EDITION

 800 E. 96th Street, Indianapolis, Indiana, 46240 USA

Sams Teach Yourself Java 2 in 24 Hours, Third Edition

Copyright © 2003 by Sams Publishing

International Standard Book Number: 0-672-32460-1

Library of Congress Catalog Card Number: 2002106457

Printed in the United States of America

First Printing: October 2002

05   04

Trademarks

Warning and Disclaimer

ACQUISITIONS EDITOR
Kathryn Purdum

DEVELOPMENT EDITOR
Scott Meyers

MANAGING EDITOR
Charlotte Clapp

PROJECT EDITORS
Elizabeth Finney
Katelyn Cozatt

COPY EDITORS
Seth Kerney
Lindsey Rue

INDEXER
Erika Millen

TECHNICAL EDITOR
John Purdum

TEAM COORDINATOR
Amy Patton

INTERIOR DESIGNER
Gary Adair

COVER DESIGNER
Aren Howell

PAGE LAYOUT
D&G Limited, LLC

Contents at a Glance

Contents

About the Author

Rogers Cadenhead is a writer, Web application developer, and the most valuable player in an NBA playoff game[*]. He has written 15 books on Internet-related topics, including *Sams Teach Yourself Java 2 in 21 Days*, *Sams Teach Yourself Microsoft FrontPage 2002 in 24 Hours*, and *How to Use the Internet*. He maintains this book's official World Wide Web site at http://www.java24hours.com.

*Cadenhead attended Game 6 of the 1988 NBA Western Conference Finals at Reunion Arena in Dallas. The Dallas Mavericks beat the Los Angeles Lakers 105-103 to force a seventh game of the series. CBS Sports gave half the MVP award to Mavericks power forward Mark Aguirre for 23 points and 13 rebounds, and half to the sellout crowd of 17,007 for shouting a whole lot in loud voices and making enthusiastic hand gestures.

Cadenhead's statistics in the game:

PLAYER	MIN	FGM-FGA	FTM-FTA	OFF-DEF-TOT	AST	PF	ST	TO	PTS	BEERS	AVG. DECIBEL LEVEL	TRIPS TO BATHROOM
CADENHEAD	0	0-0	0-0	0 0 0	0	0	0	0	00	05	80	3

About the Technical Editor

JOHN PURDUM is a software engineer for Roche Diagnostics Corporation in Indianapolis, Indiana. Currently he is developing both stand-alone and Web-based Java applications for the Business Information Warehouse, specializing in reusable component development. Prior to his current job, he was a software engineer consultant specializing in Visual Basic and C++ development for Bank One. Programming with the Java language has been the most enlightening and fulfilling aspect of his career.

Dedication

To the Klez e-mail worm, which makes sure that I always have new email to read, even if it's gibberish from total strangers who practice unsafe computing. To the Jacksonville Jaguars offensive line, which could teach us all a lesson about finding ways to let people in instead of building walls to keep them out. To Ronald McDonald, who helped prepare my body for the next Ice Age, in which my ability to retain large amounts of heat will make it easier for me to survive. To the Texas Rangers pitching staff, who always make others feel at ease by helping them get home. And to my wife Mary and my sons Max, Eli, and Sam. What...did you think I was going to say something sarcastic about them, too?—Rogers

Acknowledgments

To the folks at Sams—especially Katie Purdum, Scott Meyers, Elizabeth Finney, John Purdum, and Seth Kerney. No author can produce a book like this on his own, regardless of what my agent told Sams during contract negotiations. Their excellent work will give me plenty to take credit for later on.

To Neil Salkind and Jessica Richards at the Studio B agency, who worked hard on my behalf in regard to this title and many others.

To my wife, Mary, and my sons, Max, Eli, and Sam. Although our family has not fulfilled my dream of becoming a high-wire trapeze team like the Flying Wallendas, I'm the world's proudest husband in a non-acrobatic family.

We Want to Hear from You!

As the reader of this book, *you* are our most important critic and commentator. We value your opinion and want to know what we're doing right, what we could do better, what areas you'd like to see us publish in, and any other words of wisdom you're willing to pass our way.

You can email or write me directly to let me know what you did or didn't like about this book—as well as what we can do to make our books stronger.

Please note that I cannot help you with technical problems related to the topic of this book, and that due to the high volume of mail I receive, I might not be able to reply to every message.

When you write, please be sure to include this book's title and author as well as your name and phone or email address. I will carefully review your comments and share them with the author and editors who worked on the book.

Email: webdev@samspublishing.com

Mail: Mark Taber
           Associate Publisher
           Sams Publishing
           201 West 103rd Street
           Indianapolis, IN 46290 USA

Reader Services

For more information about this book or others from Sams Publishing, visit our Web site at www.samspublishing.com. Type the ISBN (excluding hyphens) or the title of the book in the Search box to find the book you're looking for.

Introduction

As the author of computer books, I spend a lot of time loitering in the computer section of bookstores such as Barnes & Noble and Borders, observing the behavior of shoppers browsing through the books as if they were a hominid jawbone and I was a paleontologist.

Because of my research, I've learned that if you have picked up this book and turned to the introduction, I have around 12 more seconds before you put it down and head to the coffee bar for a double tall latte decaf skim with two shots of vanilla hold the whip.

So I'll keep this brief: This Java programming stuff is a lot easier than it looks. I'm not supposed to tell you that, because there are thousands of programmers who have used their Java skills to get high-paying jobs in software development, Internet programming, and e-commerce. The last thing any of them want is for their bosses to know that anyone who has persistence and a little free time can learn this language, the most popular programming language in use today. By working your way through each of the one-hour tutorials in *Sams Teach Yourself Java 2 in 24 Hours* you'll be able to learn Java programming quickly.

Anyone can learn how to write computer programs—even if they can't program a VCR. Java is one of the best programming languages to learn because it's a useful, powerful, modern technology that's being used by thousands of programmers around the world.

This book is aimed at non-programmers, new programmers who hated learning the subject, and experienced programmers who want to quickly get up to speed with Java. It uses Java 2 version 1.4, the current version of the language.

Java is the Tiger Woods of programming languages because of the things it makes possible. You can create programs that feature a graphical user interface, design software that makes the most of the Internet, connect to databases, add animation and sound to World Wide Web pages, and more.

This book teaches Java programming from the grounds up. It introduces the concepts in English instead of jargon, with plenty of step-by-step examples of working programs you will create. Spend 24 hours with this book and you'll be writing your own Java programs, confident in your ability to use the language and learn more about it. You also will have skills that are becoming increasingly important—such as network computing, graphical user interface design, and object-oriented programming.

These terms might not mean much to you now. In fact, they're probably the kind of things that make programming seem like a secret ritual known only to a small group of humans who have a language of their own. However, if you can use a computer to create an attractive resume, balance your checkbook, or create a home page, you can write computer programs by reading *Sams Teach Yourself Java 2 in 24 Hours*.

At this point, if you would rather have coffee than Java, please reshelve this book with the front cover facing outward on an endcap with access to a lot of the store's foot traffic.

PART I
Getting Started

Hour

Hour **1**

Becoming a Programmer

Computer programming is insanely difficult. It requires a four-year degree in computer science, thousands of dollars in computer hardware and software, a keen analytical intellect, the patience of Job, and a strong liking for caffeinated drinks. If you're a programming novice, this is probably what you've heard about computer programming. Aside from the part about caffeine, all of the rumors are greatly exaggerated.

Programming is a lot easier than most people think, although there are several reasons why you might believe otherwise:

- Computer programmers have been telling people for years that programming is hard. This belief makes it easier for us to find high-paying jobs (or so I've heard), and gives us more leeway to goof off during business hours.

- Computer programming manuals are often written in a language that only a Scrabble player could appreciate. Strange acronyms like OOP, RAD, COM, and MUMPS are used frequently along with newly invented jargon like instantiation, bytecode, and makefile.

- Many computer programming languages have been available only with software packages costing $200 or more, which is a lot of cabbage.

Because of the growth of the Internet and other factors, this is a great time to learn programming. Useful programming tools are being made available at low cost (or no cost), often as downloads from World Wide Web sites. Thousands of programmers are distributing their work under "open source" licenses so people can examine how the programs were written, correct errors, and add their own improvements.

The goal of this book is to teach programming to the person who has never tried to program before, or the person who tried programming but hated it with an intense passion. The English language will be used as much as possible instead of jargon and obscure acronyms, and all new programming terms will be thoroughly explained as they are introduced.

If I've succeeded, you will finish *Sams Teach Yourself Java 2 in 24 Hours* with enough programming skill to be a danger to yourself and others. You'll be able to write programs, dive into other programming books with more confidence, and learn programming languages more easily. You also will have developed skills with Java, the most exciting programming language to be introduced in a decade.

The first hour of this book provides some introductory material about programming and gives you instructions on how to set up your computer so you can write Java programs. The following topics will be covered:

- Choosing which programming language to learn first
- What Java is
- Using programs to boss your computer around
- How programs work
- How program errors (called *bugs*) are fixed
- Acquiring a Java development tool
- Getting ready to write programs

Choosing a Language

As you might have surmised at this point, computer programming is not as hard as it's cracked up to be. If you're comfortable enough with a computer to create a nice-looking resume, balance a checkbook with software such as Intuit Quicken, or create your own home page on the Web, you can write programs.

The key to learning how to program is to start with the right language. The programming language you choose often depends on the tasks you want the computer to accomplish. Each language has things it is well-suited for, as well as things that are difficult—perhaps impossible—to do with the language. For example, many people use some form of the BASIC language when they are learning how to program because BASIC was created with beginners in mind.

> The BASIC language was invented in the 1960s to be easy for students and beginners to learn (the B in BASIC stands for *Beginner's*). The downside to using some form of BASIC is that it's easy to fall into some sloppy programming habits with the language. Those habits can make it much more difficult to write complex programs and improve them later.

Microsoft Visual Basic combines the ease of BASIC with some powerful features to aid in the design of Windows software. (VBScript, which is short for Visual Basic Script, offers the simplicity of BASIC for small programs that run in conjunction with World Wide Web pages.) Visual Basic has been used to write thousands of sophisticated programs for commercial, business, and personal use. However, Visual Basic programs can be slower than Windows programs written in other languages, such as Borland C++. This difference is especially noticeable in programs that use a lot of graphics—games, screen savers, and the like.

This book covers the Java programming language, which was developed by Sun Microsystems. Though Java is more difficult to learn than a language such as Visual Basic, it is a good starting place for several reasons. One of the biggest advantages of learning Java is that you can use it on the World Wide Web. If you're an experienced Web surfer, you have seen numerous Java programs in action. They can be used to create animated graphics, present text in new ways, play games, and help in other interactive efforts.

Another important advantage is that Java requires an organized approach for getting programs to work. The language is very particular about the way programs must be written, and it balks if programmers do not follow all of its rules. When you start writing Java programs, you might not see the language's choosy behavior as an advantage. You'll write a program and have several errors to fix before the program is finished. Some of your fixes might not be correct, and they will have to be redone. If you don't structure a program correctly as you are writing it, errors will result. In the coming hours, you'll learn about these rules and the pitfalls to avoid. The positive side of this extra effort is that your programs will be more reliable, useful, and error-free.

Java was invented by Sun Microsystems developer James Gosling as a better way to create computer programs. Gosling was unhappy with the way that the C++ programming language was working on a project he was doing, so he created a new language that did the job better. It's a matter of contentious debate whether Java is superior to other programming languages, of course, but the amount of attention paid to the language today shows that it has a large number of adherents. Book publishers obviously dig it—more than 1,000 books have been published about the language since its introduction. (This is my tenth, and I will keep writing more of them until prohibited by municipal, state, or federal law.)

Regardless of whether Java is the best language, it definitely is a great language to learn today. There are numerous resources for Java programmers on the Web, Java job openings are offered in many cities, and the language has become a major part of the Internet's past, present, and future. You'll get a chance to try out Java during Hour 2, "Writing Your First Program."

Learning Java or any other programming language makes it much easier to learn subsequent languages. Many languages are similar to each other, so you won't be starting from scratch when you dive into a new one. For instance, many C++ programmers find it fairly easy to learn Java, because Java borrows a lot of its structure and ideas from C++. Many programmers are comfortable using several different languages and will learn new ones as needed.

C++ is mentioned several times in this hour, and you might be tripping over the term wondering what it means, and more importantly, how it's pronounced. C++ is pronounced *C-Plus-Plus*, and it's a programming language that was developed by Bjarne Stroustrop and others at Bell Laboratories. C++ is an enhancement of the C programming language, hence the *Plus-Plus* part of the name. Why not just C+, then? The *Plus-Plus* part is a computer programming joke you'll understand later on.

Telling the Computer What to Do

A computer program, also called *software*, is a way to tell a computer what to do. Everything that the computer does, from booting up to shutting down, is done by a program. Windows XP is a program. *Ms. Pac-Man* is a program. The dir command used in MS-DOS to display file names is also a program. Even the Klez email worm is a program.

Computer programs are made up of a list of commands the computer handles in a specific order when the program is run. Each of these commands is called a *statement*.

If you're a science fiction fan, you're probably familiar with the concept of household robots. If not, you might be familiar with the concept of henpecked spouses. In either case, someone gives very specific instructions telling the robot or spouse what to do, something like the following:

Dear Theobald,

Please take care of these errands for me while I'm out lobbying members of Congress:

Item 1: Vacuum the living room.

Item 2: Go to the store.

Item 3: Pick up butter, lozenges, and as many bottles of Heinz E-Z Squirt green ketchup as you can carry.

Item 4: Return home.

Love,

Snookie Lumps

If you tell a loved one or artificially intelligent robot what to do, there's a certain amount of leeway in how your requests are fulfilled. If lozenges aren't available, cough medicine might be brought to you instead. Also, the trip to the store can be accomplished through a variety of routes. Computers don't do leeway. They follow instructions literally. The programs that you write will be followed precisely, one statement at a time.

The following is one of the simplest examples of a computer program, written in BASIC. Take a look at it, but don't worry yet about what each line is supposed to mean.

```
1 PRINT "Shall we play a game?"
2 INPUT A$
```

Translated into English, this program is equivalent to giving a computer the following to-do list:

Dear personal computer,

Item 1: Display the question, "Shall we play a game?"

Item 2: Give the user a chance to answer the question.

Love,

Snookie Lumps

Each of the lines in the computer program is a statement. A computer handles each statement in a program in a specific order, in the same way that a cook follows a recipe, or Theobald the robot followed the orders of Snookie Lumps when he vacuumed and shopped at the market. In BASIC, the line numbers are used to put the statements in the correct order. Other languages, such as Java, do not use line numbers, favoring different ways to tell the computer how to run a program.

Figure 1.1 shows the sample BASIC program running on the Liberty BASIC interpreter, a shareware program that can be used to develop Windows and OS/2 programs. Liberty BASIC, which was developed by Carl Gundel, is among many BASIC interpreters that can be found on the Internet for Microsoft Windows, Apple Macintosh, Unix, and Linux systems. You can find out more about it at `http://www.libertybasic.com`.

FIGURE 1.1

An example of a BASIC program running in Liberty BASIC.

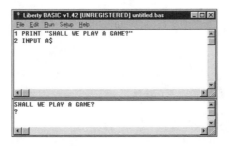

The quote "Shall we play a game?" is from the 1983 movie *WarGames*, in which a young computer programmer (portrayed by Matthew Broderick) saves mankind after nearly causing global thermonuclear war and the near-extinction of humankind. You'll learn how to do that in the next book of this series, *Sams Teach Yourself to Create International Incidents with Java in 24 Hours*.

Because of the way programs operate, it's hard to blame the computer when something goes wrong while your program runs. After all, the computer was just doing exactly what you told it to do. Unless your hardware is on the fritz, a pesky virus is attacking your system, or your operating system is having a bad day, the blame for program errors lies with the programmer. That's the bad news. The good news is that you can't do any permanent harm to your computer with the programming errors you make. No one was harmed during the making of this book, and no computers will be injured as you learn how to program with Java.

How Programs Work

Most computer programs are written in the same way that you write a letter—by typing each statement into a word processor. Some programming tools come with their own word processor, and others can be used with any text-editing software. If you don't already have a tool that can be used for Java programming, you can use the free Java 2 Software Development Kit, which you will learn about later in this hour, with any of your favorite editors.

When you have finished writing a computer program, you save the file just like saving any other document to disk. Computer programs often have their own filename extension to indicate what type of file they are. Java programs have the extension `.java`; an example of a Java program file name is `Calculator.java`.

> If you use a fancy word processing program that has features such as bold-faced text, different font sizes, and other stylistic touches, do not use those features while writing a computer program. Programs should be prepared as text files with no special formatting. For example, when using Microsoft Word to write a program, save the file in Text Only mode instead of saving it as a Word document. Notepad, a word processor that comes with Windows, saves all files as unformatted text. The vi editor on Linux systems can also be used to create text files without formatting.

To run a program you have saved as a file, you need some help. The kind of help that's needed depends on the programming language you're using. Some languages require an *interpreter* to run their programs. The interpreter is a program that interprets each line of a computer program and tells the computer what to do. Most versions of BASIC are interpreted languages. The advantage of interpreted languages is that they are faster to test. When you are writing a BASIC program, you can try it out immediately, spot any errors, fix them, and try again. The primary disadvantage is that interpreted languages run more slowly than other programs.

Other programming languages require a *compiler*. The compiler takes a computer program and translates it into a form that the computer can understand. It also does what it can to make the program run as efficiently as possible. The compiled program can be run directly without the need for an interpreter. Compiled programs run more quickly than interpreted programs, but they take more time to test. You have to write your program and compile it before trying it out. If you find an error and fix it, you must compile the program again to verify that the error is gone.

Java is unusual because it requires a compiler and an interpreter. You'll learn more about this later as you write Java programs.

How Programs Don't Work

Many new programmers become discouraged when they start to test their programs. Errors appear everywhere. Some of these are *syntax errors*, which are identified by the computer as it looks at the program and becomes confused by what you wrote. Other errors are *logic errors*, which are only noticed by the programmer as the program is being tested, if they are noticed at all. Logic errors sneak by the computer unnoticed, but they will cause it to do something unintended.

As you start to write your own programs, you will become well-acquainted with errors. They're a natural part of the process. Programming errors are called *bugs*, a term that dates back a century or more to describe errors in technical devices. The process of fixing errors has its own term also: *debugging*. Whether you want to or not, you'll get a lot of debugging experience as you learn how to write computer programs.

Next Stop: Java

Before you can start writing Java programs, you need to acquire and set up some kind of Java programming software. Although several different products are available for the development of Java programs, including many terrific ones that make programming much easier, the starting place for most new Java programmers is the Software Development Kit, a set of tools for writing, debugging, and running Java programs. All of the examples in this book were created and tested using the Kit, but they can be created with any Java development tool that supports the current version of the language.

The Software Development Kit (also referred to as the SDK) is in version 1.4 as of this writing. Whenever Sun releases a new version of Java, the first tool that supports it is the Kit.

To create all of the programs in this book, you must either use Software Development Kit 1.4 or another Java programming tool that fully supports all of version 1.4's features.

There are many different software packages that offer the capability to create Java programs, but all of these are not created equally when language support is concerned. Some of these programming tools only support Java 1.0, the initial version of the language, which was released by Sun Microsystems in late 1995. Other tools support Java 1.1, which was released in mid-1997, version 1.2 from 1998, or version 1.3 from 2000.

Some operating systems such as Mac OS X and Red Hat Linux 7.1 include a copy of the SDK, but it's probably not the current version. The kit in OS X supports version 1.3 of

Java and the one in Red Hat 7.1 supports version 1.1. Before using an SDK that was included with your operating system, make sure it supports Java version 1.4.

Users of Microsoft Windows systems may be dismayed to learn that the Software Development Kit is not graphical. You run programs from a command line (the C:\> or D:\> prompt that will be familiar to MS-DOS users) instead of using a mouse and a point-and-click environment. Figure 1.2 shows the Kit in use in an MS-DOS window on a Windows 2000 system. The Java program WarGames.java is compiled, and then it is run.

The examples in this book were prepared on the Microsoft Windows XP and Red Hat Linux operating systems. For this reason, some advice is offered for Windows and Linux users running the Software Development Kit. However, all of the Java code in this book will work regardless of the operating system you are using, as long as you have development software that supports all the features of SDK 1.4.

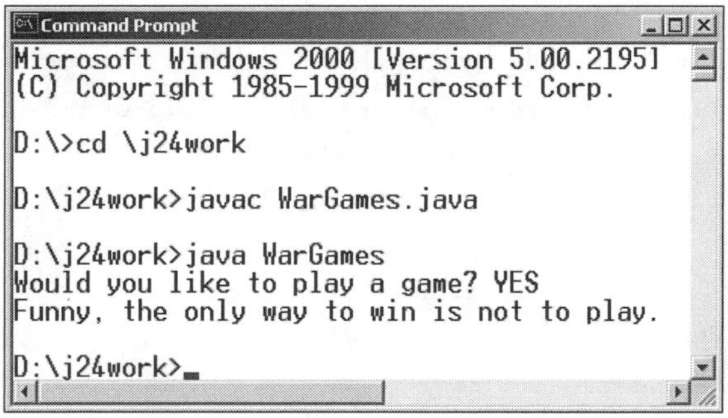

FIGURE 1.2

A program being compiled and run with the Software Development Kit.

```
Command Prompt                                    _ □ x

Microsoft Windows 2000 [Version 5.00.2195]
(C) Copyright 1985-1999 Microsoft Corp.

D:\>cd \j24work

D:\j24work>javac WarGames.java

D:\j24work>java WarGames
Would you like to play a game? YES
Funny, the only way to win is not to play.

D:\j24work>_
```

Official Documentation

Sun Microsystems offers comprehensive documentation for the Java language in Web page format. You don't need this information to use this book because each topic is discussed fully as it is introduced, but these pages will come in handy when you write your own programs.

You can download the entire documentation, but it might be more convenient to browse it as needed from Sun's Web site. The most up-to-date Java documentation is available at http://java.sun.com/j2se/1.4/docs.

Workshop: Installing a Java Development Tool

Every hour of this book ends with a workshop, a Java programming project you can undertake to enhance your knowledge of the subject matter while it is percolating in your brain.

However, you won't be doing any Java programming at all until you install a Java development tool on your computer.

If you have a program such as Borland JBuilder, IntelliJ IDEA, Sun ONE Studio, or MetroWerks CodeWarrior, you can use that to develop the tutorial programs in the next 23 hours. However, you should already have some familiarity with how to use the program—learning to use Java and a complex development tool at the same time can be daunting.

If you don't have a Java development tool, or the last paragraph scared you away from using one that you own, you can use the Java 2 Software Development Kit, which is available for free from Sun's Java Web site at `http://java.sun.com`.

Though the process is relatively straightforward, there are some configuration issues that cause problems for many people trying to get started with the kit, especially on a Windows system. To find out how to download and install the kit and fix any configuration problems that arise, read Appendix B, "Using the Java 2 Software Development Kit."

Summary

During this hour, you were introduced to the concept of programming a computer—giving it a set of instructions that tell it what to do. You also might have downloaded and installed a Java development tool that will be used as you write sample programs throughout the book.

If you are still confused about programs, programming languages, or Java in general, that's understandable at this point. Everything will make more sense to you in the next hour, "Writing Your First Program," which takes a slow trip through the process of creating a Java program.

Q&A

Q **What is it about BASIC that makes it easier to fall into bad habits while writing programs?**

A One thing you'll learn as you start writing Java programs is that you have to be organized. If you don't structure your program in the correct way, it won't work. BASIC doesn't have this kind of requirement. You can write in a disorganized manner and still get the program to work successfully. Later on, however, you'll have a much harder time figuring out how the program functions when you try to fix a bug or add an improvement.

Q **BASIC? C++? Java? What are the names of these languages supposed to mean?**

A Like many programming languages, BASIC gets its name from an acronym that describes what it is: Beginner's All Symbolic Instruction Code. C++ is a programming language that was created to be an improvement on the C language, which itself was an improvement of the B programming language. Java goes against the tradition of naming a language with an acronym or other meaningful term. It's just the name that Java's developers liked the best when brainstorming for possible monikers—beating out WebRunner, Silk, and others.

Q **Are there really more than 1,000 books about Java programming?**

A According to the official *JavaWorld* count, there are more than 2,400. The online Java magazine, which is available at `http://www.javaworld.com`, maintains a guide to all upcoming and in-print books related to Java and other Internet technology. This guide is available at `http://www.javaworld.com/javaworld/books/jw-books-index.html`.

Q **Why are interpreted languages slower than compiled ones?**

A For the same reason that a person interpreting a live speech is a lot slower than a translator interpreting a printed speech. The live interpreter has to think about each statement that's being made as it happens, while the other interpreter can work on the speech as a whole and take some shortcuts to speed up the process. Compiled languages can be much faster than interpreted languages because they can do things to make the program more efficient.

Q **Is C++ harder to learn than Java?**

A It's a matter of personal opinion, but Java does seem more approachable for beginners than C++. C++ and its predecessor C are widely regarded as "programmer's languages," meaning that they were designed for the needs of experienced programmers. There are a lot of features in C and C++ that make them faster—and more powerful—during program creation, but these features often come at the expense of understandability. Java takes a more simplified approach to programming than C++ and is probably a better place to start.

Q I am not able to install the SDK from Sun because it's a huge 25 megabyte file. How can I get the SDK?

A Sun has offered the SDK on CD for the cost of postage in the past, but that appears to have been discontinued. If you can't download the SDK over the Web, your best bet is probably to acquire a book that contains SDK 1.4 on a CD. There are several, and one of them is *Sams Teach Yourself Java 2 in 21 Days Professional Reference Edition*, *Third Edition*. The book is a more expensive hardcover, but it also includes seven bonus chapters on advanced Java topics. For more information, visit the Web site `http://www.java21pro.com`.

Quiz

Test your knowledge of the material covered in this chapter by answering the following questions.

Questions

1. Which of the following is *not* a reason that people think computer programming is painfully difficult?

    a. Programmers spread that rumor to improve their employment prospects.

    b. Jargon and acronyms are all over the place.

    c. Mind-control waves are sent out by the CIA promoting this belief.

2. What kind of tool runs a computer program by figuring out one line at a time?

    a. A slow tool

    b. An interpreter

    c. A compiler

3. Why did James Gosling hole up in his office and create Java?

    a. He was unhappy with the language he was using on a project.

    b. His rock band wasn't getting any gigs.

    c. When you can't download any MP3 files at work, the Internet is pretty dull.

Answers

1. c. Of course, the CIA could have forced me to say this.

2. b. Compilers figure out the instructions beforehand so the program can run faster.

3. a. At the time Gosling created Java, people thought that "MP3" was some kind of British secret service designation.

Activities

If you'd like to better introduce yourself to the subjects of Java and computer programming, do the following activities:

- Visit Sun's official Java site at `http://java.sun.com/java2/whatis` and read the company's introduction to the Java technology.

- Using English sentences instead of a programming language, write a set of instructions to add 10 to a number selected by a user and then multiply the result by 5. Break the instructions into as many short one-sentence lines as you can.

To see solutions to the activities at the end of each hour, visit the book's Web site at `http://www.java24hours.com`.

HOUR 2

Writing Your First Program

As you learned during Hour 1, "Becoming a Programmer," a computer program is a set of instructions that tell a computer what to do. These instructions are prepared in the same way instructions could be given to a person: You type them into a word processor. However, that's where the similarity ends. Instructions given to a computer must be written using a programming language. Dozens of computer programming languages have been created; you might have heard of some of them, such as BASIC or Pascal.

During this hour, you will create your first Java program by entering it using any word processor you like. When that's done, you will save the program, compile it, and test it out. The following topics will be covered during this hour:

- Entering a program into a word processor
- Naming a Java program with the `class` statement

- Organizing a program with bracket marks
- Storing information in a variable
- Displaying the information stored in a variable
- Saving a program
- Compiling a program
- Running a program
- Fixing errors
- Modifying a program

What You Need to Write Programs

As explained in Hour 1, to create Java programs, you must have the current version of the Software Development Kit, or another development tool that supports Java 2 version 1.4. You need something that can be used to compile and test Java programs. You also might need a word processor to write programs.

With most programming languages, computer programs are written by entering text into a word processor (also called a *text editor*). Some programming languages, such as Visual C++ from Microsoft, come with their own word processor. Several advanced tools that you could use as an alternative to the Software Development Kit, such as Borland JBuilder and Sun ONE Studio, also come with their own editors.

Java programs are simple text files without any special features, such as centered text, boldface text, or other enhancements. They can be written with any word processing program that can create text files. Microsoft Windows systems have several word processors you can use, including Notepad, WordPad, and the DOS program Edit. Apple Macintosh users can create programs with Simple Text, or other editors such as BBEdit Lite. Linux and Unix users can use vi, emacs, and others. Any of these will work fine.

You can also use more sophisticated word processors such as Microsoft Word if you remember to save the programs as text. This option has different names depending on the program you are using. In Word, the file should be saved as a file of type Text Only. Other programs call these files DOS text, ASCII text, or something similar. You'll probably have a better experience creating the programs in this book if you choose a simple word processor to work on source code rather than a sophisticated editing tool such as Word.

If you're in doubt about whether a word processor can save files as text files, you can always use one of the simple programs that come with your operating system. For instance, Windows users can rely on Notepad to create Java programs, because text files created with Notepad are always saved as text-only files.

Creating the Saluton Program

The first Java program that you create will be an application that displays a traditional greeting from the world of computer science, "Saluton mondo!"

Beginning the Program

Using your word processor, begin your Java programming career by entering each line from Listing 2.1. Don't enter the line number and colon at the beginning of each line—these are used in this book so that specific line numbers can be referred to.

LISTING 2.1   The Saluton Program

```
1: class Saluton {
2:     public static void main(String[] arguments) {
3:         // My first Java program goes here
4:     }
5: }
```

Make sure to capitalize everything exactly as shown, and use your spacebar or Tab key to insert the blank spaces in front of some lines. When you're done, save the file with the file name Saluton.java.

If you're using Windows, don't forget to put quotation marks around the filename when saving it, as in "Saluton.java". This will ensure that the file extension .txt is not added to the filename automatically.

At this point, Saluton.java contains the bare-bones form of a Java program. You will create several programs that start off exactly like this one, except for the word Saluton on Line 1. This word represents the name of your program and changes with each program you write. Line 3 should also make sense—it's a sentence in actual English. The rest is completely new, however, and each part is introduced in the following sections.

The `class` Statement

The first line of the program is the following:

```
class Saluton {
```

Translated into English, this line means, "Computer, give my Java program the name Saluton."

As you might recall from Hour 1, each instruction you give a computer is called a *statement*. The `class` statement is the way you give your computer program a name. It's also used to determine other things about the program, as you will see later. The significance of the term `class` is that Java programs are also called *classes*.

In this example, the program name `Saluton` matches the file name you gave your document, `Saluton.java`. As a rule, a Java program should have a name that matches the first part of its filename, and they should be capitalized in the same way.

If the program name doesn't match the filename, you will get an error when you try to compile some Java programs, depending on how the `class` statement is being used to configure the program. Although some programs can have a filename that doesn't match its program name, this makes it more difficult to work with the file later on.

What the `main` Statement Does

The next line of the program is the following:

```
public static void main(String[] arguments) {
```

This line tells the computer, "The main part of the program begins here." Java programs are organized into different sections, so there needs to be a way to identify the part of a program that will be handled first.

The `main` statement is the entry point to almost all Java programs. The exception are applets, programs that are run in conjunction with a World Wide Web page. Most of the programs you will write during the next several hours use `main` as the starting point.

Those Squiggly Bracket Marks

In the `Saluton` program, every line except Line 3 contains a squiggly bracket mark of some kind—either an { or an }. These brackets are a way to group parts of your program (in the same way that parentheses are used in a sentence to group words). Everything between the opening bracket, {, and the closing bracket, }, is part of the same group.

These groupings are called *blocks*. In Listing 2.1, the opening bracket on Line 1 is associated with the closing bracket on Line 5, which makes your entire program a block. You will always use brackets in this way to show the beginning and end of your programs.

Blocks can be located inside other blocks (just as parentheses are used here (and a second set is used here)). The `Saluton` program has brackets on Line 2 and Line 4 that establish another block. This block begins with the `main` statement. Everything that is inside the `main` statement's block is a command for the computer to handle when the program is run.

The following statement is the only thing located inside the block:

```
// My first Java program goes here
```

This line is a placeholder. The `//` at the beginning of the line tells the computer to ignore this line—it is put in the program solely for the benefit of humans who are looking at the program's text. Lines that serve this purpose are called *comments*.

Right now, you have written a complete Java program. It can be compiled, but if you run it, nothing will happen. The reason is that you have not told the computer to do anything yet. The `main` statement block contains only a line of comments, which is ignored. If the `Saluton` program is going to greet anyone, you will have to add some commands inside the opening and closing brackets of the `main` statement block.

Storing Information in a Variable

In the programs you write, one thing that's often needed is a place to store information for a brief period of time. You can do this by using a *variable*, a storage place that can hold information such as integers, floating-point numbers, true-false values, characters, and lines of text. The information stored in a variable can change, which is where the name "variable" comes from.

Load the `Saluton.java` file into your word processor (if it's not already loaded) and replace Line 3 with the following:

```
String greeting = "Saluton mondo!";
```

This statement tells the computer to store the line of text "Saluton mondo!" into a variable called `greeting`.

In a Java program, you must tell the computer what type of information a variable will hold. In this program, `greeting` is a *string*—a line of text that can include letters, numbers, punctuation, and other characters. Putting `String` in the statement `String greeting = "Saluton mondo!";` sets up the variable to hold string values.

When you enter this statement into the program, a semicolon must be included at the end of the line. Semicolons are used at the end of each statement in your Java programs. They're like periods at the end of a sentence; the computer uses them to determine when one statement ends and the next one begins.

Displaying the Contents of a Variable

If you ran the program at this point, it wouldn't display anything. The command to store a line of text in the greeting variable occurs behind the scenes. To make the computer show that it is doing something, you can display the contents of that variable.

Insert another blank line in the Saluton program after the String greeting = "Saluton mondo!"; statement. Use that space to enter the following statement:

```
System.out.println(greeting);
```

This statement tells the computer to display the value stored in the greeting variable. The System.out.println statement tells the computer to display a line on the system output device. In this case, the system output device is your computer monitor.

If you learned to type on a typewriter rather than a computer, watch out for hitting the "1" key as an alternative to the "l" key (lowercase "L"). A1though your cerebra1 cortex is perfect1y happy to treat the numera1 as the 1etter when it appears, the computer isn't as adaptab1e as your brain. Your program won't compile if you use print1n instead of println, for example.

Saving the Finished Product

Your program should now resemble Listing 2.2, although you might have used slightly different spacing in Lines 3–4. Make any corrections that are needed and save the file as Saluton.java. Keep in mind that all Java programs are created as text files and are saved with the .java file extension.

LISTING 2.2   The Finished Version of the Saluton Program

```
1: class Saluton {
2:     public static void main(String[] arguments) {
3:         String greeting = "Saluton mondo!";
4:         System.out.println(greeting);
5:     }
6: }
```

When the computer runs this program, it will run each of the statements in the `main` statement block on Lines 3 and 4. Listing 2.3 shows what the program would look like if it were written in the English language instead of Java.

LISTING 2.3 A Line-by-Line Breakdown of the `Saluton` Program

```
1: The Saluton program begins here:
2:     The main part of the program begins here:
3:         Store the text "Saluton mondo!" in a String variable named greeting
4:         Display the contents of the variable greeting
5:     The main part of the program ends here.
6: The Saluton program ends here.
```

Compiling the Program into a Class File

Before you can try out the program, it must be compiled. The term *compile* might be unfamiliar to you now, but you will become quite familiar with it in the coming hours. When you compile a program, you take the instructions you have given the computer and convert them into a form the computer can better understand. You also make the program run as efficiently as possible. Java programs must be compiled before you can run them. With the Software Development Kit, programs are compiled using the `javac` program.

The `javac` program, like all programs included with the Software Development Kit, is a command-line utility. You run the program by using your keyboard to type a command at a place that can accept the input. This place is what the term *command-line* refers to.

Because most Linux usage is handled at the command-line, readers with that operating system will be familiar with how the Kit's programs are used. Anyone who used MS-DOS prior to the introduction of Windows has also used a command line.

Many Windows users might not be aware that their operating system includes a command-line feature of its own: the MS-DOS window.

To compile the `Saluton` program using the Software Development Kit, go to a command-line and open the folder on your system where the `Saluton.java` file is located, then type the following at the command line:

```
javac Saluton.java
```

If the program compiles successfully, a new file called `Saluton.class` is created in the same folder as `Saluton.java`. If you have any error messages, refer to the following section, "Fixing Errors." All Java programs are compiled into class files, which are given the .class file extension. A Java program can be made up of several classes that work together, but in a simple program such as Saluton only one class is needed.

> Did you ever have a relative, spouse, or other loved one who only says something when things go wrong? (Me neither.) A Java compiler only speaks up when there's an error to complain about. If you compile a program successfully without any errors, nothing happens in response.

Fixing Errors

If errors exist in your program when you compile it, a message is displayed that explains each error and the line on which it occurred. The following output illustrates an attempt to compile a program that has an error, and the error messages that is displayed as a result:

```
C:\J24Work>javac Saluton.java
Saluton.java:4: cannot resolve symbol.
symbol  : method print1n (java.lang.String)
location: class java.io.PrintStream
        System.out.print1n(greeting);
                  ^
1 error

C:\J24Work>
```

Error messages displayed by the javac tool include the following information:

- The name of the Java program
- The number of the line where the error was found
- The type of error
- The line where the error was found

As you learned during the past hour, errors in programs are called bugs. Finding those errors and squashing them is called *debugging*. The following is another example of an error message you might see when compiling the Saluton program:

```
Saluton.java:4: cannot resolve symbol.
symbol  : variable greting
location: class Saluton
        System.out.println(greting);
                  ^
```

In this example, the 4 that follows the file name `Saluton.java` indicates that the error is on Line 4. This is where having a line-numbering word processor comes in handy—you can jump more easily to the Java statement that's associated with the error.

The actual error message, `cannot resolve symbol` in this case, can often be confusing to new programmers. In some cases, the message can be confusing to any programmer. When the error message doesn't make sense to you, take a look at the line where the error occurred.

For instance, can you determine what's wrong with the following statement?

```
System.out.println(greeting);
```

The problem is that there's a typo in the variable name, which should be `greeting` instead of `greting`.

If you get error messages when compiling the `Saluton` program, double-check that your program matches Listing 2.2, and correct any differences you find. Make sure that everything is capitalized correctly, and that all punctuation marks (such as {, }, and ;) are included.

Often, a close look at the statement included with the error message is enough to reveal the error, or errors, that need to be fixed.

> This book's official Web site at `http://www.java24hours.com` includes source files for all programs that you create. If you can't find any typos or other reasons for errors in the `Saluton` program, go to the book's Web site and download `Saluton.java` from the Hour 2 page. Try to compile that file, too.

If the Java compiler responds with error messages such as `Bad command or filename`, `error: Can't read`, `Class not found`, or `NoClassDef`, the most likely culprit is that your Software Development Kit needs to be reconfigured—a common situation on Windows systems. For help fixing this, read Appendix B, "Using the Java 2 Software Development Kit."

Workshop: Running a Java Program

To run the Java program you have just created, you must use a Java interpreter such as `java`, the command-line tool included with the Software Development Kit. An interpreter makes the computer follow the instructions you gave it when you wrote the program.

To run a Java program, the command `java` is followed by a space and the name of the class file that contains the program. Although the class file's name includes the `.class` extension, this part of the name must be left off when running the program with the Java interpreter.

To see whether the `Saluton` program does what you want, run the class. If you're using the kit, go to the folder that contains the `Saluton.class` file, and type the following at a command line:

```
java Saluton
```

Even though the program's filename is `Saluton.class`, you don't include the file extension `.class` in the command.

When the program runs, it should state the following:

```
Saluton mondo!
```

If you see this text, you have just written your first working Java program. Your computer has just greeted the world, a tradition in the field of computer programming that's as important to many of us as caffeine, short-sleeved dress shirts, and the *Star Wars* films.

> You may be asking yourself why "Saluton mondo!" is a traditional greeting, especially if you have tried using it in a conversation with other programmers and received funny looks in response. It's the phrase "Hello world!" in Esperanto, an artificial language created by Ludwig Zamenhof in 1887 to facilitate international communication. The author uses it here in the hope that more computers will be inspired to learn Esperanto.

Summary

During this hour, you got your first chance to create a Java program. You learned that to develop a Java program you need to complete these three basic steps:

1. Write the program with a word processor.
2. Compile the program.
3. Tell the interpreter to run the program.

Along the way, you were introduced to some basic computer programming concepts such as compilers, interpreters, blocks, statements, and variables. These things will become clearer to you in successive hours. As long as you got the `Saluton` program to work during this hour, you're ready to proceed.

Q&A

Q **In MS-DOS, I seem to recall that there is a control key command to retype the previous line that you had typed in. Do you happen to know that command?**

A On any Windows version but XP, enter the command `doskey`. This causes all subsequent commands you type in to be saved, and you can navigate backwards and forwards through these saved commands by using the up arrow and down arrow keys on your keyboard. Windows XP doesn't require `doskey`—the feature is turned on automatically when you open a command-line window.

Q **I have several word processing programs on my system. Which should I use to write Java programs?**

A Any of them will suffice, as long as the program can save files as text without any special formatting. A word processor that shows the line number your cursor is located on is especially useful. (Microsoft Word, for example, shows the line number at the bottom edge of the window along with the column number.) Because the `javac` compiler lists line numbers with its error messages, the line-numbering feature helps you debug a program more quickly.

Q **How important is it to put the right number of blank spaces on a line in a Java program?**

A Spacing is strictly for the benefit of people looking at a computer program—the Java compiler could care less. You could have written the `Saluton` program without using blank spaces or used the Tab key to indent lines, and it would compile successfully. Although the number of spaces in front of the lines isn't important, you should use consistent spacing in your Java programs. Spacing makes it easier for you to see how a program is organized and to which programming block a statement belongs. When you start writing more sophisticated programs, you'll find it much more difficult to do without spacing.

Q **A Java program has been described as a class, and it also has been described as a group of classes. Which is it?**

A Both. The simple Java programs you create during the next few hours will create a single file with the extension `.class`. You can run these with the `java` interpreter. Java programs can also be made up of a set of classes that work together. In fact, even simple programs like `Saluton` use other Java classes behind the scenes. This topic will be fully explored during Hour 10, "Creating Your First Object."

Q **If semicolons are needed at the end of each statement, why does the comment line // My first Java program goes here not end with a semicolon?**

A Comments are completely ignored by the compiler. If you put // on a line in your program, this tells the Java compiler to ignore everything to the right of the // on that line. The following example shows a comment on the same line as a statement:

```
System.out.println(greeting); // hello, world!
```

In this example, the compiler will handle the statement
`System.out.println(greeting);` and ignore the comments afterward.

Q **What is a character?**

A A *character* is a single letter, number, punctuation mark or other symbol. Examples are *T*, *5*, and *%*. Characters are stored in variables as text.

Q **I get an Invalid argument error message when I use the javac tool to compile the Saluton program. What can I do to correct this?**

A You are probably leaving off the .java extension and typing the following command:

```
javac Saluton
```

Make sure you are in the same folder as the file Saluton.java, and type the following command to compile the program:

```
javac Saluton.java
```

Q **I couldn't find any errors in the line where the compiler noted an error. What can I do?**

A The line number displayed with the error message isn't always the place where an error needs to be fixed in your program. Examine the statements that are directly above the error message to see whether you can spot any typos or other bugs. The error usually is within the same programming block.

Quiz

Test your knowledge of the material covered in this chapter by answering the following questions.

Questions

1. When you compile a Java program, what are you doing?
   a. Saving it to disk
   b. Converting it into a form the computer can better understand
   c. Adding it to your program collection

2. What is a variable?

    a. Something that wobbles but doesn't fall down

    b. Text in a program that the compiler ignores

    c. A place to store information in a program

3. What is the process of fixing errors called?

    a. Defrosting

    b. Debugging

    c. Decomposing

Answers

1. b. Compiling converts a `.java` file into a `.class` file or set of `.class` files.

2. c. Variables are one place to store information; later you'll learn about others, such as arrays and constants. Weebles wobble but they don't fall down, and comments are text in a program that the compiler ignores.

3. b. Because errors in a computer program are called bugs, fixing those errors is called debugging. Some programming tools come with a tool called a debugger that helps you fix errors.

Activities

If you'd like to explore the topics covered in this hour a little more fully, try the following activities:

- You can translate the English phrase "Hello world!" into other languages using the AltaVista Web site Babelfish, located at `http://babel.altavista.com`. Write a program that enables your computer to greet the world in a language such as French, Italian, or Portuguese.

- Go back to the `Saluton` program and add one or two errors. For example, take a semicolon off the end of a line, or change the text `println` on one line to `print1n`. Save the program and try to compile it. Compare the error messages you get to the errors you caused.

To see solutions to these activities, visit the book's Web site at `http://www.java24hours.com`.

HOUR 3

Vacationing in Java

Before you venture further into Java programming, it's worthwhile to learn more about the language and see what Java programmers are doing today. One of the reasons that Java became popular so quickly was because it could be used to offer programs on the World Wide Web. Though Java has outgrown its origins as a language focused on Web programs, you can still find some interesting examples of how Java is used on the Web.

During this hour, we'll take a look at some sites that feature Java programs and talk about the history and development of the language.

To go on this vacation, you need a Web browser that can handle Java programs. The current versions of Microsoft Internet Explorer, Mozilla, Netscape Navigator, and the Opera browser can run Java programs that are found on Web pages.

If you're using a current version of Netscape Navigator or Microsoft Internet Explorer and it isn't working with Java programs, check your setup configuration from one of the program's pull-down menus. Make sure your browser software has Java enabled in its settings.

Load your browser software of choice, put on your best batik shirt, and get ready to vacate. Because you won't be leaving your house, you won't get a chance to experience the simpler pleasures of tourism: odd driving rituals, exotic food, exotic members of the opposite sex, exotic members of the opposite sex with food, and so on. But look on the bright side: no antibacterial shots, traveler's checks, or passports are required either.

The following topics will be covered during this hour:

- A definition of the Java language
- The benefits of using Java
- Some examples of Java at work
- An explanation of object-oriented programming
- Sites of note for Java programmers

 The sightseeing examples you visit during today's vacation are just a small sampling of the Java programs in use on the Web. A search of the AltaVista Web search database finds more than 7.8 million pages that have included a Java program as of this writing.

First Stop: Sun Microsystems

The Java vacation begins at a place you'll be visiting regularly, now that you're a Java programmer: the Web site of Sun Microsystems, the company that developed the Java language. To get there, go to http://java.sun.com.

A Java program that runs as part of a Web page is called an *applet*. Applets are placed on pages like other elements of a page—a markup language called HTML is used to define where the program should be displayed, how big it is, and what the program does when it runs.

The Java division of Sun Microsystems is responsible for the advancement of the Java language and the development of related software. As you might expect of a proud parent, Sun uses Java applets on its site. There's a glossary applet that's a guide to the site, several applets that are free for your own use, and others.

The sample applets include an animated clock and a shopping cart assistant. Java can be a great attention-getter, creating content dynamically that changes as a page is being viewed in a Web browser. Figure 3.1 shows the clock and other sample applets.

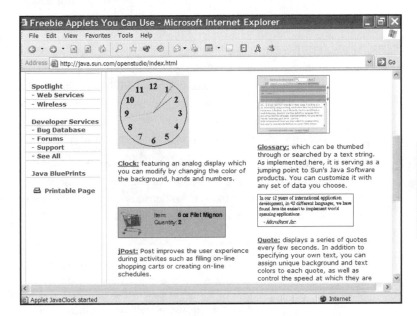

Sun's Java site is the place to find the latest released versions of the Software Development Kit, as well as other programmer's resources. This site also has press releases about Java-related products, full documentation for Java, and sample Java programs that run on the Web. Sun Microsystems first made Java available for free via this Web site in 1995, and it's still the first place to look for each new development kit and addition to the language.

A Brief History of Java

Sun co-founder Bill Joy called Java "the end result of fifteen years of work to produce a better, more reliable way to write computer programs." Java's creation was a little more complicated than that.

Java was developed in 1990 by Sun engineer James Gosling as a language to use as the brains for smart appliances (interactive TVs, omniscient ovens, and the like). Gosling was unhappy with the results he was getting by writing programs with C++, another programming language, so he holed up in his office and wrote a new language to better suit his needs.

Today, many of us like writing programs with Java, so we have no incentive to create our own programming languages. As a result, we have more time to hole up in our offices and play *EverQuest* instead.

At the time, Gosling named his language Oak after a tree he could see from his office window. The language was part of Sun's strategy to make millions when interactive TV became a multimillion-dollar industry. That still hasn't happened today (though TiVo, ReplayTV, and WebTV are making a game attempt), but something completely different took place for Gosling's new language. Just as Sun was ready to scrap Oak development and scatter its workers to other parts of the company, the World Wide Web became popular.

In a fortuitous circumstance, many of the qualities that made Gosling's language good on its appliance project made it suitable for adaptation to the World Wide Web. Sun developers devised a way for programs to be run safely from Web pages and chose a catchy new name to accompany the language's new focus: Java.

You might have heard that Java is an acronym that stands for Just Another Vague Acronym. You also might have heard that it was named for the developers' love of coffee, especially the percolating product from a shop near Sun's offices. Actually, the story behind Java's naming contains no secret messages or declarations of liquid love. Instead, Java was chosen for the same reason that comedian Jerry Seinfeld likes to say the word *salsa*. It sounds cool.

Although Java can be used for many other things, the Web provided the showcase it needed to capture international attention. A programmer who puts a Java program on a Web page makes it instantly accessible to the entire Web-surfing planet. Because Java was the first technology that could offer this capability, it became the first computer language to receive star treatment in the media. When the language really rose to prominence in 1996, you had to be in solitary confinement or a long-term orbital mission to avoid hearing about Java.

There have been five major releases of the Java language:

- Fall 1995: Java 1.0—A version best suited for use on the World Wide Web that showed potential for expansion into other types of programming
- Spring 1997: Java 1.1—An upgrade to the language that included numerous improvements to the way user interfaces are created and handled

- Summer/Fall 1998: Java 2, version 1.2—A version more than three times as large as Java 1.0, with enhancements that make the language a worthy competitor to other general-purpose programming languages
- Fall 2000: Java 2, version 1.3—A release supporting faster running Java programs and enhanced multimedia features, as well as the first official support for Java development on the Linux operating system
- Spring 2002: Java 2, version 1.4—A substantial upgrade with a much-requested feature called assertions to improve software reliability, expanded networking support, and XML processing

Going to School with Java

As a medium that offers a potential audience of millions, the World Wide Web includes numerous resources for educators and schoolchildren. Because Java programs can offer a more interactive experience than standard Web pages, some programmers have used the language to write learning programs for the Internet.

For one of the strongest examples of this use of Java, visit `http://www.npac.syr.edu/ projects/vishuman/VisibleHuman.html`.

This Web site uses data from the National Library of Medicine's Visible Human Project. The project is a database of thousands of cross-sectional images of human anatomy. A Java program is being used to enable users to search the collection and view images. Instead of making requests by text commands, users make the requests to see different parts of the body by using the mouse, and the results are shown immediately in graphic detail. The Java program is shown in Figure 3.2.

Numerous educational programs are available for many different computer systems, but what makes this program remarkable is its versatility. The Visible Human Project tool is similar in function and performance to CD-ROM software that users might run on their computer systems. However, it is run directly from a Web page. No special installation is needed, and unlike most CD-ROM software, it isn't limited to PC-compatible and Macintosh systems. Just like Web pages, Java programs can be run on any computer system that can handle them.

To be able to handle Java programs, a Web browser must have a Java interpreter. The interpreter included with a browser serves a similar function as the interpreter you used to run the Saluton program during Hour 2, "Writing Your First Program." The difference is that a browser's interpreter can only run Java programs that are set up to run on Web

3

pages and cannot handle programs set up to run from the command line. Currently, Java-enabled browsers are available for most systems, including PCs running a version of Microsoft Windows, Apple Macintosh systems, SPARC workstations, and computers running the Linux operating system.

FIGURE 3.2

Images from the National Library of Medicine's Visible Human Project can be viewed interactively on the Web using a Java program.

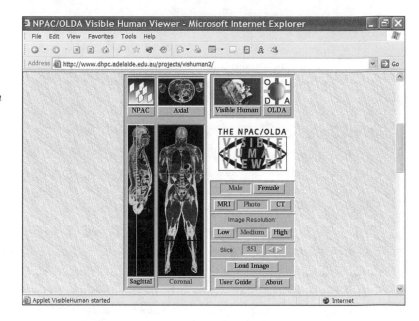

The primary Java-capable browsers in use today are Microsoft Internet Explorer, Netscape Navigator, Mozilla, and Opera. Although versions of these browsers support Java, none of them offer built-in support for Java 2. Browser developers have not been able to keep up with new versions of the language as quickly as Sun produces them, and at this time, it appears that all of the companies have given up trying to support anything beyond Java 1.1.

To make it possible for Java programmers to rely on Java 2 support in browsers, Sun has developed the Java Plug-in, a Java interpreter that works as a browser enhancement. By specifying in the coding of Web pages that this interpreter should be used instead of the one built into the browser, Java programmers can take advantage of all features of the language in their Web-based programs.

The Java Plug-in is more than 5 megabytes in size, so it would take more than 45 minutes for a user on a slow Internet connection to download and install the program. However, Sun includes it with the Software

Development Kit and other products, so it may already be installed on your computer. If not, you can download and install it as part of the Java Runtime Environment: Visit the Web page `http://java.sun.com/getjava/`.

A Java program such as the Visible Human Project database does not have to be written for a specific computer system. This advantage is called *platform independence*. Java was created to work on multiple systems. Originally, Java's developers believed it needed to be multiplatform because it would be used on a variety of appliances and other electronic devices.

The programs you write with Java can be run on a variety of computer systems without requiring any extra work from you. This advantage is one of the primary reasons so many people are learning to write Java programs and are using them on software projects. Many professional software companies are using Java for the same reason. Under the right circumstances, Java can remove the need to create specific versions of a program for different computer systems. The potential audience for software grows with a multiplatform solution such as Java.

Lunch in JavaWorld

If you didn't lose your appetite after searching through the innards of a visible human, take a lunch break with *JavaWorld*, an online magazine for Java programmers and other Internet developers. The *JavaWorld* Web site is available at `http://www.javaworld.com`.

JavaWorld offers how-to articles, news stories related to Java development, and other features in each monthly edition. One of the advantages of the publication's Web format is that it can display functional Java programs in conjunction with articles. Figure 3.3 shows a Java "poetry magnet board" in a tutorial that describes how it is written.

 JavaWorld occasionally moves things around, but at the time of this writing, you can go directly to the poetry magnet board tutorial at `http://www.javaworld.com/jw-04-1998/jw-04-step.html`. If that page is unavailable, use the site's search engine to look for the word "poetry."

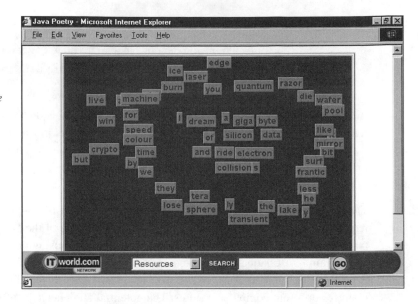

FIGURE 3.3
*A JavaWorld how-to
article on how to cre-
ate a "poetry magnet
board" includes a
working example of the
program.*

In addition to offering information of benefit to Java programmers, *JavaWorld* publishes articles and commentary about the language and its development. One issue that has been hotly debated since Java's release is whether the language is secure. Security is important because of the way Java programs work when they are placed on a Web page. The Java programs you have tried during this hour were downloaded to your computer. When the program was finished downloading, it ran on your computer. It was as though someone sat down at your computer, popped in a disk, and ran their own program.

Unless you know a whole lot of people, most of the Web pages you visit will be published by strangers. In terms of security, running their programs isn't a lot different than letting the general public use your computer on alternate weekends. If the Java language did not have safeguards to prevent abuse, its programs could introduce viruses onto your system, delete files, play the collected works of Britney Spears, and do other undesirable things. Java includes several different types of security to make sure that its programs are safe when run from Web pages.

The main security is provided by the following general restrictions on Java programs running over the Web:

- No program can open, read, write, or delete files on the user's system.
- No program can run other programs on the user's system.

- All windows created by the program will be identified clearly as Java windows. This identification prevents someone from creating a fake window asking for the user's name and password.
- Programs cannot make connections to Web sites other than the one from which they came.
- All programs will be verified to make sure that nothing was modified after they were compiled.

The general consensus among Java developers is that the language has enough safeguards in place to be usable over the Web. Several security holes have been found, often by programming security experts, and these holes have been dealt with quickly by Sun or the Web browser programmers. Because *JavaWorld* covers the latest news of note in the Java development community, it is a good way to keep track of any security issues that arise.

> None of the safeguards in place are a complete block against malicious programs. Just as loopholes have been found in the past, more will undoubtedly be found in the future. If you are concerned about running Java programs through your Web browser, you can turn off Java support in current versions of Navigator, Internet Explorer, and Opera, though you will be missing a lot of interactive content on the Web.

Version 2 of the Java language introduced a more flexible security policy for programs that run in a browser. You can designate some companies and programmers as "trusted developers," which enables their Java programs to run in your browser without the restrictions that normally would be in place.

This system of trust is established through the use of *digital signatures*, files that clearly identify the author of a Java program. These signatures are created in collaboration with independent verification groups like VeriSign, which has a World Wide Web site at `http://www.verisign.com`.

If you have ever authorized an ActiveX control to run in Internet Explorer, you have worked with a similar system of trust and identity verification.

Taking in a Ballgame at ESPN.com

The first afternoon stop on the Java tour will be a trip to the old ballgame. ESPN.com, one of the leading sports sites on the World Wide Web, is using Java to present baseball games as they happen in a visual, pitch-by-pitch fashion. To see how baseball is played in cyberspace, visit http://espn.com.

The Java program called ESPN GameCast presents each pitch in a major league game. Runners are shown on base, player changes are reflected immediately, and all stats in the game are updated in real time. It's a high-tech throwback to the period in the early 20th century when a large outdoor sign would be updated by hand with the score, men on base, and other information about an out-of-town game as it happened.

ESPN's GameCast program is a unique way to follow live games. Figure 3.4 shows GameCast after the last pitch in a thrilling 19-7 win by the Texas Rangers over the Boston Red Sox. (As a Rangers fan, I have to be thrilled about a win, because you never know when it's going to happen again.)

FIGURE 3.4

The Texas Rangers defeat the Boston Red Sox 19-7 in a game broadcast through ESPN GameCast, a Java program that displays comprehensive information about a game while it is taking place.

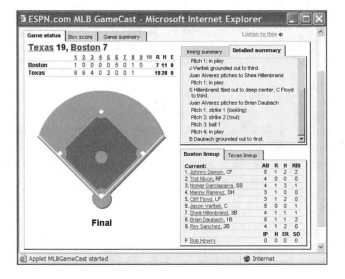

One of the things you might notice about ESPN GameCast is that it updates the day's scores from other games as you are using the program. This update is relatively easy to do because the Java language is multithreaded. *Multithreading* is a way for the computer to do more than one thing at the same time. One part of a program takes care of one task, another part takes care of a different task, and the two parts can pay no attention to each other. Each part of a program in this example is called a *thread*.

In a program such as ESPN GameCast, the league scoreboard along the top edge of the window could run in its own thread. The rest of the program could be another thread. If you use an operating system such as Microsoft Windows XP, you're using a type of this behavior when you run more than one program at the same time. If you're at work and you surf the Web for European aerobics videos in one window while running a company sales report in another window and making a long-distance call to a friend, congratulate yourself—you're multithreading!

Getting Down to Business

At this point in your travels, you might be getting the impression that Java is primarily of use to baseball fans and those who have body parts to show the world. Although those two subject areas are enough to keep most of us entertained for days, the next stop on our trip shows an example of Java getting down to business.

Direct your Web browser to `http://www.uralbeacon.co.uk/zoomchart`. This example is a financial charting tool presented as a Java program. Historical price and average data is displayed, and users can drag the mouse over an area on a chart to define a new portion of the data to chart, as shown in Figure 3.5.

Unlike other stock analysis programs that require the installation of software on the computers of each employee who needs access, the use of Java enables Ural Beacon to make the program available to anyone with a Web browser—all the employees would have to do is access the company's Web site.

FIGURE 3.5

A Java program from Ural Beacon that is used to analyze financial data such as stock market prices.

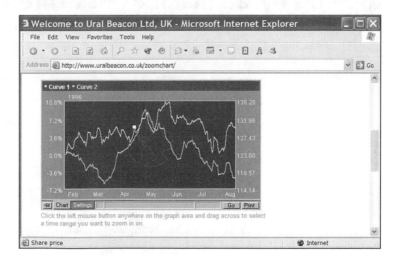

A program such as Ural Beacon's charting applet can be thought of in several different ways. One way is to think of a program as an object—something that exists in the world, takes up space, and has certain things it can do. Java, like the C++ language, uses object-oriented programming, as you will see during Hour 10, "Creating Your First Object." Object-oriented programming (OOP) is a way to design computer programs. A program is thought of as a group of objects. Each object handles a specific task and knows how to speak to other objects. For example, a word processing program could be set up as the following group of objects:

- A document object, which is the area where you type in text
- A spell-checking object, which can look over the document object to find any possible spelling errors
- A printer object, which handles the printing of the document
- A menu object, a mouse object, and many others

The word processing software is a collection of all the objects necessary to get work done.

OOP is a powerful way to create programs, and it makes the programs you write more useful. Consider word processing software. If the programmer wants to use the spell-checking capabilities of that program with some other software, the spell-checking object is ready for use with the new program. No changes need to be made.

Stopping by Gamelan to Ask Directions

This world tour of Java programs is being led by a professional who is well-versed in the hazards and highlights of Web-based travel. You'll be venturing out on your own trips soon, so it's worthwhile to stop at one of the best guides currently available for the tourist who wants to see Java, Gamelan at `http://softwaredev.earthweb.com/java`.

Gamelan features one of the most comprehensive directories of Java programs, programming resources, and other information related to the language. Many of the programs visited during this hour were originally found on a trek through the searchable database maintained by Gamelan. Updates are made on a daily basis, so this is another place you'll be visiting often as you develop your Java programming skills.

One of the best uses of Gamelan for programmers is to see what programs are available that offer source code. In case you're unfamiliar with the term, *source code* is another name for the text files that are used to create computer programs. The `Saluton.java` file you developed during Hour 2 is an example of source code.

Gamelan's Java Applet Ratings Service (JARS), a directory of Java applets and other resources at the Web address `http://www.jars.com`, often includes programs that are accompanied by the source code used to create them. After you have finished your first 24 hours as a Java programmer, you ought to take a look at some of these programs. Figure 3.6 shows the ratings service being used to search for "3D graphics" resources.

FIGURE 3.6

The Java Applet Ratings Service, a part of Gamelan, offers information on hundreds of Java applets and other resources.

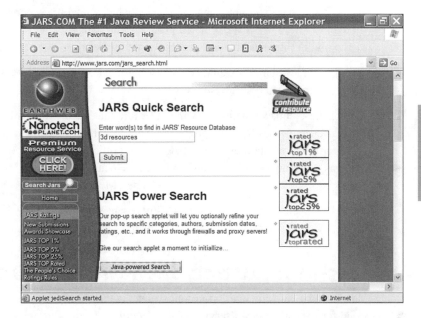

The large number of Java programs listed in JARS shows that the language has become adopted quickly by thousands of programmers around the world. Part of the reason is that Java's popularity inspires people to learn it, which is the same principle that caused parachute pants and break dancing to be briefly popular in the mid-80s. Another reason for the swiftly growing population of Java programmers is the simplicity of the language.

One of the goals of Java's design was to make it easier to learn than C++, the language James Gosling was having fits with on Sun's smart-appliance project. Much of Java is based on C++, so programmers who have learned to use that language will find it easier to learn Java. However, some of the elements of C++ that are the hardest to learn—and the hardest to use correctly—have been removed from Java.

For people who are learning programming for the first time, Java might be easier to learn than C++ would be. Also, Java will not work if its variables and other elements of a program are used incorrectly. This adherence to rules can be painful for experienced programmers, but it forces everyone to develop good habits as they create programs.

Some languages are created to make it easier for experienced programmers to harness the capabilities of the computer in their programs. These languages include shortcuts and other features that programming veterans easily understand. Java does not use these features, preferring to make the language as simple as an object-oriented programming language can be. Java was created to be easy to learn, easy to debug, and easy to use.

Because the first experience that most people had with Java was on the Web, it is often thought of strictly as a Web-related programming language. However, Java is not limited to use on the Internet. You can use it to write any kind of software.

Java 2 includes numerous enhancements that make Java a worthy competitor to languages such as Microsoft Visual C++.

One of these enhancements is Swing, a feature that makes it possible to create sophisticated user interfaces for Java programs. These interfaces have a special feature called *look-and-feel* that enables a Java program to mimic the appearance of different operating systems. Programs can be written to look like Windows software, Motif software, or even Java's own look-and-feel, which is nicknamed Metal.

Sun Microsystems has put its emphasis in recent years on turning Java into a fully capable software development language no matter where the program will run.

Workshop: Putting Java on Your Desktop

The last stop on your whirlwind tour of Java is the Yahoo! News Ticker, an applet developed for the online news service of the Yahoo! Web site. Put on your fedora and redirect your Web browser to `http://www.cadenhead.org/javaticker`.

The Yahoo! News Ticker is a Java program that provides constant headline updates. The News Ticker is viewed on your system's desktop as a stand-alone window, which you can keep open while your browser is minimized. Figure 3.7 shows the ticker on a Windows XP desktop.

FIGURE 3.7

News headlines and ads are presented in a desktop window with the Yahoo! News Java Ticker program.

Police: Calif. Girls Rescued at Last Min

Summary

Once you're completely caught up on the news events that have taken place during your world-in-a-day jaunt, it's time to put away your luggage and get ready for a return to programming.

More Web sites and other items of note for Java programmers are described in Appendix E, "Where to Go From Here: Java Resources."

Q&A

Q Can I use the sample Java programs from the Sun Microsystems Web site on my own home page?

A Sun encourages the use of its sample programs on Web sites. In addition to the programs available at `http://java.sun.com`, take a look at the folders that were created when you installed the Software Development Kit on your system. If you installed the demo programs along with the Kit, you will find more than two dozen sample programs along with the `.java` files that were used to compile them. These programs can be a valuable resource when you're working on your own Java programs later.

Q What is the difference between Java applets and ActiveX controls?

A ActiveX, an extension of Microsoft technology called the Component Object Model, offers support for interactive Web programs that are similar in function to Java programs. They are placed on Web pages and run when browsers are equipped to handle them. The primary differences are that ActiveX relies on a system to verify the identity of ActiveX programmers and ActiveX programs are not downloaded each time they are encountered. Unlike Java programs, an ActiveX program stays on a user's system. Also, an ActiveX program is not restricted in what it can do on a system, while Java programs run from Web pages face very strong restrictions in what they can do.

Q I ran a useful Java program on a Web page. Can I run it on my system without the browser?

A Under most circumstances, no. Java programs typically are developed to run on a Web page or to run from the command line. A program can be written so that it works in both ways, but most of the programs you will find in a directory such as EarthWeb do not include this functionality. You'll learn much more about the different types of Java programs during Hour 4, "Understanding How Java Programs Work."

Q Is there a print edition of *JavaWorld*?

A *JavaWorld* is distributed strictly through the World Wide Web. However, several newsstand magazines are available that cover the language, including *Java Report*, *Java Developer's Journal*, *Dr. Dobb's Journal*, and others.

Q Can a Java program I run on a Web page give my computer a virus?

A Because of general security restrictions that prevent Web programs from reading, writing, or modifying files, there's no way for a virus to be transmitted from a Java program on a Web page to your system unless you gave the program full permission to access the hard drive on your system. Java programs you download and run from the command line have the same risk of viruses as any program you download. If you're using programs received over the Internet, you need to acquire a good antivirus program and use it regularly.

Quiz

If your mind hasn't taken a vacation by this point in the hour, test your knowledge of this chapter with the following questions.

Questions

1. How did object-oriented programming get its name?

    a. Programs are considered to be a group of objects working together.

    b. People often object because it's hard to master.

    c. Its parents named it.

2. Which of the following isn't a part of Java's security?

    a. Web programs cannot run programs on the user's computer.

    b. The identity of a program's author is always verified.

    c. Java windows are labeled as Java windows.

3. What is a program's capability to handle more than one task called?

    a. schizophrenia

    b. multiculturalism

    c. multithreading

Answers

1. a. It's also abbreviated as OOP.

2. b. ActiveX programs verify the author of the program, but this security method is not implemented as a standard security measure of Java. Programmers can use digital signatures and an identity verifying company like VeriSign in Java, but it isn't required.

3. c. This also is called multitasking, but the term *multithreading* is used in conjunction with Java because an independently running part of a program is called a thread.

Activities

Before unpacking your luggage, you can explore the topics of this hour more fully with the following activities:

- Use the Java Applet Ratings Service Web site at http://www.jars.com to find out what card games have been developed using the language.

- Find the sample Java programs by searching Sun's official Java site and download one of them to your computer.

When solutions can be provided for the activities in this book, they'll be presented on the book's Web site at http://www.java24hours.com.

3

HOUR 4

Understanding How Java Programs Work

An important distinction to make in Java programming is where your program is supposed to be running. Some programs are intended to work on your computer; you type in a command or click an icon to start them up. Other programs are intended to run as part of a World Wide Web page. You encountered several examples of this type of program during the previous hour's whirlwind vacation.

Java programs that run locally on your own computer are called *applications*. Programs that run on Web pages are called *applets*. During this hour, you'll learn why that distinction is important, and the following topics will be covered:

- How applications work
- Organizing an application
- Sending arguments to an application
- How applets work

- The required parts of an applet
- Sending parameters to an applet
- Using HTML tags to put an applet on a page

Creating an Application

Although Java has become well-known because it can be used in conjunction with World Wide Web pages, you can also use it to write any type of computer program. The Saluton program you wrote during Hour 2, "Writing Your First Program," is an example of a Java application.

To try out another program, use your word processor to open up a new file and enter everything from Listing 4.1. Remember not to enter the line numbers and colons along the left side of the listing; these items are used to make parts of programs easier to describe in the book. When you're done, save the file as Root.java, making sure to save it in text-only or plain ASCII text format.

LISTING 4.1 The Full Text of Root.java

```
1: class Root {
2:     public static void main(String[] arguments) {
3:         int number = 225;
4:         System.out.println("The square root of "
5:             + number
6:             + " is "
7:             + Math.sqrt(number) );
8:     }
9: }
```

The Root application accomplishes the following tasks:

- Line 3: An integer value of 225 is stored in a variable named number.
- Lines 4–7: This integer and its square root are displayed. The Math.sqrt(number) statement in Line 7 displays the square root.

Before you can test out this application, you need to compile it using the Software Development Kit's javac compiler or the compiler included with another Java development environment. If you're using the SDK, go to a command line, open the folder that contains the Root.java file, then compile Root.java by entering the following at a command line:

```
javac Root.java
```

If you have entered Listing 4.1 without any typos, including all punctuation and every word capitalized exactly as shown, it should compile without any errors. The compiler responds to a successful compilation by not responding with any message at all.

Java applications are compiled into a class file that can be run by a Java interpreter. If you're using the SDK, you can run the compiled `Root.class` file by typing this command:

```
java Root
```

The output should resemble the following:

OUTPUT   `The square root of 225 is 15.0`

When you run a Java application, the interpreter looks for a `main()` block and starts handling Java statements at that point. If your program does not have a `main()` block, the interpreter will respond with an error.

Sending Arguments to Applications

Because Java applications are run from a command line, you can send information to applications at the same time you run them. The following example uses the `java` interpreter to run an application called `DisplayTextFile.class`, and it sends two extra items of information to the application, `readme.txt` and `/p`:

```
java DisplayTextFile readme.txt /p
```

Extra information you can send to a program is called an *argument*. The first argument, if there is one, is provided one space after the name of the application. Each additional argument is also separated by a space.

If you want to include a space inside an argument, you must put quotation marks around the argument, as in the following:

```
java DisplayTextFile readme.txt /p "Page Title"
```

This example runs the `DisplayTextFile` program with three arguments: `readme.txt`, `/p`, and `Page Title`. The quote marks prevent `Page` and `Title` from being treated as separate arguments.

You can send as many arguments as you want to a Java application. In order to do something with them, however, you have to write some statements in the application to handle them.

4

To see how arguments work in an application, create a new file in your word processor called `Blanks.java`. Enter the text of Listing 4.2 into the file and save it when you're done. Compile the program, correcting any errors that are caused by typos.

LISTING 4.2   The Full Text of `Blanks.java`

```
1: class Blanks {
2:     public static void main(String[] arguments) {
3:         System.out.println("The " + arguments[0]
4:             + " " + arguments[1] + " fox "
5:             + "jumped over the "
6:             + arguments[2] + " dog.");
7:     }
8: }
```

To try out the `Blanks` application, run it with a Java interpreter such as the SDK's `java` tool. Give it three adjectives of your own choosing as arguments, as in the following example:

```
java Blanks retromingent purple lactose-intolerant
```

The application uses the adjectives to fill out a sentence. Here's the one produced by the preceding three arguments:

 `The retromingent purple fox jumped over the lactose-intolerant dog.`

Try it with some of your own adjectives, making sure to always include at least three of them.

Arguments are a useful way to customize the performance of a program. They are often used to configure a program so it runs a specific way. Java stores arguments in *arrays*, groups of related variables that all hold the same information. You'll learn about arrays during Hour 9, "Storing Information with Arrays."

Applet Basics

When the Java language was introduced in 1995, the language feature that got the most attention was applets, Java programs that run on a World Wide Web page. Before Java, Web pages were a combination of text, images, and forms that used gateway programs running on the computer that hosted the pages. These gateway programs required special access to the Web server presenting the page, so most Web users did not have the ability to use them. Writing them required even more expertise.

In contrast, programmers of all skill levels can write Java applets, and you'll write several during the span of these 24 hours. You can test them with any Web browser that handles Java programs, and put one on a Web page without requiring any special access from a Web provider. The Java programs you toured during the previous hour were all applets. Their structure differs from applications in several important ways, and they are designed specifically for presentation on the World Wide Web.

> Because the applets you'll write in this book use Java 2, these applets must be run with a browser that supports the most current version of the language. During Hour 17, "Creating Interactive Web Programs," you'll learn how to set up a browser to use the Java Plug-in to run Java 2 applets. All applets can also be tested with the appletviewer tool that is included with the Software Development Kit.

Unlike applications, applets do not have a main() block. Instead, they have several different sections that are handled depending on what is happening in the applet, as detailed fully during Hour 17. Two of the sections are the init() block statement and the paint() block. init() is short for initialization, and it is used to take care of anything that needs to be set up as an applet first runs. The paint() block is used to display anything that should be displayed.

To see an applet version of the Root application, create a new file in your word processor and call it RootApplet.java. Enter the code in Listing 4.3 and save it when you're done.

LISTING 4.3 The Full Text of RootApplet.java

```
 1: import java.awt.*;
 2:
 3: public class RootApplet extends javax.swing.JApplet {
 4:     int number;
 5:
 6:     public void init() {
 7:         number = 225;
 8:     }
 9:
10:     public void paint(Graphics screen) {
11:         Graphics2D screen2D = (Graphics2D) screen;
12:         screen2D.drawString("The square root of " +
13:             number +
14:             " is " +
15:             Math.sqrt(number), 5, 50);
16:     }
17: }
```

Compile this file using your Java development software. If you are using the `javac` compiler tool in the SDK, type the following at a command line:

```
javac RootApplet.java
```

This program contains a lot of the same statements as the `Root` application that did the same thing. The main difference is in how it is organized—the `main()` block has been replaced with an `init()` block and a `paint()` block.

> The sample programs in this hour are provided primarily to introduce you to the way Java programs are structured. Some aspects of these programs will be introduced fully later, so don't feel like you're falling behind. The main purpose of this hour is to get the programs to compile and see how they function when you run them.

Unlike applications, compiled Java applets cannot be tested using a Java interpreter. You have to put them on a Web page and view that page in one of two ways:

- Use a Web browser that can handle Java 2 applets by using Sun's Java Plug-in, which requires special configuration of the Web page.
- Use the `appletviewer` tool that comes with the Software Development Kit.

To create a Web page that can display the `RootApplet` program, return to your word processor and create a new file. Enter Listing 4.4 in that file and save it as `RootApplet.html`.

LISTING 4.4   The Full Text of `RootApplet.html`

```
1: <applet code="RootApplet.class" height=100 width=300>
2: </applet>
```

This Web page contains the bare minimum needed to display a Java applet on a Web page. The `<APPLET>` tag is used to specify that a Java program is being put on the page, the `code` attribute provides the name of the applet, and the `height` and `width` attributes describe the size of the applet's display area. These items will be described in detail during Hour 17.

To see this applet using the `appletviewer` tool included with Software Development Kit, type the following at a command line:

```
appletviewer RootApplet.html
```

To see it using your computer's default Web browser, type the following instead:

```
RootApplet.html
```

You can also load this page in your browser: Choose File, Open, then navigate to the folder that contains RootApplet.html and select the file.

Figure 4.1 shows what the applet looks like when loaded with Internet Explorer.

FIGURE 4.1

The RootApplet applet displayed with a Web browser.

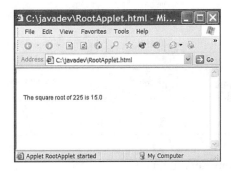

If you try to load this page with your Web browser and get an error, the most likely cause is that your browser is not yet equipped with the Java Plug-in. To correct this, visit the Web page http://java.sun.com/getjava to download and install the free Java Runtime Environment, which includes the Java Plug-in.

Sending Parameters to Applets

Java applets are never run from the command line, so you can't specify arguments the way you can with applications. Applets use a different way to receive information at the time the program is run. This information is called *parameters*, and you can send parameters through the HTML page that runs the applet. You have to use a special HTML tag for parameters called <PARAM>.

To see how the Blanks application would be rewritten as an applet, open your word processor, enter the text of Listing 4.5, then save the file as BlanksApplet.java.

LISTING 4.5 The Full Text of BlanksApplet.java

```
1: import java.awt.*;
2:
3: public class BlanksApplet extends javax.swing.JApplet {
4:     String parameter1;
```

LISTING 4.5 continued

```
 5:        String parameter2;
 6:        String parameter3;
 7:
 8:        public void init() {
 9:            parameter1 = getParameter("adjective1");
10:            parameter2 = getParameter("adjective2");
11:            parameter3 = getParameter("adjective3");
12:        }
13:
14:        public void paint(Graphics screen) {
15:            screen.drawString("The " + parameter1
16:                + " " + parameter2 + " fox "
17:                + "jumped over the "
18:                + parameter3 + " dog.", 5, 50);
19:        }
20: }
```

Save the file and then compile it. Using the SDK, you can accomplish this by typing the following at the command line:

```
javac BlanksApplet.java
```

Before you can try out this applet, you need to create a Web page that displays the BlanksApplet applet after sending it three adjectives as parameters. Open your word processor and enter Listing 4.6, saving it as BlanksApplet.html.

LISTING 4.6 The Full Text of BlanksApplet.html

```
1: <applet code="BlanksApplet.class" height=80 width=500>
2: <param name="adjective1" value="lachrymose">
3: <param name="adjective2" value="magenta">
4: <param name="adjective3" value="codependent">
5: </applet>
```

Save the file when you're done, and load the page using Internet Explorer, the SDK's appletviewer, or another browser equipped with the Java Plug-in. The output should resemble Figure 4.2. Change the values of the value attribute in Lines 2–4 of the BlanksApplet.html file, replacing "lachrymose", "magenta", and "codependent" with your own adjectives, then save the file and run the program again. Try this several times, and you'll see that your program is now flexible enough to handle any adjectives, no matter how well or how poorly they describe the strange relationship between the fox and the dog.

FIGURE 4.2

The BlanksApplet *program displayed with a Web browser.*

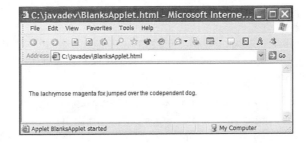

You can use as many parameters as needed to customize the operation of an applet, as long as each has a different NAME attribute specified along with the <PARAM> tag.

Workshop: Viewing the Code Used to Run Applets

As a short workshop to better familiarize yourself with the <APPLET> tag and how it can be used to alter the performance of an applet, visit this book's World Wide Web site at http://www.java24hours.com.

Load this site by using one of the Web browsers that can run Java applets, such as Microsoft Internet Explorer, Netscape Navigator, or Mozilla. Go to the section of the site labeled "Hour 4 Showcase," and you'll be given a guided tour through several working examples of applets. These applets were written with Java version 1.0, so they can be run with any browser that supports Java, even if it isn't equipped with the Java Plug-in.

On each of the pages in the Hour 4 Showcase, you can use a pull-down menu command to view the HTML tags that were used to create the page:

- In Internet Explorer or Opera, choose View, Source.
- In Navigator or Mozilla, choose View, Page Source.

Compare the parameters that are used with each applet to the way the applet runs.

Appendix F, "This Book's Web Site," describes other things you can find on the book's site. The Web site is intended as a complement to the material covered in this book, and a way to find out about corrections, revisions, or other information that make these 24 hours more productive.

4

Summary

During this hour, you got a chance to create both a Java application and an applet. These two types of programs have several important differences in the way they function and the way they are created.

Both kinds of Java programs can be easily customized at the time they are run. Applications use arguments, which are specified on the command line at the time the program is run. Applets use parameters, which are included on the Web page that displays the applet by using HTML tags.

The next several hours will continue to focus on applications as you become more experienced as a Java programmer. Applications are quicker to test because they don't require you to create a Web page to view them; they can be easier to create as well.

Q&A

Q Can a single Java program be both an applet and an application?

A It is possible to make a program serve as both applet and application, but it's often an unwieldy solution unless the program is simple. An applet could be set up to run as an application also by including a `main()` block in the applet, but you would not be able to use the `init()` block or `paint()` block in the automatic fashion they are used in an applet. Most programs are written as either an application or as an applet, rather than attempting to do both.

Q Do all arguments sent to a Java application have to be strings?

A Java makes all arguments into strings for storage when an application runs. When you want to use one of these arguments as an integer or some other non-string type, you have to convert the value. You'll learn how to do this during Hour 11, "Describing What Your Object Is Like."

Q I get errors when I try to load `RootApplet.html` into either Mozilla or Microsoft Internet Explorer. What's the problem?

A In most cases, the problem is that the browser isn't equipped to run Java 2 applets. Internet Explorer and Netscape Navigator have built-in support for Java 1.0, the first widely available version of the language, and partial support for Java 1.1. Sun offers a Java Plug-in that makes it possible for both leading browsers to support Java 2 applets, but it only works if the Web page containing the applet is equipped to work with the plug-in. When you're in doubt about why an applet won't work in a browser, try loading it with the `appletviewer` tool included with the Software Development Kit. If it works in `appletviewer`, the problem is with the browser rather than your Java applet.

Q Why don't Java applets require the same kind of special access as gateway programs?

A Java applets don't have the same access requirements because they don't pose the same risk to a Web hosting provider. Gateway programs don't have much security in place to prevent the program from attempting to do harmful things to the machine presenting the Web page. Java applets, on the other hand, have strict restrictions to prevent them from being used to write harmful programs. Also, Java programs do not run on the Web site's machine—they run on the system of the person viewing the page. This means that the Web site's machine will not slow down due to numerous people running a Java applet on a page.

Quiz

Test your knowledge of the material covered in this chapter by answering the following questions.

4

Questions

1. Which type of Java program can be run by a Java interpreter?

    a. applets

    b. applications

    c. both

2. What special HTML tag is used to put a Java program onto a Web page?

    a. `<APPLET>`

    b. `<PROGRAM>`

    c. `<RUN>`

3. If you get into a fight with someone over the way to send information to a Java application, what are you doing?

    a. Struggling over strings

    b. Arguing about arguments

    c. Feudin' for functionality

Answers

1. c. Both. Web browsers use their own built-in interpreters or the Java Plug-in. Applications use a command-line interpreter such as the `java` tool in the SDK.

2. a. The `<APPLET>` tag is used along with the `<PARAM>` tag to send parameters to the applet. You'll learn about a second tag that can be used to present applets during Hour 17.

3. b. Can't we all just get along?

Activities

If you'd like to apply your acumen of applets and applications, the following activities are suggested:

- Check out EarthWeb's Java Applet Ratings Service Web site at `http://www.jars.com` and use the search term `headline` to see links and descriptions to all of the applets that have been written to display news headlines. Each of these applets use parameters to modify the text that is displayed.

- Write a Java applet that can handle a parameter named `X` and a parameter named `Y`. Display the two parameters in a `drawString()` statement like the one in the `BlanksApplet` program.

To see a Java program that implements the second activity, visit the book's Web site at `http://www.java24hours.com`.

PART II

Learning the Basics of Programming

Hour

HOUR 5

Storing and Changing Information in a Program

In Hour 2, "Writing Your First Program," you used a *variable*, a special storage place that is used to hold information. The information stored in variables can be changed as your program runs, which is why they're called variables.

Your first program stored a string of text in a variable called greeting. Strings are only one type of information that can be stored in variables. They can also hold characters, integers, floating-point numbers, and other things.

During this hour, you'll learn more about using variables in your Java programs, including the following topics:

- Creating variables
- The different types of variables
- Storing values into variables

- Using variables in mathematical expressions
- Putting one variable's value into another variable
- Increasing and decreasing a variable's value

Statements and Expressions

Computer programs are a set of instructions that tell the computer what to do. Each of these instructions is called a statement. The following example from a Java program is a statement:

```
int HighScore = 400000;
```

You can use brackets to group a set of statements together in a Java program. These groupings are called *block statements*. Consider the following portion of a program:

```
1: public static void main(String[] arguments) {
2:     int a = 3;
3:     int b = 4;
4:     int c = 8 * 5;
5: }
```

Lines 2–4 of this example are a block statement. The opening bracket on Line 1 denotes the beginning of the block, and the closing bracket on Line 5 denotes the end of the block.

Some statements are called *expressions* because they involve a mathematical expression. Line 4 in the preceding example is an expression because it sets the value of the c variable equal to 8 multiplied by 5. You'll be working with several different types of expressions throughout the coming sections.

Assigning Variable Types

Variables are the main way that a computer remembers something as it runs a program. The Saluton program in Hour 2 used the greeting variable to hold "Saluton mondo!", a message in Esperanto. The computer needed to remember that text a little later, so that the message could be displayed.

In a Java program, variables are created with a statement that must include two things:

- The name of the variable
- The type of information the variable will store

To see the different types of variables and how they are created, load the word processor you're using to write programs and set it up to start a new file. You will be creating a program called Variable.

Give your new file the name Variable.java and start writing the program by entering the following lines:

```
class Variable {
    public static void main(String[] arguments) {
        // Coming soon: variables
    }
}
```

Go ahead and save these lines before making any changes.

Integers and Floating-Point Numbers

So far, the Variable program has a main() block with only one statement in it—the comment line // Coming soon: variables. Delete the comment line and enter the following statement in its place:

```
int tops;
```

This statement creates a variable named tops. It does not specify a value for tops, so the variable is an empty storage space for the moment. The int text at the beginning of the statement designates tops as a variable that will be used to store integer numbers. You can use the int type to store most of the nondecimal numbers you will need in your computer programs. It can hold any integer from –2.14 billion to 2.14 billion.

Create a blank line after the int tops; statement and add the following statement:

```
float gradePointAverage;
```

This statement creates a variable with the name gradePointAverage. The float text stands for floating-point numbers. Floating-point variables are used to store numbers that might contain a decimal point.

A floating-point variable can be used to store a grade point average, such as 2.25, to pick a number that's dear to my heart. It also can be used to store a number such as 0, which is the percentage chance of getting into a good graduate school with that grade point average, despite my really good cover letter and a compelling written recommendation from my parole officer.

5

Characters and Strings

Because all the variables you have dealt with so far are numeric, you might have the impression that all variables are used as a storage place for numbers. Think again. You can also use variables to store text. Two types of text can be stored as variables: characters and strings. A *character* is a single letter, number, punctuation mark, or other symbol. Most of the things you can use as characters are shown on your computer's keyboard. A *string* is a group of characters.

Your next step in creating the `Variable` program is to create a `char` variable and a `String` variable. Add these two statements after the line `float gradePointAverage;`:

```
char key = 'C';
String productName = "Larvets";
```

When you are using character values in your program, such as in the previous example, you must put single quotation marks on both sides of the character value being assigned to a variable. You must surround string values with double quotation marks. These quotation marks are needed to prevent the character or string from being confused with a variable name or other part of a statement. Take a look at the following statement:

```
String productName = Larvets;
```

This statement might look like a statement that tells the computer to create a string variable called `productName` and give it the text value of `Larvets`. However, because there are no quotation marks around the word `Larvets`, the computer is being told to set the `productName` value to the same value as a variable named `Larvets`.

> If you're wondering about Larvets, the product mentioned in this section, it's a snack made from edible worms that have been killed, dried, and mixed with the same kinds of nuclear flavoring as Doritos chips. You can order Larvets in three flavors—BBQ, cheddar cheese, and Mexican spice—from the mail-order retailer HotLix at the Web site `http://www.hotlix.com/ larvets.htm` or by calling 1-800-EAT-WORM.

After adding the `char` and `String` statements, your program will resemble Listing 5.1. Make any changes that are needed and be sure to save the file. This program does not produce anything to display, but you should compile it with your Java compiler to make sure it was created correctly.

LISTING 5.1   The Variable Program

```
1: class Variable {
2:    public static void main(String[] arguments) {
3:        int tops;
4:        float gradePointAverage;
5:        char key = 'C';
6:        String productName = "Larvets";
7:    }
8: }
```

To compile the program using the SDK compiler, type the following command:

```
javac Variable.java
```

The last two variables in the Variable program use the = sign to assign a starting value when the variables are created. You can use this option for any variables you create in a Java program. For more information, see the section called "Storing Information in Variables" later in this hour.

Although the other variable types are all lowercase letters (int, float, and char), the capital letter is required in the word String when creating string variables. A string in a Java program is somewhat different from the other types of information you will use in variables. You'll learn about this distinction in Hour 6, "Using Strings to Communicate."

Other Numeric Variable Types

The variables you have been introduced to so far will be the main ones you use during this book and probably for most of your Java programming. There are a few other types of variables you can use in special circumstances.

You can use three other variable types with integers. The first, byte, can be used for integer numbers that range from –128 to 127. The following statement creates a variable called escapeKey with an initial value of 27:

```
byte escapeKey = 27;
```

The second, short, can be used for integers that are smaller in size than the int type. A short integer can range from –32,768 to 32,767, as in the following example:

```
short roomNumber = 222;
```

Another of the numeric variable types, long, is typically used for integers that are too big for the int type to hold. A long integer can be almost any size: If the number has five commas or fewer when you write it down, it can fit into a `long`. Some six-comma numbers can fit as well.

There are two numeric types for decimal numbers: `float`, which can handle numbers with around 38 digits to the right or left of the decimal point, and `double`, which supports even more digits—as many as 324.

The `boolean` Variable Type

Java has a special type of variable called `boolean` that can only be used to store the value `true` or the value `false`. At first glance, a `boolean` variable might not seem particularly useful unless you plan to write a lot of computerized true-or-false quizzes. However, `boolean` variables will be used in a variety of situations in your programs. The following are some examples of questions that `boolean` variables can be used to answer:

- Has the user pressed a key?
- Is the game over?
- Is this the first time the user has done something?
- Is the bank account overdrawn?
- Have all ten images been displayed onscreen?
- Can the rabbit eat Trix?

The following statement is used to create a `boolean` variable called `gameOver`:

```
boolean gameOver = false;
```

This variable has the starting value of `false`, and a statement such as this one can be used in a game program to indicate that the game isn't over yet. Later on, when something happens to end the game (such as the destruction of all the player's acrobatic Italian laborers), the `gameOver` variable can be set to `true`. Although the two possible `boolean` values—`true` and `false`—look like strings in a program, you should not surround them with quotation marks. Hour 7, "Using Conditional Tests to Make Decisions," describes `boolean` variables more fully.

Boolean numbers are named for George Boole, who lived from 1815 to 1864. Boole, a mathematician who was mostly self-taught until late adulthood, invented Boolean algebra, a fundamental part of computer programming, digital electronics, and logic. One imagines that he did pretty well on true-false tests as a child.

Naming Your Variables

Variable names in Java can begin with a letter, underscore character (_), or a dollar sign ($). The rest of the name can be any letters or numbers, but you cannot use blank spaces. You can give your variables any names you like under those rules, but you should be consistent in how you name variables. This section outlines the generally recommended naming method for variables.

> Java is case-sensitive when it comes to variable names, so you must always capitalize variable names in the same way throughout a program. For example, if the gameOver variable is used as GameOver somewhere in the program, the use of GameOver will cause an error when you compile the program.

For starters, the name you give a variable will describe its purpose in some way. The first letter should be lowercase, and if the variable name has more than one word, make the first letter of each subsequent word a capital letter. For instance, if you wanted to create an integer variable to store the all-time high score in a game program, you can use the following statement:

```
int allTimeHighScore;
```

You can't use punctuation marks or spaces in a variable name, so neither of the following will work:

```
int all-TimeHigh Score;
int all Time High Score;
```

If you tried to use these names in a program, the Java compiler would respond with an error.

Storing Information in Variables

You can put a value into a variable at the same time that you create the variable in a Java program. You can also put a value in the variable at any time later in the program.

To set up a starting value for a variable upon its creation, use the equal sign (=). The following is an example of creating a floating-point variable called pi with the starting value of 3.14:

```
double pi = 3.14;
```

5

All variables that store numbers can be set up in a similar fashion. If you're setting up a character or a string variable, quotation marks must be placed around the value as shown previously.

You can also set one variable equal to the value of another variable if they both are of the same type. Consider the following example:

```
int mileage = 300;
int totalMileage = mileage;
```

First, an integer variable called `mileage` is created with a starting value of `300`. In the second line, an integer variable called `totalMileage` is created with the same value as `mileage`. Both variables will have the starting value of `300`. In future hours, you will learn how to convert one variable's value to the type of another variable.

> If you do not give a variable a starting value, you must give it a value before you try to use it. If you don't, when you attempt to compile your program, the `javac` compiler will respond with an error message such as the following:
>
> ```
> WarGame.java:7: Variable warships may not have been initialized.
>                     warships = warships + 10;
>                     ^
>
> 1 error
> ```

Another naming convention in Java is to capitalize the names of variables that will not change in value. These variables are called *constants*. The following creates three constants:

```
int TOUCHDOWN = 7;
int FIELDGOAL = 3;
int PAT = 1;
```

Because constants never change in value, you might wonder why one should ever be used—you can just use the value assigned to the constant instead. One of the advantages of using constants is that they can make a program easier to understand. For example, the variables `Font.BOLD` and `Font.ITALIC` are constants that hold integer values representing the style of the current font.

Workshop: Using Expressions

As you worked on a particularly unpleasant math problem in school, did you ever complain to a higher power, protesting that you would never use this knowledge in your life?

Sorry to break this to you, but all your teachers were right—those math skills are going to be used in your computer programming.

That's the bad news. The good news is that the computer will do any of the math you ask it to do. As mentioned earlier in this hour, any instructions you give a computer program involving math are called expressions. Expressions will be used frequently in your computer programs. You can use them for tasks such as the following:

- Changing the value of a variable
- Counting the number of times something has happened in a program
- Using a mathematical formula in a program

As you write computer programs, you will find yourself drawing on your old math lessons as you use expressions. Expressions can use addition, subtraction, multiplication, division, and modulus division.

To see expressions in action, return to your word processor and close the Variable.java file if it is still open. Create a new file and save it as Elvis.java. The Elvis program creates a fictional person whose weight loss and gain can be tracked with mathematical expressions. Instead of adding statements to the program piece-by-piece, enter the full text of Listing 5.2 into the word processor. Each part of the program will be discussed in turn.

LISTING 5.2 The Elvis Program

```
 1: class Elvis {
 2:     public static void main(String[] arguments) {
 3:         int weight = 250;
 4:         System.out.println("Elvis weighs " + weight);
 5:         System.out.println("Elvis visits all-you-can-eat rib joint.");
 6:         System.out.println("Elvis throws Thanksgiving luau.");
 7:         weight = weight + 10;
 8:         System.out.println("Elvis now weighs " + weight);
 9:         System.out.println("Elvis discovers aerobics.");
10:         weight = weight - 15;
11:         System.out.println("Elvis now weighs " + weight);
12:         System.out.println("Elvis falls into washing machine during "
13:             + "shrink cycle.");
14:         weight = weight / 3;
15:         System.out.println("Elvis now weighs " + weight);
16:         System.out.println("Oops! Elvis clones himself 12 times.");
17:         weight = weight + (weight * 12);
18:         System.out.println("The 13 Elvii now weigh " + weight);
19:     }
20: }
```

5

When you're done, save the file and compile the program. If you're using the SDK, in the same folder as the `Elvis.java` file, type the following at a command line to compile the `Elvis` application:

```
javac Elvis.java
```

If it compiles without any errors, you will not see any output; `javac` only responds if something goes wrong. If you do see error messages, check the line number that is listed in each error message to look for typos. Correct any typos you find and compile the program.

Next, run the program. SDK users should type the following at a command line:

```
java Elvis
```

Listing 5.3 shows the output for this program.

LISTING 5.3   The Output of the `Elvis` Program

```
Elvis weighs 250
Elvis visits all-you-can-eat rib joint.
Elvis throws Thanksgiving luau.
Elvis now weighs 260
Elvis discovers aerobics.
Elvis now weighs 245
Elvis falls into washing machine during shrink cycle.
Elvis now weighs 81
Oops! Elvis clones himself 12 times.
The 13 Elvii now weigh 1053
```

As in the other programs you have created, the `Elvis` program uses a `main()` block statement for all its work. This statement can be broken into the following five sections:

1. Lines 3–4: The initial weight of Elvis is set to 250.

2. Lines 5–8: Elvis gains weight.

3. Lines 9–11: Elvis loses weight.

4. Lines 12–15: Elvis reduces in size dramatically.

5. Lines 16–18: Elvis multiplies.

Line 3 creates the `weight` variable and designates it as an integer variable with `int`. The variable is given the initial value `250` and used throughout the program to monitor Elvis' weight.

The next line is similar to several other statements in the program:

```
System.out.println("Elvis weighs " + weight);
```

The `System.out.println()` command displays a string that is contained within its parenthesis marks. In the preceding line, the text `"Elvis weighs"` is displayed, followed by the value of the `weight` variable. There are numerous `System.out.println()` statements in the program. If you're still unclear about how these statements work, look at each of them in Listing 5.2 and compare them to the corresponding lines in Listing 5.3.

All About Operators

Four different mathematical expressions are used in the `Elvis` program—to add weight to Elvis, subtract weight from Elvis, divide Elvis, and finish off with some multiplied Elvii. Each of these expressions uses symbols (+, -, *, /, and %) called *operators*. You will be using these operators to crunch numbers throughout your Java programs.

An addition expression in Java uses the + sign, as in Line 7 of your program:

```
weight = weight + 10;
```

This line sets the `weight` variable equal to its current value plus 10. Because the `weight` was set to 250 when it was created, Line 7 changes `weight` to 260.

A subtraction expression uses the - sign, as in Line 10:

```
weight = weight - 15;
```

This expression sets the `weight` variable equal to its current value minus 15. The `weight` variable is now equal to 245.

A division expression uses the / sign, as in Line 14:

```
weight = weight / 3;
```

The `weight` variable is set to its current value divided by 3 and rounded down because `weight` is an integer. The `weight` variable is now equal to 81.

There's another expression you can use to find the remainder of a division. When the value of the `weight` variable was divided by 3 in Line 14, a remainder of 2 was discarded in order for `weight` to remain as an integer value. To find a remainder from a division expression, use the % operator. You can use the following statement to find the remainder of 245 divided by 3:

```
int remainder = 245 % 3;
```

5

A multiplication expression uses the * sign. Line 17 uses a multiplication expression as part of a more complicated statement:

```
weight = weight + (weight * 12);
```

The weight * 12 part of the expression multiplies weight by 12. The full statement takes the current value of weight and adds it to weight multiplied by 12. This example shows how more than one expression can be combined in a statement. The result is that weight becomes 1,053—in other words, 81 + (81 * 12).

Incrementing and Decrementing a Variable

A common task in programs is to change the value of a variable by one. You can increase the value by one, which is called *incrementing* the variable, or decrease the value by one, which is *decrementing* the variable. There are operators to accomplish each of these tasks.

To increment the value of a variable by one, use the ++ operator, as in the following statement:

```
x++;
```

This statement adds one to the value stored in the x variable.

To decrement the value of a variable by one, use the - - operator:

```
y--;
```

This statement reduces y by one.

You also can put the increment and decrement operators in front of the variable name, as in the following statements:

```
++x;
--y;
```

Putting the operator in front of the variable name is called *prefixing*, and putting it after the name is called *postfixing*. You probably have many cherished memories of grade school language lessons, when you learned about prefixes such as "pre-", "extra-", and "de-". A prefixed operator is like a prefix in a word—it comes first. Postfixed operators lag behind. (If your memories of those classes are not-so-cherished, you must not have sat behind Mary Beth Farkas.)

Although it might seem redundant for Java to include both prefixed and postfixed operators, the difference becomes important when you use the increment and decrement operators inside an expression.

Consider the following statements:

```
int x = 3;
int answer = x++ * 10;
```

What does the `answer` variable equal after these statements are handled? You might expect it to equal 40—which would be true if 3 was incremented by 1, which equals 4, and then 4 was multiplied by 10.

However, `answer` is set to 30. The reason is that the postfixed operator was used instead of the prefixed operator.

When a postfixed operator is used on a variable inside an expression, the variable's value won't change until after the expression has been completely evaluated. The statement `int answer = x++ * 10` does the same thing, in the same order, as the following two statements:

```
int answer = x * 10;
x++;
```

The opposite is true of prefixed operators. If they are used on a variable inside an expression, the variable's value changes before the expression is evaluated.

Consider the following statements:

```
int x = 3;
int answer = ++x * 10;
```

This does result in the `answer` variable being equal to 40. The prefixed operator causes the value of the x variable to be changed before the expression is evaluated. The statement `int answer = ++x * 10` does the same thing, in order, as these statements:

```
x++;
int answer = x * 10;
```

At this point, you might be ready to say, "Prefixing, postfixing, incrementing, decrementing—let's call the whole thing off!" It's easy to become exasperated with the ++ and — operators, because they're not as straightforward as many of the concepts you'll encounter in this book.

There's some good news: You don't need to use the increment and decrement operators in your own programs. You can achieve the same results by using the + and - operators. Incrementing and decrementing are useful shortcuts, but taking the longer route in an expression is fine, too.

5

During Hour 1, "Becoming a Programmer," the name of the C++ programming language was described as a joke you'd understand later. Now that you've been introduced to the increment operator ++, you have all the information you need to figure out why C++ has two plus signs in its name instead of just one. Prepare to laugh: Because C++ adds new features and functionality to the C programming language, it can be considered an incremental increase to C. Hence the name C++. After you work through all 24 hours of this book, you also will be able to tell jokes that are incomprehensible to more than 99 percent of the world's population.

Operator Precedence

When you are using an expression with more than one operator, you need to know what order the computer will use as it works out the expression. Consider the following statements:

```
int y = 10;
x = y * 3 + 5;
```

Unless you know what order the computer will use when working out the math in the last statement, you cannot be sure what the x variable will be set to. It could be set to either 35 or 80, depending on whether y * 3 is evaluated first or 3 + 5 is evaluated first.

The following order is used when working out an expression:

1. Incrementing and decrementing take place first.
2. Multiplication, division, and modulus division occur next.
3. Addition and subtraction follow.
4. Comparisons take place next.
5. The equal sign (=) is used to set a variable's value.

Because multiplication takes place before addition, you can revisit the previous example and come up with the answer:

```
int y = 10;
x = y * 3 + 5;
```

In the last statement, y is multiplied by 3 first, which equals 30, and then 5 is added. The x variable is set to 35.

Comparisons will be discussed during Hour 7. The rest has been described during this hour, so you should be able to figure out the result of the following statements:

```
int x = 5;
int number = x++ * 6 + 4 * 10 / 2;
```

These statements set the `number` variable equal to 50.

How does the computer come up with this total? First the increment operator is handled, and x++ sets the value of the x variable to 6. However, make note of the fact that the ++ operator is postfixed after x in the expression. This means that the expression is evaluated with the original value of x.

Because the original value of x is used before the variable is incremented, the expression becomes the following:

```
int number = 5 * 6 + 4 * 10 / 2;
```

Now, multiplication and division are handled from left to right. First, 5 is multiplied by 6, 4 is multiplied by 10, and that result is divided by 2 (4 * 10 / 2). The expression becomes the following:

```
int number = 30 + 20;
```

This expression results in the `number` variable being set to 50.

If you want an expression to be evaluated in a different order, you can use parentheses to group parts of an expression that should be handled first. For example, the expression x = 5 * 3 + 2; would normally cause x to equal 17 because multiplication is handled before addition. However, look at a modified form of that expression:

```
x = 5 * (3 + 2);
```

In this case, the expression within the parentheses is handled first, so the result equals 25. You can use parentheses as often as needed in an expression.

Summary

Now that you have been introduced to variables and expressions, you can give a wide range of instructions to your computer in a program. With the skills you have developed during this hour, you can write programs that accomplish many of the same tasks as a calculator, handling sophisticated mathematical equations with ease.

Numbers are only one kind of thing that can be stored in a variable. You also can store characters, strings of characters, and special `true` or `false` values called `boolean` variables. The next hour will expand your knowledge of `String` variables and how they are used.

5

Q&A

Q Is a line in a Java program the same thing as a statement?

A No. Although the programs you will create in this book put one statement on each line, this is done to make the programs easier to understand; it's not required. The Java compiler does not consider lines, spacing, or other formatting issues when compiling a program. The compiler just wants to see semicolons at the end of each statement. You can put more than one statement on a line, although this makes a program more difficult for humans to understand when they read its source code. For this reason, it is not generally recommended.

Q Is there a reason to set up a variable without giving it a value right away?

A For many of the simple programs you will be creating in the first several hours, no. However, there are many circumstances where it makes more sense to give a variable a value at some point later in the program. One example would be a calculator program. The variable that stores the result of a calculation will not be needed until a user tries out the program's calculator buttons. You will not need to set up an initial value when a `result` variable is created.

Q What's the specific range for the `long` variable type?

A In Java, a `long` integer variable can be anything from –9,223,372,036,854,775,808 to 9,223,372,036,854,775,807. This range ought to give your mathematical expressions plenty of breathing room when you can't use `int`, which has a range of –2,147,483,648 to 2,147,483,647.

Q Why should the first letter of a variable name be lowercase, as in `gameOver`?

A It makes the variable easier to spot among all the other elements of a Java program. Also, by following a consistent style in the naming of variables, you eliminate errors that can occur when you use a variable in several different places in a program. The style of naming used in this book has become popular since Java's release.

Q Can two variables have the same letters but different capitalization, as in `highScore` and `HighScore`?

A Each of the differently capitalized names would be treated as its own variable, so it's possible to use the same name twice in this way. However, it seems likely to cause a lot of confusion when you or someone else is attempting to figure out how the program works. It also increases the likelihood of using the wrong variable name somewhere in your program, which is an error that will not be caught during compilation. Errors such as that that make it into the finished product are called *logic errors*. They must be caught by an attentive programmer during testing.

Quiz

Test your knowledge of variables, expressions, and the rest of the information in this hour by answering the following questions.

Questions

1. What do you call a group of statements that is contained with an opening bracket and a closing bracket?

    a. A block statement

    b. Groupware

    c. Bracketed statements

2. A `boolean` variable is used to store `true` or `false` values.

    a. True

    b. False

    c. No, thanks. I already ate.

3. What characters cannot be used to start a variable name?

    a. A dollar sign

    b. Two forward slash marks (//)

    c. A letter

Answers

1. a. The grouped statements are called a *block statement*, or a *block*.

2. a. `true` and `false` are the only answers a `boolean` variable can store.

3. b. Variables can start with a letter, a dollar sign ($), or an underscore character (_).

5

Activities

You can review the topics of this hour more fully with the following activities:

- Expand the `Elvis` program to track the weight if it were incremented upward by one pound for three straight days.

- Create a short Java program that uses an x integer and a y integer and displays the result of x squared plus y squared.

To see Java programs that implement these activities, visit the book's Web site at
`http://www.java24hours.com`.

Hour 6

Using Strings to Communicate

In the film *The Piano*, Holly Hunter portrays Ada, a young Scottish woman who marries badly. A mute since the age of six, Ada can only express herself fully by playing her prized possession, a piano.

Like Ada, your computer programs are capable of quietly doing their work and never stopping for a chat—or piano recital—with humans. However, if *The Piano* teaches us anything, it is that communication ranks up there with food, water, and shelter as an essential need. (It also teaches us that Harvey Keitel has a lot of body confidence, but that's a matter for another book.)

Java programs don't have access to a piano. They use strings as the primary means to communicate with users. *Strings* are collections of text—letters, numbers, punctuation, and other characters. During this hour, you will learn all about working with strings in your Java programs. The following topics will be covered:

- Using strings to store text
- Displaying strings in a program

- Including special characters in a string
- Pasting two strings together
- Including variables in a string
- Some uses for strings
- Comparing two strings
- Determining the length of a string
- Changing a string to upper- or lowercase

Storing Text in Strings

Strings are a common feature in computer programming because they provide a way to store text and present it to users. The most basic element of a string is a character. A *character* is a single letter, number, punctuation mark, or other symbol.

In Java programs, a character is one of the types of information that can be stored in a variable. Character variables are created with the char type in a statement such as the following:

```
char keyPressed;
```

This statement creates a variable named keyPressed that can store a character. When you create character variables, you can set them up with an initial value, as in the following:

```
char quitKey = '@';
```

Note that the value of the character must be surrounded by single quotation marks. If it isn't, the Java compiler will respond with an error when the program is compiled.

A string is a collection of characters. You can set up a variable to hold a string value by using the String text and the name of the variable, as in the following statement:

```
String fullName = "Ada McGrath Stewart";
```

This statement creates a string variable called fullName and stores the text Ada McGrath Stewart in it, which is the full name of Hunter's pianist. A string is denoted with double quotation marks around the text in a Java statement. These quotation marks will not be included in the string itself.

Unlike the other types of variables you have used—int, float, char, boolean, and so on—the name of the String type is capitalized.

The reason for this is that strings are somewhat different than the other variable types in Java. Strings are a special resource called objects, and the types of all objects are capitalized. You'll be learning about objects during Hour 10, "Creating Your First Object." The important thing to note during this hour is that strings are different than the other variable types, and because of this difference, `String` is capitalized when strings are used in a statement.

Displaying Strings in Programs

The most basic way to display a string in a Java program is with the `System.out.println()` statement. This statement takes any strings and other variables inside the parentheses and displays them. The following statement displays a line of text to the system output device, which is the computer's monitor:

```
System.out.println("Silence affects everyone in the end.");
```

The preceding statement would cause the following text to be displayed:

```
Silence affects everyone in the end.
```

Displaying a line of text on the screen is often called printing, which is what `println()` stands for—"print this line." You can use the `System.out.println()` statement to display text within double quotation marks and also to display variables, as you will see. Put all the material you want to be displayed within the parentheses.

Another way to display text is to call `System.out.print()`. This statement displays strings and other variables inside the parentheses, but unlike `System.out.println()`, it allows subsequent statements to display text on the same line.

You can use `System.out.print()` several times in a row to display several things on the same line, as in this example:

```
System.out.print("She ");
System.out.print("never ");
System.out.print("said ");
System.out.print("another ");
System.out.println("word.");
```

These statements cause the following text to be displayed:

```
She never said another word.
```

6

Using Special Characters in Strings

When a string is being created or displayed, its text must be enclosed within double quotation marks to indicate the beginning and end of the string. These quotation marks are not displayed, which brings up a good question: What if you want to display double quotation marks?

To display them, Java has created a special code that can be put into a string: \". Whenever this code is encountered in a string, it is replaced with a double quotation mark. For example, examine the following:

```
System.out.println("Jane Campion directed \"The Piano\" in 1993.");
```

This code is displayed as the following:

```
Jane Campion directed "The Piano" in 1993.
```

You can insert several special characters into a string in this manner. The following list shows these special characters; note that each is preceded by a backslash (\).

Special characters	Display
\'	Single quotation mark
\"	Double quotation mark
\\	Backslash
\t	Tab
\b	Backspace
\r	Carriage return
\f	Formfeed
\n	Newline

The newline character causes the text following the newline character to be displayed at the beginning of the next line. Look at this example:

```
System.out.println("Music by\nMichael Nyman");
```

This statement would be displayed as the following:

```
Music by
Michael Nyman
```

Pasting Strings Together

When you use the System.out.println() statement and handle strings in other ways, you will sometimes want to paste two strings together. You do this by using the same operator that is used to add numbers: +.

The + operator has a different meaning in relation to strings. Instead of trying to do some math, it pastes two strings together. This action can cause strings to be displayed together, or it can make one big string out of two smaller ones.

Concatenation is a word used to describe this action, because it means to link two things together. You'll probably see this term in other books as you build your programming skills, so it's worth knowing. However, pasting is the term used here to describe what happens when one string and another string decide to get together. Pasting sounds like fun. Concatenating sounds like something that should never be done in the presence of an open flame.

The following statement uses the + operator to display a long string:

```
System.out.println("\"\'The Piano\' is as peculiar and haunting as any" +
    " film I've seen.\"\n\t— Roger Ebert, \'Chicago Sun-Times\'");
```

Instead of putting this entire string on a single line, which would make it harder to understand when you look at the program later, the + operator is used to break up the text over two lines of the program's Java text file. When this statement is displayed, it will appear as the following:

```
"'The Piano' is as peculiar and haunting as any film I've seen."
    — Roger Ebert, 'Chicago Sun-Times'
```

Several special characters are used in the string: \", \', \n, and \t. To better familiarize yourself with these characters, compare the output with the System.out.println() statement that produced it.

Using Other Variables with Strings

Although you can use the + operator to paste two strings together, as demonstrated in the preceding section, you will use it more often to link strings and variables. Take a look at the following:

```
int length = 121;
char rating = 'R';
System.out.println("Running time: " + length + " minutes");
System.out.println("Rated " + rating);
```

6

This code will be displayed as the following:

```
Running time: 121 minutes
Rated R
```

This example displays a unique facet about how the + operator works with strings. It can cause variables that are not strings to be treated just like strings when they are displayed.

The variable `length` is an integer set to the value `121`. It is displayed between the strings `Running time:` and `minutes`. The `System.out.println()` statement is being asked to display a string plus an integer, plus another string. This statement works because at least one part of the group is a string. The Java language offers this functionality to make displaying information easier.

One thing you might want to do with a string is paste something to it several times, as in the following example:

```
String searchKeywords = "";
searchKeywords = searchKeywords + "drama ";
searchKeywords = searchKeywords + "romance ";
searchKeywords = searchKeywords + "New Zealand";
```

This code would result in the `searchKeywords` variable being set to `drama romance New Zealand`. The first line creates the `searchKeywords` variable and sets it to be an empty string, because there's nothing between the double quotation marks. The second line sets the `searchKeywords` variable equal to its current string, plus the string `drama` added to the end. The next two lines add `romance` and `New Zealand` in the same way.

As you can see, when you are pasting more text at the end of a variable, the name of the variable has to be listed twice. Java offers a shortcut to simplify this process a bit: the `+=` operator. The `+=` operator combines the functions of the `=` and `+` operators. With strings, it is used to add something to the end of an existing string. The `searchKeywords` example can be shortened by using `+=`, as shown in the following code:

```
String searchKeywords = "";
searchKeywords += "drama ";
searchKeywords += "romance ";
searchKeywords += "New Zealand";
```

This code produces the same result: `searchKeywords` is set to `drama romance New Zealand`.

Advanced String Handling

In addition to creating strings, pasting them together, and using them with other types of variables, there are several different ways you can examine a string variable and change its value. These advanced features are possible because strings are objects in the Java language. Working with strings develops skills you'll be using to work with other objects later.

Comparing Two Strings

One thing you will be testing often in your programs is whether one string is equal to another. You do this by using `equals()` in a statement with both of the strings, as in this example:

```
String favorite = "piano";
String guess = "ukelele";
System.out.println("Is Ada's favorite instrument a " + guess + "?");
System.out.println("Answer: " + favorite.equals(guess));
```

This example uses two different string variables. One, `favorite`, is used to store the name of Ada's favorite instrument: a piano. The other, `guess`, is used to store a guess as to what her favorite might be. The guess is that Ada prefers the ukelele.

The third line displays the text `Is Ada's favorite instrument a` followed by the value of the guess variable, and then a question mark. The fourth line displays the text `Answer:` and then contains something new:

```
favorite.equals(guess)
```

This part of the statement is known as a method. A *method* is a way to accomplish a task in a Java program. This method's task is to determine if one string, `favorite`, has the same value as another string, `guess`. If the two string variables have the same value, the text `true` will be displayed. If not, the text `false` will be displayed. The following is the output of this example:

```
Is Ada's favorite instrument a ukelele?
Answer: false
```

Determining the Length of a String

It can also be useful at times to determine the length of a string in characters. You do this by using the `length()` method. This method works in the same fashion as the `equals()` method, except that only one string variable is involved. Look at the following example:

```
String cinematographer = "Stuart Dryburgh";
int nameLength = cinematographer.length();
```

This example sets `nameLength`, an integer variable, equal to 15. The `cinematographer.length()` method counts the number of characters in the string variable called `cinematographer`, and this count is assigned to the `nameLength` integer variable.

6

Changing a String's Case

Because computers take everything literally, it's easy to confuse them. Although a human would recognize that the text *Harvey Keitel* and the text *HARVEY KEITEL* are referring to the same thing, most computers would disagree. For instance, the equals() method discussed previously in this hour would state authoritatively that *Harvey Keitel* is not equal to *HARVEY KEITEL*.

To get around some of these obstacles, Java has methods that display a string variable as all uppercase letters (toUpperCase()) or all lowercase letters (toLowerCase()). The following example shows the toUpperCase() method in action:

```
String baines = "Harvey Keitel";
String change = baines.toUpperCase();
```

This code sets the string variable change equal to the baines string variable converted to all uppercase letters—HARVEY KEITEL, in other words. The toLowerCase() method works in the same fashion but returns an all-lowercase string value.

Note that the toUpperCase() method does not change the case of the string variable it is called on. In the preceding example, the baines variable will still be equal to Harvey Keitel.

Looking for a String

Another common task when handling strings is to see whether one string can be found inside another. This is useful when you're looking for specific text in a large number of strings (or a very large string).

To look inside a string, use its indexOf() method. Put the string you are looking for inside the parentheses. If the string is not found, indexOf() produces the value -1. If the string is found, indexOf() produces an integer that represents the position where the string begins. Positions in a string are numbered upwards from 0, beginning with the first character in the string. (In the string "The Piano", the text "Piano" begins at position 3.)

One possible use of the indexOf() method would be to search the entire script of *The Piano* for the place where Ada's domineering husband tells her daughter Flora, "You are greatly shamed and you have shamed those trunks."

If the entire script of *The Piano* was stored in a string called script, you could search it for part of that quote with the following statement.

```
int position = script.indexOf("you have shamed those trunks");
```

If that text can be found in the script string, position will equal the position at which the text "you have shamed those trunks" begins. Otherwise, it will equal -1.

The `indexOf()` method is *case sensitive*, which means that it only looks for text capitalized exactly like the search string. If the string contains the same text capitalized differently, `indexOf()` produces the value -1.

Workshop: Presenting Credits

In *The Piano*, Ada McGrath Stewart was thrown into unfamiliar territory when she moved from Scotland to New Zealand to marry a stranger who didn't appreciate her ivory tickling. You might have felt similarly lost with some of the topics introduced during this hour.

As a workshop to reinforce the string-handling features that have been covered, you will write a Java program to display credits for a feature film. You have three guesses as to the movie chosen, and if you need a hint, it starts with a *The* and ends with a musical instrument that can be used to express the repressed passion of attractive mutes.

Load the word processor you're using to write Java programs and create a new file called `Credits.java`. Enter the text of Listing 6.1 into the word processor and save the file when you're done.

LISTING 6.1 The `Credits` Program

```
 1: class Credits {
 2:     public static void main(String[] arguments) {
 3:         // set up film information
 4:         String title = "The Piano";
 5:         int year = 1993;
 6:         String director = "Jane Campion";
 7:         String role1 = "Ada";
 8:         String actor1 = "Holly Hunter";
 9:         String role2 = "Baines";
10:         String actor2 = "Harvey Keitel";
11:         String role3 = "Stewart";
12:         String actor3 = "Sam Neill";
13:         String role4 = "Flora";
14:         String actor4 = "Anna Paquin";
15:         // display information
16:         System.out.println(title + " (" + year + ")\n" +
17:             "A " + director + " film.\n\n" +
18:             role1 + "\t" + actor1 + "\n" +
19:             role2 + "\t" + actor2 + "\n" +
20:             role3 + "\t" + actor3 + "\n" +
21:             role4 + "\t" + actor4);
22:     }
23: }
```

6

Before you attempt to compile the program, look over the program and see whether you can figure out what it's doing at each stage. Here's a breakdown of what's taking place:

- Line 1 gives the Java program the name `Credits`.

- Line 2 begins the `main()` block statement in which all of the program's work gets done.

- Line 3 is a comment statement explaining that you're going to set up the film's information in subsequent lines.

- Lines 4–14 set up variables to hold information about the film, its director, and its stars. One of the variables, `year`, is an integer. The rest are string variables.

- Line 15 is another comment line for the benefit of humans like us who are examining the program.

- Lines 16–21 are one long `System.out.println()` statement. Everything between the first parenthesis on Line 16 and the last parenthesis on Line 21 is displayed onscreen. The newline text (\n) causes the text after it to be displayed at the beginning of a new line. The tab text (\t) inserts tab spacing in the output. The rest are either text or string variables that should be shown.

- Line 22 ends the `main()` block statement.

- Line 23 ends the program.

If you're using the SDK, you can attempt to compile the program by going to the folder that contains `Credits.java` and typing this command:

```
javac Credits.java
```

If you do not see any error messages, the program has compiled successfully, and you can run it with the following command:

```
java Credits
```

If you do encounter error messages, correct any typos you find in your version of the `Credits` program and try again to compile it.

Listing 6.2 shows the output of the `Credits application`: a rundown of the film, year of release, director, and the four lead performers from *The Piano*. Be glad that you didn't have to present the credits for an ensemble film. A program detailing Robert Altman's *Short Cuts*, the 1993 film with more than 25 lead characters, could hog an hour of typing alone.

LISTING 6.2 The Output of the Credits Program

```
The Piano (1993)
A Jane Campion film.

Ada      Holly Hunter
Baines   Harvey Keitel
Stewart  Sam Neill
Flora    Anna Paquin
```

If this hour's trivia related to *The Piano* and the films of director Jane Campion has sparked your curiosity, or if you just dig quiet women in braids, visit the following World Wide Web sites:

- Magnus Hjelstuen's unofficial *The Piano* Web site, with cast descriptions, storyline discussion, and comprehensive details about his favorite movie can be found at http://www.fys.uio.no/~magnushj/Piano/.
- The Internet Movie Database, a voluminous and searchable database of movies, TV shows, actors, directors, and other related topics, can be found at http://www.imdb.com.

Summary

Once your version of Credits works like the one shown in Listing 6.2, give yourself some credit, too. You're writing longer Java programs and dealing with more sophisticated issues each hour. Like variables, strings are something you'll use every time you sit down to write a program.

At the beginning of *The Piano*, Ada lost her piano when her new husband refused to make his Maori laborers carry it home. Luckily for you, the ability to use strings in your Java programs cannot be taken away by an insensitive newlywed, or anyone else. You'll be using strings in many ways to communicate with users.

6

Q&A

Q How can I set the value of a string variable to be blank?

A A pair of double quotation marks without any text between them is considered to be an empty string. You can set a string variable equal to this upon its creation or in other parts of your programs. The following code creates a new string variable called adaSays and sets it to nothing:

```
String adaSays = "";
```

Q Is there a way to make the text in one `println()` statement start right at the end of the text in the preceding `println()` statement? I don't want the second `println()` statement to start at the beginning of a new line, but it always does.

A Java automatically ends each `System.out.println()` statement with its own new line, so the only way to prevent this is to use a statement that includes all of the text you want to display, or use the `System.out.print()` statement, which displays a string without ending it with a newline character automatically. The `Credits` program from the workshop has an example of a `println()` statement that includes several different lines of output. Take a look at it and see whether it fits what you want to do.

Q I can't seem to get the `toUpperCase()` method to change a string so that it's all capital letters. What am I doing wrong?

A When you call a `String` object's `toUpperCase()` method, it doesn't actually change the `String` object it is called on. Instead, it creates a new string that is all uppercase letters. Consider the following statements:

```
String firstName = "Nessie";
String changeName = firstName.toUpperCase();
System.out.println("First Name: " + firstName);
```

This example will output the text `First Name: Nessie` because `firstName` contains the original string. If you switched the last statement to display the `changeName` variable instead, it would output `First Name: NESSIE`.

Q If the + operator is used with strings to link up two different strings, can you add the numeric value of one string to the value of another?

A You can use the value of a `String` variable as an integer only by using a method that converts the string's value into a numeric form. This procedure is called *casting*, because it recasts existing information, in this case a string, as a different type of information. You'll learn about casting during Hour 11, "Describing What Your Object Is Like."

Q Is it necessary to use += instead of + when adding some text to a string variable?

A Not at all. The += operator is strictly for the benefit of programmers who want to use it as a shortcut. If you're more comfortable using the + operator when pasting some added text to a string variable, you ought to stick with it. The time and convenience you can gain by using += will be lost pretty quickly if it causes you to make errors in your program.

Q Isn't there some kind of == operator that can be used to determine if two strings have the same value, as in daughter == "Flora"?

A As you will discover during the next hour, "Using Conditional Tests to Make Decisions," the == operator can be used with all the variable types except for strings. The reason for the difference is that strings are objects. Java treats objects differently than other types of information, so special methods are necessary to determine whether one string is equal to another.

Q Do all methods in Java display true or false in the same way that the equals() method does in relation to strings?

A Methods have different ways of making a response after they are used. When a method sends back a value, as the equals() method does, it's called *returning* a value. The equals() method is set to return a Boolean value. Other methods might return a string, an integer, another type of variable, or nothing at all.

Quiz

The following questions will test your knowledge of the care and feeding of a string.

Questions

1. My friend concatenates. Should I report him to the authorities?

    a. No. It's only illegal during the winter months.

    b. Yes, but not until I sell the story to *Real TV* first.

    c. No. All he's doing is pasting two strings together in a program.

2. Why is the word String capitalized, while int and others are not?

    a. String is a full word, but int ain't.

    b. Like all objects in Java, String has a capitalized name.

    c. Poor quality control at Sun Microsystems.

3. Which of the following characters will put a single quote in a string?

    a. <QUOTE>

    b. \'

    c. '

6

Answers

1. c. Concatenation is just another word for pasting, joining, melding, or otherwise connecting two strings together. It uses the + and += operators.

2. b. The types of objects available in Java are all capitalized, which is the main reason variable names have a lowercase first letter. It makes it harder to mistake them for objects.

3. b. The single backslash is what begins one of the special characters that can be inserted into strings.

Activities

You can review the topics of this hour more fully with the following activities:

*   Write a short Java program called Favorite that puts the code from this hour's "Comparing Two Strings" section into the main() block statement. Test it out to make sure it works as described and says that Ada's favorite instrument is not the ukelele. When you're done, change the initial value of the guess variable from ukelele to piano. See what happens.

*   Modify the Credits program so that the names of the director and all performers are displayed entirely in uppercase letters.

To see Java programs that implement these activities, visit the book's Web site at http://www.java24hours.com.

HOUR 7

Using Conditional Tests to Make Decisions

Writing a computer program has been compared to telling a household robot what to do. You provide the computer a list of instructions, called *statements*, and these instructions are followed to the letter. You can tell the computer to work out some unpleasant mathematical formulas, and it will work them out for you. Tell it to display some information, and it will dutifully respond.

However, there are times when you need the computer to be more selective about what it does. For example, if you have written a program to balance your checkbook, you might want the computer to display a warning message if your account is overdrawn. The warning could be something along the lines of Hear that bouncing noise? It's your checks. The computer should display this message only if your account is overdrawn. If it isn't, the message would be both inaccurate and emotionally upsetting.

The way to accomplish this task in a Java program is to use a statement called a conditional. *Conditionals* cause something to happen in a program only if a specific condition is met. During this hour, you'll learn how to use three differ-ent types of conditional statements: `if`, `else`, and `switch`. The following topics will be covered:

- Testing to see whether conditions are met
- Using the `if` statement for basic conditional tests
- Using other statements in conjunction with `if`
- Testing whether one value is greater than or less than another
- Testing whether two values are equal or unequal
- Using `else` statements as the opposite of `if` statements
- Chaining several conditional tests together
- Using the `switch` statement for complicated conditional tests
- Creating complicated tests with the ternary operator

Testing a Condition

Whenever a Java program makes a decision, it does so by employing a conditional state-ment. During this hour, you'll be checking the condition of several things in your Java programs using the conditional statements `if`, `else`, `switch`, `case`, and `break`. You will also be using several conditional operators: `==`, `!=`, `<`, `>`, and `?`, along with `boolean` vari-ables.

`if` Statements

If you want to test a condition in a Java program, the most basic way is with an `if` state-ment. As you learned previously, the `boolean` variable type is used to store only two pos-sible values: `true` or `false`. The `if` statement works along the same lines, testing to see whether a condition is true or false, and taking action only if the condition is true.

You use `if` along with a condition to test, as in the following statement:

```
if (account < 0.01)
    System.out.println("Hear that bouncing noise? It's your checks");
```

Although this code is listed on two lines, it's one statement. The first part uses `if` to determine whether the `account` variable is less than 0.01 (1 cent) by using the `<` operator. The second part displays the text `Hear that bouncing noise? It's your checks`.

The second part of an `if` statement will be run only if the first part is true. In the preced-ing example, if the `account` variable has a value of `0.01` or higher, the `println` statement will be ignored. Note that the condition you test with an `if` statement must be surrounded by parentheses, as in (`account < 0.01`).

> If you're not sure why if (`account < 0.01`) is not a statement, note that there is no semicolon at the end of the line. In Java programs, semicolons are used to show where one statement ends and the next one begins. In the preceding example, the semicolon does not appear until after the `println` portion of the statement. If you put a semicolon after the `if` portion, as in if (`account < 0.01`);, you'll cause a logic error in your program that can be hard to spot. Take care regarding semicolons when you start using the `if` statement.

The less-than operator, <, is one of several different operators you can use with conditional statements. You'll become more familiar with the `if` statement as you use it with some of the other operators.

Less Than and Greater Than Comparisons

In the preceding section, the < operator is used the same way it was used in math class: as a less-than sign. There is also a greater-than conditional operator: >. This operator is used in the following statements:

```
if (elephantWeight > 780)
    System.out.println("Elephant too fat for tightrope act.");
if (elephantTotal > 12)
    cleaningExpense = cleaningExpense + 150;
```

The first `if` statement tests whether the value of the `elephantWeight` variable is greater than 780. The second `if` statement tests whether the `elephantTotal` variable is greater than 12.

One thing to understand about `if` statements is that they often cause nothing to happen in your programs. If the two preceding statements are used in a program where `elephantWeight` is equal to 600 and `elephantTotal` is equal to 10, the rest of the `if` statements will be ignored.

There will be times when you want to determine whether something is less than or equal to something else. You can do this with the <= operator, as you might expect; use the >= operator for greater-than-or-equal-to tests. Here's an example:

```
if (account <= 0)
    System.out.println("Hear that bouncing noise? It's your checks");
```

7

This revision of the checkbook example mentioned previously should be a bit easier to understand. It tests whether account is less than or equal to the value 0, and taunts the user if it is.

Equal and Not Equal Comparisons

Another condition to check in a program is equality. Is a variable equal to a specific value? Is one variable equal to the value of another? These questions can be answered with the == operator, as in the following statements:

```
if (answer == rightAnswer)
    studentGrade = studentGrade + 10;

if (studentGrade == 100)
    System.out.println("Such a show off!");
```

The operator used to conduct equality tests has two equal signs: ==. It's very easy to confuse this operator with the = operator, which is used to give a value to a variable. Always use two equal signs in a conditional statement.

You can also test inequality—whether something is not equal to something else. This is accomplished with the != operator, as shown in the following example:

```
if (answer != rightAnswer)
    score = score - 5;
```

You can use the == and != operators reliably with every type of variable except one: strings. To see whether one string has the value of another, use the equals() method described during Hour 6, "Using Strings to Communicate."

Organizing a Program with Block Statements

Up to this point, all of the if statements have been followed with a single instruction, such as the println() method. In many cases, you will want to perform more than one action in response to an if statement. To do this, you'll use the { and } characters to create a block statement. I believe the technical term for these characters is "squiggly bracket marks."

Block statements are statements that are organized into a group. Previously, you have seen how block statements are used to mark the beginning and end of the main() block of a Java program. Each statement within the main() block is handled when the program is run. Listing 7.1 is an example of a Java program with a block statement used to denote the `main()` block. The block statement begins with the opening bracket { on Line 2 and ends with the closing bracket } on Line 11. Load your word processor and enter the text of Listing 7.1 as a new file.

LISTING 7.1 The Game Program

```
1: class Game {
2:     public static void main(String[] arguments) {
3:         int total = 0;
4:         int score = 7;
5:         if (score == 7)
6:             System.out.println("You score a touchdown!");
7:         if (score == 3)
8:             System.out.println("You kick a field goal!");
9:         total = total + score;
10:         System.out.println("Total score: " + total);
11:     }
12: }
```

Save this file as `Game.java` and compile it. If you're using the SDK, you can compile it by typing the following command:

```
javac Game.java
```

When you run the program, the output should resemble Listing 7.2.

LISTING 7.2 The Output of the Game Program

```
You score a touchdown!
Total score: 7
```

You also can use block statements in conjunction with `if` statements to make the computer do more than one thing if a conditional statement is true. The following is an example of an `if` statement that includes a block statement:

```
if (playerScore > 9999) {
    playerLives++;
    System.out.println("Extra life!");
    difficultyLevel = difficultyLevel + 5;
}
```

The brackets are used to group all statements that are part of the `if` statement. If the variable `playerScore` is greater than 9,999, three things will happen:

7

- The value of the `playerLives` variable increases by one (because the increment operator ++ is used).
- The text `Extra life!` is displayed.
- The value of the `difficultyLevel` variable is increased by 5.

If the variable `playerScore` is not greater than 9,999, nothing will happen. All three statements inside the `if` statement block will be ignored.

if-else Statements

There are times when you want to do something if a condition is true and do something else if the condition is false. You can do this by using the `else` statement in addition to the `if` statement, as in the following example:

```
if (answer == correctAnswer) {
    score += 10;
    System.out.println("That's right. You get 10 points.");
}
else {
    score -= 5;
    System.out.println("Sorry, that's wrong. You lose 5 points.");
}
```

The `else` statement does not have a condition listed alongside it, unlike the `if` statement. Generally, the `else` statement is matched with the `if` statement that immediately comes before it in a Java program. You also can use `else` to chain several `if` statements together, as in the following example:

```
if (grade == 'A')
    System.out.println("You got an A. Great job!");
else if (grade == 'B')
    System.out.println("You got a B. Good work!");
else if (grade == 'C')
    System.out.println("You got a C. You'll never get into a good "
        + "college!");
else
    System.out.println("You got an F. You'll do well in Congress!");
```

By putting together several different `if` and `else` statements in this way, you can handle a variety of conditions. In the preceding example, a specific message is sent to A students, B students, C students, and future legislators.

switch Statements

The if and else statements are good for situations with only two possible conditions, but there are times when you have more than two options that need to be considered. With the preceding grade example, you saw that if and else statements can be chained to handle several different conditions.

Another way to do this is to use the switch statement. You can use it in a Java program to test for a variety of different conditions and respond accordingly. In the following example, the grade example has been rewritten with the switch statement to handle a complicated range of choices:

```
switch (grade) {
    case 'A':
        System.out.println("You got an A. Great job!");
        break;
    case 'B':
        System.out.println("You got a B. Good work!");
        break;
    case 'C':
        System.out.println("You got a C. You'll never get into a good "
            + "college!");
        break;
    default:
        System.out.println("You got an F. You'll do well in Congress!");
}
```

The first line of the switch statement specifies the variable that will be tested—in this example, grade. Then the switch statement uses the { and } brackets to form a block statement.

Each of the case statements checks the test variable in the switch statement against a specific value. The value used in a case statement must be either a character or an integer. In this example, there are case statements for the characters 'A', 'B', and 'C'. Each of these has one or two statements that follow it. When one of these case statements matches the variable listed with switch, the computer handles the statements after the case statement until it encounters a break statement.

For example, if the grade variable has the value of B, the text You got a B. Good work! will be displayed. The next statement is break, so no other part of the switch statement will be considered. The break statement tells the computer to break out of the switch statement.

7

The `default` statement is used as a catch-all if none of the preceding `case` statements is true. In this example, it will occur if the `grade` variable does not equal `'A'`, `'B'`, or `'C'`. You do not have to use a `default` statement with every `switch` block statement you use in your programs. If it is omitted, nothing will happen if none of the `case` statements has the correct value.

> One thing you might want to do with `switch` is to make each case statement represent a range of values. As an example, in a grading program, you might want to use an integer called `numberGrade` and test for `case numberGrade > 89:`. Unfortunately, this isn't possible in Java because each case statement must refer to a single value. You'll have to use a series of `if` statements or `if-else` statements when you aren't working with a bunch of different one-value conditions.

The Conditional Operator

The most complicated conditional statement is one that you might not find reasons to use in your programs: the ternary operator. If you find it too confusing to implement in your own programs, take heart—you can use other conditionals to accomplish the same thing.

You can use the ternary operator when you want to assign a value or display a value based on a conditional test. For example, in a video game, you might need to set the `numberOfEnemies` variable based on whether the `skillLevel` variable is greater than 5. One way to do this is with an `if-else` statement:

```
if (skillLevel > 5)
    numberOfEnemies = 10;
else
    numberOfEnemies = 5;
```

A shorter way to do this is to use the ternary operator, which is `?`. A ternary operator has five parts:

- The condition to test, surrounded by parentheses, as in `(skillLevel > 5)`
- A question mark (`?`)
- The value to use if the condition is true
- A colon (`:`)
- The value to use if the condition is false

To use the ternary operator to set the value of numberOfEnemies based on skillLevel, you could use the following statement:

```
numberOfEnemies = (skillLevel > 5) ? 10 : 5;
```

You also can use the ternary operator to determine what information to display. Consider the example of a program that displays the text Mr. or Ms. depending on the value of the gender variable. You could do this action with another if-else statement:

```
if (gender.equals("male"))
    System.out.print("Mr.");
else
    System.out.print("Ms.");
```

A shorter method is to use the ternary operator to accomplish the same thing, as in the following:

```
System.out.print( (gender.equals("male")) ? "Mr." : "Ms." );
```

The ternary operator can be useful, but it's also the hardest conditional in Java to understand. As you learn Java, you won't encounter any situations where the ternary operator must be used instead of if and else statements.

Workshop: Watching the Clock

This hour's workshop gives you another look at each of the conditional tests you can use in your programs. For this project, you will use Java's built-in timekeeping feature, which keeps track of the current date and time, and present this information in sentence form.

Run the word processor you're using to create Java programs and give a new document the name ClockTalk.java. This program is long, but most of it consists of long conditional statements. Type the full text of Listing 7.3 into the word processor and save the file as ClockTalk.java when you're done.

LISTING 7.3   The ClockTalk Program

```
 1: import java.util.*;
 2:
 3: class ClockTalk {
 4:     public static void main(String[] arguments) {
 5:         // get current time and date
 6:         Calendar now = Calendar.getInstance();
 7:         int hour = now.get(Calendar.HOUR_OF_DAY);
 8:         int minute = now.get(Calendar.MINUTE);
 9:         int month = now.get(Calendar.MONTH) + 1;
```

7

LISTING 7.3 continued

```
10:          int day = now.get(Calendar.DAY_OF_MONTH);
11:          int year = now.get(Calendar.YEAR);
12:
13:          // display greeting
14:          if (hour < 12)
15:              System.out.println("Good morning.\n");
16:          else if (hour < 17)
17:              System.out.println("Good afternoon.\n");
18:          else
19:              System.out.println("Good evening.\n");
20:
21:          // begin time message by showing the minutes
22:          System.out.print("It's");
23:          if (minute != 0) {
24:              System.out.print(" " + minute + " ");
25:              System.out.print( (minute != 1) ? "minutes" :
26:                  "minute");
27:              System.out.print(" past");
28:          }
29:
30:          // display the hour
31:          System.out.print(" ");
32:          System.out.print( (hour > 12) ? (hour - 12) : hour );
33:          System.out.print(" o'clock on ");
34:
35:          // display the name of the month
36:          switch (month) {
37:              case 1:
38:                  System.out.print("January");
39:                  break;
40:              case 2:
41:                  System.out.print("February");
42:                  break;
43:              case 3:
44:                  System.out.print("March");
45:                  break;
46:              case 4:
47:                  System.out.print("April");
48:                  break;
49:              case 5:
50:                  System.out.print("May");
51:                  break;
52:              case 6:
53:                  System.out.print("June");
54:                  break;
55:              case 7:
56:                  System.out.print("July");
57:                  break;
```

LISTING 7.3 continued

```
58:            case 8:
59:                System.out.print("August");
60:                break;
61:            case 9:
62:                System.out.print("September");
63:                break;
64:            case 10:
65:                System.out.print("October");
66:                break;
67:            case 11:
68:                System.out.print("November");
69:                break;
70:            case 12:
71:                System.out.print("December");
72:        }
73:
74:        // display the date and year
75:        System.out.println(" " + day + ", " + year + ".");
76:    }
77: }
```

Save the file when you're done, and attempt to compile it (SDK users can enter `javac ClockTalk.java` at the command line). Correct any typos that cause error messages to occur during the attempted compilation. After the program compiles correctly, look over Lines 13–75 before going over the description of the program. See whether you can get a good idea about what is taking place in each of these sections and how the conditional tests are being used.

With the exception of Lines 6–11, the `ClockTalk` program contains material that has been covered up to this point. After a series of variables are set up to hold the current date and time, a series of `if` or `switch` conditionals are used to determine what information should be displayed.

This program contains several uses of `System.out.println()` and `System.out.print()` to display strings.

Lines 6–11 refer to a `Calendar` variable called now. The `Calendar` variable type is capitalized, just as `String` is capitalized in a program that uses strings. The reason for the capitalization is that `Calendar` is an object.

You'll learn how to create and work with objects during Hour 10, "Creating Your First Object." For this hour, focus on what's taking place in Lines 6–11 rather than how it's happening.

7

The ClockTalk program is made up of the following sections:

- Line 1 enables your program to use a class that is needed to track the current date and time: java.util.Calendar.

- Lines 3–4 begin the ClockTalk program and its main() statement block.

- Line 6 creates a Calendar object called now that contains the current date and time of your system. The now object will change each time you run this program (unless, of course, the physical laws of the universe are altered and time stands still).

- Lines 7–11 create variables to hold the hour, minute, month, day, and year. The values for these variables are pulled from the Calendar object, which is the storehouse for all of this information. These variables are used in the subsequent sections as the program displays information.

- Lines 14–19 display one of three possible greetings: Good morning., Good afternoon., or Good evening. The greeting to display is selected based on the value of the hour variable.

- Lines 22–28 display the current minute along with some accompanying text. First, the text It's is displayed in Line 22. If the value of minute is equal to 0, Lines 24–27 are ignored because of the if statement in Line 23. This statement is necessary because it would not make sense for the program to tell someone that it's 0 minutes past an hour. Line 24 displays the current value of the minute variable. A ternary operator is used in Lines 25–26 to display either the text minutes or minute, depending on whether minute is equal to 1. Finally, in Line 27 the text past is displayed.

- Lines 30–33 display the current hour by using another ternary operator. This ternary conditional statement in Line 32 causes the hour to be displayed differently if it is larger than 12, which prevents the computer from stating things like 15 o'clock.

- Lines 35–72, almost half of the program, are a long switch statement that displays a different name of the month based on the integer value stored in the month variable.

- Lines 74–75 finish off the display by showing the current date and the year.

- Lines 76–77 close out the main() statement block and then the entire ClockTalk program.

When you run this program, the output should resemble the following code, with changes based on the current date and time. For example, if the program was run on 7/5/2002 at 11:36 p.m., it would display the following text:

```
Good evening.
```

```
It's 36 minutes past 11 o'clock on July 5, 2002.
```

Run the program several times to see how it keeps up with the clock. If the time doesn't match the time on your computer, the Java interpreter might be using the wrong time zone to determine the current time. When the interpreter does not know the default time zone to use, it uses Greenwich Time instead.

The following statements set the current time zone:

```
TimeZone tz = TimeZone.getTimeZone("EST");
TimeZone.setDefault(tz);
```

The setDefault() method should be used before calendar or any other date-related items are created.

The first statement creates a TimeZone object called tz. The text EST is sent as an argument to the getTimeZone() method, and this causes TimeZone to be set up for Eastern Standard Time.

The second statement sets the time zone by calling the setDefault() method of the TimeZone class. If you're having trouble finding the right time zone arguments, the following statements display all valid zones recognized by Java on your system:

```
String[] ids = TimeZone.getAvailableIDs();
for (int i = 0; i < ids.length; i++)
    System.out.println(ids[i].toString());
```

The ClockTalk program uses the Gregorian calendar system that has been used throughout the Western world for many years to determine the date and time. It was introduced in 1582 when Pope Gregory XIII moved the Julian calendar system forward 10 days—turning Oct. 5, 1582, into Oct. 15, 1582. This was needed because the calendar was moving out of alignment with the seasons due to discrepancies in the Julian system (which had to be small comfort to anyone who had a birthday on October 6 through October 14). Java also supports the use of alternate calendar systems—if you're looking for a class that supports the Arabic, Buddhist, Japanese, or Hebrew calendar systems, visit the International Components for Unicode for Java site at the Web address http://oss.software.ibm.com/icu4j/.

7

Summary

Now that you can use conditional statements, the overall intelligence of your Java programs has improved greatly. Your programs can now evaluate information and use it to react differently in different situations, even if information changes as the program is running. They can decide between two or more alternatives based on specific conditions.

Programming a computer forces you to break a task down into a logical set of steps to undertake any decisions that must be made. Using the if statement and other conditionals in programming also promotes a type of logical thinking that can reap benefits in other aspects of your life:

- "*If* he is elected president in November, I will seek a Cabinet position, *else* I will move to Canada."
- "*If* my blind date is attractive, I'll pay for dinner at an expensive restaurant, *else* we will go to Edgar's Taco Barn."
- "*If* I violate my probation, the only team that will draft me is the Dallas Cowboys."

Q&A

Q The if statement seems like the one that's most useful. Is it possible to use only if statements in programs and never use the others?

A It's possible to do without else or switch, and many programmers never use the ternary operator ?. However, else and switch often are beneficial to use in your programs because they make them easier to understand. A set of if statements chained together can become unwieldy.

Q An if statement is described as either a single statement or as a conditional statement followed by another statement to handle if the condition is true. Which is it?

A The point that might be confusing is that if statements and other conditionals are used in conjunction with other statements. The if statement makes a decision, and the other statements do work based on the decision that is made. The if statement combines a conditional statement with one or more other types of Java statements, such as statements that use the println() method or create a variable.

Q **In the `ClockTalk` program, why is 1 added to `Calendar.MONTH` to get the current month value?**

A This is necessary because of a quirk in the way that the `Calendar` class represents months. Instead of numbering them from 1 to 12 as you might expect, `Calendar` numbers months beginning with 0 in January and ending with 11 in December. Adding 1 causes months to be represented numerically in a more understandable manner.

Q **During this hour, opening and closing brackets { and } are not used with an `if` statement if it is used in conjunction with only one statement. Isn't it mandatory to use brackets?**

A No. Brackets can be used as part of any `if` statement to surround the part of the program that's dependent on the conditional test. Using brackets is a good practice to get into because it prevents a common error that might take place when you revise the program. If you add a second statement after an `if` conditional and don't add brackets, unexpected errors will occur when the program is run.

Q **Will the SDK's Java compiler catch the error when a = operator is used with a conditional instead of a ==?**

A Often it will not, and it results in a real doozy of a logic error. These errors only show up when a program is being run and can be discovered only through observation and testing. Because the = operator is used to assign a value to a variable, if you use `name = "Fernando"` in a spot in a program where you mean to use `name == "Fernando"`, you could wipe out the value of the `name` variable and replace it with `Fernando`. When the value stored in a variable changes unexpectedly, it can cause subtle and unexpected errors.

Q **Does `break` have to be used in each section of statements that follow a `case`?**

A You don't have to use `break`. If you do not use it at the end of a group of statements, all of the remaining statements inside the `switch` block statement will be handled, regardless of the `case` value they are being tested with.

Q **Why do you sometimes use single-quotation marks after a case statement and sometimes leave them off?**

A The value associated with a case statement must be either a character or an integer. The single-quotation marks surround a `char` value and are not used with an `int` value, so they differentiate between these two data types—for example, `case '1':` looks for the '1' character and `case 1:` looks for the integer value of `1`.

7

Quiz

The following questions will see what condition you're in after studying conditional statements in Java.

Questions

1. Conditional tests result in either a true or false value. Which variable type does this remind you of?

   a. None. They're unique.

   b. The `long` variable type.

   c. The `boolean` type.

2. Which statement is used as a catch-all category in a `switch` block statement?

   a. `default`

   b. `otherwise`

   c. `onTheOtherHand`

3. What's a conditional?

   a. The thing that repairs messy split ends and tangles after you shampoo.

   b. Something in a program that tests whether a condition is true or false.

   c. The place where you confess your sins to a neighborhood religious figure.

Answers

1. c. The `boolean` variable type can only equal `true` or `false`, making it similar to conditional tests.

2. a. `default` statements will be handled if none of the other `case` statements matches the `switch` variable.

3. b. The other answers describe conditioner and a confessional.

Activities

To improve your conditioning in terms of Java conditionals, review the topics of this hour with the following activities:

- Remove the `break` statement from one of the lines in the `ClockTalk` program, and then compile it and see what happens when you run it. Try it again with a few more `break` statements removed.

- Create a short program that stores a value of your choosing from 1 to 100 in an integer variable called grade. Use this grade variable with a conditional statement to display a different message for all A, B, C, D, and F students. Try it first with an if statement, and then try it with a switch statement.

To see Java programs that implement these activities, visit the book's Web site at http://www.java24hours.com.

7

HOUR 8

Repeating an Action with Loops

One of the more annoying punishments for schoolchildren is to make them write something over and over again on paper or a chalkboard.

On *The Simpsons*, in one of his frequent trips to the board, Bart Simpson had to write, "I am not certified to remove asbestos" dozens of times. This kind of punishment might work on children, but it definitely would fail to be punitive to a computer, which can repeat a task with ease.

Computer programs are ideally suited to do the same thing over and over again because of loops. A *loop* is a statement or set of statements that will be repeated in a program. Some loops take place a fixed number of times. Others take place indefinitely.

There are three loop statements in Java: for, do, and while. These statements are often interchangeable in a program because each can be made to work like the others. The choice to use a loop statement in a program often depends on personal preference, but it's beneficial to learn how all three work. You can frequently simplify a loop section of a program by choosing the right statement.

The following topics will be covered during this hour:

- Using the `for` loop
- Using the `while` loop
- Using the `do-while` loop
- Exiting a loop prematurely
- Naming a loop

for Loops

In the Java programs that you write, you will find many circumstances in which a loop is useful. You can use them to keep doing something several times, such as an antivirus program that opens each new email you receive to look for any viruses. You also can use them to cause the computer to do nothing for a brief period, such as an animated clock that displays the current time once per minute.

To create and control loops, you use a *loop statement*. A loop statement causes a computer program to return to the same place more than once. If the term seems unusual to you, think of what a stunt plane does when it loops: It completes a circle and returns to the place where it started the loop.

The most complex of the loop statements is `for`. The `for` loop is often used in cases where you want to repeat a section of a program for a fixed amount of times. It also can be used if the number of times the loop should be repeated is based on the value of a variable. The following is an example of a `for` loop:

```
for (int dex = 0; dex < 1000; dex++) {
    if (dex % 12 == 0) System.out.println("#: " + dex);
}
```

This loop displays every number from 0 to 999 that is evenly divisible by 12.

Every `for` loop has a variable that is used to determine when the loop should begin and end. This variable often is called the *counter*. The counter in the preceding loop is a variable called `dex`.

The example illustrates the three parts of a `for` statement:

- The initialization section: In the first part, the `dex` variable is given an initial value of 0.

8

- The conditional section: In the second part, there is a conditional test like one you might use in an `if` statement. The test is `dex < 1000`.

- The change section: The third part is a statement that changes the value of the `dex` variable by using the increment operator.

In the initialization section, you can set up the counter variable you want to use in the `for` statement. You can even create the variable inside the `for` statement, as the preceding example does with the integer variable named `dex`. You can also create the variable elsewhere in the program. In any case, the variable should be given a starting value in this section of the `for` statement. The variable will have this value when the loop starts.

The conditional section contains a test that must remain `true` for the loop to continue looping. Once the test is `false`, the loop will end. In this example, the loop will end when the `dex` variable is equal to or greater than 1,000.

The last section of the `for` statement contains a Java statement that changes the value of the counter variable in some way. This statement is handled each time the loop goes around. The counter variable has to change in some way or the loop will never end. For instance, in this example, `dex` is incremented by one using the increment operator `++` in the change section. If `dex` was not changed, it would stay at its original value, 0, and the conditional `dex < 1000` would always be true.

The statements inside the bracket marks, { and }, are also executed during each trip through the loop. The bracketed area is usually where the main work of the loop takes place, although some loops do all their work in the change section.

The preceding example had the following statement within the { and } marks:

```
if (dex % 12 == 0) System.out.println("#: " + dex);
```

This statement will be executed 1,000 times. The loop starts by setting the `dex` variable equal to 0. It then adds 1 to `dex` during each pass through the loop and stops looping when `dex` is no longer less than 1,000. Every time `dex` is evenly divisible by 12, the number is displayed next to the text #:.

An unusual term you might hear in connection with loops is *iteration*. An iteration is a single trip through a loop. The counter variable that is used to control the loop is often called an *iterator*.

As you have seen with `if` statements, a `for` loop does not require brackets if it contains only a single statement. This is shown in the following example:

```
for (int p = 0; p < 500; p++)
    System.out.println("I am not certified to remove asbestos");
```

This loop will display the text "I am not certified to remove asbestos" 500 times. Although brackets are not required around a single statement inside a loop, you can use them if desired as a way of making the program easier to understand.

The first program you create during this hour will display the first 200 multiples of 9: 9×1, 9×2, 9×3, and so on, up to 9×200. Because this task is so repetitious, it should be handled with a loop statement such as `for`.

Open your word processor and create a new file. Enter the text of Listing 8.1 and save the file as `Nines.java` when you're done.

LISTING 8.1   The Full Text of Nines.java

```
1: class Nines {
2:     public static void main(String[] arguments) {
3:         for (int dex = 1; dex <= 200; dex++) {
4:             int multiple = 9 * dex;
5:             System.out.print(multiple + " ");
6:         }
7:     }
8: }
```

The `Nines` program contains a `for` statement in Line 3. This statement has three parts:

- The initialization section: `int dex = 1`, which creates an integer variable called dex and gives it an initial value of 1.

- The conditional section: `dex <= 200`, which must be true during each trip through the loop. When it is not true, the loop ends.

- The change section: `dex++`, which increments the dex variable by one during each trip through the loop.

Compile and run the program. If you are using the SDK, you can handle these tasks by using the following commands:

```
javac Nines.java
java Nines
```

8

This program produces the following output:

OUTPUT
```
9 18 27 36 45 54 63 72 81 90 99 108 117 126 135 144 153 162 171
180 189 198 207 216 225 234 243 252 261 270 279 288 297 306 315
324 333 342 351 360 369 378 387 396 405 414 423 432 441 450 459
468 477 486 495 504 513 522 531 540 549 558 567 576 585 594 603
612 621 630 639 648 657 666 675 684 693 702 711 720 729 738 747
756 765 774 783 792 801 810 819 828 837 846 855 864 873 882 891
900 909 918 927 936 945 954 963 972 981 990 999 1008 1017 1026
1035 1044 1053 1062 1071 1080 1089 1098 1107 1116 1125 1134 1143
1152 1161 1170 1179 1188 1197 1206 1215 1224 1233 1242 1251 1260
1269 1278 1287 1296 1305 1314 1323 1332 1341 1350 1359 1368 1377
1386 1395 1404 1413 1422 1431 1440 1449 1458 1467 1476 1485 1494
1503 1512 1521 1530 1539 1548 1557 1566 1575 1584 1593 1602 1611
1620 1629 1638 1647 1656 1665 1674 1683 1692 1701 1710 1719 1728
1737 1746 1755 1764 1773 1782 1791 1800
```

The for loop statement is extremely useful. You'll get a lot of practice using it in upcoming hours, because several of the tutorial programs and workshops make use of these loops.

Because many Java statements end with a semicolon, an easy mistake to make is putting a semicolon at the end of a for statement, as in the following:

```
for (int i = 0; i < 100; i++); {
    value = value + i;
}
```

Look closely at the closing parenthesis in this example. It is followed by a semicolon, which will prevent the loop from running correctly. The semicolon puts the statements in the brackets, value = value + i;, outside the loop. As a result, nothing will happen as the for loop is handled. The program will compile without any errors, but you won't get the results you expect when it runs.

while Loops

The while loop does not have as many different sections to set up as the for loop. The only thing it needs is a conditional test, which accompanies the while statement. The following is an example of a while loop:

```
while (gameLives > 0) {
    // the statements inside the loop go here
}
```

This loop will continue repeating until the gameLives variable is no longer greater than 0.

The while statement tests the condition at the beginning of the loop, before any statements in the loop have been handled. For this reason, if the tested condition is false when a program reaches the while statement for the first time, the statements inside the loop will be ignored.

If the while condition is true, the loop goes around once and tests the while condition again. If the tested condition never changes inside the loop, the loop will keep looping indefinitely.

The following statements cause a while loop to display the same line of text several times:

```
int limit = 5;
int count = 1;
while (count < limit) {
    System.out.println("Frodo lives!");
    count++;
}
```

A while loop uses one or more variables that are set up before the loop statement. In this example, two integer variables are created: limit, which has a value of 5, and count, which has a value of 1.

The while loop displays the text Frodo lives! four times. If you gave the count variable an initial value of 6 instead of 1, the text would never be displayed.

do-while Loops

The do-while loop is similar in function to the while loop, but the conditional test goes in a different place. The following is an example of a do-while loop:

```
do {
    // the statements inside the loop go here
} while ( gameLives > 0 );
```

Like the previous while loop, this loop will continue looping until the gameLives variable is no longer greater than 0. The do-while loop is different because the conditional test is conducted after the statements inside the loop, instead of before them.

When the do loop is reached for the first time as a program runs, the statements between the do and the while are handled automatically. Then the while condition is tested to determine whether the loop should be repeated. If the while condition is true, the loop goes around one more time. If the condition is false, the loop ends. Something must happen inside the do and while statements that changes the condition tested with while, or the loop will continue indefinitely. The statements inside a do-while loop will always be handled at least once.

The following statements cause a do-while loop to display the same line of text several times:

```
int limit = 5;
int count = 1;
do {
    System.out.println("Frodo lives!");
    count++;
while (count < limit)
```

Like a while loop, a do-while loop uses one or more variables that are set up before the loop statement.

The loop displays the text Frodo lives! four times. If you gave the count variable an initial value of 6 instead of 1, the text would be displayed once, even though count is never less than limit.

If you're still confused about the difference between a while loop and a do-while loop, engage in a little role-playing and pretend you're a teenager who wants to borrow your father's car. If you are a teenager, all the better. There are two strategies that you can take:

1. Borrow the car first and tell Dad later that you did it.
2. Ask Dad before you borrow the car.

Strategy 1 has an advantage over Strategy 2: even if Dad doesn't want to let you use the car, you get to borrow it once.

The do-while loop is like Strategy 1 because something happens once even if the loop condition is false the first time while is encountered.

The while loop is like Strategy 2 because nothing will happen unless the while condition at the beginning is true. It all depends on the situation in your program.

Sams Publishing makes no warranties express nor implied that your father will be happy if you borrow his car without telling him first.

Exiting a Loop

The normal way to exit a loop is for the condition that is tested to become `false`. This is true of all three types of loops in Java: `for`, `while`, and `do-while`. However, there might be times when you want a loop to end immediately, even if the condition being tested is still `true`. You can do this with a `break` statement, as shown in the following code:

```
int index = 0;
while (index <= 1000) {
    index = index + 5;
    if (index == 400)
        break;
    System.out.println("The index is " + index);
}
```

The condition tested in the `while` loop sets it up to loop until the value of the `index` variable is greater than 1,000. However, a special case causes the loop to end earlier than that: If `index` equals 400, the `break` statement is executed, ending the loop immediately.

Another special-circumstance statement you can use inside a loop is `continue`. The `continue` statement causes the loop to exit its current trip through the loop and start over at the first statement of the loop. Consider the following loop:

```
int index = 0;
while (index <= 1000) {
    index = index + 5;
    if (index == 400)
        continue;
    System.out.println("The index is " + index);
}
```

In this loop, the statements will be handled normally unless the value of `index` equals 400. In that case, the `continue` statement causes the loop to go back to the `while` statement instead of proceeding normally to the `System.out.println()` statement. Because of the `continue` statement, the loop will never display the following text:

```
The index is 400
```

You can use the `break` and `continue` statements with all three kinds of Java loop statements.

Naming a Loop

Like other statements in Java programs, loops can be put inside of each other. The following shows a `for` loop inside a `while` loop:

```
int points = 0;
int target = 100;
while (target <= 100) {
    for (int i = 0; i < target; i++) {
        if (points > 50)
            break;
        points = points + i;
    }
}
```

In this example, the break statement will cause the for loop to end if the points variable is greater than 50. However, the while loop will never end, because target is never greater than 100.

In this case (and others), you might want to break out of both loops. To make this possible, you have to give the outer loop—in this example, the while statement—a name. To name a loop, put the name on the line before the beginning of the loop and follow it with a colon (:).

Once the loop has a name, you can use the name after the break or continue statement to indicate to which loop the break or continue statement applies. Although the name of the loop is followed by a colon at the spot where the loop begins, the colon is not used with the name in a break or continue statement.

The following example repeats the previous one with the exception of one thing: If the points variable is greater than 50, both loops are ended.

```
int points = 0;
int target = 100;
targetloop:
while (target <= 100) {
    for (int i = 0; i < target; i++) {
        if (points > 50)
            break targetloop;
        points = points + i;
    }
}
```

Complex for Loops

Most for loops are directly comparable to the ones used up to this point in the hour. They can also be a little more complex if you want to work with more than one variable in the for statement.

Each section of a for loop is set off from the other sections with a semicolon (;). A for loop can have more than one variable set up during the initialization section, and more than one statement in the change section, as in the following:

```
int i, j;
for (i = 0, j = 0; i * j < 1000; i++, j += 2) {
    System.out.println(i + " * " + j + " = " + i * j);
}
```

These multiple statement sections of the `for` loop are set off by commas, as in
`i = 0, j = 0`. This loop will display a list of equations where the `i` variable is multiplied by the `j` variable. The `i` variable increases by one, and the `j` variable increases by
two during each trip through the loop. Once `i` multiplied by `j` is no longer less than
1,000, the loop will end.

Sections of a `for` loop can also be empty. An example of this would be if the counter
variable has already been created with an initial value in another part of the program, as
in the following:

```
for ( ; displayCount < endValue; displayCount++) {
    // loop statements would be here
}
```

Workshop: Teaching Your Computer a Lesson

This hour's workshop provides evidence that you cannot punish your computer in the
same way that Bart Simpson is punished at the beginning of each episode of *The
Simpsons*. Pretend you're a teacher and the computer is a kid who contaminated your
morning cup of coffee with Thorium 230.

Even if you're the most strident liberal, you realize that the computer must be taught a
lesson—it's not acceptable behavior to give the teacher radiation poisoning. Your computer must be punished, and the punishment is to display the same sentence over and
over again.

The `Repeat` program will use a loop statement to handle a `System.out.println()` statement again and again. Once the computer has been dealt this punishment for 1,000,000
sentences or one minute, whichever comes first, it can stop running and think about the
error of its ways.

A topic of heated debate here at Sams concerns whether the punishment is
severe enough. Thorium is a silver-white metal that has a half-life of 80,000
years. Some scientists believe that it is as toxic as plutonium, and if it finds a
home in someone's liver, bone marrow, or lymphatic tissue, Thorium 230 can
cause cancer, leukemia, or lung cancer. A student who irradiates a teacher
probably should receive three hours of in-school detention, at least.

8

Use your word processor to create a new file called Repeat.java. Enter the text of Listing 8.2 and save the file when you're done.

LISTING 8.2   The Full Source Code of Repeat.java

```
 1: import java.util.*;
 2:
 3: class Repeat {
 4:     public static void main(String[] arguments) {
 5:         String sentence = "Thorium 230 is not a toy.";
 6:         int count = 1;
 7:         Calendar start = Calendar.getInstance();
 8:         int startMinute = start.get(Calendar.MINUTE);
 9:         int startSecond = start.get(Calendar.SECOND);
10:         start.roll(Calendar.MINUTE, true);
11:         int nextMinute = start.get(Calendar.MINUTE);
12:         int nextSecond = start.get(Calendar.SECOND);
13:         while (count < 1000000) {
14:             System.out.println(sentence);
15:             GregorianCalendar now = new GregorianCalendar();
16:             if (now.get(Calendar.MINUTE) >= nextMinute)
17:                 if (now.get(Calendar.SECOND) >= nextSecond)
18:                     break;
19:             count++;
20:         }
21:         System.out.println("\nI wrote the sentence " + count
22:             + " times.");
23:         System.out.println("I have learned my lesson.");
24:     }
25: }
```

The following things are taking place in this program:

- Line 1: The import statement makes the java.util group of classes available to this program. You're going to use one of these classes, Calendar, in order to keep track of time while the program is running.

- Lines 3 and 4: The Repeat class is declared, and the main() block of the program begins.

- Lines 5 and 6: The sentence variable is set up with the text of the punishment sentence, and the count variable is created with a value of 1.

- Line 7: Using the Calendar class, which keeps track of time-related information, the start variable is created with the current time as its value.

- Lines 8 and 9: The get() method of the Calendar class is used to retrieve the current minute and second and store them in the variables startMinute and startSecond.

- Line 10: The Calendar roll() method is used to roll the value of the start variable one minute forward in time.

- Lines 11 and 12: The get() method is used again to retrieve the minute and second for start and store them in the variables nextMinute and nextSecond.

- Line 13: The while statement begins a loop using the count variable as the counter. When count hits 1,000,000, the loop will end.

- Line 14: The punishment text, stored in the string variable sentence, is displayed.

- Line 15: Using the Calendar class, the now variable is created with the current time.

- Lines 16–18: Using one if statement inside of another, the program tests to see if one minute has passed by comparing the current minute and second to the values of nextMinute and nextSecond. If it has passed, break ends the while loop.

- Line 19: The } marks the end of the while loop.

- Lines 20–22: The computer displays the number of times it repeated the punishment sentence and claims to be rehabilitated.

- Lines 24 and 25: The main() block of the program and the program are closed out with } marks.

Compile the program with the javac compiler tool or another compiler and then give it a try. Using the SDK, you can run it by typing the following at the command line:

```
java Repeat
```

Run this program several times to see how many sentences are displayed in a minute's time. The Repeat program is an excellent way to see whether your computer is faster than mine. During the testing of this workshop program, Repeat usually displayed around 390,000 sentences in a minute's time. If your computer displays the sentence more times than mine does, don't just send me your condolences. Buy more of my books so I can upgrade.

Summary

The information presented in this chapter is material you will be coming back to again and again and again when you write programs. Loops are a fundamental part of most programming languages. In several of the hours to come, you get a chance to manipulate graphics so you can produce animated effects. You couldn't do this without loops.

As you might expect, every one of Bart Simpson's chalkboard punishments has been documented on the World Wide Web. Visit `http://www.snpp.com/guides/chalk-board.openings.html` to see the list along with a Java applet that draws sayings on a green chalkboard.

Q&A

Q **Should the counter variable used in a `for` loop be created inside the `for` statement or before the loop begins?**

A The only time the counter should be created outside of the `for` loop, or any other loop for that matter, is when it needs to be used in another part of the program. A variable that is created in a loop or other kind of block statement only exists inside that block. You can't use the value in any other part of the program. This is good programming practice because it makes it harder to misuse variables—you can't set their value in one part of the program and use them somewhere else incorrectly. The concept of a variable existing in one part of a program and not existing anywhere else is called *scope*, and it's covered fully during Hour 11, "Describing What Your Object Is Like."

Q **The term *initialization* has been used in several places. What does it mean?**

A It means to give something an initial value and set it up. When you create a variable and assign a starting value to it, you are initializing the variable.

Q **If a loop never ends, how does the program stop running?**

A Usually in a program where a loop does not end, something else in the program is set up to stop execution in some way. For example, a loop could continue indefinitely while the program waits for the user to click a button labeled `Quit`.

One bug that crops up often is an *infinite loop*, a loop that never stops because of a programming mistake. If one of the Java programs you run from the command line is stuck in an infinite loop, press Ctrl+C.

Quiz

The following questions will test your knowledge of loops. In the spirit of the subject matter, repeat each of these until you get them right.

Questions

1. What must be used to separate each section of a `for` statement?

    a. commas

    b. semicolons

    c. off-duty police officers

2. Which statement causes a program to go back to the statement that began a loop and then keep going from there?

    a. `continue`

    b. `next`

    c. `skip`

3. When it comes to borrowing a car from your father, what lesson did you learn during this hour?

    a. Don't even think about it.

    b. Speak softly and carry a big stick.

    c. It's better to beg forgiveness than to ask permission.

Answers

1. b. Commas are used to separate things within a section, but semicolons separate sections.

2. a. The `break` statement ends a loop entirely, and `continue` skips to the next go-round of the loop.

3. c. Though I'm not sure my father has completely forgiven me for that incident in 1987.

Activities

If your head isn't going in circles from all this looping, review the topics of this hour with the following activities:

- Modify the `Repeat` program so that it uses a `for` loop instead of a `while` loop, and compare the efficiency of each approach.

- Write a short program using loops that finds the first 400 numbers that are multiples of 13.

To see Java programs that implement these activities, visit the book's Web site at `http://www.java24hours.com`.

PART III
Working with Information in New Ways

Hour

HOUR 9

Storing Information with Arrays

No one benefited more from the development of the computer than Santa Claus. For centuries, humankind has put an immense burden on him to gather and process information. Old St. Nick has to keep track of the following things:

- Naughty children
- Nice children
- Gift requests
- Homes with impassable chimneys
- Women who want more from Santa than Mrs. Claus is willing to let him give
- Countries that shoot unidentified aircraft first and ask questions later

Computers were a great boon at the North Pole. They are ideal for the storage, categorization, and study of information.

The most basic way that information is stored in a computer program is by putting it into a variable. However, this method is limited to relatively simple usage. If Santa had to give each naughty child his or her own variable name, he'd be working on the program for the next 12 holiday seasons at least, to say nothing of the effect on his jolly disposition.

The list of naughty children is an example of a collection of similar information. Each child's name is a string of text or some kind of Santa Information System ID number. To keep track of a list of this kind, you can use arrays.

Arrays are groups of related variables that share the same type. You can have arrays of any type of information that can be stored as a variable. Arrays can be used to keep track of more sophisticated types of information than a single variable, but they are almost as easy to create and manipulate as variables.

The following topics will be covered during this hour:

- Creating an array
- What a dimension of an array is
- Giving a value to an array element
- Changing the information in an array
- Making multidimensional arrays
- Sorting an array

Creating Arrays

Arrays are variables that are grouped together under a common name. The term *array* should be familiar to you, though the meaning might not be so clear—think of a salesman showing off his array of fabulous cleaning products, or a game show with a dazzling array of prizes. Like variables, arrays are created by stating the type of the variable being organized into the array and the name of the array. The difference lies in the addition of the square bracket marks [and].

You can create arrays for any type of information that can be stored as a variable. For example, the following statement creates an array of string variables:

```
String[] naughtyChild;
```

Here are two more examples:

```
int[] reindeerWeight;
boolean[] hostileAirTravelNations;
```

Java is flexible about where the square brackets are placed when an array is being created. You can put them after the variable name, instead of after the variable type, as in the following:

```
String niceChild[];
```

To make arrays easier for humans to spot in your programs, you should probably stick to one style rather than switching back and forth, though Java allows both styles of usage.

9

The previous examples create arrays, but they do not store any values in them initially. To do this, you must either use the new statement along with the variable type or store values in the array within { and } marks. You also must specify how many different items will be stored in the array. Each item in an array is called an *element*. The following statement creates an array and sets aside space for the values that it will hold:

```
int[] elfSeniority = new int[250];
```

This example creates an array of integers called elfSeniority. The array has 250 elements in it that can be used to store the months that each of Santa's elves has been employed at the Pole. If the rumors are true and Santa runs a union shop, this information is extremely important to keep track of.

When you create an array with the new statement, you must specify the number of elements. Each element of the array is given an initial value when it is set up with new; the value depends on the type of the array. All numeric arrays have the value 0, char arrays have the value '\0', and boolean arrays have the value false. A String array and all other objects are created with the initial value of null.

For arrays that are not extremely large, you can set up their initial values at the same time that you create them. The following example creates an array of strings and gives them initial values:

```
String[] reindeerNames = { "Dasher", "Dancer", "Prancer", "Vixen",
    "Comet", "Cupid", "Donder", "Blitzen" };
```

The information that should be put into elements of the array is placed between { and } brackets, with commas separating each element. The number of elements in the array is not specified in the statement because it is set to the number of elements in the comma-separated list. Each element of the array in the list must be of the same type. The preceding example uses a string for each of the reindeer names.

Once the array is created, you cannot make more space and add another variable to the array. Even if you recall the most famous reindeer of all, you couldn't add "Rudolph" as the ninth element of the `reindeerNames` array. A Java compiler won't let poor Rudolph join in any `reindeerNames`.

Using Arrays

You use arrays in a program as you would use any variable, except for the element number in between the square brackets next to the array's name. Once you refer to the element number, you can use an array element anywhere a variable could be used. The following statements all use arrays that have already been defined in this hour's examples:

```
elfSeniority[193] += 1;
niceChild[94287612] = "Max";
if (hostileAirTravelNations[currentNation] == true)
    sendGiftByMail();
```

An important thing to note about arrays is that the first element of an array is numbered 0 instead of 1. This means that the highest number is one less than you might expect. For example, consider the following statement:

```
String[] topGifts = new String[10];
```

This statement creates an array of string variables that are numbered from 0 to 9. If you referred to `topGifts[10]` somewhere else in the program, you would get an error message like the following when you run the program:

```
Exception in thread "main" java.lang.ArrayIndexOutOfBoundsException:
        at Gift.main(Gift.java:4);
```

Like all of the error messages encountered in Java, this one's a bit hard to decipher. The key thing to note is the part that mentions an exception, because *exceptions* are another word for errors in Java programs. This exception is an "array out of bounds" error, which means that a program tried to use an array element that doesn't exist within its defined boundaries.

If you want to check the upper limit of an array during a program so you can avoid going beyond that limit, you can use a variable called `length` that is associated with each array that is created. The `length` variable is an integer that contains the number of elements an array can hold. The following example creates an array and then reports its length:

```
String[] reindeerNames = { "Dasher", "Dancer", "Prancer", "Vixen",
    "Comet", "Cupid", "Donder", "Blitzen", "Rudolph" };
System.out.println("There are " + reindeerNames.length + " reindeer.");
```

In this example, the value of `reindeerNames.length` is 9, which means that the highest element number you can specify is 8.

There are two primary ways to work with text in Java: a string or an array of characters. When you're working with strings, one useful technique is to put each character in a string into its own element of a character array. To do this, call the string's toCharArray() method, which produces a char array with the same number of elements as the length of the string.

This hour's first project is an application that uses both of the techniques introduced in this section. The NoSpaces program displays a string with all space characters (' ') replaced with periods ('.').

9

Enter the text of Listing 9.1 in your word processor and save the file as NoSpaces.java.

LISTING 9.1 The Full Text of NoSpaces.java

```
1: class NoSpaces {
2:     public static void main(String[] arguments) {
3:         String mostFamous = "Rudolph the Red-Nosed Reindeer";
4:         char[] mfl = mostFamous.toCharArray();
5:         for (int dex = 0; dex < mfl.length; dex++) {
6:             char current = mfl[dex];
7:             if (current != ' ') {
8:                 System.out.print(current);
9:             } else {
10:                System.out.print('.');
11:            }
12:        }
13:    }
14: }
```

Compile and run this program using your Java development environment. The following commands can be used with the SDK:

```
javac NoSpaces.java
java NoSpaces
```

This program produces the following output:

```
Rudolph.the.Red-Nosed.Reindeer
```

The NoNames application stores the text Rudolph the Red-Nosed Reindeer in two places: a string called mostFamous, and a char array called mfl. The array is created in Line 4 by calling the toCharArray() method of mostFamous, which fills an array with one element for each character in the text. The character R goes into element 0, u into element 1, d into element 2, and so on, up to r in element 29.

The for loop in Lines 5–12 looks at each character in the mfl array. If the character is not a space, it is displayed. If it is a space, a . character is displayed instead.

Multidimensional Arrays

The arrays you have been introduced to thus far in the hour all have one dimension, so you can retrieve an element using a number ranging from 0 to the largest element number in the array. Some types of information require more dimensions to store adequately as arrays. An example would be the (x,y) coordinate system. If you needed to store a list of x and y coordinates that have a point marked on them, you could use a two-dimensional array. One dimension of the array could store the x coordinate, and the other dimension could store the y coordinate.

To create an array that has two dimensions, you must use an additional set of square brackets when creating and using the array. Consider the following:

```
boolean[][] selectedPoint = new boolean[50][50];
selectedPoint[4][13] = true;
selectedPoint[7][6] = true;
selectedPoint[11][22] = true;
```

This example creates an array of Boolean values called selectedPoint. The array has 50 elements in its first dimension and 50 elements in its second dimension, so there are 2,500 individual array elements that can hold values (50 multiplied by 50). When the array is created, each element is given the default value of false. Three elements are then given the value of true: a point at the (x,y) position of (4,13), one at (7,6), and one at (11,22).

Arrays can have as many dimensions as you need, but keep in mind that they take up a lot of memory if they're extremely large. Creating the 50×50 selectedPoint array was equivalent to creating 2,500 individual variables.

Sorting an Array

When you have grouped a bunch of similar items together into an array, one of the things you can do easily is rearrange items. The following statements switch the values of two elements in an integer array called numbers:

```
int temp = numbers[5];
numbers[5] = numbers[6];
numbers[6] = temp;
```

These statements result in numbers[5] and numbers[6] trading values with each other. The integer variable called temp is used as a temporary storage place for one of the values being swapped.

The most common reason to rearrange elements of an array is to sort them into a specific order. *Sorting* is the process of arranging a list of related items into a set order. An example would be sorting a list of numbers from lowest to highest.

Santa Claus, the world's biggest user of lists, might want to use sorting to rearrange the order of gift recipients according to last name. This order could determine who receives gifts first on Christmas Eve, with people such as Willie Aames and Paul Azinger raking in their Yuletide plunder much earlier than alphabetical unfortunates such as Dweezil Zappa and Jim Zorn. (As someone whose last name begins with "C," I'm not necessarily opposed to this practice).

Sorting an array is easy in Java because the Arrays class does all of the work for you. Arrays, which is part of the java.util group of classes, can rearrange arrays of all variable types as well as strings.

To use the Arrays class in a program to sort an array, undertake the following steps:

- Use the import java.util.*; statement to make all of the java.util classes available in the program.
- Create the array.
- Use the sort() method of the Arrays class to rearrange an array.

An array of variables that is sorted by the Arrays class will be rearranged into ascending numerical order. This will be easy to see with an array of numbers such as float values. Characters and strings will be arranged according to the alphabet, with the first letters such as A, B, and C coming first, and the last letters such as X, Y, and Z coming last.

Listing 9.2 contains a short program that sorts five names. Enter this with your word processor and save the file as Name.java. Make sure not to overlook Line 1. If you do, the program will fail to compile because the Arrays class in Line 11 can't be found.

LISTING 9.2 The Full Source Code of Name.java

```
1: import java.util.*;
2:
3: class Name {
4:     public static void main(String[] arguments) {
5:         String names[] = { "Peter", "Patricia", "Hunter", "Sarah",
6:             "Gabe", "Gina", "Rob", "John", "Zoey", "Tammy", "Robert",
7:             "Sean", "Paschal", "Kathy", "Neleh", "Vecepia" };
```

LISTING 9.2   continued

```
 8:          System.out.println("The original order:");
 9:          for (int i = 0; i < names.length; i++)
10:              System.out.println(i + ": " + names[i]);
11:          Arrays.sort(names);
12:          System.out.println("The new order:");
13:          for (int i = 0; i < names.length; i++)
14:              System.out.println(i + ": " + names[i]);
15:      }
16: }
```

After you have created this source file, compile it. Using the SDK, you can compile it at a command line by entering this command:

```
javac Name.java
```

This Java program displays a list of five names in their original order, sorts the names, and then redisplays the list.

The following output is produced:

```
The original order:
0: Peter
1: Patricia
2: Hunter
3: Sarah
4: Gabe
5: Gina
6: Rob
7: John
8: Zoey
9: Tammy
10: Robert
11: Sean
12: Paschal
13: Kathy
14: Neleh
15: Vecepia
The new order:
0: Gabe
1: Gina
2: Hunter
3: John
4: Kathy
5: Neleh
6: Paschal
7: Patricia
8: Peter
```

```
 9: Rob
10: Robert
11: Sarah
12: Sean
13: Tammy
14: Vecepia
15: Zoey
```

When you're working with strings and the basic types of variables such as integers and floating-point numbers, you can only sort them by ascending order using the Arrays class. You can write code to do your own sorts by hand if you desire a different arrangement of elements during a sort, or if you want better efficiency than the Arrays class provides.

> There are numerous sorting techniques that have been created for use in computer programs. The Arrays class uses a technique called a "tuned quicksort," which was described by Jon L. Bentley and M. Douglas McIlroy in a 1993 issue of *Software-Practice and Experience*. Different techniques have their own names, including the heap sort, tree sort, and bubble sort. Jason Harrison has a Web page that uses Java to visually demonstrate the speed of different sorting techniques. To see it, visit the Web address http://www.cs.ubc.ca/spider/harrison/Java/sorting-demo.html.

Workshop: Array of Prizes, Indeed

Watch the syndicated game show *Wheel of Fortune* for any length of time and you'll be surprised at how predictable the contestants are.

In the years that this show has been one of the world's most successful television programs, fortune seekers have worked the puzzle-solving process into an exact science.

Wheel contestants typically guess the same letters when they are starting out on a puzzle: R, S, T, L, and N. In the final round, when these letters and the vowel E are given to the players right away, they usually choose four other letters: C, D, M, and the vowel O.

The reason for this predictability is that these are the letters that appear most often in English words. The contestants are stifling their desire for spontaneity in order to better their chances to win a trip to Bermuda, cash, and a Yamaha Waverunner.

In case you're unfamiliar with the show, *Wheel of Fortune* is a game in which three contestants try to guess the letters of a phrase, name, quote, or other memorable item. If they get a letter right and it's a consonant, they win the amount of money they spun on a big wheel. To re-create the experience, play hangman with some of your friends in front of a studio audience, hand out random amounts of money when someone guesses a letter in the secret word or phrase, and give the winner a new Chevy Suburban.

Your Java workshop during this hour will test the most-common-letter theory by looking at as many different phrases and expressions as you care to type. An array will be used to count the number of times that each letter appears. When you're done, the program will present each letter and the number of times it appears in the phrases you entered. It also will present some clues about which letters to avoid entirely (unless you suspect that a puzzle's answer is the Aztec priest-ruler Quetzalcoatl or the fire god Xiuhtecuhtle).

Open up a new file in your word processor and call it Wheel.java. Enter Listing 9.2 and save the file when you're done.

LISTING 9.2 The Full Source Code of Wheel.java

```
 1: class Wheel {
 2:     public static void main(String[] arguments) {
 3:         String phrase[] = {
 4:             "A STITCH IN TIME SAVES NINE",
 5:             "DON'T EAT YELLOW SNOW",
 6:             "JUST DO IT",
 7:             "EVERY GOOD BOY DOES FINE",
 8:             "I WANT MY MTV",
 9:             "HOW 'BOUT THEM COWBOYS",
10:             "PLAY IT AGAIN, SAM",
11:             "FROSTY THE SNOWMAN",
12:             "ONE MORE FOR THE ROAD",
13:             "HOME FIELD ADVANTAGE",
14:             "VALENTINE'S DAY MASSACRE",
15:             "GROVER CLEVELAND OHIO",
16:             "WONDERFUL WORLD OF DISNEY",
17:             "COAL MINER'S DAUGHTER",
18:             "WILL IT PLAY IN PEORIA"
19:         };
20:         int[] letterCount = new int[26];
21:         for (int count = 0; count < phrase.length; count++) {
22:             String current = phrase[count];
23:             char[] letters = current.toCharArray();
24:             for (int count2 = 0;  count2 < letters.length; count2++) {
25:                 char lett = letters[count2];
```

LISTING 9.2   continued

```
26:                         if ( (lett >= 'A') & (lett <= 'Z') ) {
27:                             letterCount[lett - 'A']++;
28:                         }
29:                     }
30:                 }
31:         for (char count = 'A'; count <= 'Z'; count++) {
32:             System.out.print(count + ": " +
33:                         letterCount[count - 'A'] +
34:                         "\t");
35:         }
36:         System.out.println();
37:     }
38: }
```

After you compile the file and run it, the output should resemble Listing 9.3.

LISTING 9.3   Output of the Wheel Program

A: 22	B: 3	C: 5	D: 13	E: 28	F: 6	G: 5	H: 8	I: 18
J: 1	K: 0	L: 13	M: 10	N: 19	O: 27	P: 3	Q: 0	R: 13
S: 15	T: 19	U: 4	V: 7	W: 9	X: 0	Y: 10	Z: 0	

The following things are taking place in the Wheel program:

- Lines 1 and 2: The Wheel program and the main() block of the program begin.
- Lines 3–19: Phrases are stored in a string array called phrase. Every phrase between the { on Line 3 and the } on Line 19 will be stored in its own element of the array, beginning with A STITCH IN TIME SAVES NINE in phrase[0].
- Line 20: An integer array called letterCount is created with 26 elements. This array will be used to store the number of times each letter appears. The order of the elements is from A to Z. letterCount[0] will store the count for letter A, letterCount[1] will store the count for B, and so on, up to letterCount[25] for Z.
- Line 21: A for loop is begun that cycles through the phrases stored in the phrase array. The phrase.length variable is used in the for statement to end the loop after the last phrase is reached.
- Line 22: A string variable named current is created and set with the value of the current element of the phrase array.
- Line 23: A character array is created that stores all of the characters in the current phrase.

- Line 24: A `for` loop is begun that cycles through the letters of the current phrase. The `letters.length` variable is used to end the loop after the last letter is reached.
- Line 25: A character variable called `lett` is created with the value of the current letter. In addition to their text value, characters have a numeric value. Because elements of an array are numbered, the numeric value of each character will be used to determine its element number.
- Lines 26–28: An `if` statement is used to weed out all characters that are not part of the alphabet, such as punctuation and spaces. An element of the `letterCount` array is increased by 1 depending on the numeric value of the current character, which is stored in `lett`. The numeric values of the alphabet range from 65 for `'A'` to 90 for `'Z'`. Because the `letterCount` array begins at 0 and ends at 25, `'A'` (65) is subtracted from `lett` to determine which array element to increase.
- Line 29: One pass through the inner `for` loop ends, and the loop returns to Line 24 to get the next letter in the current phrase, if there is one.
- Line 30: One pass through the outer `for` loop ends, and the loop returns to Line 21 to get the next phrase, if there is one.
- Line 31: A `for` loop is used to cycle through the alphabet from `'A'` to `'Z'`.
- Lines 32–34: The current letter is displayed followed by a semicolon and the number of times the letter appeared in the phrases stored in the `phrase` array. The `\t` inserts a tab character.
- Line 35: One pass through the `for` loop ends, and the loop returns to Line 31 to get the next character in the alphabet, unless `'Z'` has been reached.
- Lines 36–38: A blank line is displayed, followed by the end of the program's `main()` block, and the end of the program.

This workshop project shows how two nested `for` loops can be used to cycle through a group of phrases one letter at a time. Java attaches a numeric value to each character; this value is easier to use than the character inside arrays.

The numeric values associated with each of the characters from A to Z are those used by the ASCII character set. ASCII is a standard method of arranging and numbering letters, numbers, punctuation, and other symbols that can be represented by a computer. The ASCII character set is part of Unicode, the full character set supported by the Java language. Unicode includes support for more than 60,000 different characters used in the world's written languages.

Using the length variable makes it possible for you to add as many phrases as desired within the { and } marks. The letters in each of the new phrases you add will be analyzed, and you can build up a better idea of what it takes to make a small fortune in 30 minutes on television.

Summary

Arrays make it possible to store complicated types of information in a program and manipulate that information. They're ideal for anything that can be arranged in a list and can be accessed easily using the loop statements that you learned about during Hour 8, "Repeating an Action with Loops."

To be honest, the information processing needs of Santa Claus probably have outgrown arrays. There are more children being manufactured each year, and the gifts they want are increasing in complexity and expense. Pokémon alone created a logistical nightmare at the North Pole.

Your programs are likely to use arrays to store information that is unwieldy to work with using variables, even if you're not making any lists or checking them twice.

Q&A

Q Do arrays have to begin with an element 0, or can they range from a higher minimum number to a higher maximum number, such as 65 to 90?

A They don't have to begin at element 0, but it is more efficient to do so because it takes up less memory in the computer to store arrays that begin with 0. You can use arrays of a higher index number simply by referring to the numbers you want to use. For example, if you created a for loop that cycled from array element 65 to element 90, you could disregard any other element numbers. However, there still will be array elements numbered from 0 to 64 taking up space in memory, even if you don't use them for anything.

Q Is the numeric range of the alphabet, from 65 for A to 90 for Z, part of the basic Java language? If so, what are 1 through 64 reserved for?

A The numbers 1 through 64 include numerals, punctuation marks, and some unprintable characters, such as linefeed, newline, and backspace. A number is associated with each printable character that can be used in a Java program, as well as some unprintable ones. Java uses the Unicode numbering system, which supports more than 60,000 different characters from the different languages of the world. The first 127 characters are from the ASCII character set, which you might have used in another programming language.

Q Why are some errors called exceptions?

A The significance of the term is that a program normally runs without any problems, and the exception signals an exceptional circumstance that must be dealt with. Exceptions are warning messages that are sent from within a Java program. In the Java language, the term *error* is sometimes confined to describe error conditions that take place within the interpreter running a program. You learn more about both subjects during Hour 18, "Handling Errors in a Program."

Q In a multidimensional array, is it possible to use the `length` variable to measure different dimensions other than the first?

A You can test any dimension of the array. For the first dimension, use `length` with the name of the array, as in `x.length`. Subsequent dimensions can be measured by using `length` with the `[0]` element of that dimension. Consider an array called `data` that was created with the following statement:

```
int[][][] data = new int[12][13][14];
```

The dimensions of this array can be measured by using the `data.length` variable for the first dimension, `data[0].length` for the second, and `data[0][0].length` for the third.

Q Can the `length` variable be set to increase or decrease the size of an array after it has been created?

A There's no way to modify the size of an array after it has been created; `length` is strictly used to find out an array's upper boundary.

Quiz

If your brain were an array, you could test its `length` by answering each of the following questions about arrays.

Questions

1. What types of information are arrays best suited for?

    a. lists

    b. pairs of related information

    c. trivia

2. What variable can be used to check the upper boundary of an array?

    a. `top`

    b. `length`

    c. `limit`

3. Who is the famous Aztec priest-ruler?

    a. Quisp

    b. Quetzalcoatl

    c. Quichelorraine

Answers

1. a. Lists that contain nothing but the same type of information—strings, numbers, and so on—are well-suited for storage in arrays.

2. b. The length variable contains a count of the number of elements in an array.

3. b. It's also the name of a god of learning and civilization who is depicted as an approaching storm whose winds kick up dust before the rain comes.

Activities

To give yourself an array of experiences to draw from later, you can expand your knowledge of this hour's topics with the following activities:

- Create a program that uses a multidimensional array to store student grades. The first dimension should be a number for each student, and the second dimension should be for each student's grades. Display the average of all the grades earned by each student and an overall average for every student.

- Write a program that stores the first 400 numbers that are multiples of 13 in an array.

To see Java programs that implement these activities, visit the book's Web site at http://www.java24hours.com.

HOUR 10

Creating Your First Object

One of the more fearsome examples of jargon that you'll encounter during these 24 hours is *object-oriented programming*. This is a complicated term that describes, in an elegant way, what a computer program is and how it works.

Before object-oriented programming, computer programs were usually described under the simplest definition you've learned in this book: sets of instructions that are listed in a file and handled in some kind of reliable order. Whether the program is big or small, the programmer's job is largely the same—write instructions for each thing the computer must do. By thinking of a program as a collection of objects instead, you can figure out the tasks a program must accomplish and assign the tasks to the objects where they best belong.

During this hour, the following topics will be covered:

- Understanding objects
- Describing an object with attributes

- Determining how objects behave
- Combining objects
- Inheriting from other objects
- Creating an object
- Converting objects and other types of information

How Object-Oriented Programming Works

The programs you create with Java can be thought of as objects, just like physical objects that exist in the real world. Objects exist independently of other objects, interact in specific ways, and can often be combined with other objects to form something. Examples of objects in the real world include ham sandwiches, the Nixon tapes, a stereo receiver, and my father-in-law Clint. Examples of objects in a computer include a Web browser, the Java compiler, an MP3 file, and a Macromedia Flash plug-in.

If you think of a computer program as a group of objects that interact with each other, you can often come up with a better design for the program that's more reliable, easier to understand, and reusable in other projects.

Later in this book you will create a Java program that displays pie graphs—circles with different-colored pie slices to represent data (Figure 10.1). A pie chart is an object that is made up of smaller objects—individual slices of different colors, a legend identifying what each slice represents, and a title.

FIGURE 10.1

A Java program that displays a pie chart.

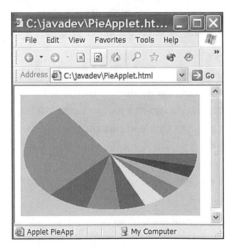

Each object has things that make it different from other objects. Pie charts are circular, while bar graphs represent data as a series of rectangles instead of pie slices. If you break down computer programs in the same way you have broken down a pie chart, you are engaging in object-oriented programming. It's a much less complicated concept than it originally sounds.

In object-oriented programming, an object contains two things: attributes and behavior. *Attributes* are things that describe the object and show how it is different from other objects. *Behavior* is what an object does.

You create objects in Java by using a class as a template. A *class* is a master copy of the object that is consulted to determine which attributes and behavior an object should have. The term *class* should be familiar to you, because every Java program you have written thus far has been called a class. Every program you create with Java will be a class because each one can be used as a template for the creation of new objects. As an example, any Java program that uses strings is using objects created from the String class. This class contains attributes that determine what a String object is and behavior that controls what String objects can do.

With object-oriented programming, a computer program is a group of objects that work together to get something done. Some simple programs might seem as though they consist of only one object—the class file. However, even those programs are using other objects to get work done.

Objects in Action

Consider the case of a program that displays a pie chart. A PieChart object could consist of the following:

- Behavior to calculate how big each pie slice should be in the chart
- Behavior to draw the chart
- An attribute to store the title of the chart

When you compare a pie chart in the real world to a PieChart object in a computer program, it might seem odd to ask the PieChart object to draw itself. Graphs don't draw themselves in the real world. However, objects in object-oriented programming work for themselves whenever possible. This quality makes them more useful because you can incorporate them in other programs without having as many things to teach them. If a PieChart object did not know how to draw itself, for instance, every time you used that PieChart object somewhere, you would have to create behavior to draw it.

For another example of object-oriented programming, consider the autodialer program that Matthew Broderick's character used in *WarGames* to find computers he could break into. If you're unfamiliar with the term, an *autodialer* is software that uses a modem to dial a series of phone numbers in sequence. The purpose of such a program is to find other computers that answer their own phone, so you can call them up later to see what they are.

Using an autodialer today practically guarantees you'll be on a first-name basis with your local phone company. In the early 80s, it was a good way to be rebellious without actually leaving the house. David Lightman (the character portrayed by Broderick) used his autodialer to look for a video game company's private computer system so he could play the company's new game before it was released. Instead, Lightman found a secret government computer that could play everything from chess to Global Thermonuclear War.

An autodialer, like any computer program, can be thought of as a group of objects that work together. It could be broken down into the following:

- A `Modem` object, which knows how to make the modem dial a number and how to report when another computer system has answered a call
- A `Monitor` object, which keeps track of what numbers were called and which ones were successful, and can save this information for later inspection

Each object exists independently of the other. The `Modem` object does its job without requiring any help from the `Monitor` object.

One of the advantages of having a completely independent `Modem` object is that it could be used in other programs that need modem functionality. If David Lightman returns to hacking in *WarGames 2003* after a bitter divorce from Jennifer Mack (Ally Sheedy's character), he could use the `Modem` object as part of an elaborate ATM fraud scheme.

Another reason to use self-contained programs such as objects is that they are easier to debug. Computer programs quickly become unwieldy in size. If your program is just one big list of instructions, you can't change one part without making sure it won't damage the performance of other parts that are dependent on it. If you're debugging something like a `Modem` object, though, you know it's not dependent on anything else. You can focus on making sure the `Modem` object does the job it's supposed to do and holds the information that it needs to do its job.

For these reasons, object-oriented programming is becoming the norm in many areas of software development. Learning an object-oriented language like Java as your first programming language can be an advantage in some ways because you're not unlearning the habits of other styles of programming. The main disadvantage is that an object-oriented

language can be more challenging to learn than a non-object-oriented language such as
Visual Basic.

What Objects Are

As stated, objects are created by using a class of objects as a guideline. The following is
an example of a class:

```
public class Modem {
}
```

Any object created from this class can't do anything because it doesn't have any attributes or behavior yet. You need to add those or this class that won't be terribly useful. You
could expand the class into the following:

```
public class Modem {
    int speed;

    public void displaySpeed() {
        System.out.println("Speed: " + speed);
    }
}
```

The Modem class now should be recognizable to you because it looks a lot like the programs you have written during Hours 1 through 9. The Modem class begins with a class
statement, as your programs have, except that it has a public statement alongside it. The
public statement means that the class is available for use by the public—in other words,
by any program that wants to use Modem objects.

The first part of the Modem class creates an integer variable called speed. This variable is
an attribute of the object; the name is one of the things that distinguishes a modem from
other modems.

The second part of the Modem class is a method called displaySpeed(). This method is
some of the object's behavior. It contains one statement: a System.out.println() statement that displays the modem's speed value along with some text.

If you wanted to use a Modem object in a program, you would create the object much like
you would create a variable. You could use the following statement:

```
Modem com = new Modem();
```

This statement creates a Modem object called com. You can now use the object in the program; you can set its variables and call its methods. To set the value of the speed variable of the com object, you could use the following statement:

```
com.speed = 28800;
```

10

To make this modem display its speed by calling the `displaySpeed()` method, you could use the following code:

```
com.displaySpeed();
```

The `Modem` object named `com` would respond to this statement by displaying the text `Speed: 28800`.

Understanding Inheritance

One of the biggest advantages to using object-oriented programming is *inheritance*, which is the way one object can inherit behavior and attributes from other objects that are similar to it.

When you start creating objects for use in other programs, you will find that some new objects you want are a lot like other objects that have already been developed. For example, if David Lightman does not run afoul of the law because of his ATM scheme, he might want to create an object that can handle error correction and other advanced modem features that weren't around back in 1983 when *WarGames* was released.

Lightman could create a new `ErrorCorrectionModem` object by copying the statements of the `Modem` object and revising them. However, if most of the behavior and attributes of `ErrorCorrectionModem` are the same as those of `Modem`, this is a lot of unnecessary work. It also means that Lightman will have to maintain two separate programs if something needs to be changed or debugged later. Through inheritance, a programmer can create a new class of objects by defining only how it is different from an existing class. Lightman could make `ErrorCorrectionModem` inherit from `Modem`, and all he would have to write are the things that make error-correction modems different than previous modems.

The way a class of objects inherits from another class is through the `extends` statement. The following is a skeleton of an `ErrorCorrectionModem` class that inherits from the `Modem` class:

```
class ErrorCorrectionModem extends Modem {
    // program goes here
}
```

Building an Inheritance Hierarchy

Inheritance, which enables a variety of related classes to be developed without a lot of redundant work, can be passed down from one class to another class to another class. This system of classes is called a class hierarchy, and all of the standard classes you can use in your Java programs are part of a hierarchy.

Understanding a hierarchy is easier if you understand what subclasses and superclasses are. A class that inherits from another class is called a *subclass*, and the class that is inherited from is called a *superclass*.

In the preceding *WarGames* example, the Modem class is the superclass of the ErrorCorrectionModem class, and ErrorCorrectionModem is the subclass of Modem. A class can have more than one class that inherits from it in the hierarchy—another subclass of Modem could be ISDNModem, since ISDN modems have behavior and attributes that make them different from error-correcting modems. If there were a subclass of ErrorCorrectionModem such as InternalErrorCorrectionModem, it would inherit from all classes above it in the hierarchy—both ErrorCorrectionModem and Modem. These inheritance relationships are shown in Figure 10.2.

FIGURE 10.2

An example of a class hierarchy.

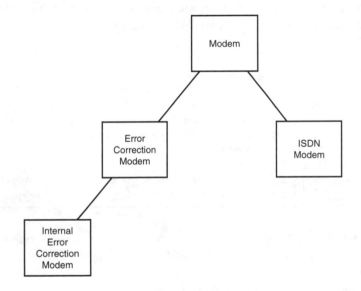

10

The programs you write as you are learning about Java won't use complicated class hierarchies. However, the classes that are part of the standard Java language make full use of inheritance. Understanding it is essential to working with the classes that are part of the Java language. You'll learn more about inheritance during Hour 12, "Making the Most of Existing Objects."

Converting Objects and Simple Variables

One of the most common tasks you'll need to accomplish in Java is to convert information from one form into another. There are several types of conversions you can do:

- Converting an object into another object
- Converting a simple variable into another type of variable
- Using an object to create a simple variable
- Using a simple variable to create an object

Simple variables are the basic data types you learned about during Hour 5, "Storing and Changing Information in a Program." These types include int, float, char, long, and double.

When using a method or an expression in a program, you must use the right type of information that's expected by these methods and expressions. A method that expects a Calendar object must receive a Calendar object, for instance. If you used a method that takes a single integer argument and you sent it a floating-point number instead, an error would occur when you attempted to compile the program.

> There is one area in which Java is less particular: strings. When a method such as System.out.println() requires a string argument, you can use the + operator to combine several different types of information in that argument. As long as one of the things being combined is a string, the combined argument will be converted into a string. This makes the following statements possible:
>
> ```
> float sentence = 17.5F;
> System.out.println("My sentence has been reduced to "
>     + sentence + "years.");
> ```

Converting information into a new form in a program is called *casting*. Casting produces a new value that is a different type of variable or object than its source. You don't actually change the value of a variable or object when it is cast. Instead, a new variable or object is created in the format you need.

The terms *source* and *destination* are useful when discussing the concept of casting. The source is some kind of information in its original form—whether its a variable or an object. The destination is the converted version of the source in its new form.

Casting Simple Variables

With simple variables, casting occurs most commonly between numeric variables, such as integers and floating-point numbers. There's one type of variable that cannot be used in any casting: Boolean values.

To cast information into a new format, you precede it with the new format surrounded by parenthesis marks. For example, if you wanted to cast something into a `long` variable, you would precede it with `(long)`.

For example, the following statements cast a `float` value into an `int`:

```
float source = 7.06F;
int destination = (int)source;
```

In a variable cast where the destination holds larger values than the source, the value is converted easily. An example is when a `byte` is cast into an `int`. A `byte` holds values from –128 to 127, while an `int` holds values from –2.14 billion to 2.14 billion. No matter what value the `byte` variable holds, there's plenty of room for it in a new `int` variable.

You can sometimes use a variable in a different format without casting it at all. For example, `char` variables can be used as if they were `int` variables. Also, `int` variables can be used as if they were `long` variables, and anything can be used as a `double`.

A character can be used as an `int` variable because each character has a corresponding numeric code that represents its position in the character set. As an example, if the variable `k` has the value 67, the cast `(char)k` produces the character value `'C'` because the numeric code associated with a capital `C` is 67, according to the ASCII character set. The ASCII character set is part of the Unicode character standard adopted by the Java language.

In most cases, because the destination provides more room than the source, the information is converted without changing its value. The main exceptions occur when an `int` or `long` variable is cast to a `float`, or a `long` is cast into a `double`.

When you are converting information from a larger variable type into a smaller type, you must explicitly cast it, as in the following statements:

```
int xNum = 103;
byte val = (byte)xNum;
```

Casting is used to convert an integer value called `xNum` into a `byte` variable called `val`. This is an example where the destination variable holds a smaller range of values than the source variable. A `byte` holds integer values ranging from -128 to 127, and an `int` holds a much larger range of integer values: -2.14 billion to 2.14 billion.

When the source variable in a casting operation has a value that isn't allowed in the destination variable, Java will change the value to make the cast fit successfully. This can produce unexpected results if you're not expecting the change.

10

Casting Objects

Objects can be cast into other objects as long as the source and destination are related by inheritance. One class must be a subclass of the other.

Some objects do not require casting at all. An object can be used where any of its superclasses are expected. For example, because all objects in Java are subclasses of the Object class, you can use any object as an argument when an Object is expected.

You can also use an object where one of its subclasses is expected. However, because subclasses usually contain more information than their superclasses, you might lose some of this information. If the object doesn't have a method that the subclass would contain, an error will result if that missing method is used in the program.

To use an object in the place of one of its subclasses, you must cast it explicitly with statements such as the following:

```
JWindow win = new JWindow();
JFrame top = new (JFrame)win;
```

This casts a JWindow object called win into a JFrame object. You won't lose any information in the cast, but you gain all the methods and variables the subclass defines.

Converting Simple Variables to Objects and Back

One thing you can't do is cast an object to a simple variable or a simple variable to an object. These types of information are too different in Java for them to be substituted for each other.

Instead, there are classes in the java.lang package for each of the simple variable types: Boolean, Byte, Character, Double, Float, Integer, Long, and Short. All of these classes are capitalized, which serves as a reminder that they are objects, rather than simple variable types.

Using class methods defined in each of these classes, you can create an object using a variable's value as an argument. The following statement creates an Integer object with the value 5309:

```
Integer suffix = new Integer(5309);
```

After you have created an object like this, you can use it like any other object. When you want to use that value again as a simple variable, the class has methods for this also. For example, to get an int value from the preceding suffix object, the following statement can be used:

```
int newSuff = suffix.intValue();
```

This statement causes the newSuff variable to have the value 5309, expressed as an int value. One of the most commonplace casts from an object to a variable is when you have a string that should be used in a numeric way. This is done by using the parseInt() method of the Integer class, as in the following example:

```
String count = "25";
int myCount = Integer.parseInt(count);
```

This converts a string with the text 25 into an integer with the value 25.

The next project you will create is an application that converts a string value in a command-line argument to a numeric value, a common technique when you're taking input from a user at the command line.

Enter the text of Listing 10.1 in your word processor and save the file as NewRoot.java.

LISTING 10.1   The Full Text of NewRoot.java

```
 1: class NewRoot {
 2:     public static void main(String[] arguments) {
 3:         int number = 100;
 4:         if (arguments.length > 0)
 5:             number = Integer.parseInt( arguments[0] );
 6:         System.out.println("The square root of "
 7:             + number
 8:             + " is "
 9:             + Math.sqrt(number) );
10:     }
11: }
```

Compile the application using the javac tool included with the Software Development Kit or another compiler. When you run the program, specify an integer as a command-line argument, as in the following command:

```
java NewRoot 196
```

The program will display the number and its square root, as in this example:

```
The square root of 196 is 14.0
```

The NewRoot application is an expansion of an earlier tutorial from Hour 4, "Understanding How Java Programs Work." The Root program in that hour displayed the square root of the integer 225.

That program would have been more useful if it took a number submitted by a user and displayed its square root. This requires conversion from a string to an integer. All command-line arguments are stored as elements of a `String` array, so you must be able to convert them to numbers before using them in mathematical expressions.

To create an integer value based on the contents of a string, the `Integer.parseInt()` method is called with the string as the only argument, as in Line 5:

```
number = Integer.parseInt( arguments[0] );
```

Since `arguments[0]` holds the first command-line argument submitted when the application was run, the value of number will be an integer based on that string.

Workshop: Creating an Object

To see a working example of classes and inheritance, you will create classes that represent two types of objects: cable modems, which will be implemented as the `CableModem` class, and DSL modems, which will be implemented as the `DslModem` class.

For the sake of simplicity, the workshop will focus on a few simple attributes and behavior for these objects:

- Each object should have a speed and be able to display it when asked.
- Each object should be able to connect to the Internet.

One thing that cable modems and DSL modems have in common is that they both have a speed. Since it is something they share, it could be put into a class that is the superclass of both the `CableModem` and `DslModem` classes. Call this class `Modem`. Using your word processor, create a new file and save it as `Modem.java`. Enter Listing 10.2 and save the file.

LISTING 10.2   The Full Text of `Modem.java`

```
1: public class Modem {
2:     int speed;
3:
4:     public void displaySpeed() {
5:         System.out.println("Speed: " + speed);
6:     }
7: }
```

Compile this file with `javac` or another compiler to produce a file called `Modem.class`. Although you cannot run this program with the interpreter, you will be able to use it in other classes. You now have a `Modem` class that can handle one of the things that the `CableModem` and `DslModem` classes have in common. By using the `extends` statement when you are creating the CableModem and DslModem classes, you can make each of them a subclass of Modem.

Start a new file in your word processor and save it as CableModem.java. Enter Listing 10.3 and then save and compile the file.

LISTING 10.3   The Full Text of CableModem.java

```
1: public class CableModem extends Modem {
2:      String method = "cable connection";
3:
4:      public void connect() {
5:          System.out.println("Connecting to the Internet ...");
6:          System.out.println("Using a " + method);
7:      }
8: }
```

Create a third file with your word processor, and save it as DslModem.java. Enter Listing 10.4 and then save and compile the file when you're done.

LISTING 10.4   The Full Text of DslModem.java

```
1: public class DslModem extends Modem {
2:      String method = "DSL phone connection";
3:
4:      public void connect() {
5:          System.out.println("Connecting to the Internet ...");
6:          System.out.println("Using a " + method);
7:      }
8: }
```

Once you have compiled all three of these files, you will have three class files: Modem.class, CableModem.class, and DslModem.class. However, you cannot run any of these class files with java or another Java interpreter because they do not have main() blocks. You need to create a short Java program to test out the class hierarchy you have just built.

Return to your word processor and create a new file called TestModems.java. Enter Listing 10.5.

LISTING 10.5   The Full Text of `TestModems.java`

```
 1: class TestModems {
 2:     public static void main(String[] arguments) {
 3:         CableModem roadRunner = new CableModem();
 4:         DslModem bellSouth = new DslModem();
 5:         roadRunner.speed = 500000;
 6:         bellSouth.speed = 400000;
 7:         System.out.println("Trying the cable modem:");
 8:         roadRunner.displaySpeed();
 9:         roadRunner.connect();
10:         System.out.println("Trying the DSL modem:");
11:         bellSouth.displaySpeed();
12:         bellSouth.connect();
13:     }
14: }
```

Save and compile the file when you're done. When you run it, the output should resemble the following:

OUTPUT
```
Trying the cable modem:
Speed: 500000
Connecting to the Internet ...
Using a cable connection
Trying the DSL modem:
Speed: 400000
Connecting to the Internet ...
Using a DSL phone connection
```

The following things are taking place in the program:

- Lines 3–4: Two new objects are created—a `CableModem` object called `roadRunner`, and a `DslModem` object called `bellSouth`.

- Line 5: The `speed` variable of the `CableModem` object named `roadRunner` is set to `500000`.

- Line 6: The `speed` variable of the `DslModem` object named `bellSouth` is set to `400000`.

- Line 8: The `displaySpeed()` method of the `roadRunner` object is called. This method is inherited from `Modem`—even though it isn't present in the `CableModem` class, you can call it.

- Line 9: The `connect()` method of the `roadRunner` object is called.

- Line 11: The `displaySpeed()` method of the `bellSouth` object is called.

- Line 12: The `connect()` method of the `bellSouth` object is called.

Summary

After creating your first class of objects and arranging several classes into a hierarchy, you ought to be more comfortable with the term *object-oriented programming*. You will be learning more about object behavior and attributes in the next two hours as you start creating more sophisticated objects.

Terms such as *program*, *class*, and *object* will make more sense as you become more experienced with this style of development. Object-oriented programming is a concept that takes some time to get used to. Once you have mastered it, you'll find that it's an effective way to design, develop, and debug computer programs.

Q&A

10

Q Can classes inherit from more than one class?

A It's possible with some programming languages, but not Java. Multiple inheritance is a powerful feature, but it also makes object-oriented programming a bit harder to learn and use. Java's developers decided to limit inheritance to one superclass for any class, although a class can have numerous subclasses. One way to compensate for this limitation is to inherit methods from a special type of class called an interface. You'll learn more about interfaces during Hour 19, "Creating a Threaded Program."

Q Why are object-oriented programs easier to debug?

A Object-oriented programs enable you to focus on a smaller part of a computer program when figuring out where an error is happening. Because a related group of tasks are handled by the same object, you can focus on that object if the tasks aren't being performed correctly. You don't have to worry about any other parts of the program.

Q When would you want to create a class that isn't `public`?

A The main time you would not want to make a class of objects available to other programs is when the class is strictly for the use of one program you're writing. If you're creating a game program and your `ReloadRayGun` class of objects is highly specific to the game you're writing, it could be a private class. To keep a class from being `public`, leave off the `public` statement in front of `class`.

Quiz

The following questions will test your knowledge of objects and the programs that use them.

Questions

1. What statement is used to enable one class to inherit from another class?

    a. `inherits`

    b. `extends`

    c. `handitover`

2. Why are compiled Java programs saved with the `.class` file extension?

    a. Java's developers think it's a classy language.

    b. It's a subtle tribute to the world's teachers.

    c. Every Java program is a class.

3. What are the two things that make up an object?

    a. attributes and behavior

    b. commands and data files

    c. spit and vinegar

Answers

1. b. The `extends` statement is used because the subclass is an extension of the attributes and behavior of the superclass and of any superclasses above that in the class hierarchy.

2. c. Your programs will always be made up of at least one main class and any other classes that are needed.

3. a. In a way, b. is also true because commands are comparable to behavior, and data files are analogous to attributes.

Activities

If you don't object, you can `extends` your knowledge of this hour's topics with the following activities:

- Create an `AcousticModem` class with a speed of 300 and its own `connect()` method.

- Rewrite the `DslModem` and `CableModem` classes so that they both inherit the `connect()` method from the `Modem` class. Make sure that they still display the same output that they did in the workshop.

To see Java programs that implement these activities, visit the book's Web site at `http://www.java24hours.com`.

HOUR 11

Describing What Your Object Is Like

As you learned during last hour's introduction to object-oriented programming, an object is a way of organizing a program so that it has everything it needs to accomplish a task. Objects need two things to do their jobs: attributes and behavior.

Attributes are the information stored within an object. They can be variables such as integers, characters, Boolean values, or other objects such as String and Calendar objects. Behavior is the groups of statements used to handle specific jobs within the object. Each of these groups is called a *method*.

Up to this point, you have been working with the methods and variables of objects without knowing it. Any time your statement had a period in it that wasn't a decimal point or part of a string, chances are an object was involved. You'll see this during this hour as the following topics are covered:

- Creating variables for an object
- Creating variables for a class
- Using methods with objects and classes

- Calling a method in a statement
- Returning a value with a method
- Creating constructor methods
- Sending arguments to a method
- Using `this` to refer to an object
- Creating new objects
- Putting one object inside another object

Creating Variables

For the purposes of this hour's examples, you'll be looking at a class of objects called `Virus` whose sole purpose in life is to reproduce in as many places as possible—much like some of the people I knew in college. A `Virus` has several different things it needs in order to do its work, and these will be implemented as the behavior of the class. The information that's needed for the methods will be stored as attributes.

> This hour will not teach actual virus writing, though it might provide some insight into how virus programs work as they wreak havoc on the file systems of the computer-loving world. This publisher had scheduled *Sams Teach Yourself Virus Programming in a Three-Day Weekend* for next spring, but the book has been postponed because the author's hard drive was unexpectedly erased by an email from someone who said "I love you" but had a funny way of showing it.

The attributes of an object represent any variables needed in order for the object to function. These variables could be simple data types such as integers, characters, and floating-point numbers, or they could be arrays or objects of classes such as `String` or `Calendar`. An object's variables can be used throughout its program, in any of the methods the object includes. You create variables immediately after the `class` statement that creates the class and before any methods.

One of the things that a `Virus` object needs is a way to indicate that a file already has been infected. Some computer viruses change the field that stores the time a file was last modified; for example, a virus might move the time from `13:41:20` to `13:41:61`. Because no normal file would be saved on the 61st second of a minute, the time is a sign that the file was infected. The `Virus` object will use `86` as the seconds field of a file's modification time because "86 it" is slang that means to throw something away—exactly the kind of unpleasant antisocial connotation we're going for. The value will be stored in an integer variable called newSeconds.

The following statements begin a class called Virus with an attribute called newSeconds and two other attributes:

```
public class Virus {
    public int newSeconds = 86;
    public String author = "Sam Snett";
    int maxFileSize = 30000;
}
```

All three variables are attributes for the class: newSeconds, maxFileSize, and author.

Putting a statement such as public in a variable declaration is called *access control*, because it determines how other objects made from other classes can use that variable— or if they can use it at all.

The newSeconds variable has a starting value of 86, and the statement that creates it has public as the first part of the statement. Making a variable public makes it possible to modify the variable from another program that is using the Virus object. If the other program attaches special significance to the number 92, for instance, it can change newSeconds to that value. The following statements create a Virus object called influenza and set its newSeconds variable:

```
Virus influenza = new Virus();
influenza.newSeconds = 92;
```

In the Virus class, the author variable also is public, so it can be changed freely from other programs. The other variable, maxFileSize, can only be used within the class itself.

When you make a variable in a class public, the class loses control over how that variable is used by other programs. In many cases, this might not be a problem. For example, the author variable can be changed to any name or pseudonym that identifies the author of the virus, and the only restriction is aesthetic. The name might eventually be used on court documents if you're prosecuted, so you don't want to pick a dumb one. *The State of Ohio v. LoveHandles* doesn't have the same ring to it as *Ohio v. MafiaBoy*.

Restricting access to a variable keeps errors from occurring if the variable is set incorrectly by another program. With the Virus class, if newSeconds is set to a value of 60 or less, it won't be reliable as a way to tell that a file is infected. Some files might be saved with that number of seconds regardless of the virus, and they'll look infected to Virus. If the Virus class of objects needs to guard against this problem, you need to do these two things:

11

- Switch the variable from `public` to `protected` or `private`, two other statements that provide more restrictive access.
- Add behavior to change the value of the variable and report the value of the variable to other programs.

A `protected` variable can only be used in the same class as the variable, any subclasses of that class, or by classes in the same package. A *package* is a group of related classes that serve a common purpose. An example is the `java.util` package, which contains classes that offer useful utility functions, such as date and time programming and file archiving. When you use the `import` statement in a Java program with an asterisk, as in `import java.util.*;`, you are making the classes of a package available for use in that program.

A `private` variable is restricted even further than a `protected` variable—it only can be used in the same class. Unless you know that a variable can be changed to anything without affecting how its class functions, you probably should make the variable `private` or `protected`.

The following statement makes `newSeconds` a `private` variable:

```
private int newSeconds = 86;
```

If you want other programs to use the `newSeconds` variable in some way, you'll have to create behavior that makes it possible. This task will be covered later in the hour.

There also is another type of access control: the lack of any `public`, `private`, or `protected` statement when the variable is created.

In the programs you have created prior to this hour, you didn't specify any of these statements. When no access control is specified, the variable is available to be used only by any classes in the same package. This is often called default or package access, although there are no statements used to declare it specifically when creating a variable.

Creating Class Variables

When you create an object, it has its own version of all variables that are part of the object's class. Each object created from the `Virus` class of objects has its own version of the `newSeconds`, `maxFileSize`, and `author` variables. If you modified one of these variables in an object, it would not affect the same variable in another `Virus` object.

There are times when an attribute has more to do with an entire class of objects than a specific object itself. For example, if you wanted to keep track of how many `Virus` objects were being used in a program, it would not make sense to store this value repeat-edly in each Virus object. Instead, you can use a class variable to store this kind of infor-mation. You can use this kind of variable with any object of a class, but only one copy of the variable exists for the whole class. The variables you have been creating for object thus far can be called *object variables*, because they are tied to a specific object. *Class variables* refer to a class of the objects as a whole.

Both types of variables are created and used in the same way, except that static is used in the statement that creates class variables. The following statement creates a class vari-able for the Virus example:

```
static int virusCount = 0;
```

Changing the value of a class variable is no different than changing an object's variables. If you have a Virus object called tuberculosis, you could change the class variable virusCount with the following statement:

```
tuberculosis.virusCount++;
```

Because class variables apply to an entire class instead of a specific object, you can use the name of the class instead:

```
Virus.virusCount++;
```

Both statements accomplish the same thing, but there's an advantage to using the name of the class when working with class variables. It shows immediately that virusCount is a class variable instead of an object's variable, because you can't refer to object variables using the name of a class. If you always use object names when working with class vari-ables, you won't be able to tell whether they are class or object variables without looking carefully at the source code of the class.

Creating Behavior with Methods

Attributes are the way to keep track of information about a class of objects, but they don't take any action. For a class to actually do the things it was created to do, you must create behavior. Behavior describes all of the different sections of a class that accomplish specific tasks. Each of these sections is called a *method*.

You have been using methods throughout your programs up to this point without know-ing it, including one in particular: println(). This method displays text onscreen. Like variables, methods are used in connection with an object or a class. The name of the object or class is followed by a period and the name of the method, as in screen2D.drawString() or Integer.parseInt().

11

> The `System.out.println()` method might seem confusing because it has two periods instead of one. This is because two classes are involved in the statement—the `System` class and the `PrintStream` class. The `System` class has a variable called `out` that is a `PrintStream` object. `println()` is a method of the `PrintStream` class. The `System.out.println()` statement means, in effect, "Use the `println()` method of the `out` variable of the `System` class." You can chain together references to variables and methods in this way.

Declaring a Method

You create methods with a statement that looks similar to the statement that begins a class. Both can take arguments between parentheses after their names, and both use { and } marks at the beginning and end. The difference is that methods can send back a value after they are handled. The value can be one of the simple types such as integers or Boolean values, or it can be a class of objects. If a method should not return any value, use the `void` statement.

The following is an example of a method the `Virus` class can use to infect files:

```
public boolean infectFile(String filename) {
    boolean success = false;
    // file-infecting statements would be here
    return success;
}
```

The `infectFile()` method is used to add a virus to a file. This method takes a single argument, a string variable called `filename`, and this variable represents the file that should be attacked. The actual code to infect a file is omitted here due to the author's desire to stay on the good side of the U.S. Secret Service. The only thing you need to know is that if the infection is a success, the `success` variable is set to a value of `true`.

By looking at the statement that begins the method, you can see `boolean` preceding the name of the method, `infectFile`. This statement signifies that a `boolean` value will be sent back after the method is handled. The `return` statement is what actually sends a value back. In this example, the value of `success` is returned.

When a method returns a value, you can use the method as part of an assignment statement. For example, if you created a `Virus` object called `malaria`, you could use statements such as these:

```
if (malaria.infectFile(currentFile))
    System.out.println(currentFile + " has been infected!");
else
    System.out.println("Curses! Foiled again!");
```

Any method that returns a value can be used at any place a value or variable could be used in a program.

Earlier in the hour, you switched the newSeconds variable to private to prevent it from being set by other programs. However, because you're a virus writer who cares about people, you still want to make it possible for newSeconds to be used if it is used correctly. The way to do this is to create public methods in the Virus class that read the value of newSeconds or write a new value to newSeconds. These new methods should be public, unlike the newSeconds variable itself, so they can be called by other programs. The new methods will be able to work with newSeconds because they are in the same class as the variable.

Consider the following two methods:

```
public int getSeconds() {
    return newSeconds;
}

public void setSeconds(int newValue) {
    if (newValue > 60)
        newSeconds = newValue;
}
```

The getSeconds() method is used to send back the current value of newSeconds. The getSeconds() method is necessary because other programs can't even look at a private variable such as newSeconds. The getSeconds() method does not have any arguments, but it still must have parentheses after the method name. Otherwise, when you were using getSeconds in a program, the method would look no different than a variable.

The setSeconds() method takes one argument, an integer called newValue. This integer contains the value that a program wants to change newSeconds to. If newValue is greater than 60, the change will be made. The setSeconds() method has void preceding the method name, so it does not return any kind of value.

In this example, the Virus class controls how the newSeconds variable can be used by other classes. This process is called *encapsulation*, and it's a fundamental concept of object-oriented programming. The better your objects are able to protect themselves against misuse, the more useful they will be when you use them in other programs.

Similar Methods with Different Arguments

As you have seen with the setSeconds() method, you can send arguments to a method to affect what it does. Different methods in a class can have different names, but methods can also have the same name if they have different arguments.

Two methods can have the same name if they have a different number of arguments, or the specific arguments are of different variable types. For example, it might be useful for the `Virus` class of objects to have two `tauntUser()` methods. One could have no arguments at all and would deliver a generic taunt. The other could specify the taunt as a string argument. The following statements could implement these methods:

```
void tauntUser() {
    System.out.println("The problem is not with your set, but "
        + "with yourselves.");
}

void tauntUser(String taunt) {
    System.out.println(taunt);
}
```

Constructor Methods

When you want to create an object in a program, the new statement is used, as in the following example:

```
Virus typhoid = new Virus();
```

This statement creates a new `Virus` object called `typhoid`. When you use the new statement, a special method of that object's class is called. This method is called a *constructor* because it handles the work required to create the object. The purpose of a constructor is to set up any variables and other things that need to be established for the object to function properly.

Constructor methods are defined like other methods, except that they cannot return a value as other methods do. The following are two constructor methods for the `Virus` class of objects:

```
public Virus() {
    author = "Ignoto";
    maxFileSize = 30000;
}

public Virus(String name, int size) {
    author = name;
    maxFileSize = size;
}
```

Like other methods, constructors can use the arguments they are sent as a way to define more than one constructor in a class. In this example, the first constructor would be called when a new statement such as the following is used:

```
Virus mumps = new Virus();
```

The other constructor could be called only if a string and an integer were sent as arguments with the new statement, as in this example:

```
Virus rubella = new Virus("April Mayhem", 60000);
```

If you don't include any constructor methods in a class, it will inherit a single constructor method with no arguments from its superclass. There also might be other constructor methods that it inherits, depending on the superclass used.

In any class, there must be a constructor method that has the same number and type of arguments as the new statement that's used to create objects of that class. In the example of the Virus class, which has Virus() and a Virus(String name, int size) constructors, you only could create Virus objects with two different types of new statements: one without arguments and one with a string and an integer as the only two arguments.

Class Methods

Like class variables, class methods are a way to provide functionality associated with an entire class instead of a specific object. Use a class method when the method does nothing that affects an individual object of the class. One example that you have used in a previous hour was the parseInt() method of the Integer class. This method is used to convert a string to a variable of the type int, as in the following:

```
int time = Integer.parseInt(timeText);
```

To make a method into a class method, use static in front of the method name, as in the following:

```
static void showVirusCount() {
    System.out.println("There are " + virusCount + " viruses.");
}
```

The virusCount class variable was used earlier to keep track of how many Virus objects have been created by a program. The showVirusCount() method is a class method that displays this total, and it should be called with a statement such as the following:

```
Virus.showVirusCount();
```

Variable Scope Within Methods

When you create a variable or an object inside a method in one of your classes, it is usable only inside that method. The reason for this is the concept of *variable scope*. Scope is the section in which a variable exists in a program. If you go outside of the part of the program defined by the scope, you can no longer use the variable.

11

The { and } statements in a program define the boundaries for a variable. Any variable created within these marks cannot be used outside of them. For example, consider the following statements:

```
if (numFiles < 1) {
    String warning = "No files remaining.";
}
System.out.println(warning);
```

This example does not work correctly because the warning variable was created inside the brackets of the if block statement. Those brackets define the scope of the variable. The warning variable does not exist outside of the brackets, so the System.out.println() method cannot use it as an argument.

When you use a set of brackets inside another set of brackets, you'll need to pay attention to the scope of the variables with which you are working. Take a look at the following example:

```
if (infectedFiles < 5) {
    int status = 1;
    if (infectedFiles < 1) {
        boolean firstVirus = true;
        status = 0;
    } else {
        firstVirus = false;
    }
}
```

In this example the status variable can be used anywhere, but the firstVirus variable will cause a compiler error. Because firstVirus is created within the scope of the if (infectedFiles < 1) statement, it doesn't exist inside the scope of the else statement that follows.

To fix the problem, firstVirus must be created outside both of these blocks so that its scope includes both of them. One solution would be to create firstVirus at the same time that status is created.

Rules that enforce scope make programs easier to debug because scope limits the area in which a variable can be used. This reduces one of the most common errors that can crop up in many programming languages: the same variable being used two different ways in different parts of a program. By enforcing restrictive rules for a variable's scope, the Java language makes it more difficult to misuse a variable.

The concept of scope applies to methods also, because they are defined by an opening bracket and closing bracket. A variable created inside a method cannot be used in other methods. You can only use a variable in more than one method if it was created as an object variable or class variable after the `class` statement at the beginning of the program.

Putting One Class Inside Another

Although a Java program is sometimes called a class, there are many occasions when a program requires more than one class to get its work done. A multiclass program consists of a main class and any helper classes that are needed. These helper classes earn their name by helping the main class do its work.

An example might be a Java applet that displays a scrolling headline as part of its graphical user interface. The headline could be an independent object in the program, just like other interface elements such as buttons and scroll bars. It makes sense to put the headline into its own class, rather than including its variables and methods in the `applet` class.

When you divide a program into multiple classes, there are two ways to define the helper classes. One way is to define each class separately, as in the following example:

```
public class WreakHavoc {
    String author = "Ignoto";

    public void infectFile() {
        VirusCode vic = new VirusCode(1024);
    }
}

class VirusCode {
    int vSize;

    VirusCode(int size) {
        vSize = size;
    }
}
```

In this example, the `VirusCode` class is being used as a helper of the `WreakHavoc` class. Helper classes will often be defined in the same `.java` source file as the class they're assisting. When the source file is compiled, multiple class files will be produced. The preceding example would produce the files `WreakHavoc.class` and `VirusCode.class`.

If more than one class is defined in the same source file, only one of the classes can be `public`. The other classes should not have `public` in their class statements. Also, the name of the source file should match the name of the `public` class. In the preceding example, the name should be `WreakHavoc.java`.

11

When creating a main class and a helper class, you can also put the helper inside the main class. When this is done, the helper class is called an *inner class*.

An inner class is placed within the opening bracket and closing bracket of another class.

```
public class WreakMoreHavoc {
    String author = "Ignoto";

    public void infectFile() {
        VirusCode vic = new VirusCode(1024);
    }

    class VirusCode {
        int vSize;

        VirusCode(int size) {
            vSize = size;
        }
    }
}
```

An inner class can be used in the same manner as any other kind of helper class. The main difference—other than its location—is what happens after the compiler gets through with these classes. Inner classes do not get the name indicated by their `class` statement. Instead, the compiler gives them a name that includes the name of the main class.

In the preceding example, the compiler produces `WreakHavoc.class` and `WreakHavoc$VirusCode.class`.

> This section illustrates one of the simplest examples of how an inner class can be defined and used. Inner classes are an advanced feature of Java that you won't encounter often as you first learn the language. The functionality they offer can be accomplished by using helper classes defined separately from a main class, and that's the best course to take as you're starting out in programming.

Using the `this` Keyword

Because you can refer to variables and methods in other classes along with variables and methods in your own classes, the variable you're referring to can become confusing in some circumstances. One way to make things a little more clear is with the `this` statement. The `this` statement is a way to refer in a program to the program's own object.

When you are using an object's methods or variables, you put the name of the object in front of the method or variable name, separated by a period. Consider these examples:

```
Virus chickenpox = new Virus();
chickenpox.name = "LoveHandles";
chickenpox.setSeconds(75);
```

These statements create a new `Virus` object called `chickenpox`, set the `name` variable of `chickenpox`, and then call the `setSeconds()` method of `chickenpox`.

There are times in a program when you need to refer to the current object—in other words, the object represented by the program itself. For example, inside the `Virus` class, you might have a method that has its own variable called `author`:

```
void public checkAuthor() {
    String author = null;
}
```

A variable called `author` exists within the scope of the `checkAuthor()` method, but it isn't the same variable as an object variable called `author`. If you wanted to refer to the current object's `author` variable, you have to use the `this` statement, as in the following:

```
System.out.println(this.author);
```

By using `this`, you make it clear to which variable or method you are referring. You can use `this` anywhere in a class that you would refer to an object by name. If you wanted to send the current object as an argument in a method, for example, you could use a statement such as the following:

```
verifyData(this);
```

In many cases, the `this` statement will not be needed to make it clear that you're referring to an object's variables and methods. However, there's no detriment to using `this` any time you want to be sure you're referring to the right thing.

Workshop: Using Class Methods and Variables

At the insistence of every attorney and management executive in the Pearson family of computer publishers, the workshop for this hour will not be the creation of a working virus program. Instead, you'll create a simple `Virus` object that can do only one thing: count the number of `Virus` objects that a program has created and report the total.

Load your word processor and create a new file called `Virus.java`. Enter Listing 11.1 into the word processor and save the file when you're done.

11

LISTING 11.1   The Full Text of `Virus.java`

```
 1: public class Virus {
 2:     static int virusCount = 0;
 3:
 4:     public Virus() {
 5:         virusCount++;
 6:     }
 7:
 8:     static int getVirusCount() {
 9:         return virusCount;
10:     }
11: }
```

Compile the file and return to your word processor. To test out this new `Virus` class, you need to create a second class that can create `Virus` objects.

The `VirusLook` class is a simple application that creates `Virus` objects and then counts the number of objects that have been created with the `getVirusCount()` class method of the `Virus` class.

Open up a new file with your word processor and enter Listing 11.2. Save the file as `VirusLook.java` when you're done.

LISTING 11.2   The Full Text of `VirusLook.java`

```
 1: class VirusLook {
 2:     public static void main(String[] arguments) {
 3:         int numViruses = Integer.parseInt(arguments[0]);
 4:         if (numViruses > 0) {
 5:             Virus[] virii = new Virus[numViruses];
 6:             for (int i = 0; i < numViruses; i++)
 7:                 virii[i] = new Virus();
 8:             System.out.println("There are " + Virus.getVirusCount()
 9:                 + " viruses.");
10:         }
11:     }
12: }
```

The `VirusLook` class is an application that takes one argument when you run it at the command line: the number of `Virus` objects to create. The following is an example of a command that can be used to run the application:

```
java VirusLook 200
```

Arguments are read into an application using a string array that's sent to the `main()` method. In the `VirusLook` class, this occurs in Line 2.

To work with an argument as an integer, it must be converted from a `String` object to an integer. This requires the use of the `parseInt()` class method of the `Integer` class. In Line 3, an `int` variable named `numViruses` is created from the first argument sent to the program on the command line.

If the `numViruses` variable is greater than 0, the following things take place in the `VirusLook` application:

- Line 5: An array of `Virus` objects is created with the `numViruses` variable determining the number of objects in the array.
- Lines 6–7: A `for` loop is used to call the constructor method for each `Virus` object in the array.
- Lines 8–9: After all of the `Virus` objects have been constructed, the `getVirusCount()` class method of the `Virus` class is used to count the number of its objects that have been created. This should match the argument that was set when the `VirusLook` application was run.

If the `numViruses` variable is not greater than 0, nothing happens in the `VirusLook` application.

After you compile the `VirusLook.java` file, test it with any command-line argument you'd like to try. The number of `Virus` objects that can be created depends on the memory that's available on your system when you run the `VirusLook` application. On the author's system, anything above 5.6 million viruses causes the program to crash after displaying an `OutOfMemoryError` message.

If you don't specify more `Virus` objects than your system can handle, the output should be something like the following:

```
There are 125000 viruses.
```

Summary

You now have completed two of the three hours devoted to object-oriented concepts in this book. You've learned how to create an object, give behavior and attributes to the object and its class of objects, and convert objects and variables into other forms by using casting.

11

Thinking in terms of objects is one of the tougher challenges of the Java programming language. Once you start to understand it, however, you realize that the entire language makes use of objects and classes.

During the next hour, you'll learn how to give your objects parents and children.

Q&A

Q Can constructor methods send back a value like other methods?

A No, because there's no way to receive that value. Unlike other methods that can be used as part of an equation, the argument of a method, or other statements, constructors are only handled in response to a new statement. There's no way for that statement to receive a value that would be sent by the method.

Q Do you have to create an object to use class variables or methods?

A Because class variables and methods aren't associated with a specific object, you don't need to create an object solely for the purpose of using them. The use of the `Integer.parseInt()` method is an example of this because you don't have to create a new `Integer` object just to convert a string to an `int` value.

Q Is there a list of all the built-in methods that Java supports?

A Sun offers full documentation for all classes in the Java language, including all the public methods you can use. The documentation is in HTML format, so you can browse easily through the classes to see what methods and variables they include. Visit the Java 2 version 1.4 documentation Web page at `http://java.sun.com/j2se/1.4/docs/api`. During the preparation of this book, I spent enough time at this part of Sun's Web site to qualify for California residency.

Q When I run the `VirusLook` application without an argument, the program crashes with an `ArrayIndexOutOfBoundsException` error. What can I do to correct this?

A This error occurs because of the effort to call the `Integer.parseInt()` method with a null string as the value of `arguments[0]`. One solution would be to test the value of `arguments[0]` with an `if` statement and call `Integer.parseInt()` only if `arguments[0]` is not null. This would require a default value for the `numViruses` variable. Arguments often require some kind of testing to make sure they have acceptable values before you use them.

Q What's the difference between the `Integer` object and the `int` variable type?

A The first is an object, and the second is a simple variable type. Each of the variable types, such as `char`, `int`, and `float`, has a corresponding object. The object is used when you want to make use of an object's methods or treat the variable like an object. Because an `Integer` object can do things in a program that the `int` variable type cannot, it is convenient to have both.

Quiz

The following questions will see if you have the attributes and behavior to understand object-oriented programming techniques.

Questions

1. In a Java class, a method is an example of what?

   a. Attributes

   b. Statements

   c. Behavior

2. If you want to make a variable a class variable, what statement must you use when it is created?

   a. `new`

   b. `public`

   c. `static`

3. What is the name for the part of a program in which a variable lives?

   a. Its nest

   b. The scope

   c. Variable valley

Answers

1. c. A method is made up of statements, but it's an example of behavior.

2. c. If the `static` statement is left off, the variable will be an object variable instead of a class variable.

3. b.

Activities

If all this talk of viruses didn't make you sick, you can increase your knowledge of this hour's topics with the following activity:

- Add a `private` variable to the `Virus` class that stores an integer called `newSeconds`. Create methods to return the value of `newSeconds` and change the value of `newSeconds` only if the new value is between `60` and `100`.

- Write a Java application that takes an argument as a string, converts it to a float variable, converts that to a `Float` object, and finally turns that into an `int` variable. Run it a few times with different arguments to see what results.

To see Java programs that implement these activities, visit the book's Web site at `http://www.java24hours.com`.

HOUR 12

Making the Most of Existing Objects

This might be a surprise to you, but your Java objects are ideally suited for childbearing. When you create a program as an object—a set of attributes and behavior—you have designed something that's ready to pass these qualities on to offspring. Like most offspring, these child objects will take on a lot of the attributes and behavior of their parent. They can also do some things differently than their parent does; some extra attributes and behavior can be added that Pop is incapable of.

This system is called *inheritance*, and it's something every superclass (parent) gives to its subclasses (children). Inheritance is one of the most useful aspects of object-oriented programming, and you'll be learning more about it during this hour.

Another useful aspect of object-oriented programming is the capability to create an object that can be used with different programs. Reusability speeds up the software development process and makes it easier to develop error-free, reliable programs. Using Java and special development tools, you'll be able to develop JavaBeans—completely reusable Java objects that are easily incorporated into programs.

The following topics will be covered:

- Superclasses and subclasses
- An inheritance hierarchy
- Overriding methods
- Creating a subclass
- Developing JavaBeans

The Power of Inheritance

Without knowing it, you have used inheritance every time you used one of the standard Java classes such as String or Math. Java classes are organized into a pyramid-shaped hierarchy of classes in which all classes descend from the Object class.

A class of objects inherits from all superclasses that are above it. To get a working idea of how this operates, you'll look at the JApplet class. This class is a superclass of all Swing applets, Java programs written to run on the World Wide Web. The JApplet class, which is used to create Java 2 applets, is a subclass of Applet.

A partial family tree of JApplet is shown in Figure 12.1. Each of the boxes is a class, and the lines connect a superclass to any subclasses below it.

FIGURE 12.1

The family tree of the Applet *class.*

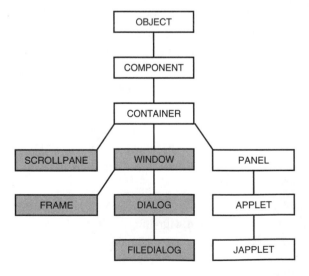

At the top is the Object class. JApplet has five superclasses above it in the hierarchy: Applet, Panel, Container, Component, and Object. The JApplet class inherits attributes and behavior from each of these classes because each is directly above it in the hierarchy of superclasses. JApplet does not inherit anything from the five shaded classes in Figure 12.1, which include Dialog and Frame, because they are not above it in the hierarchy.

If this seems confusing, think of the hierarchy as a family tree. JApplet will inherit from its parent, the parent's parent, and on upward. It even might inherit some things from its great-great-grandparent, Object. The JApplet class won't inherit from its siblings or its cousins, however.

Setting up a complicated hierarchy of classes is a difficult thing, but it makes it easier to create new programs later. The amount of work you need to do to write a new class of objects is reduced. Creating a new class boils down to the following task: You only have to define the ways in which it is different from an existing class. The rest of the work is done for you.

As an example, consider the popular video game *Tetris*. Since the game was invented by Soviet mathematician Alexey Pajitnov, it has been adapted for dozens of different operating systems, processors, and programming languages—including several different Java adaptations. In case you somehow avoided *Tetris* during the past decade by lapsing into a coma or falling into a deep meditative trance, the game works as follows: Blocks of different shapes fall from the top of the screen, and you must organize them into unbroken horizontal lines before they stack up too high.

The Java source file for several adaptations of *Tetris* is available for your use. If you wanted to create a new version of *Tetris* based on one of these existing classes, you could make your game a subclass of an existing *Tetris* game. All you would have to do is create the things that are new or different about your version, and you'd end up with a new game.

Inheriting Behavior and Attributes

The behavior and attributes of a class are a combination of two things: its own behavior and attributes, and all the behavior and attributes it inherits from its superclasses.

The following are some of the behavior and attributes of Applet:

- The equals() method determines whether an JApplet object has the same value as another object.
- The setBackground() method sets the background color displayed on the applet window.

12

- The `add()` method adds user interface components such as buttons and text fields to the applet.
- The `setLayout()` method defines how the applet's graphical user interface will be organized.

The `JApplet` class can use all of these methods, even though `setLayout()` is the only one it didn't inherit from another class. The `equals()` method is defined in `Object`, `setBackground()` comes from `Component`, and `add()` comes from `Container`.

Overriding Methods

Some of the methods defined in the `JApplet` class of objects were also defined in one of its superclasses. As an example, the `update()` method is set up in both the `JApplet` class and the `Component` class. This method was originally used in Java 1.0 to control whether the applet window is cleared out before anything is drawn in it. In Java 2, the `JApplet` class has its own `update()` method that never clears the applet window. When a method is defined in a subclass and its superclass, the subclass method is used. This enables a subclass to change, replace, or completely wipe out some of the behavior or attributes of its superclasses. In the case of `update()`, the purpose was to wipe out some behavior present in a superclass.

Creating a new method in a subclass to change behavior inherited from a superclass is called *overriding* the method. You need to override a method any time the inherited behavior will produce an undesired result.

Establishing Inheritance

You establish a class as the subclass of another class with the `extends` statement, as in the following:

```
class AnimatedLogo extends javax.swing.JApplet {
    // behavior and attributes go here
}
```

The `extends` statement establishes the `AnimatedLogo` class of objects as a subclass of `JApplet`, using the full class name of `javax.swing.JApplet`. As you will see during Hour 17, "Creating Interactive Web Programs," all Swing applets must be subclasses of `JApplet` because they need the functionality this class provides to run on a World Wide Web page.

One method that `AnimatedLogo` will have to override is the `paint()` method, which is used to draw all things that are shown on the program's display area. The `paint()` method is implemented by the `Component` class and is passed all the way down to

`AnimatedLogo`. However, the `paint()` method does not do anything. It exists so that subclasses of `Component` have a method they can use when something must be displayed when that subclass is running.

To override a method, you must start the method in the same way it started in the superclass from which it was inherited. A `public` method must remain public, the value sent back by the method must be the same, and the number and type of arguments to the method must not change.

The `paint()` method of the `Component` class begins as follows:

```
public void paint(Graphics g) {
```

When `AnimatedLogo` overrides this method, it must begin with a statement like this:

```
public void paint(Graphics screen) {
```

The only difference is in the name of the `Graphics` object, which does not matter when determining if the methods are created in the same way. These two statements match because the following things match:

- Both `paint()` methods are `public`.
- Both methods return no value, as declared by the use of the `void` statement.
- Both have a `Graphics` object as their only argument.

Using `this` and `super` in a Subclass

Two keywords that are extremely useful in a subclass are `this` and `super`.

As you learned during the previous hour, the `this` keyword is used to refer to the current object. When you're creating a class and you need to refer to the specific object created from that class, `this` can be used, as in the following statement:

```
this.title = "Cagney";
```

This statement sets the object's `title` variable to the text `Cagney`.

The `super` keyword serves a similar purpose: It refers to the immediate superclass of the object. `super` can be used in several different ways:

- To refer to a constructor method of the superclass, as in `super("Adam", 12)`.
- To refer to a variable of the superclass, as in `super.hawaii = 50`.
- To refer to a method of the superclass, as in `super.dragNet()`.

One of the ways you'll use the `super` keyword is in the constructor method of a subclass. Because a subclass inherits all the behavior and attributes of its superclass, you have to

12

associate each constructor method of that subclass with a constructor method of its superclass. Otherwise, some of the behavior and attributes might not be set up correctly, and the subclass won't be able to function properly.

To make sure that this happens, the first statement of a subclass constructor method must be a call to a constructor method of the superclass. This requires the super keyword, as in the following statements:

```
public ReadFiles(String name, int length) {
    super(name,length);
}
```

This example is the constructor method of a subclass, and it uses super(name,length) to call a comparable constructor in its superclass.

> If you don't use super to call a constructor method in the superclass, the program still might compile and run successfully. If no superclass constructor is called, Java automatically calls one with no arguments when the subclass constructor begins. If this superclass constructor doesn't exist or provides unexpected behavior, errors will result, so it's much better to call a super-class constructor yourself.

Working with Existing Objects

One of the things you have learned about object-oriented programming is how it encourages reuse. If you develop an excellent spell-checking object for use with one Java programming project, it should be possible to incorporate that object into another project without modification.

If a Java class is well-designed, it's possible to make that class available for use in other programs. As long as the class is documented thoroughly, a programmer should be able to work with that class as if it were part of the official Java language itself.

This is an idea that has great potential for software developers. The more objects available for use in your programs, the less work you have to do when creating your own software. If there's an excellent spell-checking object that suits your needs, you can use it instead of writing your own. Ideally, you can even give your boss a false impression about how long it took to add spell-checking functionality to your project, and use this extra time to make personal long-distance calls from the office.

The author of this book, like many in his profession, is self-employed and works out of his home. Please keep this in mind when evaluating his advice on how to conduct yourself in the workplace.

When Java was first introduced, the system of sharing objects was largely an informal one. Programmers developed their objects to be as independent as possible and protected them against misuse through the use of private variables and public methods to read and write those variables.

Sharing objects becomes more powerful when there's a standard for developing reusable objects. The benefits of a standard include the following:

- There's less need to document how an object works, because anyone who knows the standard already knows a lot about how it functions.

- Development tools can be designed that follow the standard, making it possible to work more easily with these objects.

- Two objects that follow the standard will be able to interact with each other without special programming to make them compatible.

The standard for developing reusable objects in Java is called JavaBeans, and each individual object is called a Bean.

Developing JavaBeans

JavaBeans are Java classes designed specifically for the purpose of being reused. These reusable classes, which are called software components in many programming languages, are developed under a standard set of rules.

12

Developing Beans requires a programming tool in addition to the Software Development Kit. Sun Microsystems offers two tools that demonstrate the technology, the Bean Builder and JavaBeans Development Kit, at http://java.sun.com/beans/software.

There are also several programs that make it possible to develop Beans and incorporate them into programs, including Borland JBuilder, NetBeans, Sun ONE Studio, and IBM VisualAge for Java.

The JavaBeans Development Kit, also called the BDK, includes the BeanBox, a visual tool that is used to add Beans to a Java program and make those Beans work with each other. The BeanBox, which is a Java program itself, is shown in Figure 12.2.

FIGURE 12.2

Using the BeanBox to create a Java program out of several Beans.

In Figure 12.2, the BeanBox is being used to link together three Beans: Two buttons and an animated Bean that displays the Java mascot, an anthropomorphic cuspid named Duke, juggling some giant beans. A lot of JavaBeans programming can be accomplished by using a tool like the BeanBox—some projects can be accomplished entirely with the mouse and no coding of your own classes.

Bean programming is a specialized aspect of Java that's best learned after you have mastered the basics of the language. However, a beginning programmer can accomplish a lot by working with existing Beans, so you'll benefit by becoming more familiar with JavaBeans as you learn to program.

You'll be developing skills throughout this book that are directly applicable to JavaBeans programming. A prime example is encapsulation, which you learned about during the previous hour. Using methods to read and write the values of a variable is a fundamental part of JavaBeans development.

During the previous hour, you saw how `getSeconds()` and `setSeconds()` methods could be used in a class to read and write a variable called `newSeconds`:

```
public int getSeconds() {
    return newSeconds;
}

public void setSeconds(int newValue) {
    if (newValue > 60)
        newSeconds = newValue;
}
```

If the `newSeconds` variable is `private`, these methods are an example of encapsulation. One of the rules of JavaBeans programming is to limit access to object variables according to the following rules:

- The variable should be `private`.
- A `public` method to read the variable should begin with `get`, end with a name that describes the variable being read, and return the same type of data as the variable.
- A `public` method to write the variable should begin with `set`, end with a name that describes the variable being written, and return `void`.
- If there are both reading and writing methods, they should end with the same name to describe the variable.

The preceding example follows all of these rules with the `getSeconds` and `setSeconds` methods. Because of this, if these methods are part of a Bean, the `newSeconds` variable can be manipulated directly within a tool like the BeanBox.

In Figure 12.3, the Properties window shows a `seconds` property that can be changed from within the BeanBox. This shows up because a `setSeconds()` method exists in a Bean that's selected in the main BeanBox window.

FIGURE 12.3

Manipulating a Bean's variables with the BeanBox's Properties window.

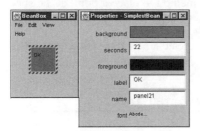

Much of the work that's done creating JavaBeans is for the benefit of programmers using a development environment such as the BeanBox. The more a Bean can be customized, the more useful it is.

Following the `set` and `get` rules for using an object variable is a first step towards making a class a Bean, and they demonstrate the kind of programming that JavaBeans requires.

These rules make sense for all object-oriented programming that you do because they present a useful and safe interface between an object and the other classes that will use it. You'll learn more skills that are useful in Bean development during Hour 22, "Playing Sound Files."

12

Workshop: Creating a Subclass

To see an example of inheritance at work, you will create a class called Point3D that represents a point in three-dimensional space. A two-dimensional point can be expressed with an (x,y) coordinate. Applets use an (x,y) coordinate system to determine where text and graphics should be displayed. Three-dimensional space adds a third coordinate, which can be called z.

The Point3D class of objects should do three things:

- Keep track of an object's (x,y,z) coordinate.
- Move an object to a new (x,y,z) coordinate when needed.
- Move an object by a certain amount of x, y, and z values as needed.

Java already has a standard class that represents two-dimensional points; it's called Point. It has two integer variables called x and y that store a Point object's (x,y) location. It also has a move() method to place a point at the specified location, and a translate() method to move an object by an amount of x and y values.

Run your word processor and create a new file called Point3D.java. Enter the text of Listing 12.1 into the file, and save it when you're done.

LISTING 12.1   The Full Text of Point3D.java

```
 1: import java.awt.*;
 2:
 3: public class Point3D extends Point {
 4:     public int z;
 5:
 6:     public Point3D(int x, int y, int z) {
 7:         super(x,y);
 8:         this.z = z;
 9:     }
10:
11:     public void move(int x, int y, int z) {
12:         this.z = z;
13:         super.move(x, y);
14:     }
15:
16:     public void translate(int x, int y, int z) {
17:         this.z += z;
18:         super.translate(x, y);
19:     }
20: }
```

After you compile this file with a Java compiler such as `javac`, you will have a class you can use in programs. The `Point3D` class does not have a `main()` block statement, so you cannot run it with the `java` interpreter.

The `Point3D` class only has to do work that isn't being done by its superclass, `Point`. This primarily involves keeping track of the integer variable z, and receiving it as an argument to the `move()` method, `translate()` method, and `Point3D()` constructor method.

All of the methods use the keywords `super` and `this`. The `this` statement is used to refer to the current `Point3D` object, so `this.z = z;` in Line 8 sets the object variable z equal to the z value that was sent as an argument to the method in Line 6.

The `super` statement refers to the superclass of the current object, `Point`. It is used to set variables and call methods that were inherited by `Point3D`. The statement `super(x,y)` in Line 7 calls the `Point(x,y)` constructor in the superclass, which then sets the (x,y) coordinates of the `Point3D` object. Because `Point` already is equipped to handle the x and y axes, it would be redundant for the `Point3D` class of objects to do the same thing.

To test out the `Point3D` class you have compiled, create a program that uses `Point` and `Point3D` objects and moves them around. Create a new file in your word processor and enter Listing 12.2 into it. Save the file as `TryPoints.java`.

LISTING 12.2 The Full Text of `TryPoints.java`

```
 1: import java.awt.*;
 2:
 3: class TryPoints {
 4:     public static void main(String[] arguments) {
 5:         Point object1 = new Point(11,22);
 6:         Point3D object2 = new Point3D(7,6,64);
 7:
 8:         System.out.println("The 2D point is located at (" + object1.x
 9:             + ", " + object1.y + ")");
10:         System.out.println("\tIt's being moved to (4, 13)");
11:         object1.move(4,13);
12:         System.out.println("The 2D point is now at (" + object1.x
13:             + ", " + object1.y + ")");
14:         System.out.println("\tIt's being moved -10 units on both the x "
15:             + "and y axes");
16:         object1.translate(-10,-10);
17:         System.out.println("The 2D point ends up at (" + object1.x
18:             + ", " + object1.y + ")\n");
19:
20:         System.out.println("The 3D point is located at (" + object2.x
21:             + ", " + object2.y + ", " + object2.z +")");
```

12

LISTING 12.2   continued

```
22:          System.out.println("\tIt's being moved to (10, 22, 71)");
23:          object2.move(10,22,71);
24:          System.out.println("The 3D point is now at (" + object2.x
25:              + ", " + object2.y + ", " + object2.z +")");
26:          System.out.println("\tIt's being moved -20 units on the x, y "
27:              + "and z axes");
28:          object2.translate(-20,-20,-20);
29:          System.out.println("The 3D point ends up at (" + object2.x
30:              + ", " + object2.y + ", " + object2.z +")");
31:      }
32: }
```

After you compile this file and run it with a Java interpreter, the following output should be displayed:

OUTPUT

```
The 2D point is located at (11, 22)
     It's being moved to (4, 13)
The 2D point is now at (4, 13)
     It's being moved -10 units on both the x and y axes
The 2D point ends up at (-6, 3)

The 3D point is located at (7, 6, 64)
     It's being moved to (10, 22, 71)
The 3D point is now at (10, 22, 71)
     It's being moved -20 units on the x, y and z axes
The 3D point ends up at (-10, 2, 51)
```

Summary

When people talk about the miracle of birth, they're probably not speaking of the way a superclass can give birth to subclasses or the way behavior and attributes are inherited in a hierarchy of classes.

However, if the real world worked the same way that object-oriented programming does, every grandchild of Mozart could choose to be a brilliant composer. All descendants of Mark Twain could wax poetic about Mississippi riverboat life. Every skill your direct ancestors worked to achieve would be handed to you without an ounce of toil.

On the scale of miracles, inheritance isn't quite up to par with continuing the existence of a species or getting a good tax break. However, it's an effective way to design software with a minimum of redundant work.

Another timesaver you may come to rely on are JavaBeans, objects that are ready-made for use in other programs. Whether you're using Beans that were developed by other programmers or designing your own, you have one more way to achieve something with fewer ounces of actual toil.

Q&A

Q Can a class have more than one superclass so that it inherits additional methods and behavior?

A It is possible with some object-oriented programming languages, but not Java. One of the goals when Java was developed was to provide a simpler language than an object-oriented language such as C++, and limiting inheritance to a single superclass was one way to achieve this. You can use a special type of class called an interface to inherit behavior that isn't received from superclasses.

Q Most Java programs created up to this point have not used `extends` to inherit from a superclass. Does this mean they exist outside of the class hierarchy?

A All classes you create in Java are part of the hierarchy because the default superclass for the programs you write is `Object` when the `extends` keyword is not used. The `equals()` and `toString()` methods of all classes are part of the behavior that automatically is inherited from `Object`.

Q Are JavaBeans anything like ActiveX controls?

A JavaBeans and Microsoft ActiveX are different answers to the question, "What's the best way to create reusable software components?" ActiveX is a simplified adaptation of the Component Object Model, a complex standard for software component programming that can be implemented in many different programming languages. ActiveX controls can be developed with several different languages, including Java. One of the things a JavaBeans programmer learns is how to turn a Bean into an ActiveX control.

12

Q When is the full name of a class, such as `java.applet.Applet`, needed in an `extends` clause instead of a shorter name such as `Applet`?

A You must use the full name whenever you don't use an `import javax.swing.JApplet;` or `import.javax.swing.*;` statement at the beginning of your program. The `import` statement is used solely to make it easier to refer to class names in programs. Each class of objects in Java has a full name that identifies the group of classes to which it belongs. For instance, the `Math` class is part of the `java.lang` group of classes. A group of classes is also called a *package*.

Quiz

To determine what kind of knowledge you inherited from the past hour's work, answer the following questions.

Questions

1. If a superclass handles a method in a way you don't want to use in the subclass, what can you do?

    a. Delete the method in the superclass.

    b. Override the method in the subclass.

    c. Write a nasty letter to the editor of the *San Jose Mercury News* hoping that Java's developers will read it.

2. Which of the following is not a benefit of JavaBeans?

    a. Objects can be shared easily with other programmers.

    b. A Bean can be used with any development tool that supports the standard.

    c. They cause emissions that violate stringent air quality standards in most countries.

3. What statement can you use to refer to the methods and variables of the current object?

    a. `this`

    b. `that`

    c. `theOther`

Answers

1. b. Because you can override the method, you don't have to change any aspect of the superclass or the way it works.

2. c. You're thinking of an entirely different type of bean. This question is dedicated to my father, who is prohibited by local statute from eating Ranch Style Beans in a poorly ventilated environment.

3. a.

Activities

If a fertile imagination has birthed in you a desire to learn more, you can spawn more knowledge of inheritance with the following activities:

- Create a Point4D class that adds a t coordinate to the (x,y,z) coordinate system created by the Point3D class. The t coordinate stands for time, so you will need to ensure that it is never set to a negative value.

- Take the members of a football team's offense—lineman, wide receiver, tight end, running back, and quarterback. Design a hierarchy of classes that represent the skills of these players, putting common skills higher up in the hierarchy. For example, blocking is behavior that should probably be inherited by the linemen and tight end classes, and speed is something that should be inherited by wide receivers and running backs.

To see Java programs that implement these activities, visit the book's Web site at http://www.java24hours.com.

12

PART IV
Programming a Graphical User Interface

Hour

HOUR **13**

Building a Simple User Interface

Because of the popularity of Microsoft Windows and Apple Macintosh systems, computer users have come to expect certain things from their software. It should feature a graphical user interface, take user input from a mouse, and work like other programs.

These expectations are a far cry from the heyday of MS-DOS and other command-line systems, when the user interface varied greatly with each program you used, and point-and-click was something photographers did.

Programs that use a graphical user interface and mouse control are called *windowing software*. Although you probably have been using a command-line interface to write Java programs, during this hour you create windowing programs using a group of classes called Swing.

The following topics will be covered:

- Using user interface components such as buttons
- Using labels, text fields, and other components

- Grouping components together
- Putting components inside other components
- Opening and closing windows
- Testing an interface

Swing and the Abstract Windowing Toolkit

Because Java is a cross-platform language that enables you to write programs for many different operating systems, its windowing software must be flexible. Instead of catering only to the Microsoft Windows-style of windowing or the Apple Macintosh version, it must handle both along with other platforms.

With Java, the development of a program's user interface is based on two sets of classes: the Abstract Windowing Toolkit and Swing. These classes enable you to create a graphical user interface and receive input from the user.

Swing and the Abstract Windowing Toolkit include everything you need to write programs that use a graphical user interface, which is also called a GUI (pronounced *gooey*, as in Huey, Dewey, and Louie). With Java's windowing classes, you can create a GUI that includes all of the following and more:

- Buttons, check boxes, labels, and other simple components
- Text fields, sliders, and other more complex components
- Pull-down menus and pop-up menus
- Windows, frames, dialog boxes, and applet windows

During this hour and the next, you will create and organize graphical user interfaces in Java. Afterwards in Hour 15, "Responding to User Input," you will enable those interfaces to receive mouse clicks and other user input.

Using Components

In Java, every part of a graphical user interface is represented by a class in the Swing or Abstract Windowing Toolkit packages. There is a `JButton` class for buttons, a `JWindow` class for windows, a `JTextField` class for text fields, and so on.

To create and display an interface, you create objects, set their variables, and call their methods. The techniques are the same as those you used during the previous three hours as you were introduced to object-oriented programming.

When you are putting a graphical user interface together, you work with two kinds of objects: components and containers. A *component* is an individual element in a user interface, such as a button or slider. A *container* is a component that can be used to hold other components.

The first step in creating an interface is to create a container that can hold components. In an application, this container is often a frame or a window. You will use another, the applet window, in Hour 17, "Creating Interactive Web Programs."

Frames and Windows

Windows and frames are containers that can be displayed on a user's desktop. Windows are simple containers that do not have a title bar or any of the other buttons normally along the top edge of a graphical user interface. Frames are windows that include all of these common windowing features users expect to find when they run software—such as buttons to close, expand, and shrink the window.

These containers are created using Swing's JWindow and JFrame classes. To make the Swing package of classes available in a Java program, use the following statement:

```
import javax.swing.*;
```

One way to make use of a frame in a Java application is to make the application a sub-class of JFrame. Your program will inherit the behavior it needs to function as a frame. The following statements create a subclass of JFrame:

```
import javax.swing.*;

public class MainFrame extends JFrame {
    public MainFrame() {
        // set up the frame
    }
}
```

This class creates a frame, but doesn't set it up completely. In the frame's constructor method, you must do several actions when creating a frame:

- Call a constructor method of the superclass, JFrame.
- Set up the title of the frame.
- Set up the size of the frame.
- Define what happens when the frame is closed by a user.

You also must make the frame visible, unless for some reason it should not be displayed when the application begins running.

13

All of these things can be handled in the frame's constructor method. The first thing the method must contain is a call to one of the constructor methods of JFrame, using the super statement. Here's an example:

```
super();
```

The preceding statement calls the JFrame constructor with no arguments. You can also call it with the title of your frame as an argument:

```
super("Main Frame");
```

This sets the title of the frame, which appears in the title bar along the top edge, to the specified string. In this example, the text greeting "Main Frame" will appear.

If you don't set up a title in this way, you can call the frame's setTitle() method with a String as an argument:

```
setTitle("Main Frame");
```

The size of the frame can be established by calling its setSize() method with two arguments: the width and height. The following statement sets up a frame that is 350 pixels wide and 125 pixels tall:

```
setSize(350, 125);
```

Another way to set the size of a frame is to fill it with components and then call the frame's pack() method with no arguments, as in this example:

```
pack();
```

The pack() method sets the frame up based on the preferred size of each component inside the frame. Every interface component has a preferred size, though this is sometimes disregarded depending on how components have been arranged within a container. You don't need to explicitly set the size of a frame before calling pack()—the method sets it to an adequate size before the frame is displayed.

Every frame is displayed with a button along the title bar that can be used to close the frame. On a Windows system, this button appears as an X in the upper-right corner of the frame. To define what happens when this button is clicked, call the frame's setDefaultCloseOperation() method with one of four JFrame class variables as an argument:

- setDefaultCloseOperation(JFrame.EXIT_ON_CLOSE)—Exit the program when the button is clicked.
- setDefaultCloseOperation(JFrame.DISPOSE_ON_CLOSE)—Close the frame, dispose of the frame object, and keep running the application.

- setDefaultCloseOperation(JFrame.DO_NOTHING_ON_CLOSE)—Keep the frame open and continue running.
- setDefaultCloseOperation(JFrame.HIDE_ON_CLOSE)—Close the frame and continue running.

The last thing that's required is to make the frame visible: call its setVisible() method with true as an argument:

```
setVisible(true);
```

This opens the frame at the defined width and height. You can also call it with false to stop displaying a frame.

Listing 13.1 contains the source code described in this section. Enter these statements and save the file as SalutonFrame.java.

LISTING 13.1   The Full Text of SalutonFrame.java

```
 1: import javax.swing.*;
 2:
 3: public class SalutonFrame extends JFrame {
 4:     public SalutonFrame() {
 5:         super("Saluton mondo!");
 6:         setSize(350, 100);
 7:         setDefaultCloseOperation(JFrame.EXIT_ON_CLOSE);
 8:         setVisible(true);
 9:     }
10:
11:     public static void main(String[] arguments) {
12:         SalutonFrame sal = new SalutonFrame();
13:     }
14: }
```

Lines 11–13 of Listing 13.1 contain a main() method, which turns this frame class into an application that can be run at the command line. After you compiling this into a class, run the application with the following command:

```
java SalutonFrame
```

Figure 13.1 shows the result. The only thing that SalutonFrame displays is a title—the Esperanto greeting "Saluton mondo!" The frame is an empty window, because it doesn't contain any other components yet.

13

FIGURE **13.1**

Displaying a frame in an application.

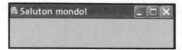

To add components to a frame, window, or an applet, you must work with the content pane of these containers. A *content pane* is the area in a container that can hold other components. They are represented in Java by the `Container` class, which is part of the Abstract Windowing Toolkit. To make the toolkit available in your Java classes, use the following `import` statement:

```
import java.awt.*;
```

Using a content pane requires three steps:

- Create a pane by calling a container's `getContentPane()` method, which produces a `Container` object that represents the pane.
- Create components and add them to the pane by calling the pane's `add()` method.
- Call `setContentPane()` with your pane as an argument.

You will work with content panes in the next section.

Buttons

One simple component you can add to a container is a `JButton` object. `JButton`, like the other components you'll be working with during this hour, is part of the `java.awt.swing` package. A `JButton` object is a clickable button with a label that describes what clicking the button will do. This label can be text, graphics, or both. The following statement creates a `JButton` called `okButton` and gives it the text label `OK`:

```
JButton okButton = new JButton("OK");
```

After a component such as `JButton` is created, it should be added to a container. In a container such as a frame, the following statement creates a `Container` object called `pane` and sets it up with the value of the container's content pane:

```
Container pane = getContentPane();
```

Because the `pane` object represents a content pane for a container, components can be added to this object by calling its `add()` method. The component to add should be the only argument to this method. For example, the previously created `okButton` object could be added to the `pane` container with the following statement:

```
pane.add(okButton);
```

When you add components to a container, you do not specify the place in the container where the component should be displayed. The arrangement of components is decided by an object called a layout manager. The simplest of these managers is the FlowLayout class, which is part of the java.awt package.

To make a container use a specific layout manager, you must first create an object of that layout manager's class. A FlowLayout object is created with a statement, such as the following:

```
FlowLayout fff = new FlowLayout();
```

Once a layout manager has been created, the container's setLayoutManager() method is called to associate the manager with the container. The only argument to this method should be the layout manager object, as in the following example:

```
pane.setLayoutManager(fff);
```

This statement designates the fff object as the layout manager for the pane container.

Listing 13.2 contains a Java application that displays a frame with three buttons.

LISTING 13.2   The Full Text of Playback.java

```
 1: import javax.swing.*;
 2: import java.awt.*;
 3:
 4: public class Playback extends JFrame {
 5:     public Playback() {
 6:         super("Playback");
 7:         setSize(225, 80);
 8:         setDefaultCloseOperation(JFrame.EXIT_ON_CLOSE);
 9:         setVisible(true);
10:         Container pane = getContentPane();
11:         FlowLayout flo = new FlowLayout();
12:         pane.setLayout(flo);
13:         JButton play = new JButton("Play");
14:         JButton stop = new JButton("Stop");
15:         JButton pause = new JButton("Pause");
16:         pane.add(play);
17:         pane.add(stop);
18:         pane.add(pause);
19:         setContentPane(pane);
20:     }
21:
22:     public static void main(String[] arguments) {
23:         Playback pb = new Playback();
24:     }
25: }
```

13

When you run this application at a command line, your output should resemble Figure 13.2. You can click each of the buttons, but nothing happens in response because your program does not contain any methods to receive user input—that's covered during Hour 15.

FIGURE **13.2**
*Displaying buttons
on a graphical user
interface.*

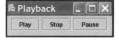

Many of the user components available as part of Swing can be added to a container in this manner.

> Because so many different user interface components must be introduced during this hour, the full source code used to create each figure is not listed here. You can find full versions of each program on the book's Web site at http://www.java24hours.com on the Hour 13 page.

Labels and Text Fields

A JLabel component displays information that cannot be modified by the user. This information can be text, a graphic, or both. These components are often used to label other components in an interface, hence the name. They are often used to identify text fields.

A JTextField component is an area where a user can enter a single line of text. You can set up the width of the box when you create the text field.

The following statements create a JLabel component and JTextField object and add them to a container:

```
JLabel pageLabel = new JLabel("Web page address: ", JLabel.RIGHT);
JTextField pageAddress = new JTextField(20);
FlowLayout flo = new FlowLayout();
Container pane = getContentPane();
pane.setLayout(flo);
pane.add(pageLabel);
pane.add(pageAddress);
setContentPane(pane);
```

Figure 13.3 shows this label and text field side-by-side. Both of the statements in this example use an argument to configure how the component should look. The pageLabel

label is set up with the text Web page address: and a JLabel.RIGHT argument. This last value indicates that the label should appear flush right. JLabel.LEFT aligns the label text flush left, and JLabel.CENTER centers it. The argument used with JTextField indicates that the text field should be approximately 20 characters wide. You can also specify default text that will appear in the text field with a statement such as the following:

```
JTextField state = new JTextField("TX", 2);
```

This statement would create a JTextField object that is two characters wide and has the text TX in the field.

FIGURE 13.3

Displaying labels and text fields.

Check Boxes

A JCheckBox component is a box next to a line of text that can be checked or unchecked by the user. The following statements create a JCheckBox object and add it to a container:

```
JCheckBox jumboSize = new JCheckBox("Jumbo Size");
FlowLayout flo = new FlowLayout();
Container pane = getContentPane();
pane.setLayout(flo);
pane.add(jumboSize);
setContentPane(pane);
```

The argument to the JCheckBox() constructor method indicates the text to be displayed alongside the box. If you wanted the box to be checked, you could use the following statement instead:

```
JCheckBox jumboSize = new JCheckBox("Jumbo Size", true);
```

A JCheckBox can be presented singly or as part of a group. In a group of check boxes, only one can be checked at a time. To make a JCheckBox object part of a group, you have to create a ButtonGroup object. Consider the following:

```
JCheckBox frogLegs = new JCheckBox("Frog Leg Grande", true);
JCheckBox fishTacos = new JCheckBox("Fish Taco Platter", false);
JCheckBox emuNuggets = new JCheckBox("Emu Nuggets", false);
FlowLayout flo = new FlowLayout();
Container pane = getContentPane();
ButtonGroup meals = new ButtonGroup();
meals.add(frogLegs);
meals.add(fishTacos);
meals.add(emuNuggets);
pane.setLayout(flo);
pane.add(jumboSize);
```

13

```
pane.add(frogLegs);
pane.add(fishTacos);
pane.add(emuNuggets);
setContentPane(pane);
```

This creates three check boxes that are all grouped under the `ButtonGroup` object called `meals`. The `Frog Leg Grande` box is checked initially, but if the user checked one of the other meal boxes, the check next to `Frog Leg Grande` would disappear automatically. Figure 13.4 shows the different check boxes from this section.

FIGURE 13.4
Displaying check box components.

Combo Boxes

A `JComboBox` component is a pop-up list of choices that can also be set up to receive text input. When both options are enabled, you can select an item with your mouse or use the keyboard to enter text instead. The combo box serves a similar purpose to a group of check boxes, except that only one of the choices is visible unless the pop-up list is being displayed.

To create a `JComboBox` object, you have to add each of the choices after creating the object, as in the following example:

```
JComboBox profession = new JComboBox();
FlowLayout flo = new FlowLayout();
Container pane = getContentPane();
profession.addItem("Butcher");
profession.addItem("Baker");
profession.addItem("Candlestick maker");
profession.addItem("Fletcher");
profession.addItem("Fighter");
profession.addItem("Technical writer");
pane.setLayout(flo);
pane.add(profession);
setContentPane(pane);
```

This example creates a single `JComboBox` component that provides six choices from which the user can select. When one is selected, it appears in the display of the component. Figure 13.5 shows this example while the pop-up list of choices is being displayed.

FIGURE **13.5**
Displaying combo box components.

To enable a `JComboBox` component to receive text input, its `setEditable()` method must be called with an argument of `true`, as in the following statement:

```
profession.setEditable(true);
```

This method must be called before the component is added to a container.

Text Areas

A `JTextArea` component is a text field that enables the user to enter more than one line of text. You can specify the width and height of the component. For example, the following statements create a `JTextArea` component with an approximate width of 40 characters and a height of 8 lines, and then add the component to a container:

```
JTextArea comments = new JTextArea(8, 40);
FlowLayout flo = new FlowLayout();
Container pane = getContentPane();
pane.setLayout(flo);
pane.add(comments);
setContentPane(pane);
```

Figure 13.6 shows this example in a frame.

FIGURE **13.6**
Displaying text area components.

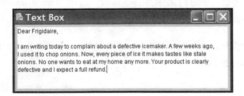

13

You can specify a string in the `JTextArea()` constructor method to be displayed in the text area. You can use the newline character `\n` to send text to the next line, as in the following:

```
JTextArea desire = new JTextArea("I should have been a pair\n"
    + "of ragged claws.", 10, 25);
```

Text area components behave in ways you might not expect—they expand in size when the user reaches the bottom of the area, and do not include scrollbars along the right edge or bottom edge. To implement the kind of text areas you see in other windowing software, you must place the area inside a container called a scroll pane, as you will see in Hour 16, "Building a Complex User Interface."

Panels

The last of the components you'll learn to create during this hour are panels, which are created in Swing using the JPanel class. JPanel objects are the simplest kind of container you can use in a Swing interface. The purpose of JPanel objects is to subdivide a display area into different groups of components. When the display is divided into sections, you can use different rules for how each section is organized.

You can create a JPanel object and add it to a container with the following statements:

```
JPanel topRow = new JPanel();
FlowLayout flo = new FlowLayout();
Container pane = getContentPane();
pane.setLayout(flo);
pane.add(topRow);
```

Panels are often used when arranging the components in an interface, as you'll see in Hour 14, "Laying Out a User Interface."

Unlike other containers, panels do not have a content pane. Instead, you can add components by calling the panel's add() method directly. You can also assign a layout manager directly to the panel by calling its setLayout() method.

Panels can also be used when you need an area in an interface to draw something, such as an image from a graphics file.

Another convenient use of JPanel is to create your own components that can be added to other classes. This is demonstrated in this hour's workshop.

Workshop: Creating Your Own Component

As you may recall, one of the main advantages of object-oriented programming is the capability to reuse classes in different projects. For this hour's workshop, you will create a special panel component that can be reused in different Java programs. The component, ClockPanel, displays the current date and time in a manner similar to the ClockTalk project from Hour 7, "Using Conditional Tests to Make Decisions."

The first step in creating your own user interface component is to decide the existing component from which to inherit. The ClockPanel component is most like a panel, so it will be a subclass of JPanel.

The ClockPanel class is defined in Listing 13.3. This class represents panel components that include a label displaying the current date and time. Enter the text of Listing 13.3 and save the file as ClockPanel.java.

LISTING 13.3 The Full Text of ClockPanel.java

```
 1: import javax.swing.*;
 2: import java.awt.*;
 3: import java.util.*;
 4:
 5: public class ClockPanel extends JPanel {
 6:     public ClockPanel() {
 7:         super();
 8:         String currentTime = getTime();
 9:         JLabel time = new JLabel("Time: ");
10:         JLabel current = new JLabel(currentTime);
11:         add(time);
12:         add(current);
13:     }
14:
15:     String getTime() {
16:         String time;
17:         // get current time and date
18:         Calendar now = Calendar.getInstance();
19:         int hour = now.get(Calendar.HOUR_OF_DAY);
20:         int minute = now.get(Calendar.MINUTE);
21:         int month = now.get(Calendar.MONTH) + 1;
22:         int day = now.get(Calendar.DAY_OF_MONTH);
23:         int year = now.get(Calendar.YEAR);
24:
25:         String monthName = "";
26:         switch (month) {
27:             case (1):
28:                 monthName = "January";
29:                 break;
30:             case (2):
31:                 monthName = "February";
32:                 break;
33:             case (3):
34:                 monthName = "March";
35:                 break;
36:             case (4):
37:                 monthName = "April";
38:                 break;
39:             case (5):
```

13

LISTING 13.3   continued

```
40:                      monthName = "May";
41:                      break;
42:                  case (6):
43:                      monthName = "June";
44:                      break;
45:                  case (7):
46:                      monthName = "July";
47:                      break;
48:                  case (8):
49:                      monthName = "August";
50:                      break;
51:                  case (9):
52:                      monthName = "September";
53:                      break;
54:                  case (10):
55:                      monthName = "October";
56:                      break;
57:                  case (11):
58:                      monthName = "November";
59:                      break;
60:                  case (12):
61:                      monthName = "December";
62:              }
63:          time = monthName + " " + day + ", " + year + " "
64:              + hour + ":" + minute;
65:          return time;
66:      }
67: }
```

The getTime() method in Lines 15–66 contains the same technique for retrieving the current date and time as the ClockTalk application from Hour 7. The panel is created in the constructor method in Lines 6–13. The following things are taking place:

- Line 8: The date and time are retrieved by calling getTime() and storing the value it returns in a String variable called currentTime.
- Line 9: A new label named time is created with the text "Time: ".
- Line 10: currentTime is used as the text of new label component called current.
- Line 11: The time label is added to the clock panel by calling the panel's add() method with the label as an argument.
- Line 12: The current label is added to the panel in the same manner.

The ClockPanel class cannot be run at a command line. To use it, you must create a Java program that includes an object of this class in its graphical user interface. This could be an application that displays a frame, an applet, or any other kind of program that features a GUI.

To try out this panel, create the ClockFrame application, which is contained in Listing 13.4.

LISTING 13.4 The Full Text of ClockFrame.java

```
 1: import java.awt.*;
 2: import javax.swing.*;
 3:
 4: public class ClockFrame extends JFrame {
 5:     public ClockFrame() {
 6:         super("Clock");
 7:         setSize(225, 125);
 8:         setDefaultCloseOperation(JFrame.EXIT_ON_CLOSE);
 9:         Container pane = getContentPane();
10:         FlowLayout flo = new FlowLayout();
11:         pane.setLayout(flo);
12:         ClockPanel time = new ClockPanel();
13:         pane.add(time);
14:         setContentPane(time);
15:         setVisible(true);
16:     }
17:
18:     public static void main(String[] arguments) {
19:         ClockFrame sal = new ClockFrame();
20:     }
21: }
```

When you run the application, it should resemble Figure 13.7.

FIGURE 13.7

Displaying a clock panel component.

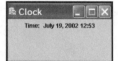

13

Summary

Users have come to expect a point-and-click, visual environment for the programs they run. This expectation makes creating software more of a challenge, but Java puts these capabilities into your hands with its user interface classes. Swing and the Abstract Windowing Toolkit provide all the classes you will need to provide a working, useful GUI in the tradition of Windows and Macintosh software—regardless of what kind of setup you're using to run Java programs.

During the next hour, you'll learn more about the design of a graphical user interface as you work with layout managers, classes that are used to specify how components are arranged within a container.

Q&A

Q How are components arranged if I don't assign a layout manager to a container?

A In a simple container such as a panel, components are arranged using FlowLayout by default—each component is added in the same manner that words are displayed on a page, from left to right until there is no more room, then on the next line down in the same manner. Frames, windows, and applets use the GridLayout default layout style you will learn about during the next hour.

Q Why does the time in the ClockFrame program never change?

A The time that is displayed in a ClockPanel object is set up when the panel is created. For the date and time to change over a period of time, you need to call getTime() frequently and change what the panel displays each time. This involves some techniques you will learn during Hour 24, "Creating Animation."

Quiz

If your brain hasn't been turned into a GUI mush with this hour's toil, test your skills by answering the following questions.

Questions

1. Which user component is used as a container to hold other components?

    a. TupperWare

    b. JPanel

    c. Choice

2. Which of the following must be done first within a container?

    a. Establish a layout manager

    b. Add components

    c. Doesn't matter

3. What part of a frame can contain other components?

    a. The whole frame

    b. None of the frame

    c. The frame's content pane

Answers

1. b. `JPanel`. You can add components to the panel, then add the panel to another container such as a frame.

2. a. You must specify the layout manager before the components so you can add them in the correct way.

3. c. The pane is a `Container` object, and you call the object's `add()` method to add components to it.

Activities

To interface further with the subject of GUI design, undertake the following activity:

- Modify the `SalutonFrame` application so that it displays "Saluton Mondo!" in the frame's main area instead of the title bar.

- Create a frame that contains another frame and make both of them visible at the same time.

To see Java programs that implement these activities, visit the book's Web site at `http://www.java24hours.com`.

13

HOUR 14

Laying Out a User Interface

When you begin designing graphical user interfaces for your Java programs, one obstacle you face is that your components can move around. Whenever a container changes size—such as when a user resizes a frame—the components within the container will rearrange themselves to fit within its new dimensions.

This fluidity works in your favor, because it takes into account the differences in how interface components are displayed on different operating systems. On the same Java program, a clickable button might look different in Windows than it does in Linux or Mac OS. This is a departure from languages such as Microsoft Visual Basic, where you normally specify exactly where a component will appear and what it looks like.

Components are organized in an interface by using a set of classes called layout managers. These classes define how components will be displayed within a container—during the previous hour, you used the FlowLayout class to arrange components. Each container in an interface can have its own layout manager.

The following topics will be covered:

- Creating a layout manager
- Assigning a layout manager to a container
- Using panels to organize components in an interface
- Working with unusual layouts
- Creating a prototype for a Java application

Using Layout Managers

In Java, the placement of components within a container depends on the size of other components and the height and width of the container. The layout of buttons, text fields, and other components can be affected by the following things:

- The size of the container
- The size of other components and containers
- The layout manager that is being used

There are several layout managers you can use to affect how components are shown. The default manager for panels is the FlowLayout class, which was used during the previous hour.

Under FlowLayout, components are dropped onto an area in the same way words are organized on a printed page in English—from left to right, then on to the next line when there's no more space.

To set up a container to work under FlowLayout:

- Create a Container object and a FlowLayout object.
- Set up the container's layout manager by calling the Container object's setLayout() method with the FlowLayout object as an argument.
- Call setContentPane() with the Container as an argument.

The following example could be used in a frame so that it will employ flow layout when components are added:

```
Container pane = getContentPane();
FlowLayout topLayout = new FlowLayout();
pane.setLayout(topLayout);
setContentPane(pane);
```

You can also set up a layout manager to work within a specific container, such as a JPanel object. You can do this by using the setLayout() method of that container object. The following statements create a JPanel object called inputArea and set it up to use FlowLayout as its layout manager:

```
JPanel inputArea = new JPanel();
FlowLayout inputLayout = new FlowLayout();
inputArea.setLayout(inputLayout);
```

To give you an idea of how the different layout managers work, a simple application will be shown under each of the classes. The Crisis application has a graphical user interface with five buttons. Load your word processor and open up a new file called Crisis.java. Enter Listing 14.1 and save the file when you're done.

LISTING 14.1   The Full Text of Crisis.java

```
 1: import java.awt.*;
 2: import javax.swing.*;
 3:
 4: public class Crisis extends JFrame {
 5:     JButton panicButton = new JButton("Panic");
 6:     JButton dontPanicButton = new JButton("Don't Panic");
 7:     JButton blameButton = new JButton("Blame Others");
 8:     JButton mediaButton = new JButton("Notify the Media");
 9:     JButton saveButton = new JButton("Save Yourself");
10:
11:     public Crisis() {
12:         super("Crisis");
13:         setSize(308, 128);
14:         setDefaultCloseOperation(JFrame.EXIT_ON_CLOSE);
15:         Container pane = getContentPane();
16:         FlowLayout flo = new FlowLayout();
17:         pane.setLayout(flo);
18:         pane.add(panicButton);
19:         pane.add(dontPanicButton);
20:         pane.add(blameButton);
21:         pane.add(mediaButton);
22:         pane.add(saveButton);
23:         setVisible(true);
24:     }
25:
26:     public static void main(String[] arguments) {
27:         Crisis cr = new Crisis();
28:     }
29: }
```

14

After compiling the `Crisis` application, you can run it with the following command:

```
java Crisis
```

Figure 14.1 shows the application running.

The `FlowLayout` class uses the dimensions of its container as the only guideline for how to lay out components. Resize the window of the application to see how components are instantly rearranged. Make the window twice as wide, and you'll see all of the `JButton` components are now shown on the same line. Java programs will often behave differently when their display area is resized.

The `GridLayout` Manager

The `GridLayout` class organizes all components in a container into a specific number of rows and columns. All components are allocated the same amount of size in the display area, so if you specify a grid that is three columns wide and three rows tall, the container will be divided into nine areas of equal size.

The following statements create a container and set it to use a grid layout that is two columns wide and three rows tall:

```
Container pane = getContentPane();
GridLayout grid = new GridLayout(2, 3);
pane.setLayout(grid);
```

Figure 14.2 shows what the `Crisis` application would look like if it used grid layout.

Some of the labels in Figure 14.2 display text that has been shortened—if the text is wider than the area available in the component, the label will be shortened using ellipses (…).

GridLayout places all components as they are added into a place on a grid. Components are added from left to right until a row is full, and then the leftmost column of the next grid is filled.

The BorderLayout Manager

The next layout manager left to experiment with is the BorderLayout class. The following statements create a container that uses border layout, placing components at specific locations within the layout:

```
Container pane = getContentPane();
BorderLayout crisisLayout = new BorderLayout();
pane.setLayout(crisisLayout);
pane.add(panicButton, BorderLayout.NORTH);
pane.add(dontPanicButton, BorderLayout.SOUTH);
pane.add(blameButton, BorderLayout.EAST);
pane.add(mediaButton, BorderLayout.WEST);
pane.add(saveButton, BorderLayout.CENTER);
```

Figure 14.3 shows how this looks in the Crisis application.

FIGURE 14.3

Arranging components using border layout.

The BorderLayout manager arranges components into five areas: four denoted by compass directions and one for the center area. When you add a component under this layout, the add() method includes a second argument to specify where the component should be placed. This argument should be one of five class variables of the BorderLayout class: NORTH, SOUTH, EAST, WEST, and CENTER are used for this argument.

Like the GridLayout class, BorderLayout devotes all available space to the components. The component placed in the center is given all the space that isn't needed for the four border components, so it's usually the largest.

Separating Components with Insets

As you are arranging components within a container, you might want to move components away from the edges of the container. This is accomplished using Insets, an object that represents the border area of a container.

14

The Insets class, which is part of the java.awt package, has a constructor method that takes four arguments: the space to leave at the top, left, bottom, and right on the container. Each argument is specified using pixels, the same unit of measure employed when defining the size of a frame.

The following statement creates an Insets object:

```
Insets around = new Insets(10, 6, 10, 3);
```

The around object represents a container border that is 10 pixels inside the top edge, 6 pixels inside the left, 10 pixels inside the bottom, and 3 pixels inside the right.

To make use of an Insets object in a container, you must override the container's getInsets() method. This method has no arguments and returns an Insets object, as in the following example:

```
public Insets getInsets() {
        Insets squeeze = new Insets(50, 20, 15, 20);
        return squeeze;
    }
```

Figure 14.4 shows how this would change one of the preceding examples, the BorderLayout-managed interface shown in Figure 14.2.

FIGURE 14.4

Using insets to add space around components.

The container shown in Figure 14.4 has an empty border that's 20 pixels from the left edge, 15 pixels from the bottom edge, 20 pixels from the right edge, and 50 pixels from the top edge.

That last measurement isn't an error, though you may think it is after looking at Figure 14.4 again. Visually, the top and bottom border both look about the same size. There's a reason for this: A JFrame container automatically has a top inset value of 35 to make room for the frame's title bar. When you override getInsets() and set your own values, anything less than 35 will cause the container to display components underneath the title bar. You must create an Insets object with a top value of at least 35 for the container's contents to be fully visible.

Workshop: Laying Out an Application

The layout managers you have seen thus far were applied to a container's entire content pane; the setLayout() method of the pane was used, and all components followed the same rules. This setup can be suitable for some programs, but as you try to develop a graphical user interface with Swing and the Abstract Windowing Toolkit, you will often find that none of the layout managers fit.

One way around this problem is to use a group of JPanel objects as containers to hold different parts of a graphical user interface. You can set up different layout rules for each of these parts by using the setLayout() methods of each JPanel. Once these panels contain all of the components they need to contain, the panels can be added directly to the content pane.

This hour's workshop will be to develop a full interface for the program you will write during the next hour. The program is a Lotto number cruncher that will assess a user's chance of winning one of the multimillion-dollar Lotto contests in the span of a lifetime. This chance will be determined by running random six-number Lotto drawings again and again until the user's numbers turn up as a big winner. Figure 14.5 shows the GUI you will be developing for the application.

FIGURE 14.5
Displaying the graphical user interface of the LottoMadness *application.*

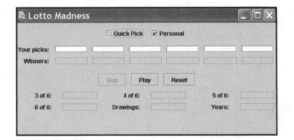

Create a new file in your word processor called LottoMadness.java. Enter Listing 14.2 and save the file when you're done.

LISTING 14.2   The Full Text of LottoMadness.java

```
1: import java.awt.*;
2: import javax.swing.*;
3:
4: public class LottoMadness extends JFrame {
5:
6:     // set up row 1
7:     JPanel row1 = new JPanel();
```

14

LISTING **14.2**   continued

```
 8:     ButtonGroup option = new ButtonGroup();
 9:     JCheckBox quickpick = new JCheckBox("Quick Pick", false);
10:     JCheckBox personal = new JCheckBox("Personal", true);
11:     // set up row 2
12:     JPanel row2 = new JPanel();
13:     JLabel numbersLabel = new JLabel("Your picks: ", JLabel.RIGHT);
14:     JTextField[] numbers = new JTextField[6];
15:     JLabel winnersLabel = new JLabel("Winners: ", JLabel.RIGHT);
16:     JTextField[] winners = new JTextField[6];
17:     // set up row 3
18:     JPanel row3 = new JPanel();
19:     JButton stop = new JButton("Stop");
20:     JButton play = new JButton("Play");
21:     JButton reset = new JButton("Reset");
22:     // set up row 4
23:     JPanel row4 = new JPanel();
24:     JLabel got3Label = new JLabel("3 of 6: ", JLabel.RIGHT);
25:     JTextField got3 = new JTextField();
26:     JLabel got4Label = new JLabel("4 of 6: ", JLabel.RIGHT);
27:     JTextField got4 = new JTextField();
28:     JLabel got5Label = new JLabel("5 of 6: ", JLabel.RIGHT);
29:     JTextField got5 = new JTextField();
30:     JLabel got6Label = new JLabel("6 of 6: ", JLabel.RIGHT);
31:     JTextField got6 = new JTextField(10);
32:     JLabel drawingsLabel = new JLabel("Drawings: ", JLabel.RIGHT);
33:     JTextField drawings = new JTextField();
34:     JLabel yearsLabel = new JLabel("Years: ", JLabel.RIGHT);
35:     JTextField years = new JTextField();
36:
37:     public LottoMadness() {
38:         super("Lotto Madness");
39:         setSize(550, 270);
40:         setDefaultCloseOperation(JFrame.EXIT_ON_CLOSE);
41:         GridLayout layout = new GridLayout(5, 1, 10, 10);
42:         Container pane = getContentPane();
43:         pane.setLayout(layout);
44:
45:         FlowLayout layout1 = new FlowLayout(FlowLayout.CENTER,
46:             10, 10);
47:         option.add(quickpick);
48:         option.add(personal);
49:         row1.setLayout(layout1);
50:         row1.add(quickpick);
51:         row1.add(personal);
52:         pane.add(row1);
53:
54:         GridLayout layout2 = new GridLayout(2, 7, 10, 10);
55:         row2.setLayout(layout2);
```

LISTING 14.2 continued

```
56:            row2.setLayout(layout2);
57:            row2.add(numbersLabel);
58:            for (int i = 0; i < 6; i++) {
59:                numbers[i] = new JTextField();
60:                row2.add(numbers[i]);
61:            }
62:            row2.add(winnersLabel);
63:            for (int i = 0; i < 6; i++) {
64:                winners[i] = new JTextField();
65:                winners[i].setEditable(false);
66:                row2.add(winners[i]);
67:            }
68:            pane.add(row2);
69:
70:            FlowLayout layout3 = new FlowLayout(FlowLayout.CENTER,
71:                10, 10);
72:            row3.setLayout(layout3);
73:            stop.setEnabled(false);
74:            row3.add(stop);
75:            row3.add(play);
76:            row3.add(reset);
77:            pane.add(row3);
78:
79:            GridLayout layout4 = new GridLayout(2, 3, 20, 10);
80:            row4.setLayout(layout4);
81:            row4.add(got3Label);
82:            got3.setEditable(false);
83:            row4.add(got3);
84:            row4.add(got4Label);
85:            got4.setEditable(false);
86:            row4.add(got4);
87:            row4.add(got5Label);
88:            got5.setEditable(false);
89:            row4.add(got5);
90:            row4.add(got6Label);
91:            got6.setEditable(false);
92:            row4.add(got6);
93:            row4.add(drawingsLabel);
94:            drawings.setEditable(false);
95:            row4.add(drawings);
96:            row4.add(yearsLabel);
97:            years.setEditable(false);
98:            row4.add(years);
99:            pane.add(row4);
100:            setContentPane(pane);
101:            setVisible(true);
102:        }
103:
```

14

LISTING 14.2 continued

```
104:    public static void main(String[] arguments) {
105:        LottoMadness frame = new LottoMadness();
106:    }
107: }
```

After you compile this application, run it to see how the LottoMadness application will work. Even though you haven't added any statements that make the program do anything yet, you can make sure that the graphical interface is organized correctly and collects the information you need.

This application uses several different layout managers. If you look carefully at each of the components, you might be able to determine which manager is in use in the different areas of the program. To get a clearer picture of how the application's user interface is laid out, take a look at Figure 14.6. The interface is divided into five horizontal rows which are separated by horizontal black lines in the figure. Each of these rows is a JPanel object, and the overall layout manager of the application organizes these rows into a GridLayout of five rows and one column.

FIGURE 14.6

Dividing the LottoMadness *application into panels.*

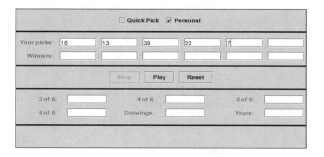

Within the rows, different layout managers are used to determine how the components should appear. Rows 1 and 3 use FlowLayout objects. Lines 45–46 of the program show how these are created:

```
FlowLayout layout1 = new FlowLayout(FlowLayout.CENTER,
    10, 10);
```

Three arguments are used with the FlowLayout() constructor method. The first argument, FlowLayout.CENTER, indicates that the components should be centered within their container—the horizontal Panel on which they are placed. The last two components specify the width and height that each component should be moved away from other components. Using a width of 10 pixels and a height of 10 pixels puts a small amount of extra distance between the components.

Row 2 of the interface is laid out into a grid that is two rows tall and seven columns wide. The GridLayout() constructor also specifies that components should be set apart from other components by 10 pixels in each direction. Lines 54–55 set up this grid:

```
GridLayout layout2 = new GridLayout(2, 7, 10, 10);
row2.setLayout(layout2);
```

Row 4 uses GridLayout to arrange components into a grid that is two rows tall and three columns wide.

The LottoMadness application uses several of the components described during this hour. Lines 7–35 are used to set up objects for all of the components that make up the interface. The statements are organized by row. First, a JPanel object for the row is created, and then each component that will go on the row is set up. This code creates all of the components and containers, but they will not be displayed unless an add() method is used to put them onto the application's content pane.

In Lines 45–100, the components are added. Lines 45–52 are indicative of the entire LottoMadness() constructor method:

```
FlowLayout layout1 = new FlowLayout(FlowLayout.CENTER,
    10, 10);
option.add(quickpick);
option.add(personal);
row1.setLayout(layout1);
row1.add(quickpick);
row1.add(personal);
pane.add(row1);
```

After a layout manager object is created, it is used with the setLayout() method of the row's JPanel object—row1 in this case. Once the layout has been specified, components are added to the JPanel by using its add() method. Once all of the components have been placed, the entire row1 object is added to the frame's content pane by calling its own add() method.

Summary

When you design a Java program's graphical user interface for the first time, you may have trouble believing that it's an advantage for components to move around. There's an appeal to seeing something exactly in the way you designed it—a feature that's called WYSIWYG, an acronym for "What You See Is What You Get."

Because Java was designed to run on a wide variety of operating systems and computing environments, interface layout was designed to be TNTWTMLL—There's No Telling What This Might Look Like.

14

Layout managers provide a way to develop an attractive graphical user interface that is flexible enough to handle differences in presentation.

During the next hour, you'll learn more about the function of a graphical user interface. You'll get a chance to see the LottoMadness interface in use as it churns through lottery drawings and tallies up winners.

Q&A

Q Why are some of the text fields in the LottoMadness application shaded in gray while others are white?

A The setEditable() method has been used on the gray fields to make them impossible to edit. The default behavior of a text field is to enable users to change the value of the text field by clicking within its borders and typing any desired changes. However, some fields are intended to display information rather than take input from the user. The setEditable() method prevents users from changing a field they should not modify.

Quiz

To see whether your brain cells are laid out properly, test your Java layout management skills by answering the following questions.

Questions

1. What container is often used when subdividing an interface into different layout managers?

    a. JWindow

    b. JPanel

    c. Container

2. What is the default layout manager for a panel?

    a. FlowLayout

    b. GridLayout

    c. There is no default

3. The BorderLayout class gets its name from where?

    a. The border of each component

    b. The way components are organized along the borders of a container

    c. Sheer capriciousness on the part of Java's developers

Answers

1. b. `JPanel`.

2. a. Panels use flow layout, but the default manager for frames, windows, and an applet window is grid layout.

3. b. The border position of components must be specified as they are added to a container with the use of directional variables such as `BorderLayout.WEST` and `BorderLayout.EAST`.

Activities

If you'd like to keep going with the flow (and the grid and the border), undertake the following activities:

- Create a modified version of the `Crisis` application with the `panic` and `dontPanic` objects organized under one layout manager and the remaining three buttons under another.

- Make a copy of the `LottoMadness.java` file that you can rename to `NewMadness.java`. Make changes to this program so the quick pick or personal choice is a combo box and the start, stop, and reset buttons are check boxes.

To see Java programs that implement these activities, visit the book's Web site at `http://www.java24hours.com`.

14

HOUR 15

Responding to User Input

A graphical user interface you developed during the past two hours can run on its own without any changes. Buttons can be clicked, text fields filled with text, and the window can be resized with wild abandon.

Sooner or later, however, even the least discriminating user is going to be left wanting more. The graphical user interface that a program offers has to cause things to happen when a mouse-click or keyboard entry occurs. Text areas and other components must be updated to show what's happening as the program runs.

These things are possible when your Java program can respond to user events. An *event* is something that happens when a program runs, and user events are things a user causes to happen by using the mouse, keyboard, or another input device. Responding to user events is often called *event handling*, and it's the activity you'll be learning about during this hour.

The following topics will be covered:

- Making your programs aware of events
- Setting up a component so it can cause events
- Ignoring some components
- Finding out where events end up in a program
- Storing information in the interface
- Using numeric variables with text fields

Getting Your Programs to Listen

Before you can receive user input in a Java program, you must learn how to teach an object to listen. Responding to user events in a Java program requires the use of one or more `EventListener` interfaces. *Interfaces* are special classes that enable a class of objects to inherit behavior it would not be able to use otherwise.

Adding an `EventListener` interface requires two things right away. First, because the listening classes are part of the `java.awt.event` group of classes, you must make them available with the following statement:

```
import java.awt.event.*;
```

Second, the class must use the `implements` statement to declare that it will be using one or more listening interfaces. The following statement creates a class that uses `ActionListener`, an interface used with buttons and other components:

```
public class Graph extends javax.swing.JApplet implements ActionListener {
```

`EventListener` interfaces enable a component of a graphical user interface to generate user events. Without one of the listeners in place, a component cannot do anything that can be heard by other parts of a program. A program must include a listener interface for each type of component to which it wants to listen. To have the program respond to a mouse-click on a button or the Enter key being pressed in a text field, you must include the `ActionListener` interface. To respond to the use of a choice list or check boxes, You need the `ItemListener` interface to respond to the use of a choice list or check boxes.

When you require more than one interface in the same class, separate their names with commas after the `implements` statement. The following is an example:

```
public class Graph3D extends javax.swing.JApplet
    implements ActionListener, MouseListener {
    // ...
}
```

Setting Up Components to Be Heard

15

After you have implemented the interface needed for a particular component, you have to set that component to generate user events. A good example is the use of JButton objects as components. When you use a button in an interface, something has to happen in response to the click of the button.

The program that should respond to the button-click must implement the ActionListener interface. This interface listens for action events, such as a button-click or the press of the Enter key. To make a JButton object generate an event, use the addActionListener() method, as in the following:

```
JButton fireTorpedos = new JButton("Fire torpedos");
fireTorpedos.addActionListener(this);
```

This code creates the fireTorpedos button and then calls the button's addActionListener() method. The this statement used as an argument to the addActionListener() method indicates that the current object will receive the user event and handle it as needed.

> From the mail I've gotten from readers of past editions, the concept of the "current object" manages to throw some people. In an effort to catch those people, here's a few more details: This term refers to the object in which the this keyword is used. So if you called the statement fireTorpedos.addActionListener(this) in an object of the Submarine class, that object would listen for action events.

Handling User Events

When a user event is generated by a component that has a listener, a method will be called automatically. The method must be found in the class that was specified when the listener was attached to the component. For instance, in the example of the fireTorpedos object, the method must be located in the same program because the this statement was used.

Each listener has different methods that are called to receive their events. The ActionListener interface sends events to a class called actionPerformed(). The following is a short example of an actionPerformed() method:

```
public void actionPerformed(ActionEvent evt) {
    // method goes here
}
```

All action events sent in the program will go to this method. If only one component in a program can possibly send action events, you can put statements in this method to handle the event. If more than one component can send these events, you need to use the object that is sent to the method.

In this case, an `ActionEvent` object is sent to the `actionPerformed()` method. There are several different classes of objects that represent the user events that can be sent in a program. These classes have methods you can use to determine which component caused the event to happen. In the `actionPerformed()` method, if the `ActionEvent` object is named evt, you can identify the component with the following statement:

```
String cmd = evt.getActionCommand();
```

The `getActionCommand()` method sends back a string. If the component is a button, the string will be the label that is on the button. If it's a text field, the string will be the text entered in the field. The `getSource()` method sends back the object that caused the event.

You could use the following `actionPerformed()` method to receive events from three components: a `JButton` object called start, a `JTextField` called speed, and another `JTextField` called viscosity:

```
public void actionPerformed(ActionEvent evt) {
    Object source = evt.getSource();
    if (source == speed) {
        // speed field caused event
    } else if (source == viscosity) {
        // viscosity caused event
    } else
        // start caused event
```

You can use the `getSource()` method with all types of user events to identify the specific object that caused the event.

Check Box and Combo Box Events

Combo boxes and check boxes require the `ItemListener` interface. Call the component's `addItemListener()` method to make it generate these events. For example, the following statements create a check box called superSize and cause it to send out user events when selected or deselected:

```
JCheckBox superSize = new JCheckBox("Super Size", true);
superSize.addItemListener(this);
```

These events are received by the `itemStateChanged()` method, which takes an `ItemEvent` object as an argument. To see which object caused the event, you can use the `getItem()` method.

To determine whether a check box is selected or deselected, use the getStateChange() method with the constants ItemEvent.SELECTED and ItemEvent.DESELECTED. The following is an example for an ItemEvent object called item:

```
int status = item.getStateChange();
if (status == ItemEvent.SELECTED)
    // item was selected
```

To determine the value that has been selected in a JComboBox object, use getItem() and convert that value to a string, as in the following:

```
Object which = item.getItem();
String answer = which.toString();
```

Keyboard Events

One thing that's common in a game program is for the program to react immediately when a key is pressed. Several game programmers, such as Karl Hörnell, have created arcade-style Java applets on Web pages that you control through the keyboard using the arrow keys, numeric keypad, spacebar, and other keys. Keyboard events of this kind are handled through the KeyListener interface.

The first step is to register the component that receives presses of the keyboard by calling its addKeyListener() method. The argument of the method should be the object that implements the KeyListener interface—if it is the current class, you can use this as the argument.

An object that handles keyboard events must implement three methods:

- void keyPressed(*KeyEvent*)—This method is called the moment a key is pressed.
- void keyReleased(*KeyEvent*)—This method is called the moment a key is released.
- void keyTyped(*KeyEvent*)—This method is called after a key has been pressed and released.

Each of these has a KeyEvent object as an argument, and you can call this object's methods to find out more about the event. Call the getKeyChar() method to find out which key was pressed. This key is returned as a char value, and it only can be used with letters, numbers, and punctuation.

To monitor any key on the keyboard, including Enter, Home, Page Up, and Page Down, you can call getKeyCode() instead. This method returns an integer value representing the key. You can then call getKeyText() with that integer as an argument to receive a String object containing the name of the key (such as Home, F1, and so on).

Listing 15.1 contains a Java application that draws the most recently pressed key in a label by using the getKeyChar() method. The application implements the KeyListener interface, so there are keyTyped(), keyPressed(), and keyReleased() methods in the class. The only one of these that does anything is keyTyped() in Lines 22–25.

LISTING 15.1   The Full Text of KeyView.java

```
 1: import javax.swing.*;
 2: import java.awt.event.*;
 3: import java.awt.*;
 4:
 5: class KeyView extends JFrame implements KeyListener {
 6:     JTextField keyText = new JTextField(80);
 7:     JLabel keyLabel = new JLabel("Press any key in the text field.");
 8:
 9:     KeyView() {
10:         super("KeyView");
11:         setSize(350, 100);
12:         setDefaultCloseOperation(JFrame.EXIT_ON_CLOSE);
13:         keyText.addKeyListener(this);
14:         Container pane = getContentPane();
15:         BorderLayout bord = new BorderLayout();
16:         pane.add(keyLabel, BorderLayout.NORTH);
17:         pane.add(keyText, BorderLayout.CENTER);
18:         setContentPane(pane);
19:         setVisible(true);
20:     }
21:
22:     public void keyTyped(KeyEvent input) {
23:         char key = input.getKeyChar();
24:         keyLabel.setText("You pressed " + key);
25:     }
26:
27:     public void keyPressed(KeyEvent txt) {
28:         // do nothing
29:     }
30:
31:     public void keyReleased(KeyEvent txt) {
32:         // do nothing
33:     }
34:
35:     public static void main(String[] arguments) {
36:         KeyView frame = new KeyView();
37:     }
38: }
```

When you run the application, it should resemble Figure 15.1.

FIGURE **15.1**
Handling keyboard events in a program.

15

To play Karl Hörnell's Java applets, visit his Web site at http://www.javaonthebrain.com. He publishes the source code to more than a dozen programs he has written, and provides some explanatory notes for people trying to develop their own games.

Enabling and Disabling Components

You may have seen a component in a program that appears shaded instead of its normal appearance.

If you haven't seen a shaded component yet, you must have skipped Hour 14, "Laying Out a User Interface." I'm sorry to hear that. *Teach Yourself Java 2 in 23 Hours* doesn't have the same ring to it.

Shading indicates that users cannot do anything to the component because it is disabled. Disabling and enabling components as a program runs is done with the setEnabled() method of the component. A Boolean value is sent as an argument to the method, so setEnabled(true) enables a component for use, and setEnabled(false) disables a component.

The following statement creates three buttons with the labels Previous, Next, and Finish, and disables the first button:

```
JButton previousButton = new JButton("Previous");
JButton nextButton = new JButton("Next");
JButton finishButton = new JButton("Finish");
previousButton.setEnabled(false);
```

This method is an effective way to prevent a component from sending a user event when it shouldn't. For example, if you're writing a Java application that takes a user's address in text fields, you might want to disable a Save button until all of the fields have some kind of value.

Workshop: A Little Lotto Madness

To see how Swing's event-handling classes work in a Java program, you will finish
`LottoMadness`, the Lotto simulation that was begun during Hour 14.

> See what you missed if you didn't read Hour 14? It may have been my finest
> hour.

At this point, `LottoMadness` is just a graphical user interface. You can click buttons and
enter text into text boxes, but nothing happens in response. In this workshop, you will
create `LottoEvent`, a new class that receives user input, conducts lotto drawings, and
keeps track of the number of times you win anything. Once the class is complete, you
will add a few lines to `LottoMadness` so that it makes use of `LottoEvent`. It is often convenient to divide Swing projects in this manner, with the graphical user interface in one
class, and the event-handling methods in another.

The purpose of this application is to assess the user's chances of winning a six-number
lotto drawing in a lifetime. Figure 15.2 shows a screen capture of the program as it continues to run.

FIGURE **15.2**
Running the
`LottoMadness`
application.

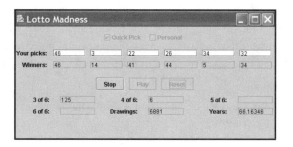

Instead of using probability to figure this problem out, the computer will take a more
anecdotal approach: It will conduct drawing after drawing after drawing until you win.
Because the 6-out-of-6 win is extremely unlikely, the program also will report on any
combination of three, four, or five winning numbers.

The interface you created includes 12 text fields for Lotto numbers and two check boxes
labeled Quick Pick and Personal. Six of the text fields are disabled from input, and they
will be used to display the winning numbers of each drawing. The other six text fields
are for the user's choice of numbers. If the user wants to select six numbers manually, he

should select the Personal check box. If he selects the Quick Pick box instead, six random numbers will appear in the text fields.

Three buttons control the activity of the program: Stop, Play, and Reset. When the Play button is pressed, the program starts a thread called `playing` and generates Lotto drawings as fast as it can. Pressing the Stop button stops the thread, and pressing Reset clears all fields so the user can start all the number-crunching over again.

The `LottoEvent` class implements three interfaces: `ActionListener`, `ItemListener`, and `Runnable`. The first two are needed to listen to user events generated by the buttons and check boxes on the application. The program does not need to listen to any events related to the text fields because they will be used strictly to store the user's choice of numbers. The user interface handles this function automatically.

The class requires the use of two packages from the Java class library: the main Swing package, `javax.swing`, and Java's event-handling package, `java.awt.event`.

The class has two instance variables:

- `gui`, a `LottoMadness` object
- `playing`, a `Thread` object that will be used to conduct continuous lotto drawings

The `gui` variable will be used to communicate with the `LottoMadness` object that contains the project's graphical user interface. When you need to make a change to the interface or retrieve a value from one of its text fields, you will use the `gui` object's instance variables.

For example, the `play` instance variable of `LottoMadness` represents the Play button. To disable this button in `LottoEvent`, the following statement can be used:

```
gui.play.setEnabled(false);
```

The following statement can be used to retrieve the value of the `JTextField` object `got3`:

```
String got3value = gui.got3.getText();
```

Listing 15.2 contains the full text of the `LottoEvent` class.

LISTING 15.2 The Full Text of `LottoEvent.java`

```
1: import javax.swing.*;
2: import java.awt.event.*;
3:
4: public class LottoEvent implements ItemListener, ActionListener,
5:     Runnable {
6:
```

LISTING 15.2   continued

```
 7:        LottoMadness gui;
 8:        Thread playing;
 9:
10:        public LottoEvent(LottoMadness in) {
11:            gui = in;
12:        }
13:
14:        public void actionPerformed(ActionEvent event) {
15:            String command = event.getActionCommand();
16:            if (command == "Play")
17:                startPlaying();
18:            if (command == "Stop")
19:                stopPlaying();
20:            if (command == "Reset")
21:                clearAllFields();
22:        }
23:
24:        void startPlaying() {
25:            playing = new Thread(this);
26:            playing.start();
27:            gui.play.setEnabled(false);
28:            gui.stop.setEnabled(true);
29:            gui.reset.setEnabled(false);
30:            gui.quickpick.setEnabled(false);
31:            gui.personal.setEnabled(false);
32:        }
33:
34:        void stopPlaying() {
35:            gui.stop.setEnabled(false);
36:            gui.play.setEnabled(true);
37:            gui.reset.setEnabled(true);
38:            gui.quickpick.setEnabled(true);
39:            gui.personal.setEnabled(true);
40:            playing = null;
41:        }
42:
43:        void clearAllFields() {
44:            for (int i = 0; i < 6; i++) {
45:                gui.numbers[i].setText(null);
46:                gui.winners[i].setText(null);
47:            }
48:            gui.got3.setText(null);
49:            gui.got4.setText(null);
50:            gui.got5.setText(null);
51:            gui.got6.setText(null);
52:            gui.drawings.setText(null);
53:            gui.years.setText(null);
54:        }
```

LISTING 15.2   continued

```
55:
56:        public void itemStateChanged(ItemEvent event) {
57:            Object item = event.getItem();
58:            if (item == gui.quickpick) {
59:                for (int i = 0; i < 6; i++) {
60:                    int pick;
61:                    do {
62:                        pick = (int) Math.floor(Math.random() * 50 + 1);
63:                    } while (numberGone(pick, gui.numbers, i));
64:                    gui.numbers[i].setText("" + pick);
65:                }
66:            } else {
67:                for (int i = 0; i < 6; i++)
68:                    gui.numbers[i].setText(null);
69:            }
70:        }
71:
72:        void addOneToField(JTextField field) {
73:            int num = Integer.parseInt("0" + field.getText());
74:            num++;
75:            field.setText("" + num);
76:        }
77:
78:        boolean numberGone(int num, JTextField[] pastNums, int count) {
79:            for (int i = 0; i < count; i++)
80:                if (Integer.parseInt(pastNums[i].getText()) == num)
81:                    return true;
82:            return false;
83:        }
84:
85:        boolean matchedOne(JTextField win, JTextField[] allPicks) {
86:            for (int i = 0; i < 6; i++) {
87:                String winText = win.getText();
88:                if ( winText.equals( allPicks[i].getText() ) )
89:                    return true;
90:            }
91:            return false;
92:        }
93:
94:        public void run() {
95:            Thread thisThread = Thread.currentThread();
96:            while (playing == thisThread) {
97:                addOneToField(gui.drawings);
98:                int draw = Integer.parseInt(gui.drawings.getText());
99:                float numYears = (float)draw / 104;
100:                gui.years.setText("" + numYears);
101:
102:                int matches = 0;
```

LISTING 15.2   continued

```
103:                for (int i = 0; i < 6; i++) {
104:                    int ball;
105:                    do {
106:                        ball = (int)Math.floor(Math.random() * 50 + 1);
107:                    } while (numberGone(ball, gui.winners, i));
108:                    gui.winners[i].setText("" + ball);
109:                    if (matchedOne(gui.winners[i], gui.numbers))
110:                        matches++;
111:                }
112:                switch (matches) {
113:                    case 3:
114:                        addOneToField(gui.got3);
115:                        break;
116:                    case 4:
117:                        addOneToField(gui.got4);
118:                        break;
119:                    case 5:
120:                        addOneToField(gui.got5);
121:                        break;
122:                    case 6:
123:                        addOneToField(gui.got6);
124:                        gui.stop.setEnabled(false);
125:                        gui.play.setEnabled(true);
126:                        playing = null;
127:                }
128:                try {
129:                    Thread.sleep(100);
130:                } catch (InterruptedException e) { }
131:            }
132:        }
133: }
```

Save Listing 15.2 as LottoEvent.java and compile it into a class file. This class cannot be run as an application—it lacks a main() method. Instead, you will create an object of this class in LottoMadness later in this workshop, and work with that object.

The LottoEvent class has one constructor: LottoEvent(LottoMadness). The LottoMadness object specified as an argument to the constructor identifies the object that is relying on LottoEvent to handle user events and conduct drawings.

The following methods are used in the class to accomplish specific tasks:

- Lines 43–54: The clearAllFields() method causes all text fields in the application to be emptied out. This method is handled when the Reset button is pressed.

- Lines 72–76: The addOneToField() method converts a text field to an integer, increments it by one, and converts it back into a text field. Because all text fields are stored as strings, you have to take special steps to use some of them as numbers.

- Lines 78–83: The numberGone() method takes three arguments—a single number from a Lotto drawing, an array that holds several JTextField objects, and a count integer. This method makes sure that each number in a drawing hasn't been selected already in the same drawing.

- Lines 85–92: The matchedOne() method takes two arguments—a JTextField object and an array of six JTextField objects. This method checks to see whether one of the user's numbers matches the numbers from the current lotto drawing.

The actionPerformed() method of the application receives the action events caused when the user presses Stop, Play, or Reset. The getActionCommand() method retrieves the label of the button that is used to determine which component was pressed. Pressing the Play button causes the startPlaying() method in Lines 24–32 to be called. This method disables four components so they do not interfere with the drawings as they are taking place. Pressing Stop causes the stopPlaying() method in Lines 34–41 to be called, which enables every component except for the Stop button.

The itemStateChanged() method receives the user events triggered by the selection of the Quick Pick or Personal check boxes. The getItem() method sends back an Object that represents the check box that was clicked. If it's the Quick Pick check box, six random numbers from 1 to 50 are assigned to the user's lotto numbers. Otherwise, the text fields that hold the user's numbers are cleared out.

The LottoEvent class uses numbers from 1 to 50 for each ball in the lotto drawings. This is established in Line 106, which multiplies the Math.random() method by 50, adds 1 to the total, and uses this as an argument to the Math.floor() method. The end result is a random integer from 1 to 50. If you replaced 50 with a different number here and on Line 62, you could use LottoMadness for lottery contests that generate a wider or smaller range of values.

One thing to note about the LottoMadness project is the lack of variables used to keep track of things like the number of drawings, winning counts, and lotto number text fields. This element of user interface programming differs from other types of programs. You can use the interface to store values and display them automatically.

To finish the project, load the LottoMadness.java file you created during the last hour into your word processor. You only need to add six lines to make it work with the LottoEvent class.

First, add a new instance variable to hold a `LottoEvent` object, using the following statement:

```
LottoEvent lotto = new LottoEvent(this);
```

Next, in the `LottoMadness()` constructor, call the `addItemListener()` and `addActionListener()` methods of each user interface component that can receive user input:

```
// Add listeners
quickpick.addItemListener(lotto);
personal.addItemListener(lotto);
stop.addActionListener(lotto);
play.addActionListener(lotto);
reset.addActionListener(lotto);
```

Listing 15.3 contains the full text of `LottoMadness.java` after you have made the changes. The lines you added are shaded—the rest is unchanged from the previous hour.

LISTING 15.3   The Full Text of `LottoMadness.java`

```
 1: import java.awt.*;
 2: import javax.swing.*;
 3:
 4: public class LottoMadness extends JFrame {
 5:
 6:     LottoEvent lotto = new LottoEvent(this);
 7:
 8:     // set up row 1
 9:     JPanel row1 = new JPanel();
10:     ButtonGroup option = new ButtonGroup();
11:     JCheckBox quickpick = new JCheckBox("Quick Pick", false);
12:     JCheckBox personal = new JCheckBox("Personal", true);
13:     // set up row 2
14:     JPanel row2 = new JPanel();
15:     JLabel numbersLabel = new JLabel("Your picks: ", JLabel.RIGHT);
16:     JTextField[] numbers = new JTextField[6];
17:     JLabel winnersLabel = new JLabel("Winners: ", JLabel.RIGHT);
18:     JTextField[] winners = new JTextField[6];
19:     // set up row 3
20:     JPanel row3 = new JPanel();
21:     JButton stop = new JButton("Stop");
22:     JButton play = new JButton("Play");
23:     JButton reset = new JButton("Reset");
24:     // set up row 4
25:     JPanel row4 = new JPanel();
26:     JLabel got3Label = new JLabel("3 of 6: ", JLabel.RIGHT);
27:     JTextField got3 = new JTextField();
28:     JLabel got4Label = new JLabel("4 of 6: ", JLabel.RIGHT);
```

LISTING 15.3   continued

```
29:     JTextField got4 = new JTextField();
30:     JLabel got5Label = new JLabel("5 of 6: ", JLabel.RIGHT);
31:     JTextField got5 = new JTextField();
32:     JLabel got6Label = new JLabel("6 of 6: ", JLabel.RIGHT);
33:     JTextField got6 = new JTextField(10);
34:     JLabel drawingsLabel = new JLabel("Drawings: ", JLabel.RIGHT);
35:     JTextField drawings = new JTextField();
36:     JLabel yearsLabel = new JLabel("Years: ", JLabel.RIGHT);
37:     JTextField years = new JTextField();
38:
39:     public LottoMadness() {
40:         super("Lotto Madness");
41:         setSize(550, 270);
42:         setDefaultCloseOperation(JFrame.EXIT_ON_CLOSE);
43:         GridLayout layout = new GridLayout(5, 1, 10, 10);
44:         Container pane = getContentPane();
45:         pane.setLayout(layout);
46:
47:         // Add listeners
48:         quickpick.addItemListener(lotto);
49:         personal.addItemListener(lotto);
50:         stop.addActionListener(lotto);
51:         play.addActionListener(lotto);
52:         reset.addActionListener(lotto);
53:
54:         FlowLayout layout1 = new FlowLayout(FlowLayout.CENTER,
55:             10, 10);
56:         option.add(quickpick);
57:         option.add(personal);
58:         row1.setLayout(layout1);
59:         row1.add(quickpick);
60:         row1.add(personal);
61:         pane.add(row1);
62:
63:         GridLayout layout2 = new GridLayout(2, 7, 10, 10);
64:         row2.setLayout(layout2);
65:         row2.setLayout(layout2);
66:         row2.add(numbersLabel);
67:         for (int i = 0; i < 6; i++) {
68:             numbers[i] = new JTextField();
69:             row2.add(numbers[i]);
70:         }
71:         row2.add(winnersLabel);
72:         for (int i = 0; i < 6; i++) {
73:             winners[i] = new JTextField();
74:             winners[i].setEditable(false);
75:             row2.add(winners[i]);
76:         }
```

LISTING 15.3 continued

```
 77:          pane.add(row2);
 78:
 79:          FlowLayout layout3 = new FlowLayout(FlowLayout.CENTER,
 80:              10, 10);
 81:          row3.setLayout(layout3);
 82:          stop.setEnabled(false);
 83:          row3.add(stop);
 84:          row3.add(play);
 85:          row3.add(reset);
 86:          pane.add(row3);
 87:
 88:          GridLayout layout4 = new GridLayout(2, 3, 20, 10);
 89:          row4.setLayout(layout4);
 90:          row4.add(got3Label);
 91:          got3.setEditable(false);
 92:          row4.add(got3);
 93:          row4.add(got4Label);
 94:          got4.setEditable(false);
 95:          row4.add(got4);
 96:          row4.add(got5Label);
 97:          got5.setEditable(false);
 98:          row4.add(got5);
 99:          row4.add(got6Label);
100:          got6.setEditable(false);
101:          row4.add(got6);
102:          row4.add(drawingsLabel);
103:          drawings.setEditable(false);
104:          row4.add(drawings);
105:          row4.add(yearsLabel);
106:          years.setEditable(false);
107:          row4.add(years);
108:          pane.add(row4);
109:          setContentPane(pane);
110:          setVisible(true);
111:      }
112:
113:      public static void main(String[] arguments) {
114:          LottoMadness frame = new LottoMadness();
115:      }
116: }
```

After you compile the LottoMadness class, run the application. If you are using the SDK, you can run it with the following command:

```
java LottoMadness
```

The application can test your lotto-playing skills for thousands of years. As you might expect, it's an exercise in futility—the chances of winning a 6-out-of-6 lotto drawing in a lifetime is extremely slim, even if you live as long as a biblical figure.

> The book's Web site at `http://www.java24hours.com` contains a link to an applet version of the `LottoMadness` program. At the time of this printing, 4,962,762 drawings have been conducted, which equals 47,719 years of twice-weekly drawings. There have been 76,433 3-out-of-6 winners, 4,038 4-out-of-6 winners, 99 5-out-of-6 winners, and 1 6-out-of-6 winner. The first person to win this fictional lottery was Bill Teer on Aug. 14, 2000, more than four years after the applet went online. His numbers were 3, 7, 1, 15, 34, and 43, and it only took him 241,225 drawings (2,319.47 years) to win.

Summary

You can create a professional-looking program with a reasonably modest amount of programming by using Swing and Java's event handling features. Although the `LottoMadness` application is longer than many of the examples you have worked in during the last 14 hours, half of the program was comprised of statements to build the interface.

If you spend some time running the application, you will become even more bitter and envious about the good fortune of the people who win these six-number lottery drawings.

My most recent run of the program indicates that I could blow $27 grand and the best 266 years of my life buying tickets, only to win a handful of 4-of-6 and 3-of-6 prizes. In comparison to those odds, the chance to make Java programming skills pay off almost seems like a sure thing.

Q&A

Q Is there a way to use different colors in an interface?

A You can use `Color` objects to change the appearance of each component in several ways. The `setBackground()` method designates the background elements, and `setForeground()` sets foreground elements. You must use these methods with the components themselves. The `setBackground()` method of the applet will not change the color of containers and components within the applet.

Q Do you need to do anything with the `paint()` method or `repaint()` to indicate that a text field has been changed?

A After the `setText()` method of a text component is used to change its value, nothing else needs to be done. Swing handles the updating necessary to show the new value.

Quiz

After the `LottoMadness` program has soured you on games of chance, play a game of skill by answering the following questions.

Questions

1. Why are action events called by that name?

   a. They occur in reaction to something else.

   b. They indicate that some kind of action should be taken in response.

   c. They honor cinematic adventurer Action Jackson.

2. What does `this` signify as the argument to an `addActionListener()` method?

   a. "This" listener should be used when an event occurs.

   b. "This" event takes precedence over others.

   c. "This" class of objects will handle the events.

3. Which component stores user input as integers?

   a. `JButton`

   b. `JTextField`

   c. Neither does

Answers

1. b. Action events include the click of a button and the selection of an item from a pull-down menu.

2. c. If the name of another class were used as an argument instead of the `this` statement, that class would receive the events and be expected to handle them.

3. c. `JTextField` and `JTextArea` components store their values as text, so their values must be converted before they can be used as integers, floating-point numbers, or other non-text values.

15

Activities

If the main event of this hour didn't provide enough action for your tastes, interface with the following activities:

- Add a text field to the LottoMadness application that works in conjunction with the Thread.sleep() statement in the LottoEvent class to slow down the rate that drawings are conducted.

- Modify the LottoMadness project so that it draws five numbers from 1 to 90.

To see Java programs that implement these activities, visit the book's Web site at http://www.java24hours.com.

Hour **16**

Building a Complex User Interface

Creating a graphical user interface with Swing involves more than learning how to use the different interface components, layout managers, and event-handling methods. You also have to spend some time familiarizing yourself with everything that Swing offers.

In the current version of Java 2, there are more than 400 different classes in Swing's `javax.swing` library and other related libraries. Many of these classes can be implemented using the same techniques you have used in the preceding three hours—all Swing containers and components share super-classes with each other, which gives them common behavior.

During this hour, you will learn about some additional components that you can use in your Swing programs:

- Scroll panes—Containers that add support for vertical and horizontal scrolling to other components
- Sliders—Components that can be used to select a number within a range of numbers

- Change listeners—Objects that can monitor changes in sliders
- Image icons—Graphics that can be used on labels, buttons, and other components
- Toolbars—Containers that can be moved around to different parts of an interface
- Menu bars, menus, and menu items—Two containers and a component used to create pull-down menus

Scroll Panes

Components in a graphical user interface are often bigger than the area available to display them. To move from one part of the component to another, vertical and horizontal scrollbars are used—this is standard behavior for a text area in software such as word processors and email programs.

In Swing, you offer scrolling by adding a component to a scroll pane, a container that is represented by the JScrollPane class in Swing.

You can create a scroll pane with the following constructors:

- JScrollPane()—Create a scroll pane with a horizontal and vertical scrollbar that appear, if they are needed
- JScrollPane(*int*, *int*)—Create a scroll pane with the specified vertical scrollbar and horizontal scrollbars
- JScrollPane(*Component*)—Create a scroll pane that contains the specified user interface component
- JScrollPane(*Component*, *int*, *int*)—Create a scroll pane with the specified component, vertical scrollbar, and horizontal scrollbar

The integers used as arguments to these constructors determine how scrollbars will be used in the pane. Use the following class variables as these arguments:

- JScrollPane.VERTICAL_SCROLLBAR_AS_NEEDED or JScrollPane.HORIZONTAL_SCROLLBAR_AS_NEEDED
- JScrollPane.VERTICAL_SCROLLBAR_NEVER or JScrollPane.HORIZONTAL_ SCROLLBAR_NEVER
- JScrollPane.VERTICAL_SCROLLBAR_ALWAYS or JScrollPane.HORIZONTAL_ SCROLLBAR_ALWAYS

If you have created a scroll pane without a component in it, you can use the pane's add(*Component*) method to add components.

After you have finished setting up a scroll pane, it should be added to a container in place of the component.

To see an application that includes a scroll pane, enter Listing 16.1 into a text editor and save it as `WriteMail.java`.

LISTING 16.1   The Full Text of `WriteMail.java`

16

```
1: import javax.swing.*;
2: import java.awt.*;
3:
4: class WriteMail extends JFrame {
5:
6:     WriteMail() {
7:         super("Write an E-Mail");
8:         setSize(370, 270);
9:         setDefaultCloseOperation(JFrame.EXIT_ON_CLOSE);
10:        Container pane = getContentPane();
11:        FlowLayout flow = new FlowLayout(FlowLayout.RIGHT);
12:        pane.setLayout(flow);
13:        JPanel row1 = new JPanel();
14:        JLabel toLabel = new JLabel("To:");
15:        row1.add(toLabel);
16:        JTextField to = new JTextField(24);
17:        row1.add(to);
18:        pane.add(row1);
19:        JPanel row2 = new JPanel();
20:        JLabel subjectLabel = new JLabel("Subject:");
21:        row2.add(subjectLabel);
22:        JTextField subject = new JTextField(24);
23:        row2.add(subject);
24:        pane.add(row2);
25:        JPanel row3 = new JPanel();
26:        JLabel messageLabel = new JLabel("Message:");
27:        row3.add(messageLabel);
28:        JTextArea message = new JTextArea(4, 22);
29:        message.setLineWrap(true);
30:        message.setWrapStyleWord(true);
31:        JScrollPane scroll = new JScrollPane(message,
32:            JScrollPane.VERTICAL_SCROLLBAR_ALWAYS,
33:            JScrollPane.HORIZONTAL_SCROLLBAR_NEVER);
34:        row3.add(scroll);
35:        pane.add(row3);
36:        JPanel row4 = new JPanel();
37:        JButton send = new JButton("Send");
38:        row4.add(send);
39:        pane.add(row4);
40:        setContentPane(pane);
41:        setVisible(true);
```

LISTING 16.1   continued

```
42:     }
43:
44:     public static void main(String[] arguments) {
45:         WriteMail mail = new WriteMail();
46:     }
47: }
```

After you compile and run the application, you should see a window like the one in Figure 16.1.

FIGURE 16.1

Displaying a scrolling text area in an application.

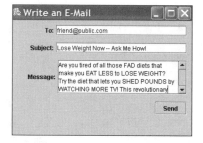

The `WriteMail` application is a graphical user interface that is used to compose an email. There is no event-handling code in the program, so you can't do anything with the data entered in the form.

The text of an email is entered in a scrolling text area, which is implemented with the following statements:

```
JTextArea message = new JTextArea(4, 22);
message.setLineWrap(true);
message.setWrapStyleWord(true);
JScrollPane scroll = new JScrollPane(message,
JScrollPane.VERTICAL_SCROLLBAR_ALWAYS,
JScrollPane.HORIZONTAL_SCROLLBAR_NEVER);
row3.add(scroll);
```

Sliders

One of the easiest ways for a user to enter numeric input is by using a slider, a component that can be dragged from side to side or up and down.

Sliders are represented in Swing by the `JSlider` class. Figure 16.2 shows what a slider component looks like.

FIGURE 16.2

Displaying a slider component.

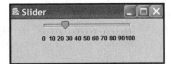

Sliders enable a number to be chosen from between a minimum and maximum range of values. These values can be displayed on a label that includes the minimum value, maximum value, and intermediate values (as shown later in Figure 16.3).

You can create a horizontal slider with one of the following constructors:

- JSlider(*int*, *int*)—Create a slider with the specified minimum value and maximum value.
- JSlider(*int*, *int*, *int*)—Create a slider with the specified minimum value, maximum value, and starting value.

To create a vertical slider, you must use a constructor method with an additional argument—the orientation of the slider. This argument should be the class variables JSlider.VERTICAL or JSlider.HORIZONTAL.

The following statement creates a vertical slider that can be used to pick a number from 1 to 1,000:

```
JSlider guess = new JSlider(JSlider.VERTICAL, 1, 1000, 500);
```

This slider starts with the caret—the part of the component used to select a number—at the 500 position.

To display a label for a slider, you must set up the information that the label will contain. Call the slider's setMajorTickSpacing(*int*) and setMinorTickSpacing(*int*) methods to determine how often a tick mark will be displayed on the label. Major ticks are displayed as a thicker line than minor ticks.

After you have set up how often tick marks will appear, call the slider's setPaintTicks(*boolean*) method with true as the argument.

You can also display the numeric value of each major tick by calling the slider's setPaintLabels(*boolean*) method with true.

The following statements can be used to create the slider shown in Figure 16.2:

```
JSlider percentage = new JSlider(0, 100, 25);
percentage.setMajorTickSpacing(10);
percentage.setMinorTickSpacing(5);
percentage.setPaintTicks(true);
percentage.setPaintLabels(true);
```

> Like other Swing components, a slider should be set up completely before you add it to the content pane or any other container. Otherwise, it may not be displayed as intended, or might not be displayed at all.

Change Listeners

To monitor the use of a slider in a Java program, you must have a class that implements the ChangeListener interface, which is part of the javax.swing.event package of classes. This interface includes only one method, which takes the following form:

```
public void stateChanged(ChangeEvent evt) {
    // statements to handle the event
}
```

To register an object as a change listener, call the addChangeListener(Object) method of the container that holds the slider. When the slider is moved, the listening object's stateChanged() method will be called.

This method is called with a ChangeEvent object that can be used to identify the slider component that was changed in value. Call the object's getSource() method and cast the object to a JSlider, as in the following statement:

```
JSlider changedSlider = (JSlider)evt.getSource();
```

In this example, evt is the ChangeEvent object that was an argument to the stateChanged() method.

When you are using a change listener, it's important to note that change events occur throughout the movement of a slider. They begin when the slider is first moved, and don't stop occurring until the slider has been released.

For this reason, you might not want to do anything in the stateChanged() method until the slider has stopped moving.

To see if a slider is currently being moved around, call its getValueIsAdjusting() method. This method returns true while movement is taking place, and false otherwise.

This technique is demonstrated in your next project, a Java application that uses three sliders to choose a color. Colors are created in Java by using the Color class, which is part of the java.awt package.

One way to create a Color object is to specify the amount of red, green, and blue in the color. Each of these can be an integer from 0 to 255, with 255 representing the maximum amount of that color.

For example, the following statement creates a `Color` object that represents the color butterscotch:

```
Color butterscotch = new Color(255, 204, 128);
```

The red value used to create this `Color` object is 255, so it contains the maximum amount of red. It also contains a large amount of green and some blue.

Colors can be represented by a range of values, so they are an ideal use for slider components.

Listing 16.2 contains the `ColorSlide` application, which has three sliders, three labels for the sliders, and a panel where the color is displayed. Enter this source code into your word processor and save the file as `ColorSlide.java`.

LISTING 16.2   The Full Text of `ColorSlide.java`

```
 1: import javax.swing.*;
 2: import javax.swing.event.*;
 3: import java.awt.*;
 4:
 5: public class ColorSlide extends JFrame implements ChangeListener {
 6:     ColorPanel canvas = new ColorPanel();
 7:     JSlider red = new JSlider(0, 255, 255);
 8:     JSlider green = new JSlider(0, 255, 0);
 9:     JSlider blue = new JSlider(0, 255, 0);
10:
11:     public ColorSlide() {
12:         super("Color Slide");
13:         setSize(270, 300);
14:         setDefaultCloseOperation(JFrame.EXIT_ON_CLOSE);
15:         setVisible(true);
16:         red.setMajorTickSpacing(50);
17:         red.setMinorTickSpacing(10);
18:         red.setPaintTicks(true);
19:         red.setPaintLabels(true);
20:         red.addChangeListener(this);
21:         green.setMajorTickSpacing(50);
22:         green.setMinorTickSpacing(10);
23:         green.setPaintTicks(true);
24:         green.setPaintLabels(true);
25:         green.addChangeListener(this);
26:         blue.setMajorTickSpacing(50);
27:         blue.setMinorTickSpacing(10);
28:         blue.setPaintTicks(true);
29:         blue.setPaintLabels(true);
30:         blue.addChangeListener(this);
31:         JLabel redLabel = new JLabel("Red: ");
32:         JLabel greenLabel = new JLabel("Green: ");
```

16

LISTING 16.2   continued

```
33:            JLabel blueLabel = new JLabel("Blue: ");
34:            GridLayout grid = new GridLayout(4, 1);
35:            FlowLayout right = new FlowLayout(FlowLayout.RIGHT);
36:            Container pane = getContentPane();
37:            pane.setLayout(grid);
38:            JPanel redPanel = new JPanel();
39:            redPanel.setLayout(right);
40:            redPanel.add(redLabel);
41:            redPanel.add(red);
42:            pane.add(redPanel);
43:            JPanel greenPanel = new JPanel();
44:            greenPanel.setLayout(right);
45:            greenPanel.add(greenLabel);
46:            greenPanel.add(green);
47:            pane.add(greenPanel);
48:            JPanel bluePanel = new JPanel();
49:            bluePanel.setLayout(right);
50:            bluePanel.add(blueLabel);
51:            bluePanel.add(blue);
52:            pane.add(bluePanel);
53:            pane.add(canvas);
54:            setContentPane(pane);
55:        }
56:
57:        public void stateChanged(ChangeEvent evt) {
58:            JSlider source = (JSlider)evt.getSource();
59:            if (source.getValueIsAdjusting() != true) {
60:                Color current = new Color(red.getValue(), green.getValue(),
61:                    blue.getValue());
62:                canvas.changeColor(current);
63:                canvas.repaint();
64:            }
65:        }
66:
67:        public Insets getInsets() {
68:            Insets border = new Insets(45, 10, 10, 10);
69:            return border;
70:        }
71:
72:        public static void main(String[] arguments) {
73:            ColorSlide cs = new ColorSlide();
74:        }
75: }
76:
77: class ColorPanel extends JPanel {
78:     Color background;
79:
80:     ColorPanel() {
```

LISTING 16.2   continued

```
81:         background = Color.red;
82:     }
83:
84:     public void paintComponent(Graphics comp) {
85:         Graphics2D comp2D = (Graphics2D)comp;
86:         comp2D.setColor(background);
87:         comp2D.fillRect(0, 0, getSize().width, getSize().height);
88:     }
89:
90:     void changeColor(Color newBackground) {
91:         background = newBackground;
92:     }
93: }
```

16

Compile and run the application. A frame will open that contains three sliders that represent the amount of red, green, and blue in a panel along the bottom edge of the frame.

Adjust the values of each slider to change the color that is displayed. Figure 16.3 shows the application being used to create North Texas Mean Green, a color that has a red value of 50, a green value of 150, and a blue value of 50, a shade that inspires students and alumni of the University of North Texas to leap to our feet and make ferocious eagle-claw hand gestures that put fear in our rivals.

FIGURE 16.3
Choosing a color using slider components.

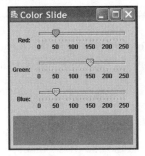

Menus

If you're creating a program that uses a frame, you can jazz it up with a *menu bar*, a set of pull-down menus that is usually displayed below the title bar.

Menus in Java are created using three components: JMenuBar, JMenu, and JMenuItem.

A JMenuItem component is an item on a menu. It serves the same purpose as a button—click an item to make something happen.

A `JMenu` container holds `JMenuItem` components, lines that separate menu items, and other interface components, such as check boxes.

A `JMenuBar` container holds `JMenu` components, displaying their names.

These three work together more closely than members of the Osmond Family. For example, you could put an Exit button on a menu so users can exit the program. This button could be put in a File menu, which is then placed in a menu bar, displaying the name File, along with other menu names below a frame's title bar.

A `JMenuItem` component can be set up using the same constructor methods as a `JButton` component: Call `JMenuItem(String)` to create an item with the text of the item as the argument.

The following statements create five menu items:

```
JMenuItem kr1 = new JMenuItem("Hold 'Em");
JMenuItem kr2 = new JMenuItem("Fold 'Em");
JMenuItem kr3 = new JMenuItem("Walk Away");
JMenuItem kr4 = new JMenuItem("Run");
JMenuItem kr5 = new JMenuItem("Count Your Money");
```

> The `kr5` item should be disabled—call `kr5.setEnabled(false)` after creating the item. You never count your money when you're sitting at the table. There'll be time enough for counting when the dealing's done.

A `JMenu` container holds menu items. To create one, call the `JMenu(String)` constructor with the menu's name as the only argument. The following statement creates a menu titled Gamble:

```
JMenu menu1 = new JMenu("Gamble");
```

After you have created a `JMenu` object, call its `add(JMenuItem)` method to add a menu item to it. Each new item will be placed at the end of the menu, so you should add items in order from top to bottom.

You can also add a text label: Call the `add(String)` method with the text as an argument.

If you'd like to add something to a menu other than a `JMenuItem` or text, call a `JMenu` object's `add(Component)` method with a user interface component. The following statements create a check box and add it to a menu:

```
JMenu view = new JMenu("View");
JCheckBox wordWrap = new JCheckBox("Word Wrap");
view.add(wordWrap);
```

Menus can also contain lines that are used to visually group related items together. To add a line separator, call the addSeparator() method, which puts a line at the end of the menu.

Using the five menu items created earlier, the following statements create a menu and fill it with those items and two separators:

```
JMenu m1 = new JMenu("Gamble");
m1.add(kr1);
m1.add(kr2);
m1.addSeparator();
m1.add(kr3);
m1.add(kr4);
m1.addSeparator();
m1.add(kr5);
```

After you have created all your menus and filled them with menu items, you're ready to add them to a frame by putting them in a JMenuBar. JMenuBar, another container, holds JMenu objects and displays each of their names, usually in a gray horizontal panel directly below an application's title bar.

To create a menu bar, call the JMenuBar() constructor method with no arguments. Call the bar's add(*JMenu)* method to add menus to the bar, beginning with the menu that should be displayed at the end of the bar. (The end is the rightmost position on a horizontal bar and the bottom position on a vertical bar.)

When the menu bar contains all of the menus it needs, add it to a frame by calling the frame's setJMenuBar(*JMenuBar)* method.

The following statement finishes off the ongoing example by creating a menu bar, adding a menu to it, then placing the bar on a frame called kenny:

```
JMenuBar jmb = new JMenuBar();
jmb.add(m1);
kenny.setJMenuBar(jmb);
```

Figure 16.4 shows what this menu looks like on an otherwise empty frame.

You already know how to handle events generated by these menu items, because JMenuItem objects function like buttons, and can generate action events when they are selected. Other components such as check boxes work the same way they do when placed in other containers.

16

FIGURE **16.4**

A frame with a menu bar.

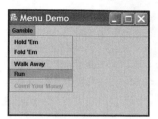

Workshop: Using Image Icons and Toolbars

One of the easiest ways to improve the visual appeal of a graphical user interface is to use *icons*, small images used to identify buttons, menu items, and other parts of an interface.

With many of the components in the Swing class library, you can label a component with an image instead of text by using the ImageIcon class in the javax.swing package.

You can create an ImageIcon from a file on your computer by calling the ImageIcon(*String*) constructor method. The argument to the method is either the name of the file or its location and name, as in these examples:

```
ImageIcon stopSign = new ImageIcon("stopsign.gif");
ImageIcon saveFile = new ImageIcon("images/savefile.gif");
```

Make note of the / separator used in path names when creating an ImageIcon object. Although some operating systems use the \ character to separate folders and file names, the ImageIcon constructor requires the / character.

The graphics file used to create the image icon must be in GIF or JPEG format. Most will be in GIF format, because it is well-suited to displaying small graphics with a limited number of colors.

The constructor method of ImageIcon will load the entire image from the file immediately—unlike other graphics-related classes you will work with during Hour 23, "Working with Graphics."

You can use image icons as labels and buttons by using the JLabel(*ImageIcon*) and JButton(*ImageIcon*) constructor methods, as in the following example:

```
ImageIcon siteLogo = new ImageIcon("siteLogo.gif");
JLabel logoLabel = new JLabel(siteLogo);
ImageIcon searchWeb = new ImageIcon("searchGraphic.gif");
JButton search = new JTextField(searchWeb);
```

Several components can have an icon and a text label. The following statement creates a button with both:

```
JButton refresh = new JButton("Refresh",
    "images/refreshIcon.gif");
```

Image icons are often used in toolbars, containers that group several components together into a row or column.

They can also be added to menus. Call the JMenuItem(*Icon*) to add an icon to a menu or JMenuItem(*String*, *Icon*) to add an icon and text.

Toolbars, which are created by using the JToolBar class in Swing, can be designed so that a user can move them from one part of a graphical user interface to another. This process is called *docking*, and these components are also called *dockable toolbars*.

You can create a toolbar with one of the following constructor methods:

- JToolBar()—Create a toolbar that will line up components in a horizontal direction
- JToolBar(*int*)—Create a toolbar that will line up components in the specified direction, which is either SwingConstants.HORIZONTAL or SwingConstants. VERTICAL.

Components are added to a toolbar in the same way they are added to other containers— the add(*Component*) method is called with the component to be added.

For a toolbar to be dockable, it must be placed in a container that uses BorderLayout as its layout manager. This layout arranges a container into north, south, east, west, and center areas. When you are using a dockable toolbar, however, the container should only use two of these: the center and only one directional area.

The toolbar should be added to the directional area. The following statements create a vertical, dockable toolbar with three icon buttons:

```
Container pane = getContentPane();
BorderLayout border = new BorderLayout();
pane.setLayout(border);
JToolBar bar = new JToolBar(SwingConstants.VERTICAL);
ImageIcon play = new ImageIcon("play.gif");
JButton playButton = new JButton(play);
ImageIcon stop = new ImageIcon("stop.gif");
JButton stopButton = new JButton(stop);
ImageIcon pause = new ImageIcon("pause.gif");
JButton pauseButton = new JButton(pause);
bar.add(playButton);
bar.add(stopButton);
bar.add(pauseButton);
```

16

```
pane.add(bar, BorderLayout.WEST);
setContentPane(pane);
```

The next project you will undertake during this hour is Tool, a Java application that includes image icons and a dockable toolbar around.

Open your text editor and enter Listing 16.3, saving the file as Tool.java.

LISTING 16.3   The Full Text of Tool.java

```
 1: import java.awt.*;
 2: import java.awt.event.*;
 3: import javax.swing.*;
 4:
 5: public class Tool extends JFrame {
 6:     public Tool() {
 7:         super("Tool");
 8:         setSize(370, 200);
 9:         setDefaultCloseOperation(JFrame.EXIT_ON_CLOSE);
10:         ImageIcon image1 = new ImageIcon("newfile.gif");
11:         JButton button1 = new JButton(image1);
12:         ImageIcon image2 = new ImageIcon("openfile.gif");
13:         JButton button2 = new JButton(image2);
14:         ImageIcon image3 = new ImageIcon("savefile.gif");
15:         JButton button3 = new JButton(image3);
16:         JToolBar bar = new JToolBar();
17:         bar.add(button1);
18:         bar.add(button2);
19:         bar.add(button3);
20:         JTextArea edit = new JTextArea(8, 40);
21:         JScrollPane scroll = new JScrollPane(edit);
22:         JPanel pane = new JPanel();
23:         BorderLayout border = new BorderLayout();
24:         pane.setLayout(border);
25:         pane.add("North", bar);
26:         pane.add("Center", scroll);
27:         setContentPane(pane);
28:         setVisible(true);
29:     }
30:
31:     public static void main(String[] arguments) {
32:         Tool frame = new Tool();
33:     }
34: }
```

The Tool application requires three graphics files that will be used to create the icons on the toolbar: newfile.gif, openfile.gif, and savefile.gif. You can find these files on the book's Web site at http://www.java24hours.com (open the Hour 16 page).

Figure 16.5 and Figure 16.6 show two different screenshots of this application as it runs. The toolbar has been moved from its original location (Figure 16.5) to another edge of the interface (Figure 16.6).

FIGURE 16.5

Using an application with a toolbar.

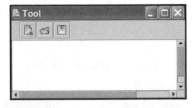

FIGURE 16.6

Moving a toolbar to a new location.

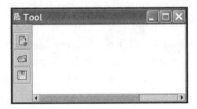

Compile the application and try it out by moving the toolbar around. You can move a toolbar by clicking its handle and dragging the toolbar to a different edge of the text area. When you release the toolbar, it will be placed along that edge and the text area will move over to make room for it.

You can also drag a dockable toolbar off an interface entirely. This causes a new window to be opened that contains the toolbar.

Sun Microsystems offers a repository of icon graphics that you can use in your own programs. The three icons used in this hour's workshop are from that collection. To view the graphics, visit the Web page http://java.sun.com/developer/techDocs/hi/repository/.

Summary

This is the last of four hours devoted to Swing, the part of the Java language that supports windowing software.

Java offers extensive support for the graphical user interface features expected by users of Microsoft Windows and Apple Macintosh systems.

Although Swing is by far the largest part of the Java class library, most of the classes are used in similar ways. Once you know how to create a component, add a component to a container, apply a layout manager to a container, and respond to user input, you can make use of many new Swing classes as you explore the language.

Q&A

Q Is there a reason to display scrollbars only when they are needed, as opposed to displaying them all the time?

A Normally, the decision is based on how you want the interface to look. Some interface designers prefer to have the scrollbars visible at all times, while others make them visible only when the component needs them.

With early implementations of scroll panes in Java 2, scrollbars would disappear in certain instances and never reappear. Though this appears to have been resolved, making scrollbars visible at all times is a way to work around a problem like this.

Q How can I find out about the rest of the Swing classes in the Java class library?

A On Sun's official Java site, the full documentation for the Java class library is published at `http://java.sun.com/j2se/1.4/docs/api/`. You can see the classes that are included in `javax.swing`, `java.awt`, and `java.awt.event`, the packages that were covered during the preceding four hours. All Swing classes and interfaces are documented, including their constructor methods, class variables, and instance variables. There are also links to some of Sun's official tutorials for Swing programmers.

Quiz

No pane, no gain: Exercise some brain muscle by answering the following questions about scroll panes, image icons, and other Swing features.

Questions

1. What graphics file formats are supported by the `ImageIcon` class?

    a. GIF

    b. GIF and JPEG

    c. GIF, PNG, and JPEG

2. What does a `JSlider` object's `getValueIsAdjusting()` method accomplish?

   a. It determines whether the slider has been changed from its original value.

   b. It determines whether the slider is currently being changed in value.

   c. Not a lot; this method is a major disappointment to its parent superclass.

3. The Swing library was named after a style of dance band jazz that was popularized in the 1930s and unexpectedly revived in the 1990s. Which of the following is not a real title of a song performed by a Swing musician?

   a. "Cement Mixer (Put-ti, Put-ti)"

   b. "Barney Google with the Goo Goo Googly Eyes"

   c. "Flat Foot Floogie (with the Floy Floy)"

16

Answers

1. b. PNG is supported with other Java classes that involve images, but graphics in this format aren't supported by `ImageIcon`.

2. b. The `getValueIsAdjusting()` method returns `true` while the slider is being moved and `false` otherwise.

3. b. "Barney Google," a hit song by Billy Rose in 1923, was too early for Swing. The other two songs are by Slim Gaillard.

Activities

To see if you've got the swing of things, try the following activities:

- Create a graphical user interface that includes a combo box in a scroll pane.

- Add event-handling to the `WriteMail` application that displays the contents of the `to`, `subject`, and `message` components using `System.out.println()` when the Send button is clicked.

To see Java programs that implement these activities, visit the book's Web site at `http://www.java24hours.com`.

PART V
Creating Multimedia Programs

Hour

HOUR 17

Creating Interactive Web Programs

Now that Java has made the transition from a child prodigy to an established language, it is being used for all kinds of large-scale business software and other applications. However, for many people, the core appeal of the language lies in a type of program that Java made possible: the applet.

Applets are programs designed to run as part of a World Wide Web page. When a Java applet is encountered on a page, it is downloaded to the user's computer and begins running.

During this hour you'll be introduced to applet programming. Programming applets with Java is much different from creating applications with Java. Because applets must be downloaded from a page each time they are run, they're smaller than most applications to reduce download time. Also, because applets run on the computer of the person using the applet, they have numerous security restrictions in place to prevent malicious or damaging code from being run.

The following topics will be covered:

- Setting up an applet
- Displaying information in an applet
- Stopping and starting an applet
- Putting an applet on a Web page
- Using applet HTML tags and attributes
- Customizing an applet with parameters on a Web page
- Receiving parameters in an applet
- Running applets with the Java Plug-in

Standard Applet Methods

The first step in the creation of an applet is to make it a subclass of JApplet, a class that's part of the Swing package, javax.swing. An applet is treated as a visual window inside a Web page, so JApplet is part of Swing alongside clickable buttons, scrollbars, and other components of a program's user interface.

JApplet is a subclass of Applet, a class in the java.applet package. Being part of this hierarchy enables the applets you write to use all the behavior and attributes they need to be run as part of a World Wide Web page. Before you begin writing any other statements in your applets, they will be able to interact with a Web browser, load and unload themselves, redraw their window in response to changes in the browser window, and handle other necessary tasks.

In applications, programs begin running with the first statement inside the main() block statement and end with the last closing bracket (}) that closes out the block. There is no main() method in a Java applet, so there is no set starting place for the program. Instead, an applet has a group of standard methods that are handled in response to specific events as the applet runs.

The following are the events that could prompt one of the applet methods to be handled:

- The program is loaded for the first time, which causes the applet's init() and start() methods to be called.
- Something happens that requires the applet window to be redisplayed, which causes the applet's paint() method to be called.
- The program is stopped by the browser, which calls the applet's stop() method.

- The program restarts after a stop, which calls the start() method.
- The program is unloaded as it finishes running, which calls the destroy() method.

The following is an example of a bare-bones applet:

```
public class Skeleton extends javax.swing.JApplet {
    // program will go here
}
```

Unlike applications, applet class files must be public because the JApplet class is also public. (If your applet uses other class files of your own creation, they do not have to be declared public.)

Your applet's class inherits all the methods that are handled automatically when needed: init(), paint(), start(), stop(), and destroy(). However, none of these methods do anything. If you want something to happen in an applet, you have to override these methods with new versions in your applet program.

Painting an Applet Window

The paint() method is used to display text, shapes, and graphics within the applet window. Whenever something needs to be displayed or redisplayed on the applet window, the paint() method handles the task. You can also force paint() to be handled with the following statement in any method of an applet:

```
repaint();
```

Aside from the use of repaint(), the main time the paint() method is handled is when something changes in the browser or the operating system running the browser. For example, if a user minimizes a Web page containing an applet, the paint() method will be called to redisplay everything that was onscreen in the applet when the applet is later restored to full size.

Unlike the other methods you will be learning about during this hour, paint() takes an argument. The following is an example of a simple paint() method:

```
public void paint(Graphics screen) {
    Graphics2D screen2D = (Graphics2D)screen;
    // display statements go here
}
```

The argument sent to the paint() method is a Graphics object. The Graphics class of objects represents an environment in which something can be displayed, such as an applet window. There's also another version of this class, Graphics2D, which supports more sophisticated graphical features.

17

In the preceding example, a `Graphics2D` object called `screen2D` is created. Instead of calling a constructor method to create the object, a technique called casting is used.

Casting is the process of creating a Java object based on an existing object. In this example, a `Graphics` object called `screen` is cast to a `Graphics2D` object called `screen2D`. To take advantage of the features of `Graphics2D` in an applet window, you must cast the `Graphics` object sent to the `paint()` method into a `Graphics2D` object.

Later this hour, you'll learn about `drawString()`, a method for the display of text that's available in both the `Graphics` and `Graphics2D` classes.

If you are using a `Graphics` or `Graphics2D` object in your applet, you have to add the following `import` statements before the `class` statement at the beginning of the source file:

```
import java.awt.Graphics;
import java.awt.Graphics2D;
```

> If you are using several classes that are a part of the `java.awt` package of classes, you can use the statement `import java.awt.*;` instead to make all of these classes available for use in your program.

Initializing an Applet

The `init()` method is handled once—and only once—when the applet is run. As a result, it's an ideal place to set up values for any objects and variables that are needed for the applet to run successfully. This method is also a good place to set up fonts, colors, and the screen's background color. Here's an example:

```
public void init() {
    Container pane = getContentPane();
    FlowLayout flo = new FlowLayout();
    pane.setLayout(flo);
    JButton run = new JButton("Run");
    pane.add(run);
    setContentPane(pane);
}
```

If you are going to use a variable in other methods, it should not be created inside an `init()` method because it will only exist within the scope of that method.

For example, if you create an integer variable called `displayRate` inside the `init()` method and try to use it in the `paint()` method, you'll get an error when you attempt to compile the program. Create any variables you need to use throughout a class as object variables right after the `class` statement and before any methods.

Starting and Stopping an Applet

At any point when the applet program starts running, the `start()` method will be handled. When a program first begins, the `init()` method is followed by the `start()` method. After that, in many instances there will never be a cause for the `start()` method to be handled again. In order for `start()` to be handled a second time or more, the applet has to stop execution at some point.

The `stop()` method is called when an applet stops execution. This event can occur when a user leaves the Web page containing the applet and continues to another page. It can also occur when the `stop()` method is called directly in a program.

Destroying an Applet

The `destroy()` method is an opposite of sorts to the `init()` method. It is handled just before an applet completely closes down and completes running.

This method is used in rare instances when something has been changed during a program and it should be restored to its original state. It's another method you'll use more often with animation than with other types of programs.

Putting an Applet on a Web Page

Applets are placed on a Web page in the same way that anything unusual is put on a page: HTML commands are used to describe the applet, and the Web browser loads it along with the other parts of the page. If you have used HTML to create a Web page, you know that it's a way to combine formatted text, images, sound, and other elements together. HTML uses special commands called tags that are surrounded by < and > marks, including `<IMG>` for the display of images, `<P>` for the insertion of a paragraph mark, and `<CENTER>` to center the text that follows until a `</CENTER>` tag is reached.

The performance of some of these HTML tags can be affected by attributes that determine how they function. For example, `SRC` is an attribute of the `<IMG>` tag, and it provides the name of the image file that should be displayed. The following is an example of an `<IMG>` tag:

```
<IMG SRC="Graduation.jpg">
```

One way to place applets on a Web page is by using an `<APPLET>` tag and several attributes. The following is an example of the HTML required to put an applet on a page:

17

```
<APPLET CODE="StripYahtzee.class" CODEBASE="javadir" HEIGHT=300 WIDTH=400>
Sorry, no dice ... this requires a Java-enabled browser.
</APPLET>
```

The CODE attribute identifies the name of the applet's class file. If more than one class file is being used with an applet, CODE should refer to the main class file that is a subclass of the JApplet class.

If there is no CODEBASE attribute, all files associated with the applet should be in the same folder as the Web page that loads the program. CODEBASE should contain a reference to the folder or subfolder where the applet and any related files can be found. In the preceding example, CODEBASE indicates that the StripYahtzee applet can be found in the javadir subfolder.

The HEIGHT and WIDTH attributes designate the exact size of the applet window on the Web page. It must be big enough to handle the things you are displaying in your applet.

In between the opening <APPLET> tag and the closing </APPLET> tag, you can provide an alternate of some kind for Web users whose browser software cannot run Java programs (less than five percent of all Web users run browsers that fall into this group). In the preceding example, the text "Sorry, no dice...this requires a Java-enabled browser" is displayed in place of the applet on a browser such as Lynx, which does not support Java. You can put instructions here on how to download a Java-enabled browser from Netscape, Microsoft, or Opera Software. You can also include hyperlinks and other HTML elements.

Another attribute you can use with applets is ALIGN. It designates how the applet will be displayed in relation to the surrounding material on the page, including text and graphics. Values include ALIGN="Left", ALIGN="Right", and others.

A Sample Applet

For your first applet, you will display the string "Saluton mondo!" in the applet window, the traditional Esperanto greeting that is becoming more traditional by the hour. You'll take a look at how applets are structured by re-creating the Saluton application from Hour 2, "Writing Your First Program," as a program that can run on a Web page.

Load your word processor and create a new file called SalutonApplet.java. Enter the text of Listing 17.1 into the file and save it when you're done.

LISTING 17.1   The Full Text of `SalutonApplet.java`

```
 1: import java.awt.*;
 2:
 3: public class SalutonApplet extends javax.swing.JApplet {
 4:     String greeting;
 5:
 6:     public void init() {
 7:         greeting = "Saluton mondo!";
 8:     }
 9:
10:     public void paint(Graphics screen) {
11:         Graphics2D screen2D = (Graphics2D)screen;
12:         screen2D.drawString(greeting, 25, 50);
13:     }
14: }
```

17

This applet does not need to use the `start()`, `stop()`, or `destroy()` methods, so they are not included in the program. Compile the program with the `javac` compiler tool, if you're an SDK user, or another tool.

Drawing in an Applet Window

Text is displayed in an applet window by using the `drawString()` method of the `Graphics2D` class, which draws text in a graphical user interface component.

The `drawString()` method is similar in function to the `System.out.println()` method that displays information to the system's standard output device.

Before you can use the `drawString()` method, you must have a `Graphics2D` object that represents the applet window.

The `paint()` method of all applets includes a `Graphics` object as its only argument. This object represents the applet window, so it can be used to create a `Graphics2D` object that also represents the window.

As you might suspect, you use casting to convert a `Graphics` object into a `Graphics2D` object. `Graphics2D` is a subclass of `Graphics`. The following statement casts a `Graphics` object named `screen` into a `Graphics2D` object named `screen2D`.

```
Graphics2D screen2D = (Graphics2D)screen;
```

You'll see a statement like this often in the `paint()` method of applets.

When you have created a `Graphics2D` object like this, you can call its `drawString()` method to display text on the area represented by the object.

The following three arguments are sent to drawString():

- The text to display, which can be several different strings and variables pasted together with the + operator
- The x position (in an (x,y) coordinate system) where the string should be displayed
- The y position where the string should be displayed

The (x,y) coordinate system in an applet is used with several methods. It begins with the (0,0) point in the upper-left corner of the applet window. Figure 17.1 shows how the (x,y) coordinate system works in conjunction with the statement on Line 12 of SalutonApplet.java.

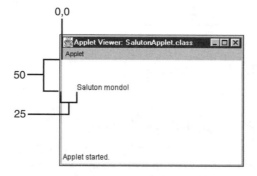

FIGURE 17.1

Drawing a string to an (x,y) position.

Testing the SalutonApplet Program

Although you have compiled the SalutonApplet program into a class file, you cannot run it using a Java interpreter such as java. If you do, you'll get an error message looking like this:

```
Exception in thread "main" java.lang.NoSuchMethodError: main
```

The error occurs because a Java interpreter runs applications by calling its main() method. Applets don't include this method. Instead, to run an applet, you need to create a Web page that loads the applet. To create a Web page, open up a new file on your word processor and call it SalutonApplet.html. Enter Listing 17.2 and then save the file.

LISTING 17.2   The Full Text of SalutonApplet.html

```
1: <html>
2: <head>
3: <title>Saluton Mondo!</title>
4: </head>
5: <body bgcolor="#000000" text="#FF00FF">
```

LISTING 17.2 continued

```
 6: <center>
 7: This a Java applet:<br>
 8: <applet code="SalutonApplet.class" height=150 width=300>
 9: You need a Java-enabled browser to see this.
10: </applet>
11: </body>
12: </html>
```

All applets you write can be tested with the `appletviewer` tool that comes with the Software Development Kit. You can see the output of the `SalutonApplet` applet by typing the following:

```
appletviewer SalutonApplet.html
```

One thing to note about `appletviewer` is that it only runs the applets that are included in a Web page, and does not handle any of the other elements, such as text and images.

Applets can also be loaded by Web browsers, if they are equipped with the Java Plug-in. To attempt this at a command line, type the following command:

```
SalutonApplet.html
```

You can also choose File, Open from the browser's menu to find and open the page.

Figure 17.2 shows a screen capture of `SalutonApplet` loaded by Internet Explorer.

FIGURE 17.2

The `SalutonApplet` *program running on a Web page.*

If you can't get this applet to run in Internet Explorer or another Web browser, the most likely reason is that the browser needs the Java Plug-in.

The Java Plug-in

Because there are now five major versions of the Java language, one of the things you must concern yourself with as an applet programmer is the version your audience can handle.

None of the leading Web browsers offer built-in support for Java 2, and that doesn't seem likely to change. Netscape Navigator, Microsoft Internet Explorer, and Opera include Java interpreters that support Java 1.0 fully and some of the features of Java 1.1.

Applet programmers who want their programs to run on Navigator and Internet Explorer can use Java 1.0. This provides the widest possible audience, but Java 1.0 is a much simpler language than Java 2, lacking many of the best features of the language, including Swing, JavaBeans, improved event-handling, JDBC, and other changes that reflect three years of feedback from Java developers.

To make it possible for Java 2 applets to be written for current browsers, Sun Microsystems offers the Java Plug-in, a substitute for each browser's built-in interpreter.

A *plug-in* is a program that works in conjunction with a Web browser to expand its functionality. Plug-ins handle a type of data that the browser normally could not handle. For example, Apple offers a plug-in to display QuickTime movies and Macromedia has released a plug-in to run Flash animation files.

If you installed the Software Development Kit, you were given a chance to install the Java Plug-in at the same time.

The Java Plug-in runs Java applets in place of the Web browser's Java interpreter. Once the Java Plug-in is installed, all future Java 2 applets will run automatically if they specify that the Plug-in should be used to run them.

The plug-in is part of the Java Runtime Environment, which can be downloaded at no cost from Sun's Java site at `http://java.sun.com/getjava/`.

The HTML tags you have learned about up to this point do not specify that the Java Plug-in be used to run applets. Browsers that are not equipped with the Java Plug-in will attempt to run the applet with their own built-in Java interpreters and fail, displaying an error message in the browser's status line.

To make an applet run on the Java Plug-in, you can use a different HTML tag to load the applet: `<OBJECT>`.

The <OBJECT> Tag

The <OBJECT> tag is used for all objects that can run as part of a Web page, including applets and other types of interactive programs. It is supported by versions 4.0 and higher of Netscape Navigator, Microsoft Internet Explorer, and the SDK appletviewer.

The tag uses several of the same attributes as the <APPLET> tag, including WIDTH, HEIGHT, ALIGN, HSPACE, and VSPACE, but not all of them. One that's missing is the CODE attribute. Instead, the <OBJECT> tag requires a new <PARAM> tag that takes the following format:

```
<PARAM NAME="Code" VALUE="AppletClassname">
```

If the name of your applet's main class file is Zork.class, the tag would be the following:

```
<PARAM NAME="Code" VALUE="Zork.class">
```

The <PARAM> tag is used to specify parameters, which are the applet's version of command-line arguments. You can have several <PARAM> tags within an applet, and all of them must be located between the beginning <OBJECT> tag and the ending </OBJECT> tag.

The <OBJECT> tag also requires the classid attribute, which identifies the Java Plug-in as the interpreter that should be used to run the applet. This attribute should always have the following value:

```
clsid:8AD9C840-044E-11D1-B3E9-00805F499D93
```

This value is a string that identifies the Java Plug-in. You'll learn more about how to use it later today.

The <OBJECT> tag also has a CODEBASE attribute that contains a Web page address for the Java Plug-in. For the current version of Java 2 (version 1.4), the CODEBASE attribute should have this value:

```
http://java.sun.com/products/plugin/autodl/jinstall-1_4_0-win.cab
```

> Later this hour, you'll learn about the <PARAM> tag and create an applet that uses several parameters.

Listing 17.3 contains a Web page that uses the <OBJECT> tag to load an applet.

17

LISTING 17.3   The Full Text of SalutonObject.html

```
 1: <html>
 2: <head>
 3: <title>Saluton Mondo!</title>
 4: </head>
 5: <body bgcolor="#000000" text="#FF00FF">
 6: <center>
 7: This a Java applet:<br>
 8: <object height=150 width=300
 9: classid="clsid:8AD9C840-044E-11D1-B3E9-00805F499D93"
10: codebase="http://java.sun.com/products/plugin/autodl/jinstall-1_4_0-
➥win.cab">
11:     <param name="Code" value="SalutonApplet.class">
12: You need a Java-enabled browser to see this.
13: </object>
14: </body>
15: </html>
```

If you load this page with a browser that supports the <OBJECT> tag, two things might happen:

- If the browser is equipped with the Java Plug-in, it runs the applet.

- If the browser is not equipped with the Java Plug-in, a dialog box opens asking if the user wants to download and install it, as shown in Figure 17.3.

FIGURE 17.3

Choosing whether to install the Java Plug-in.

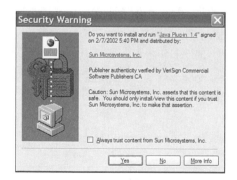

After you have installed the Java Plug-in, it runs all applets as if it was the browser's built-in Java interpreter.

Sending Parameters from a Web Page

Now that you have had some experience writing computer programs, you might be feeling one of the strongest emotions of the programmer: compiler angst. Even though it takes no more than 15 seconds to compile most programs, that time can seem interminable when you're debugging a program. Write, save, compile, Aargh—an error! Write, save, compile, Aargh! Write, save, compile, Aargh!... As this vicious cycle repeats itself, it's easy to become world-weary as a program is compiled and recompiled.

One of the driving forces behind parameter use in Java applets is the fear and loathing of compilation. Parameters enable you to change elements of an applet without editing or recompiling anything. They also make the program more useful.

Parameters are stored as part of the Web page that contains an applet. They are created using the HTML tag <PARAM> and its two attributes: NAME and VALUE. You can have more than one <PARAM> tag with an applet, but all of them must be between the opening <APPLET> tag and the closing </APPLET> tag (or the <OBJECT> and </OBJECT> tags, which also support parameters). The following is an <APPLET> tag that includes several parameters:

```
<APPLET CODE="ScrollingHeadline.class" HEIGHT=50 WIDTH=400>
<PARAM NAME="Headline1" VALUE="Dewey defeats Truman">
<PARAM NAME="Headline2" VALUE="Stix nix hix pix">
<PARAM NAME="Headline3" VALUE="Man bites dog">
</APPLET>
```

This example could be used to send news headlines to an applet that scrolls them across the screen. Because news changes all the time, the only way to create a program of this kind is with parameters. No other solution would work; just imagine how long it would take to recompile a Java program every time a National Basketball Association star player ran afoul of the law.

You use the NAME attribute to give the parameter a name. This attribute is comparable to giving a variable a name. The VALUE attribute gives the named parameter a value.

Receiving Parameters in the Applet

You have to do something in your Java program to retrieve the parameters on the Web page or they will be ignored. The getParameter() method of the JApplet class retrieves a parameter from a <PARAM> tag on a Web page. The parameter name, which is specified with the NAME attribute on the page, is used as an argument to getParameter(). The following is an example of getParameter() in action:

```
String display1 = getParameter("Headline1");
```

The getParameter() method returns all parameters as strings, so you have to convert them to other types as needed. If you want to use a parameter as an integer, you could use statements such as the following:

```
int speed;
String speedParam = getParameter("SPEED");
if (speedParam != null)
    speed = Integer.parseInt(speedParam);
```

This example sets the speed variable by using the speedParam string. You have to test for null strings before setting speed because the parseInt() method cannot work with a null string. When you try to retrieve a parameter with getParameter() that was not included on a Web page with the <PARAM> tag, it will be sent as null, which is the value of an empty string.

Workshop: Handling Parameters in an Applet

The next project you'll undertake has little practical value, except perhaps as a taunting device. The ShowWeight applet takes a person's weight and displays it under several different units. The applet takes two parameters: a weight in pounds, and the name of the person who weighs that amount. The weight is used to figure out the person's weight in ounces, kilograms, and metric tons, all of which are displayed.

Create a new file with your word processor and give it the name ShowWeight.java. Enter Listing 17.4 into the file. Then save and compile the file.

LISTING 17.4   The Full Text of ShowWeight.java

```
1: import java.awt.*;
2:
3: public class ShowWeight extends javax.swing.JApplet {
4:     float lbs = (float)0;
5:     float ozs;
6:     float kgs;
7:     float metricTons;
8:     String name = "somebody";
9:
10:     public void init() {
11:         String lbsValue = getParameter("weight");
12:         if (lbsValue != null) {
13:             Float lbsTemp = Float.valueOf(lbsValue);
14:             lbs = lbsTemp.floatValue();
15:         }
```

LISTING 17.4   continued

```
16:          String personValue = getParameter("person");
17:          if (personValue != null)
18:              name = personValue;
19:
20:          ozs = (float)(lbs * 16);
21:          kgs = (float)(lbs / 2.204623);
22:          metricTons = (float)(lbs / 2204.623);
23:      }
24:
25:      public void paint(Graphics screen) {
26:          Graphics2D screen2D = (Graphics2D) screen;
27:          screen2D.drawString("Studying the weight of " + name, 5, 30);
28:          screen2D.drawString("In pounds: " + lbs, 55, 50);
29:          screen2D.drawString("In ounces: " + ozs, 55, 70);
30:          screen2D.drawString("In kilograms: " + kgs, 55, 90);
31:          screen2D.drawString("In metric tons: " + metricTons, 55, 110);
32:      }
33: }
```

17

The init() method is where the two parameters are loaded into the applet. Because they come from the Web page as strings, they must be converted into the form you need: a floating-point number for the lbs variable, and a string for name. Converting a string to a floating-point number requires two steps: converting the string to a Float object and then converting that object to a variable of the type float.

> As you learned with strings, objects and variables are treated differently in Java programs, and there are different things you can do with them. The reason there is a Float object and a float variable type is so you can use a floating-point number as either an object or a variable. The Float object class also has useful methods, such as valueOf() and floatValue(), that you can use to convert floating-point numbers into different types of variables.

Lines 20–22 are used to convert the lbs variable into different units of measure. Each of these statements has (float) in front of the conversion equation. This is used to cast the result of the equation into a floating-point number.

The paint() method of the applet uses the drawString() method of the Graphics2D class to display a line of text onscreen. The paint() method has three arguments: the text to display, and the x and y positions where the text should be shown.

Before you can test the `ShowWeight` applet, you need to create a Web page that contains the applet. Open up a new file on your word processor and name it `ShowWeight.html`. Enter Listing 17.5 and save it when you're done.

LISTING 17.5   The Full Text of `ShowWeight.html`

```
1: <applet code="ShowWeight.class" height=170 width=210>
2: <param name="person" value="Konishiki">
3: <param name="weight" value=605>
4: </applet>
```

Use a Web browser equipped with the Java Plug-in to see the `ShowWeight` applet. This demonstration uses Konishiki as its example because the American-born sumo wrestling champion weighs in at more than 605 pounds, making him the largest of these immodest, bikini-wearing behemoths. You can substitute anyone whose weight is either exemplary or well-known. Figure 17.4 shows an example of output from the applet. As you can see, Konishiki's workout regimen doesn't include a lot of fat-free SnackWell's Devil's Food Cakes.

FIGURE 17.4

The `ShowWeight` applet loaded with Internet Explorer.

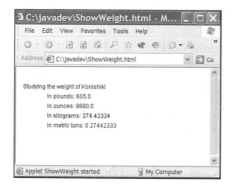

To make the applet display a different name along with a different value for the `"weight"` parameter, all you have to change is the `ShowWeight.html` file. The applet itself will continue to work correctly.

Summary

Most of the hours in this book focus on applications, primarily because most Java programmers today don't do a lot of work designing applets for the World Wide Web.

Writing applets is a good way for beginners to develop their skills as Java programmers for the following reasons:

- Applets are usually smaller in scope, making their creation a less daunting task.

- You can find thousands of sample applets on the World Wide Web, including many with the source file available from which to learn.

- You can make applets available to a global audience at low to no cost through the Web, exposing your work to more people who can offer comments and suggestions.

Q&A

Q Is there a reason why the CODEBASE attribute should be used in an <APPLET> or <OBJECT> tag?

A If all Java programs are grouped into their own subfolder, as indicated by CODEBASE, this structure might improve the way a Web site is organized, but there's no other reason why using CODEBASE is better than omitting it. The choice is a matter of personal preference.

Q What happens if the height and width specified for an applet don't leave enough room for the information that is displayed in the paint() method?

A The information will be drawn offscreen, beyond the edges of the applet window, and won't be visible at any point while the applet runs. Choosing the right dimensions for an applet is largely a matter of trial-and-error until you find the right size for both the HEIGHT and WIDTH attributes of the <APPLET> tag. You can't resize an applet window from within a Java program, so the only way to control its size is by using the HEIGHT and WIDTH attributes. Fortunately, you can change the Web page's HTML without having to recompile the Java program.

17

Quiz

The following questions test your knowledge of applets.

Questions

1. What type of argument is used with the paint() method?

   a. A Graphics object

   b. A Graphics2D object

   c. None

2. Which method is handled right before an applet finishes running?

    a. `decline()`

    b. `destroy()`

    c. `defenestrate()`

3. Why can't all variables needed in an applet be created inside the `init()` method?

    a. The scope of the variables would be limited to the method only.

    b. Federal legislation prohibits it.

    c. They can be created there without any problems.

Answers

1. a. The `Graphics` object keeps track of the behavior and attributes needed to display things on-screen in the applet window. You might create a `Graphics2D` object inside the method, but it isn't sent as an argument.

2. b.

3. a. Variables that are used in more than one method of a class should be created right after the class statement but before any methods begin.

Activities

You can apply your applet programming knowledge with the following activities:

- Write an applet in which the text that is displayed moves each time the applet window is repainted.

- Install the Java Plug-in with your preferred browser, if you're on a Windows or Solaris system, and try the sample applets provided from Sun's Java Plug-in page.

To see a Java program that implements the first activity, visit the book's Web site at `http://www.java24hours.com`.

HOUR 18

Handling Errors in a Program

No subject in this book is less popular than the one you're about to tackle: errors.

Errors—the various bugs, blunders, typos, and other problems that stop a program from running successfully—are a natural part of the software development process. "Natural" is probably the kindest word that has ever been used to describe them—in my own Java programming, when I can't find the cause of an elusive error that keeps my program from working, I use words that would make a gangsta rapper blush.

Some errors are flagged by the compiler and prevent you from creating a class. Others are noted by the interpreter in response to a problem that keeps it from running successfully.

There are two kinds of problems you will encounter in Java:

- Exceptions—Events that signal an unusual circumstance has taken place as a program runs
- Errors—Events that signal the interpreter is having problems that may be unrelated to your program

During this hour, we'll explore exceptions as the following topics are discussed:

- How to use methods that cause exceptions
- How to respond to exceptions in your Java programs
- How to create methods that ignore an exception, leaving it for another class to handle
- How to create your own exceptions

You'll also learn about a new feature of version 1.4 that helps keep errors out of your programs: assertions.

Exceptions

Although you are just learning about them now, you have probably become well-acquainted with exceptions during the previous hours of this book. These errors turn up when you write a Java program that compiles successfully but encounters a problem when it runs.

For example, a common programming mistake is to refer to an element of an array that doesn't exist, as in the following statements:

```
String[] greek = { "Alpha", "Beta", "Gamma" };
System.out.println(greek[3]);
```

In this example, the `String` array has three elements. Because the first element in an array is numbered 0 rather than 1, the first element is `greek[0]`, the second is `greek[1]` and the third is `greek[2]`. The statement to display the contents of `greek[3]` is erroneous, because that element does not exist.

The above statements will compile successfully, but when you run the program, the Java interpreter will halt with a message such as the following:

```
Exception in thread "main" java.lang.ArrayIndexOutBoundsException
        at SampleProgram.main(SampleProgram.java:4)
```

This message indicates that the application has generated an exception, which the interpreter made note of by displaying an error message and stopping the program.

This error message includes a reference to a class called `ArrayIndexOutOfBoundsException` in the `java.lang` package. This class is an *exception*, an object that is created to make note of an exceptional circumstance that has taken place in a Java program.

When a Java class encounters an exception, it alerts users of the class to the error. In this example, the user of the class is the Java interpreter.

Two terms that are used to describe this process are *throw* and *catch*. Classes and methods can throw exceptions to alert others that they have occurred. These exceptions can be caught by other classes, methods, or the Java interpreter.

All exceptions are subclasses of `Exception`, another class in the `java.lang` package. The `ArrayIndexOutOfBoundsException` does what you would expect—it lets you know you have used an array element that isn't within the array's boundaries.

There are hundreds of exceptions in Java. Many of them indicate a problem that can be fixed with a change in your program, such as the array exception. These are comparable to compiler errors—once you correct the situation, you don't have to concern yourself with the exception any longer.

Other exceptions must be dealt with every time a program runs by using five new statements: `try`, `catch`, `finally`, `throw`, and `throws`.

Catching Exceptions in a `try-catch` Block

Up to this point, you have dealt with exceptions by fixing the problem that caused them. There are times you either can't deal with an exception like this or want to handle them within a Java class.

As an introduction to why this is useful, enter the short Java application in Listing 18.1 and save it as `SumNumbers.java`.

LISTING 18.1 The Full Text of `SumNumbers.java`

```
1: class SumNumbers {
2:     public static void main(String[] arguments) {
3:         float sum = 0;
4:         for (int i = 0; i < arguments.length; i++)
5:             sum = sum + Float.parseFloat(arguments[i]);
6:         System.out.println("Those numbers add up to " + sum);
7:     }
8: }
```

You can compile this application successfully. The SumNumbers application takes one or more numbers as command-line arguments, adds all of them up, and displays the total.

Because all command-line arguments are represented by strings in a Java application, the program must convert them into floating-point numbers before adding them together. The Float.parseFloat() class method in Line 5 takes care of this, adding the converted number to a variable named sum.

Run the application with the following command (or use another Java tool where you can specify the same seven numeric arguments):

```
java SumNumbers 8 6 7 5 3 0 9
```

The application will display the following output:

OUTPUT   Those numbers add up to 38.0

Run the program several times with different numbers as arguments. It should handle all of them successfully, which might make you wonder what this has to do with exceptions.

To see the relevance, run the SumNumbers application with the following command:

```
java SumNumbers 1 3 5x
```

The third argument in this example contains a typo—there shouldn't be an x after the number 5. The SumNumbers application has no way to know this is a mistake, so it tries to add 5x to the other numbers, causing the following exception to be displayed:

```
Exception in thread "main" java.lang.NumberFormatException: 5x
        at java.lang.FloatingDecimal.readJavaFormatString(Unknown source)
        at java.lang.Float.parseFloat(Unknown source)
        at SumNumbers.main(SumNumbers:5)
```

This message is informative to the programmer developing the application, but it's not something you would want a user to see. Java programs can take care of their own exceptions by using a try-catch block.

This block statement takes the following form:

```
try {
    // statements that might cause the exception
} catch (Exception e) {
    // what to do when the exception occurs
}
```

A try-catch block should be used with any exception that you want a program to handle. The Exception object that appears in the catch statement should be one of two things:

- The class of the exception that might occur
- A superclass of several different kinds of exceptions that might occur

The try section of the try-catch block should contain the statement or statements that might throw an exception. In the SumNumbers application, the call to the Float.parseFloat() method in Line 5 will throw a NumberFormatException whenever it is used to convert a non-numeric string to a floating-point value.

To improve the SumNumbers application so that it never stops running with this kind of error, you can use a try-catch block that deals with this exception.

Open your text editor and create an application called NewSumNumbers.java from Listing 18.2.

LISTING 18.2   The Full Text of NewSumNumbers.java

```
 1: class NewSumNumbers {
 2:     public static void main(String[] arguments) {
 3:         float sum = 0;
 4:         for (int i = 0; i < arguments.length; i++) {
 5:             try {
 6:                 sum = sum + Float.parseFloat(arguments[i]);
 7:             } catch (NumberFormatException e) {
 8:                 System.out.println(arguments[i] + " is not a number.");
 9:             }
10:         }
11:         System.out.println("Those numbers add up to " + sum);
12:     }
13: }
```

After you save and compile the application, run it with a non-numeric command-line argument along with a few numbers, such as the following:

```
java NewSumNumbers 1 3 5x
```

Running it with these arguments produces the following output:

OUTPUT
```
5x is not a number
Those numbers add up to 4.0
```

The try-catch block in Lines 5–9 deals with NumberFormatException errors that are thrown by the Float.parseFloat() method. These exceptions are caught within the NewSumNumbers class, which displays an error message for any argument that is not a number.

Because the exception is handled within the class, the Java interpreter does not display an error message when something like 5x is used as a command-line argument.

You can often deal with problems related to user input and other unexpected data by using try-catch blocks.

> You can also use try and catch to deal with errors that could be fixed by making some changes to your program, such as the ArrayIndexOutOfBoundsException problem that was described earlier this hour. This isn't recommended—the easiest solution is to change your program so the error never occurs.

Catching Several Different Exceptions

try-catch blocks can be used to handle several different kinds of exceptions, even if they are thrown by different statements.

Listing 18.3 contains an application called DivideNumbers that takes two integer arguments from the command-line and uses them in a division expression.

This application must be able to deal with two potential problems in user input:

- Non-numeric arguments
- Division by zero

LISTING 18.3   The Full Text of DivideNumbers.java

```
 1: class DivideNumbers {
 2:     public static void main(String[] arguments) {
 3:         if (arguments.length == 2) {
 4:             int result = 0;
 5:             try {
 6:                 result = Integer.parseInt(arguments[0]) /
 7:                     Integer.parseInt(arguments[1]);
 8:                 System.out.println(arguments[0] + " divided by " +
 9:                     arguments[1] + " equals " + result);
10:             } catch (NumberFormatException e) {
11:                 System.out.println("Both arguments must be numbers.");
12:             } catch (ArithmeticException e) {
13:                 System.out.println("You cannot divide by zero.");
14:             }
15:         }
16:     }
17: }
```

Compile the application and try it out with some integers, floating-point numbers, and non-numeric arguments.

The `if` statement in Line 3 checks to make sure that two arguments were sent to the application. If not, the program exits without displaying anything.

The `DivideNumbers` application performs integer division, so the result will be an integer. This isn't going to be as accurate as division using floating-point numbers—in integer division, 5 divided by 2 equals 2, not 2.5.

If you use a floating-point or non-numeric argument, a `NumberFormatException` will be thrown by Lines 6–7 and caught by Lines 10–11.

If you use an integer as the first argument and a zero as the second argument, a `ArithmeticExpression` will be thrown in Lines 6–7 and caught by Lines 12–13.

Handling Something After an Exception

When you are dealing with multiple exceptions by using `try` and `catch`, there are times when you want the program to do something at the end of the block whether an exception occurred or not.

You can handle this by using a `try-catch-finally` block, which takes the following form:

```
try {
    // statements that might cause the exception
} catch (Exception e) {
    // what to do when the exception occurs
} finally {
    // statements to execute no matter what
}
```

The statement or statements within the `finally` section of the block will be executed after everything else in the block, even if an exception occurs.

One place this is useful is in a program that reads data from a file on disk, which you will do in Hour 20, "Reading and Writing Files." There are several ways an exception can occur when you are accessing data—the file might not exist, a disk error could occur, and so on. If the statements to read the disk are in a `try` section and errors are handled in a `catch` section, you can close the file in the `finally` section. This makes sure that the file will be closed whether or not an exception was thrown as it was read.

18

Throwing Exceptions

When you call a method of another class, that class can control how the method is used by throwing exceptions.

As you make use of the classes in the Java class library, the compiler will often display a message such as the following:

```
NetReader.java:14: unreported exception java.net.MalformedURLException; must be
caught or declared to be thrown
```

Whenever you see an error stating that an exception "must be caught or declared to be thrown," it indicates that the method you are trying to use throws an exception.

Any class that calls these methods, such as an application that you write, must do one of the following things:

- Handle the exception with a `try-catch` block.
- Throw the exception.
- Handle the exception with a `try-catch` block and then throw it.

Up to this point in the hour, you have seen how to handle exceptions. If you would like to throw an exception after handling it, you can use a `throw` statement followed by the exception object to throw.

The following statements handle a `NumberFormatException` error in a `catch` block and then throw the exception:

```
try {
    principal = Float.parseFloat(loanText) * 1.1F;
} catch (NumberFormatException e) {
    System.out.println(arguments[i] + " is not a number.");
    throw e;
}
```

When you throw an exception in this manner, it generally means that you have not done everything that needs to be done to take care of the exception.

An example of where this might be useful: Consider a hypothetical program called `CreditCardChecker`, an application that verifies credit card purchases. This application uses a class called `CheckDatabase`, which has the following job:

1. Make a connection to the credit card lender's computer.
2. Ask that computer if the customer's credit card number is valid.
3. Ask the computer if the customer has enough credit to make the purchase.

As the CheckDatabase class is doing its job, what happens if the credit card lender's computer doesn't answer the phone at all? This kind of error is exactly the kind of thing that the try-catch block was designed for, and it is used within CheckDatabase to handle connection errors.

If the CheckDatabase class handles this error by itself, the CreditCardChecker application won't know that the exception took place at all. This isn't a good idea—the application should know when a connection cannot be made so it can report this to the person using the application.

One way to notify the CreditCardChecker application is for CheckDatabase to catch the exception in a catch block, then throw it again with a throw statement. The exception will be thrown in CheckDatabase, which must then deal with it like any other exception.

Exception handling is a way that classes can communicate with each other in the event of an error or other unusual circumstance.

Ignoring Exceptions

The last technique that will be covered today is the laziest: how to ignore an exception completely.

A method in a class can ignore exceptions by using a throws clause as part of the method definition.

The following method throws a MalformedURLException, an error that can occur when you are working with World Wide Web addresses in a Java program:

```
public void loadURL(String address) throws MalformedURLException {
    URL page = new URL(address);
    loadWebPage(page);
}
```

The second statement in this example, URL page = new URL(address); creates a URL object, which represents an address on the Web. The constructor method of the URL class throws a MalformedURLException to indicate that an invalid address was used, so no object can be constructed. The following statement would cause one of these exceptions to be thrown:

```
URL source = new URL("http:www.java24hours.com");
```

The string http:www.java24hours.com is not a valid URL. It's missing some punctuation—two slash characters (//).

Because the loadURL() method has been declared to throw MalformedURLException errors, it does not have to deal with them inside the method. The responsibility for handling this exception falls to any class that calls the loadURL() method.

Assertions

Sun Microsystems did something in Java 2 version 1.4 that hasn't happened often in the history of the language: It added a new keyword, assert.

The assert keyword enables Java programmers to use assertions, a technique that's supposed to improve the reliability of software. An assertion is a Boolean true-or-false expression that represents something that should be true at that spot in the program. Here's an example:

```
assert speed > 55;
```

This statement asserts that the speed variable has a value greater than 55. It's another way for a programmer to say, "I expect speed to be greater than 55 at this position, and if it isn't, my program would be completely FUBAR."

> FUBAR is an acronym popular among computer programmers that means "fouled up beyond all recognition" or "fouled up beyond all repair." A saltier version that uses a different F word is even more popular.

Assertions are a way to ensure that a program is running as expected.

The assert keyword must be followed by something that produces a Boolean value: an expression, a boolean, or a method that returns a boolean. Three examples:

```
assert pointX = 0;
```

```
assert endOfFileReached;
```

```
assert network.noLongerConnected();
```

If the expression used with the assert keyword is false, an AssertionError exception will be thrown. You can make these errors more meaningful by specifying an error message in an assert statement. Add a colon and text at the end, as in this example:

```
assert temperature > 2200 : "Core breach in Sector 12!";
```

If you're using the SDK interpreter, here's how it responds to an AssertionError exception:

```
Exception in thread "main" java.lang.AssertionError: Core breach in Sector 12!
    at Nuke.power(Nuke.java:1924)
```

Assertions are offered in Java 1.4, but are turned off by default in the SDK (and presumably other tools as well).

SDK users must use command-line arguments to turn on assertion support. To compile a class that contains `assert` statements, use the `-source 1.4` option, as in the following example:

```
javac -source 1.4 Nuke.java
```

The `-source 1.4` option causes the compiler to support assertions in the class file (or files) that it produces. An error will result if you try to compile a program that contains `assert` statements but do not use this option.

You must also enable assertions when running a Java class with the SDK interpreter. The easiest way to do this is to use the `-ea` argument, which enables assertions for all classes (except those that are part of the Java class library):

```
java -ea Nuke
```

To enable assertions only in one class, follow `-ea` with a colon and the name of the class, as in this example:

```
java -ea:Nuke Nuke
```

To enable assertions only in one package, follow `-ea` with a colon and the name of the package:

```
java -ea:com.prefect.power Nuke
```

18

Workshop: Throwing and Catching Exceptions

For this hour's workshop, you will create a class that uses exceptions to tell another class about an error that has taken place.

The classes in this workshop are `HomePage`, a class that represents a personal home page on the World Wide Web, and `PageCatalog`, an application that catalogs these pages.

Enter the text of Listing 18.4 in your text editor, saving it as `HomePage.java` when you're done.

LISTING 18.4 The Full Text of `HomePage.java`

```
1: import java.net.*;
2:
3: public class HomePage {
4:     String owner;
5:     URL address;
6:     String category = "none";
7:
8:     public HomePage(String inOwner, String inAddress)
9:         throws MalformedURLException {
10:
11:         owner = inOwner;
12:         address = new URL(inAddress);
13:     }
14:
15:     public HomePage(String inOwner, String inAddress, String inCategory)
16:         throws MalformedURLException {
17:
18:         this(inOwner, inAddress);
19:         category = inCategory;
20:     }
21: }
```

Save the file and compile it, producing a `HomePage` class you can use in other programs. This class represents personal Web pages on the Web. It has three variables: `address`, a `URL` object representing the address of the page; `owner`, the person who owns the page; and `category`, a short comment describing the page's primary subject matter.

Like any class that creates `URL` objects, `HomePage` must either deal with `MalformedURLException` errors in a `try-catch` block or declare that it is ignoring these errors.

The class takes the latter course, as shown in Lines 8–9 and Lines 15–16. By using `throws` in the two constructor methods, `HomePage` removes the need to deal with `MalformedURLException` errors in any way.

To create an application that uses the `HomePage` class, return to your text editor and enter Listing 18.5. Save the file as `PageCatalog.java`.

LISTING 18.5 The Full Text of `PageCatalog.java`

```
1: import java.net.*;
2:
3: public class PageCatalog {
4:     public static void main(String[] arguments) {
```

LISTING 18.5   continued

```
 5:        HomePage[] catalog = new HomePage[5];
 6:        try {
 7:            catalog[0] = new HomePage("Carl Steadman",
 8:                "http://www.freedonia.com/~carl", "angst");
 9:            catalog[1] = new HomePage("Greg Knauss",
10:                "http://www.eod.com", "humor");
11:            catalog[2] = new HomePage("Rogers Cadenhead",
12:                "http://workbench.cadenhead.info", "programming");
13:            catalog[3] = new HomePage("Joshua Marshall",
14:                "http://www.talkingpointsmemo.com", "politics");
15:            catalog[4] = new HomePage("Matt Haughey",
16:                "a.wholelottanothing.org");
17:            for (int i = 0; i < catalog.length; i++)
18:                System.out.println(catalog[i].owner + ": " +
19:                    catalog[i].address + " — " +
20:                    catalog[i].category);
21:        } catch (MalformedURLException e) {
22:            System.out.println("Error: " + e.getMessage());
23:        }
24:    }
25: }
```

18

When you run the compiled application, the following output will be displayed:

OUTPUT   `Error: no protocol: a.wholelottanothing.org`

The `PageCatalog` application creates an array of `HomePage` objects and then displays the contents of the array. Each `HomePage` object is created using up to three arguments:

- The name of the page's owner
- The address of the page (as a `String`, not a URL)
- The category of the page

The third argument is optional, and it is not used in Lines 15–16.

The constructor methods of the `HomePage` class throw `MalformedURLException` errors when they receive a string that cannot be converted into a valid URL object. These exceptions are handled in the `PageCatalog` application by using a `try-catch` block.

To correct the problem causing the "no protocol" error, edit Line 16 so that the string begins with the text `"http://"` like the other Web addresses in Lines 7–14.

Carl Steadman: http://www.freedonia.com/~carl — angst
Greg Knauss: http://www.eod.com — humor
Rogers Cadenhead: http://workbench.cadenhead.info — programming
Joshua Marshall: http://www.talkingpointsmemo.com — politics
Matt Haughey: http://a.wholelottanothing.org — none

Summary

Now that you have put Java's exception handling techniques to use, I hope the subject of errors is a little more popular than it was at the beginning of the hour.

You can do a lot with these techniques:

- Catch an exception and deal with it
- Ignore an exception, leaving it for another class or the Java interpreter to take care of
- Catch several different exceptions in the same try-catch block
- Throw your own exception

Managing exceptions in your Java programs makes them more reliable, more versatile, and easier to use, because you don't display any cryptic error messages to people who are running your software.

Once you're comfortable handling errors, you can even use assertions to create more of them—as a safeguard against the times when your assumptions about a program are not correct.

Q&A

Q Is it possible to create your own exceptions?

A You can create your own exceptions easily by making them a subclass of an existing exception, such as Exception, the superclass of all exceptions. In a subclass of Exception, there are only two methods you might want to override: Exception() with no arguments and Exception() with a String as an argument. In the latter, the string should be a message describing the error that has occurred.

Q Why doesn't this hour cover how to throw and catch errors in addition to exceptions?

A Java divides problems into Errors and Exceptions because they differ in severity. Exceptions are less severe, so they are something that should be dealt with in your programs using try-catch or throws. Errors, on the other hand, are more serious and can't be dealt with adequately in a program.

Two examples of these errors are stack overflows and out-of-memory errors. These can cause the Java interpreter to crash, and there's no way you can fix them in your own program as the interpreter runs it.

Quiz

Although this hour is literally filled with errors, see if you can answer the following questions about them without making any errors of your own.

Questions

1. How many exceptions can a single catch statement handle?

    a. Only one

    b. Several different exceptions

    c. This answer intentionally left blank

2. When will the statements inside a finally section be run?

    a. After a try-catch block that has ended with an exception

    b. After a try-catch block that has ended without an exception

    c. Both

3. With all this talk about throwing and catching, what do the Texas Rangers need to do in the off-season?

    a. Get some more starting pitching

    b. Sign a left-handed power-hitting outfielder who can reach the short porch in right

    c. Bring in some new middle relievers

Answers

1. b. An Exception object in the catch statement can handle all exceptions of its own class and its subclasses.

2. b. The statement or statements in a finally section always are executed after the rest of a try-catch block, whether or not an exception has occurred.

3. a. Every answer is correct, but a. is more correct than the others, and will probably be correct for the next 30 years.

18

Activities

To see whether you are an exceptional Java programmer, try to make as few errors as possible in the following activities:

- Modify the `DivideNumbers` application so that it throws any exceptions that it classes, and run the program to see what happens.

- There's a `try-catch` block in the `LottoEvent` class you created in Hour 15, "Responding to User Input." Use this block as a guide to create your own `Sleep` class, which handles `InterruptedException` so other classes like `LottoEvent` don't need to deal with them.

To see Java programs that implement these activities, visit the book's Web site at `http://www.java24hours.com`.

HOUR 19

Creating a Threaded Program

A computer term that is used often to describe the hectic pace of daily life is *multitasking*, which means to do more than one thing at once—such as surfing the Web at your desk while participating in a conference call and using the Buttmaster exercise device to achieve more shapely shanks.

The term multitasking comes from the world of operating systems, where a multitasking computer is one that can run more than one program at a time.

One of the most sophisticated features of the Java language is the ability to write programs that can multitask using objects called threads.

During this hour, you'll learn how to make programs more sophisticated through the use of threads. The following topics will be covered:

- Using an interface with a program
- Creating threads
- Starting, stopping, and pausing threads
- Catching errors

Threads

In a Java program, each of the simultaneous tasks the computer handles is called a thread, and the overall process is called *multithreading*. Threading is useful in animation and many other programs.

Threads are a way to organize a program so that it does more than one thing at a time. Each task that must occur simultaneously is placed in its own thread, and this often is accomplished by implementing each task as a separate class.

Threads are represented by the Thread class and the Runnable interface, which are both part of the java.lang package of classes. Because they belong to this package, you don't have to use an import statement to make them available in your programs.

One of the simplest uses of the Thread class is to slow down how fast a program does something.

Slowing Down a Program

The Thread class has a sleep() method that can be called in any program that should stop running for a short period of time. You will often see this technique used in a program that features animation because it prevents images from being displayed faster than the Java interpreter can handle them.

To use the sleep() method, call Thread.sleep() with the number of milliseconds to pause, as in the following statement:

```
Thread.sleep(5000);
```

The preceding example will cause the Java interpreter to pause for five seconds before doing anything else. If for some reason the interpreter can't pause that long, an InterruptedException will be thrown by the sleep() method.

For this reason, you must deal with this exception in some manner when using the sleep() method. One way to do this is to place the Thread.sleep() statement inside a try-catch block:

```
try {
    Thread.sleep(5000);
} catch (InterruptedException e) {
    // wake up early
}
```

When you want a Java program to handle more than one thing at a time, you must organize the program into threads. Your program can have as many threads as needed, and they can all run simultaneously without affecting each other.

Creating a Thread

A Java class that can be run as a thread is often referred to as a *threaded class*. Although threads can be used to pause a program's execution for a few seconds, they are often used to the opposite reason: to speed up a program. If you put time-consuming tasks in their own threads, the rest of the program runs more quickly. This often is used to prevent a task from slowing down the responsiveness of a program's graphical user interface.

For example, if you have written a Swing application that loads stock market price data from disk and compiles statistics, the most time-consuming task is to load the data from disk. If threads are not used in the application, the program's interface may respond sluggishly as the data is being loaded. This can be extremely frustrating to a user, especially if the person has decided to close the application and return to more pressing matters, like a game of Windows FreeCell.

There are two ways to place a task in its own thread:

- Put the task in a class that implements the `Runnable` interface.
- Put the task in a class that is a subclass of `Thread`.

To support the `Runnable` interface, the `implements` keyword is used when the class is created, as in this example:

```
public class LoadStocks implements Runnable {
    // body of the class
}
```

When a class implements an interface, it indicates that the class supports some kind of additional behavior in addition to its own methods.

Classes that implement the `Runnable` interface must include the `run()` method, which has the following structure:

```
public void run() {
    // body of the method
}
```

The `run()` method should take care of the task that the thread was created to accomplish. In the stock-analysis example, the `run()` method could contain statements to load data from disk and compile statistics based on that data.

When a threaded application is run, the statements in its `run()` method are not executed automatically. Threads can be started and stopped in Java, and a thread won't begin running until you do two things:

19

- Create an object of the threaded class by calling the Thread constructor.

- Start the thread by calling its start() method.

The Thread constructor takes a single argument—the object that contains the thread's run() method. Often, you will use the this keyword as the argument, which indicates that the current class includes the run() method.

Listing 19.1 contains a Java application that displays a sequence of prime numbers in a text area.

LISTING 19.1   The Full Text of FindPrimes.java

```
 1: import java.awt.*;
 2: import javax.swing.*;
 3: import java.awt.event.*;
 4:
 5: class FindPrimes extends JFrame implements Runnable, ActionListener {
 6:     Thread go;
 7:     JLabel howManyLabel = new JLabel("Quantity: ");
 8:     JTextField howMany = new JTextField("400", 10);
 9:     JButton display = new JButton("Display primes");
10:     JTextArea primes = new JTextArea(8, 40);
11:
12:     FindPrimes() {
13:         super("Find Prime Numbers");
14:         setSize(400, 300);
15:         setDefaultCloseOperation(JFrame.EXIT_ON_CLOSE);
16:         Container content = getContentPane();
17:         BorderLayout bord = new BorderLayout();
18:         content.setLayout(bord);
19:         display.addActionListener(this);
20:         JPanel topPanel = new JPanel();
21:         topPanel.add(howManyLabel);
22:         topPanel.add(howMany);
23:         topPanel.add(display);
24:         content.add(topPanel, BorderLayout.NORTH);
25:         primes.setLineWrap(true);
26:         JScrollPane textPane = new JScrollPane(primes);
27:         content.add(textPane, BorderLayout.CENTER);
28:         setVisible(true);
29:     }
30:
31:     public void actionPerformed(ActionEvent evt) {
32:         display.setEnabled(false);
33:         if (go == null) {
34:             go = new Thread(this);
35:             go.start();
36:         }
```

LISTING 19.1 continued

```
37:     }
38:
39:     public void run() {
40:         int quantity = Integer.parseInt(howMany.getText());
41:         int numPrimes = 0;
42:         // candidate: the number that might be prime
43:         int candidate = 2;
44:         primes.append("First " + quantity + " primes:");
45:         while (numPrimes < quantity) {
46:             if (isPrime(candidate)) {
47:                 primes.append(candidate + " ");
48:                 numPrimes++;
49:             }
50:             candidate++;
51:         }
52:     }
53:
54:     public static boolean isPrime(int checkNumber) {
55:         double root = Math.sqrt(checkNumber);
56:         for (int i = 2; i <= root; i++) {
57:             if (checkNumber % i == 0)
58:                 return false;
59:         }
60:         return true;
61:     }
62:
63:     public static void main(String[] arguments) {
64:         FindPrimes fp = new FindPrimes();
65:     }
66: }
```

19

The FindPrimes application displays a text field, a Display Primes button, and a text area, as shown in Figure 19.1.

FIGURE 19.1
Running the
FindPrimes
application.

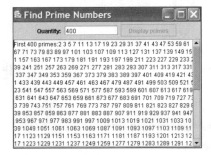

Most of the statements in the application are used to create the graphical user interface or display a sequence of prime numbers. The following statements are used to implement threads in this program:

- Line 5: The Runnable interface is supported in the FindPrimes class.

- Line 6: A Thread object is given a name (go), but isn't created yet.

- Lines 33–36: If the go thread has a value of null, which indicates the thread hasn't been created yet, a new Thread object is created under the name go. The thread is started by calling the thread's start() method, which causes the run() method of the FindPrimes class to be executed.

- Lines 39–52: The run() method looks for a sequence of prime numbers beginning with 2, displaying each one in the primes text area component by calling its append() method. The number of primes in the sequence is determined by the value in the howMany text field.

Working with Threads

You can start a thread by calling its start() method, which may lead you to believe that there's also a stop() method to bring it to a halt.

Although Java includes a stop() method in the Thread class, it has been deprecated. In Java, a *deprecated* element is a class, interface, method, or variable that has been replaced with something that works better. Anything that has been deprecated can still be used, but may be removed from the language entirely in a future version.

> It's a good idea to heed this deprecation warning. Sun Microsystems has deprecated the stop() method because it can cause problems for other threads running in the Java interpreter.

The next project you undertake will show how a thread can be stopped. The remainder of this hour covers an extended project describing the design of a threaded applet. The program you'll be writing will rotate through a list of Web site titles and the addresses used to visit them.

The title of each page and the Web address will be displayed in a continuous cycle. Users will be able to visit the currently displayed site by clicking a button on the applet window. This program operates over a period of time, displaying information about each Web site in sequence. Because of this time element, threads are the best way to control the program.

Instead of entering this program into your word processor first and learning about it afterward, you'll get a chance to enter the full text of the `Revolve` applet at the end of the hour. Before then, each section of the program will be described.

The `class` Declaration

The first thing you need to do in this applet is to use `import` to make some classes available.

The `java.awt` group of classes is needed because you'll be using one of them, `Graphics2D`, to display text onscreen. The `java.net` group will be used when you work with the Web addresses, and the `java.applet` group is needed when you tell the browser to load a new page. Finally, the `java.awt.event` group is needed to respond to mouse clicks so a user can visit one of the addresses shown, and the `java.awt.swing` package is needed because it is used to create the applet window and other user interface elements.

Use the following `import` statements:

```
import java.applet.*;
import java.awt.*;
import java.awt.event.*;
import javax.swing.*;
import java.net.*;
```

After you have used `import` to make some classes available, you're ready to begin the applet with the following statement:

```
public class Revolve extends JApplet
    implements Runnable, ActionListener {
```

This statement creates the `Revolve` class as a subclass of the `JApplet` class. It also indicates that two interfaces are supported by this class—`Runnable` and `ActionListener`. By implementing the `Runnable` class, you will be able to use a `run()` method in this applet to make a thread begin running. The `ActionListener` interface enables the applet to respond to actions the user takes with the mouse. Implementing it enables the `actionPerformed()` method to be called when a mouse button is clicked.

Setting Up Variables

The first thing to do in the `Revolve` class is create the variables and objects needed throughout the program. Create two arrays with six elements—an array of `String` objects called `pageTitle` and an array of `URL` objects called `pageLink`:

```
String[] pageTitle = new String[6];
URL[] pageLink = new URL[6];
```

19

The `pageTitle` array will store the titles of the six Web sites that will be displayed. The `URL` class of objects stores the value of a Web site address. `URL` has all the behavior and attributes needed to keep track of a Web address and use it to load the page with a Web browser. Both of these arrays are set up without any values at this point, so you'll have to provide them later.

The last three things to be created are a `Color` object named `butterscotch`, an integer variable called `current` and a `Thread` object called `runner`:

```
Color butterscotch = new Color(204, 204, 158);
int current = 0;
Thread runner;
```

`Color` objects represent colors you can use on fonts, user interface components, and other visual aspects of Swing. You'll find out how to use them during Hour 21, "Using Fonts and Color."

The `current` variable will be used to keep track of which site is being displayed so you can cycle through the sites. The `Thread` object `runner` represents the only thread this program runs. You will call methods of the `runner` object when you start, stop, and pause the operation of the applet.

Starting with `init()`

The `init()` method of an applet automatically is handled once when the applet first starts to run. In this example, this method is used to assign values to the two arrays created for this applet, `pageTitle` and `pageLink`. It also is used to create a clickable button that will appear on the applet. The method consists of the following statements:

```
public void init() {
    pageTitle[0] = "Sun's Java site";
    pageLink[0] = getURL("http://java.sun.com");
    pageTitle[1] = "Cafe au Lait";
    pageLink[1] = getURL("http://www.ibiblio.org/javafaq/");
    pageTitle[2] = "JavaWorld";
    pageLink[2] = getURL("http://www.javaworld.com");
    pageTitle[3] = "Java 2 in 24 Hours";
    pageLink[3] = getURL("http://www.java24hours.com");
    pageTitle[4] = "Sams Publishing";
    pageLink[4] = getURL("http://www.samspublishing.com");
    pageTitle[5] = "Workbench";
    pageLink[5] = getURL("http://workbench.cadenhead.info");
    Button goButton = new Button("Go");
    goButton.addActionListener(this);
    FlowLayout flow = new FlowLayout();
    Container pane = getContentPane();
```

```
        pane.setLayout(flow);
        pane.add(goButton);
        setContentPane(pane);
}
```

Strings are assigned to the six elements of the `pageTitle` array, which stores the title of each Web page. The elements of the `pageLink` array are assigned a value returned by the `getURL()` method, which you will be creating for this program.

The last seven statements of the `init()` method are used to create a button and place it on the applet window. The button has the name `goButton` and is labeled with the text `Go`.

Catching Errors as You Set Up URLs

When you set up a `URL` object, you must make sure that the text used to set up the address is in a valid format. `http://java.sun.com` and `http://www.samspublishing.com` are valid, but something such as `http:www.java-world.com` would not be because of the missing `//` marks.

The `getURL()` method takes a string of text as an argument. The string is checked to see if it's a valid Web address, and if it is, the method returns that valid address. If it's erroneous, the method sends back a `null` value. The following is the `getURL()` method:

```
URL getURL(String urlText) {
    URL pageURL = null;
    try {
        pageURL = new URL(getDocumentBase(), urlText);
    }
    catch (MalformedURLException m) { }
    return pageURL;
}
```

The first line of this method includes three things, in this order:

- The type of object or variable that is returned by the method—a `URL` object in this case. If this is `void`, no information is returned by the method.

- The name of the method—getURL.

- The argument or arguments, if any, that this method takes—only one in this example, a `String` variable called `urlText`.

The `try-catch` block deals with any `MalformedURLException` errors that occur when `URL` objects are created.

If the string variable sent to the method is a valid Web address, it will be sent back as a valid `URL` object. If not, `null` is returned. Because you were assigning values to six different `URL` objects in the `pageURL` array, the `getURL()` method makes this process easier to do.

19

Handling Screen Updates in the `paint()` Method

The `paint()` method of any applet is handled when the screen needs to be updated. This situation can be caused by the Web browser or operating system outside of the applet if they obscure part of an applet window or change its dimensions in some way. The `paint()` method can also be called manually within an applet when the screen needs to be updated.

If you put a `repaint();` statement in an applet, it forces the `paint()` method to be handled. This statement is a way you can tell the program that you have done something that requires a screen update. For example, if you are writing an animation program and you move an image from one place to another, you need to use `repaint();` so the image is shown in its new location.

The `Revolve` applet has a short `paint()` method:

```
public void paint(Graphics screen) {
    Graphics2D screen2D = (Graphics2D) screen;
    screen2D.setColor(butterscotch);
    screen2D.fillRect(0, 0, getSize().width, getSize().height);
    screen2D.setColor(Color.black);
    screen2D.drawString(pageTitle[current], 5, 60);
    screen2D.drawString("" + pageLink[current], 5, 80);
}
```

The first statement in this method creates a `screen2D` object that represents the area of the applet window where things such as strings can be drawn. All drawing will be done by calling the methods of this object.

The `setColor()` method of `Graphics2D` selects the color that will be used for subsequent drawing. The color is set to butterscotch before a rectangle is drawn that fills the entire applet window. Next, the color is set to black and lines of text are displayed on the screen at the (x,y) positions of (5,60) and (5,80). The first line that is displayed is an element of the `pageTitle` array. The second line displayed is the address of the `URL` object, which is stored in the `pageLink` array. The `current` variable is used to determine which elements of these arrays to display.

Starting the Thread

One of the objects created for this program is a `Thread` object called `runner`. For a thread to get started, a place is needed where the thread is given a value and told to begin running. In this applet, the `runner` thread will start whenever the `start()` method is handled and stop whenever `stop()` is handled.

The start() method of an applet is handled at two different times: right after the init() method and every time the program is restarted after being stopped. An applet is stopped any time a user switches from the applet page to another Web page. It starts again when a user returns to the original page. The following is the start() method of the Revolve applet:

```
public void start() {
    if (runner == null) {
        runner = new Thread(this);
        runner.start();
    }
}
```

This method does only one thing: If the runner thread is not already started, it creates a new runner thread and starts it. The runner object equals null when it has not been started yet, so you can test for this condition with the if statement.

The statement runner = new Thread(this); creates a new Thread object with one argument—the this statement. Using this makes the applet itself the program that will run in the runner thread.

The runner.start(); statement causes the thread to begin running. When a thread begins, the run() method of that thread is handled. Because the runner thread is the applet itself, the run() method of the applet is handled.

Running the Thread

The run() method is where the main work of a thread takes place. It is comparable to the main() block statement of a Java application. In the Revolve applet, the following represents the run() method:

```
public void run() {
    Thread thisThread = Thread.currentThread();
    while (runner == thisThread) {
        repaint();
        current++;
        if (current > 5)
            current = 0;
        try {
            Thread.sleep(10000);
        } catch (InterruptedException e) { }
    }
}
```

The first thing that takes place in the run() method is the creation of a Thread object called thisThread. A class method of the Thread class, currentThread(), is used to set up the value for the `thisThread` object. The `currentThread()` method keeps track of the thread that's currently running.

All of the statements in this method are part of a `while` loop that compares the `runner` object to the `thisThread` object. Both of these objects are threads, and as long as they have the same value, the `while` loop will continue looping. There's no statement inside this loop that causes the `runner` and `thisThread` objects to have different values, so it will loop indefinitely unless something outside of the loop changes one of the `Thread` objects.

The `run()` method first uses the `repaint();` statement to cause the `paint()` method to be handled. Next, the value of the `current` variable increases by one, and if `current` exceeds 5, it is set to 0 again. The `current` variable is used in the `paint()` method to determine which Web site information to display. Changing `current` causes a different site to be displayed the next time `paint()` is handled.

This method includes another `try-catch` statement that handles an error that might occur. The `Thread.sleep(10000);` statement causes a thread to pause for 10,000 milliseconds. This statement causes the thread to wait long enough for users to read the name of the Web site and its address. The `catch` statement takes care of any `InterruptedException` errors that might occur while the `Thread.sleep()` statement is being handled. These errors would occur if something interrupted the thread while it was trying to `sleep()`.

Stopping the Thread

The `stop()` method is handled any time the applet is stopped because the applet's page is exited, and it is the best place to stop the running thread. The `stop()` method for the `Revolve` applet contains the following statements:

```
public void stop() {
    if (runner != null) {
        runner = null;
    }
}
```

The `if` statement tests whether the `runner` object is equal to `null`. If it is, there isn't an active thread that needs to be stopped. Otherwise, the statement sets `runner` equal to `null`.

Setting the `runner` object to a `null` value causes it to have a different value than the `thisThread` object. When this happens, the `while` loop inside the `run()` method will stop running.

Handling Mouse Clicks

The last thing to take care of in the `Revolve` applet is event-handling: Whenever a user clicks the Go button, the Web browser should open the Web site that is listed. This is done with a method called `actionPerformed()`. The `actionPerformed()` method is called whenever the button is clicked.

The following is the `actionPerformed()` method of the `Revolve` applet:

```
public void actionPerformed(ActionEvent evt) {
    if (runner != null) {
        runner = null;
    }
    AppletContext browser = getAppletContext();
    if (pageLink[current] != null)
        browser.showDocument(pageLink[current]);
}
```

The first thing that happens in this method is that the `runner` thread is stopped in the same way it was stopped in the applet's `stop()` method. The next statement creates a new `AppletContext` object called `browser`.

An `AppletContext` object represents the environment in which the applet is being presented—in other words, the page it's located on and the Web browser that loaded the page.

The `showDocument()` method of this object is called with a single argument: a `URL` object representing a World Wide Web address. If the page represented by `pageLink[current]` is a valid address, `showDocument()` is used to request that the browser load the page.

19

Workshop: Revolving Links

Now that all aspects of the `Revolve` applet have been described, you're ready to create the program and test it. Run your word processor and create a new file called `Revolve.java`. Enter the text of Listing 19.2 and save the file when you're done.

LISTING 19.2 The Full Text of `Revolve.java`

```
1: import java.applet.*;
2: import java.awt.*;
3: import java.awt.event.*;
4: import javax.swing.*;
5: import java.net.*;
6:
7: public class Revolve extends JApplet
8:     implements Runnable, ActionListener {
```

LISTING 19.2   continued

```
 9:
10:        String[] pageTitle = new String[6];
11:        URL[] pageLink = new URL[6];
12:        Color butterscotch = new Color(255, 204, 158);
13:        int current = 0;
14:        Thread runner;
15:
16:        public void init() {
17:            pageTitle[0] = "Sun's Java site";
18:            pageLink[0] = getURL("http://java.sun.com");
19:            pageTitle[1] = "Cafe au Lait";
20:            pageLink[1] = getURL("http://www.ibiblio.org/javafaq/");
21:            pageTitle[2] = "JavaWorld";
22:            pageLink[2] = getURL("http://www.javaworld.com");
23:            pageTitle[3] = "Java 2 in 24 Hours";
24:            pageLink[3] = getURL("http://www.java24hours.com");
25:            pageTitle[4] = "Sams Publishing";
26:            pageLink[4] = getURL("http://www.samspublishing.com");
27:            pageTitle[5] = "Workbench";
28:            pageLink[5] = getURL("http://workbench.cadenhead.info");
29:            Button goButton = new Button("Go");
30:            goButton.addActionListener(this);
31:            FlowLayout flow = new FlowLayout();
32:            Container pane = getContentPane();
33:            pane.setLayout(flow);
34:            pane.add(goButton);
35:            setContentPane(pane);
36:        }
37:
38:        URL getURL(String urlText) {
39:            URL pageURL = null;
40:            try {
41:                pageURL = new URL(getDocumentBase(), urlText);
42:            } catch (MalformedURLException m) { }
43:            return pageURL;
44:        }
45:
46:        public void paint(Graphics screen) {
47:            Graphics2D screen2D = (Graphics2D) screen;
48:            screen2D.setColor(butterscotch);
49:            screen2D.fillRect(0, 0, getSize().width, getSize().height);
50:            screen2D.setColor(Color.black);
51:            screen2D.drawString(pageTitle[current], 5, 60);
52:            screen2D.drawString("" + pageLink[current], 5, 80);
53:        }
54:
55:        public void start() {
56:            if (runner == null) {
```

LISTING 19.2   continued

```
57:                     runner = new Thread(this);
58:                     runner.start();
59:             }
60:     }
61:
62:     public void run() {
63:         Thread thisThread = Thread.currentThread();
64:         while (runner == thisThread) {
65:             repaint();
66:             current++;
67:             if (current > 5)
68:                 current = 0;
69:             try {
70:                 Thread.sleep(10000);
71:             } catch (InterruptedException e) { }
72:         }
73:     }
74:
75:     public void stop() {
76:         if (runner != null) {
77:             runner = null;
78:         }
79:     }
80:
81:     public void actionPerformed(ActionEvent evt) {
82:         if (runner != null) {
83:             runner = null;
84:         }
85:         AppletContext browser = getAppletContext();
86:         if (pageLink[current] != null)
87:             browser.showDocument(pageLink[current]);
88:     }
89: }
```

19

After you compile this program with the javac or another compiler, you need to create a Web page on which to put the applet. Create a new file with your word processor and name it Revolve.html. Enter Listing 19.3 and save the file.

LISTING 19.3   The Full Text of Revolve.html

```
1: <applet code="Revolve.class" width=200 height=100>
2: </applet>
```

When you're done, you can load this file in `appletviewer` to see how the different links are displayed. You won't be able to use the Go button to visit any of the links, however, because that isn't supported in `appletviewer`.

Figure 19.2 shows what the applet looks like in Internet Explorer 6.

FIGURE **19.2**

Displaying revolving links in an applet window.

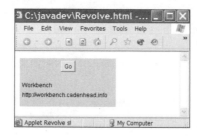

Summary

Threads are a powerful concept that is implemented with a small number of classes and interfaces in Java. By supporting multithreading in your applications and applets, you make the programs more responsive and can often speed up how quickly they perform tasks.

Even if you learned nothing else from this hour, you now have a new 21st century term to describe your frenzied lifestyle. Use it in a few sentences to see if it grabs you:

- "Boy, I was really multithreading yesterday after Mom was indicted for mail fraud."
- "I multithreaded all through lunch, and it gave me gas."
- "Not tonight, dear, I'm multithreading."

Q&A

Q Why isn't `javax.swing.JApplet` needed in the `class` statement of the `Revolve` applet?

A It isn't needed because of the `import` statement that makes all the `javax.awt.swing` classes available to the program. The only purpose of `import` is to make it easier to refer to classes in a program. If you don't use it, you have to use full class references such as `javax.swing.JApplet` instead of simply `JApplet`.

You could write all of your Java programs without using import, though it would make the source files more difficult to understand.

Q If the Revolve applet only has one thread, what's the point of using threads at all?

A Multithreading has benefits, even if it's really just one-threading. One of the main benefits is that you can start, stop, and pause a thread from within a program; you don't have the same kind of control without threads. Also, by making an applet a thread, even for a single-thread project, you make it easier to implement additional threads as needed later on.

Q Are there any reasons not to leave a pair of empty brackets after a catch statement, which causes errors to be disregarded?

A It depends on the type of error or exception being caught. In the Revolve applet, you know with both catch statements what the cause of an exception would be. Because of this knowledge, you can handle the error. In the getURL() method, the MalformedURLException would only be caused if the URL sent to the method is invalid.

Quiz

Set aside your threads (in the Java sense, not the nudity sense), and answer the following questions about multithreading in Java.

Questions

1. What interface must be implemented for a program to use threads?

    a. Runnable

    b. Thread

    c. Applet

2. If an interface contains three different methods, how many of them must be included in a class that implements the interface?

    a. None of them.

    b. All of them.

    c. I know but I'm not telling.

3. You're admiring the work of another programmer who has created a program that handles four simultaneous tasks. What should you tell him?

    a. "That's not half as exciting as the Anna Kournikova screen saver I downloaded off the Web."

    b. "You're the wind beneath my wings."

    c. "Nice threads!"

Answers

1. a. `Runnable` must be used with the `implements` statement. `Thread` is used inside a multithreaded program, but it is not needed in the class statement that begins a program.

2. b. An interface is a guarantee that the class will include all of the interface's methods.

3. c. This compliment could be confusing if the programmer is well-dressed, but let's be honest—what are the chances of that?

Activities

If this long workshop hasn't left you feeling threadbare, expand your skills with the following activities:

- If you are comfortable with HTML, create your own home page that includes the `Revolve` applet and six of your own favorite Web sites. Use the applet along with other graphics and text on the page.

- Add a button to the `FindPrimes` application that can stop the thread while the sequence of prime numbers is still being calculated.

To see Java programs that implement these activities, visit the book's Web site at `http://www.java24hours.com`.

HOUR **20**

Reading and Writing Files

There are numerous ways to represent data on a computer. You have already worked with one by creating objects—an object includes data in the form of variables and references to objects. It also includes methods that use the data to accomplish tasks.

To work with other kinds of data, such as files on your hard drive and documents on a Web server, you can use the classes of the java.io package. The "IO" part of its name stands for "input/output" and the classes are used to access a source of data, such as a hard drive, CD-ROM, or the computer's memory.

You can bring data into a program and send data out by using a communications system called streams, or objects that take information from one place to another.

During this hour, you will work with streams to do each of the following:

- Read bytes from a file into a program
- Create a new file on your computer
- Save an array of bytes to a file
- Make changes to the data stored in a file

Streams

To save data permanently within a Java program, or to retrieve that data later, you must use at least one stream.

A *stream* is an object that takes information from one source and sends it to another. The name is inspired by streams that take fish, boats, inner tube riders, and industrial pollutants from one place to another.

Streams connect a diverse variety of sources, including computer programs, hard drives, Internet servers, computer memory, and CD-ROMs. Because all these things use streams, once you learn how to work with one kind of data, you will be able to work with others in the same manner.

During this hour, you will use streams to read and write data stored in files on your computer.

There are two kinds of streams:

- Input streams, which read data from a source
- Output streams, which write data to a source

All input and output streams are made up of bytes, individual integers with values ranging from 0 to 255. You can use this format to represent data, such as executable programs, word-processing documents, and MP3 music files, but those are only a small sampling of what bytes can represent. A *byte stream* is used to read and write this kind of data.

Java class files are stored as bytes in a form called *bytecode*. The Java interpreter runs bytecode, which doesn't actually have to be produced by the Java language. It can run compiled bytecode produced by other languages, including NetRexx and JPython. You will also hear the Java interpreter referred to as the "bytecode interpreter."

A more specialized way to work with data is in the form of characters—individual letters, numbers, punctuation, and the like. A character stream can be used when you are reading and writing text files, word-processing documents, Web pages and the like.

Whether you work with a stream of bytes, characters, or other kinds of information, the overall process is the same:

- You create a stream object associated with the data.
- You call methods of the stream to either put information in the stream or take information out of it.
- You close the stream by calling the object's `close()` method.

Files

In Java, files are represented by the `File` class, which also is part of the `java.io` package. Files can be read from hard drives, floppy drives, CD-ROMs, and other storage devices.

A `File` object can represent files that already exist and files you want to create. To create a `File` object, use the name of the file as the constructor, as in this example:

```
File bookName = new File("address.dat");
```

This creates an object for a file named `address.dat` in the current folder. You can also include a path in the filename:

```
File bookName = new File("data\address.dat");
```

This example works on a Windows system, which uses the backslash (\) character as a separator in path and filenames. Linux and other Unix-based systems use a forward slash (/) character instead. To write a Java program that refers to files in a way that works regardless of the operating system, use the class variable `File.pathSeparator` instead of a forward or backslash, as in this statement:

```
File bookName = new File("data" + File.pathSeparator
    + "address.dat");
```

20

Once you have a `File` object, you can call several useful methods on that object:

- `exists()`—`true` if the file exists, `false` otherwise.
- `getName()`—The name of the file, as a `String`.
- `length()`—The size of the file, as a `long` value.

- `createNewFile()`—Creates a file of the same name, if one does not exist already.
- `delete()`—Delete the file, if it exists.
- `renameTo(File)`—Renames the file, using the name of the `File` object specified as an argument.

You also can use a `File` object to represent a folder on your system rather than a file. Specify the folder name in the `File` constructor, which can be absolute (such as "C:\MyDocuments\") or relative (such as "java\database").

Once you have an object representing a folder, you can call its `listFiles()` method to see what's inside the folder. This method returns an array of `File` objects representing every file and subfolder it contains.

Reading Data from a Stream

The first project of the hour is to read data from a file using an input stream. You can do this using the `FileInputStream` class, which represents input streams that will be read as bytes from a file.

You can create a file input stream by specifying a filename or a `File` object as the argument to the `FileInputStream()` constructor method.

The file must exist before the file input stream is created. If it doesn't, an `IOException` will be generated when you try to create the stream. Many of the methods associated with reading and writing files will generate this exception, so it's often convenient to put all statements involving the file in their own `try-catch` block, as in this example:

```
try {
    File cookie = new File("cookie.web");
    FileInputStream = new FileInputStream(cookie);
    System.out.println("Length of file: " + cookie.length());
} catch (IOException e) {
    System.out.println("Could not read file.");
}
```

File input streams read data in bytes. You can read a single byte by calling the stream's `read()` method without an argument. If no more bytes are available in the stream because you have reached the end of the file, a byte value of `-1` will be returned.

When you read an input stream, it begins with the first byte in the stream—such as the first byte in a file. You can skip some bytes in a stream by calling its `skip()` method with one argument: an `int` representing the number of bytes to skip. The following statement skips the next 1024 bytes in a stream named `scanData`:

```
scanData.skip(1024);
```

If you want to read more than one byte at a time, do the following:

- Create a byte array that is exactly the size of the number of bytes you want to read.

- Call the stream's read() method with that array as an argument. The array will be filled with bytes read from the stream.

You will create an application that reads ID3 data from an MP3 audio file. Because MP3 is such a popular format for music files, 128 bytes are often added to the end of an ID3 file to hold information about the song, such as the title, artist, and album it is from.

The ReadID3 application reads an MP3 file using a file input stream, skipping everything but the last 128 bytes. The remaining bytes are examined to see if they contain ID3 data. If they do, the first three bytes will be the numbers 84, 65, and 71.

On the ASCII character set, which is included in the Unicode Standard character set supported by Java, those three numbers represent the capital letters "T," "A," and "G," respectively.

Open the editor you have been using, and enter the text of Listing 20.1. Save the file as ReadID3.java.

LISTING 20.1 The Full Text of ReadID3.java

```
 1: import java.io.*;
 2:
 3: public class ReadID3 {
 4:     public static void main(String[] arguments) {
 5:         try {
 6:             File song = new File(arguments[0]);
 7:             FileInputStream file = new FileInputStream(song);
 8:             int size = (int)song.length();
 9:             file.skip(size - 128);
10:             byte[] last128 = new byte[128];
11:             file.read(last128);
12:             String id3 = new String(last128);
13:             String tag = id3.substring(0, 3);
14:             if (tag.equals("TAG")) {
15:                 System.out.println("Title: " + id3.substring(3, 32));
16:                 System.out.println("Artist: " + id3.substring(33, 62));
17:                 System.out.println("Album: " + id3.substring(63, 91));
18:                 System.out.println("Year: " + id3.substring(93, 97));
19:             } else
20:                 System.out.println(arguments[0] + " does not contain"
21:                     + " ID3 info.");
```

20

LISTING 20.1   continued

```
22:            file.close();
23:         } catch (Exception e) {
24:            System.out.println("Error — " + e.toString());
25:         }
26:     }
27: }
```

When you compile this source file, a `ReadID3` class file will be created. You can run this class as an application, specifying an MP3 file on your system as a command-line argument. For example:

```
java ReadID3 Everlong.mp3
```

If you have the song `Everlong.mp3` on your system (and you really should), here's an example of what the `ReadID3` application will display:

Title: Everlong
Artist: Foo Fighters
Album: The Colour and the Shape
Year: 1997

If you don't have `Everlong.mp3` on your computer (a big mistake, in my opinion), you can find other MP3 songs to examine with this application on the Web site MP3.com at `http://www.mp3.com`.

The application reads the last 128 bytes from the MP3 in Lines 10–11 of Listing 20.1, storing them in a `byte` array. This array is used in Line 12 to create a `String` object that contains the characters represented by those bytes.

If the first three characters in the string are "TAG," the MP3 file being examined contains ID3 information in a format the application understands.

In Lines 15–18, the string's `substring()` method is called to display portions of the string. The characters to display are from the ID3 format, which always puts the artist, song, title, and year information in the same positions in the last 128 bytes of an MP3 file.

Some MP3 files either don't contain ID3 information at all or contain ID3 information in a different format than application can read.

The file `Everlong.mp3` will contain readable ID3 information if you created it from a copy of *The Colour and the Shape* CD that you purchased, because programs that create MP3 files from audio CDs read song information from a music industry database called CDDB.

After everything related to the ID3 information has been read from the MP3's file input stream, the stream is closed in Line 22. You should always close streams when you are finished with them to conserve resources in the Java interpreter.

You may be tempted to find a copy of Everlong.mp3 on a service such as AudioGalaxy, WinMX, or Gnutella, three popular file-sharing services. I can understand this temptation perfectly where "Everlong" is concerned. However, according to a recent report by the Recording Industry Association of America, anyone who downloads MP3 files for CDs you do not own will immediately burst into flame. For this reason, it's better just to buy the CD and make your own legal copy for personal use only. *The Colour and the Shape* is available at Wherehouse, Sam Goody, Turtle's, Amazon.com and other leading retailers.

Buffered Input Streams

One of the ways to improve the performance of a program that reads input streams is to buffer the input. Buffering is the process of saving data in memory for use later when a program needs it. When a Java program needs data from a buffered input stream, it looks in the buffer first, which is faster than reading from a source such as a file.

To use a buffered input stream, you create an input stream such as a `FileInputStream` object, then use that object to create a buffered stream. Call the `BufferedInputStream(InputStream)` constructor with the input stream as the only argument. Data will be buffered as it is read from the input stream.

To read from a buffered stream, call its `read()` method with no arguments. An integer from 0 to 255 will be returned that represents the next byte of data in the stream. If no more bytes are available, -1 is returned instead.

As a demonstration of buffered streams, the next program you create will add a feature to Java that many programmers miss from other languages they have used: console input.

Console input is the ability to read characters from the console (also known as the command line) while running an application.

The `System` class, which contains the `out` variable used in the `System.out.print()` and `System.out.println()` statements, has a class variable called in that represents an `InputStream` object. This object receives input from the keyboard and makes it available as a stream.

20

You can work with this input stream like any other. The following statement creates a buffered input stream associated with the System.in input stream:

```
BufferedInputStream bin = new BufferedInputStream(System.in);
```

The next project, the ReadConsole class, contains a class method you can use to receive console input in any of your Java applications. Enter the text of Listing 20.2 in your editor and save the file as ReadConsole.java.

LISTING 20.2   The Full Text of ReadConsole.java

```
 1: import java.io.*;
 2:
 3: public class ReadConsole {
 4:     public static String readLine() {
 5:         StringBuffer response = new StringBuffer();
 6:         try {
 7:             BufferedInputStream bin = new
 8:                 BufferedInputStream(System.in);
 9:             int in = 0;
10:             char inChar;
11:             do {
12:                 in = bin.read();
13:                 inChar = (char) in;
14:                 if (in != -1) {
15:                     response.append(inChar);
16:                 }
17:             } while ((in != -1) & (inChar != '\n'));
18:             bin.close();
19:             return response.toString();
20:         } catch (IOException e) {
21:             System.out.println("Exception: " + e.getMessage());
22:             return null;
23:         }
24:     }
25:
26:     public static void main(String[] arguments) {
27:         System.out.print("You are standing at the end of the road ");
28:         System.out.print("before a small brick building. Around you ");
29:         System.out.print("is a forest. A small stream flows out of ");
30:         System.out.println("the building and down a gully.\n");
31:         System.out.print("> ");
32:         String input = ReadConsole.readLine();
33:         System.out.println("That's not a verb I recognize.");
34:     }
35: }
```

The `ReadConsole` class includes a `main()` method that demonstrates how it can be used. When you compile and run it as an application, the output should resemble the following:

```
You are standing at the end of the road before a small brick building.
Around you is a forest. A small stream flows out of the building and
down a gully.

> go north
That's not a verb I recognize.
```

The `ReadConsole` class contains one class method, `readLine()`, which receives characters from the console. When the Enter key is hit, `readLine()` returns a `String` object that contains all the characters that were received.

If you save the `ReadConsole` class in a folder that is listed in your `CLASSPATH` environment variable, you can call `ReadConsole.readLine()` from any Java program that you write.

> The `ReadConsole` class is also the world's least satisfying text adventure game. You can't enter the building, wade in the stream, or even wander off. For a more full-featured version of this game, which is called Adventure, visit the Interactive Fiction archive at http://www.wurb.com/if/game/1.

Writing Data to a Stream

In the `java.io` package, the classes for working with streams come in matched sets. There are `FileInputStream` and `FileOutputStreams` classes for working with byte streams, `FileReader` and `FileWriter` classes for working with character streams, and many other sets for working with other kinds of stream data.

To begin reading data from a stream of bytes, you first create a `File` object that will be associated with an output stream. This file doesn't have to exist on your system.

You can create a `FileOutputStream` in two ways. If you want to append bytes onto an existing file, call the `FileOutputStream()` constructor method with two arguments: a `File` object representing the file and the `boolean` of `true`. The bytes you write to the stream will be tacked onto the end of the file.

If you want to write bytes into a new file, call the `FileOutputStream()` constructor method with a `File` object as its only object.

Once you have an output stream, you can call different `write()` methods to write bytes to it:

20

- Call write() with a byte as its only argument to write that byte to the stream.
- Call write() with a byte array as its only argument to write all of the array's bytes to the stream.
- Specify three arguments to the write() method: a byte array, an integer representing the first element of the array to write to the stream, and the number of bytes to write.

The following statement creates a byte array with 10 bytes and writes the last five to an output stream:

```
File dat = new File("data.dat");
FileOutputStream datStream = new FileOutputStream(dat);
byte[] data = new { 5, 12, 4, 13, 3, 15, 2, 17, 1, 18 };
datStream.write(data, 5, 5);
```

After you have finished writing bytes to a stream, you close it by calling the stream's close() method.

Workshop: Writing Bytes to an MP3 File

For this hour's workshop, you will make music, but by no stretch of the imagination can it be called beautiful music.

The project is to read in all of the bytes in an MP3 file and replace a small percentage of them with altered data.

Enter the text of Listing 12.3 into an editor and save the file as TrashMP3.java when you're done.

LISTING 12.3   The Full Text of TrashMP3.java

```
 1: import java.io.*;
 2:
 3: public class TrashMP3 {
 4:     static int INTERFERENCE = 500;
 5:     static int RANDOMBYTE = 5;
 6:
 7:     public static void main(String[] arguments) {
 8:         try {
 9:             File song = new File(arguments[0]);
10:             FileInputStream file = new FileInputStream(song);
11:             File trashedSong = new File("trashed.mp3");
12:             FileOutputStream trash = new FileOutputStream(trashedSong);
13:             boolean eof = false;
14:             int count = 0;
15:             System.out.println("Creating file ...");
```

Listing 12.3 continued

```
16:              while (!eof) {
17:                  int input = file.read();
18:                  if (input == -1)
19:                      eof = true;
20:                  else {
21:                      count++;
22:                      if (count % INTERFERENCE == 0) {
23:                          int newInput = input + RANDOMBYTE;
24:                          if (newInput > 255)
25:                              newInput = newInput - 255;
26:                          trash.write(newInput);
27:                      } else
28:                          trash.write(input);
29:                  }
30:              }
31:              file.close();
32:              trash.close();
33:              System.out.println("Done");
34:          } catch (Exception e) {
35:              System.out.println("Error — " + e.toString());
36:          }
37:      }
38: }
```

When you're done, compile the file with your Java compiler. The application requires one MP3 file that will be used for ill purpose. Though you won't be altering the file itself, you will be producing a version of it that may be quite painful to hear. The file Everlong.mp3 is not recommended for this purpose.

Run the application with the name of the MP3 file as a command-line argument, as in the following SDK example:

```
java TrashMP3 MuskratLove.mp3
```

The TrashMP3 program reads in all of the data in the MP3 file, in this example the song "Muskrat Love" by the Captain and Tennille. A file input stream associated with the file is created in Lines 9–10.

The MP3 file is read in the while loop contained in Lines 16–30. A boolean variable called eof is used as the condition of the loop. As long as it is equal to false, the loop will continue executing.

In Line 17, a single byte is read. If this byte is equal to -1, the end of the MP3 file has been reached, so eof is set to true in Lines 18–19, which will cause the loop to end.

20

The altered version of the MP3 will be written to its own file, which is given the name `trashed.mp3` in Line 11. This file is associated with a file output stream in Line 12.

Data is written to the altered MP3 file in Lines 21–28. A `count` variable is used to determine when the next byte of altered data should be written.

The static variable `INTERFERENCE` determines how often a byte will be altered. It is set to 500 when it is created in Line 4, so when you run the application, every 500th byte will be trashed.

The static variable `RANDOMBYTE` determines how much the byte will be altered. In Line 23, the value of this variable is added to the byte that was read from the original file. If this value exceeds 255, it cannot be used as a byte, so Lines 24–25 make sure this doesn't happen.

The altered byte is written to the new MP3 file in Line 26. Unaltered bytes are written in Line 28.

If you have an MP3 player, you can play your handiwork by opening the folder that contains `trashed.mp3` and double-clicking its icon. The MP3 format is usually pretty resilient in the face of unauthorized tampering like this, so you probably will be able to hear the song with a few wrong notes, odd moments of bad tempo, and lots of "gleep!" and "glorp!" sound effects.

Summary

During this hour, you worked with input streams and output streams that wrote bytes, the simplest way to represent data over a stream.

There are many more classes in the `java.io` package to work with streams in other ways. There's also a package of classes called `java.net` that enables you to read and write streams over an Internet connection.

Byte streams can be adapted to many uses, because you can easily convert bytes into other data types, such as integers, characters, and strings.

The first project of this hour, the `ReadID3` application, read bytes from a stream and converted them into a string, since it was easier to read the ID3 data in this format from a song such as "Everlong" by the Foo Fighters off the album *The Colour and the Shape*.

Have I mentioned yet that you should buy the album?

Q&A

Q **Why do some of the byte stream methods in this hour use integers as arguments? Shouldn't they be using `byte` arguments?**

A There's a different between the bytes in a stream and the bytes represented by the `byte` class. A `byte` in Java has a value ranging from –128 to 127, while a byte in a stream has a value from 0 to 255. You often have to use `int` when working with bytes for this reason—it can hold the values 128 to 255, while `byte` cannot.

Quiz

To see whether you took a big enough byte from the tree of knowledge during this hour, answer the following questions about input and output streams in Java.

Questions

1. Which of the following techniques can be used to convert an array of bytes into a string?

   a. Call the array's `toString()` method.

   b. Convert each byte to a character, then assign each one to an element in a `String` array.

   c. Call the `String()` constructor method with the array as an argument.

2. What kind of stream is used to read from a file in a Java program?

   a. an input stream

   b. an output stream

   c. either

3. What method of the `File` class can be used to determine the size of a file?

   a. `getSize()`

   b. `read()`

   c. `length()`

20

Answers

1. c. You can deal with each byte individually, as suggested in answer b., but you can easily create strings from other data types.

2. a. An input stream is created from a `File` object or by providing a filename to the input stream's constructor method.

3. c. This method returns a `long` representing the number of bytes in the stream.

Activities

To experience the refreshing feeling of wading through another stream, test the waters with the following activities:

- Write an application that reads the ID3 tags of all MP3 files in a folder and renames the files using the artist, song, and album information (when it is provided).

- Write a program that reads a Java source file and writes it back without any changes under a new name.

- Buy a copy of the album *The Colour and the Shape* by the Foo Fighters.

To see Java programs that implement these activities, visit the book's Web site at `http://www.java24hours.com`.

Part VI

Creating Multimedia Programs

Hour

HOUR 21

Using Fonts and Color

A catch phrase from the television show *Saturday Night Live* during the 1980s was, "It's not how you feel, but how you look…and darling, you look MAH-ve-lous." The quote epitomized the philosophy of Fernando, comedian Billy Crystal's eternally tan and impeccably groomed character. Regardless of what was going on in Fernando's life, as long as his hair was styled properly and he was dressed for the occasion, everything was copacetic because he still looked good. Correction: MAH-ve-lous.

If you're interested in making your Java programs look MAH-ve-lous, you should know about the Font and Color classes. No self-respecting program would be seen in public without them. You'll learn about these classes during this hour as the following topics are covered:

- Using fonts in your programs
- Setting a font's style and size
- Displaying colors
- Using the color constants
- Setting up the background color

- Using sRGB values to choose colors
- Using HSB values to choose colors
- Creating special text effects using colors

Using the Font Class

Colors and fonts are represented in Java by the Color and Font classes, which both belong to the java.awt package. With these classes, you can present text in several different fonts and sizes, and change the colors of text, graphics, and other elements.

One of the principles of object-oriented programming is to make an object work for itself, and the Font and Color objects follow this rule. They store all the information that's needed to display a font or change a color, and they can handle other related tasks that are required.

There are three things you need to know about a font to display it:

- The typeface of the font: Either a descriptive name (Dialog, DialogInput, Monospaced, SanSerif, or Serif) or an actual font name (such as Arial, Courier New, or Times New Roman)
- The style of the font: bold, italic, or plain
- The size of the font, in points

Before you can display text in a certain typeface, style, and point size, you need to create a Font object that holds this information. The following statement creates a 12-point serif italic Font object:

```
Font currentFont = new Font("Serif", Font.ITALIC, 12);
```

When selecting a typeface, it's better to choose one of the descriptive names: Serif, SanSerif, and Monospaced. This enables the system running the program to designate one of its own fonts that fits the description.

You can, however, refer to specific fonts, which will only be used if they are installed on the computer of the person running your program.

You choose the style of the font by using one or more constant variables. Specifying the style as Font.PLAIN makes it non-bold and non-italic, Font.BOLD makes it bold, and Font.ITALIC makes it italic. To combine bold and italic, use Font.BOLD+Font.ITALIC, as in the following code:

```
Font headlineFont = new Font("Courier New", Font.BOLD+Font.ITALIC, 72);
```

The last argument specifies the point size of the font.

There are several ways to make use of fonts in a Java program:

- On a graphical user interface, you can call a component's setFont(*Font*) method, which designates the font as the one that will be used on all subsequent text that is displayed (until the font is changed).
- On a container such as a panel, you can override the paintComponent(*Graphics*) method and work with the Graphics object to set and display fonts.
- On an applet window, you can override the paint(*Graphics*) method as you did on Hour 17, "Creating Interactive Web Programs."

The first project you undertake during this hour draws text on a panel. This class uses the second option for using fonts—overriding a panel's paintComponent() method. Open your word processor and create a new file called Player.java, entering the text of Listing 21.1 in the file.

LISTING 21.1   The Full Text of Player.java

```
 1: import java.awt.*;
 2: import javax.swing.*;
 3:
 4: public class Player extends JFrame {
 5:     public Player() {
 6:         super("Player");
 7:         setSize(244, 286);
 8:         setDefaultCloseOperation(JFrame.EXIT_ON_CLOSE);
 9:         PlayerPanel fp = new PlayerPanel();
10:         Container pane = getContentPane();
11:         pane.add(fp);
12:         setContentPane(pane);
13:         setVisible(true);
14:     }
15:
16:     public static void main(String[] arguments) {
17:         Player frame = new Player();
18:     }
19: }
20:
21: class PlayerPanel extends JPanel {
22:     public void paintComponent(Graphics comp) {
23:         super.paintComponent(comp);
24:         Graphics2D comp2D = (Graphics2D)comp;
25:         int width = getSize().width;
26:         int height = getSize().height;
27:         Font currentFont = new Font("Dialog", Font.BOLD, 18);
28:         comp2D.setFont(currentFont);
```

21

LISTING 21.1   continued

```
29:          comp2D.drawString("ARMANDO BENITEZ", width - 185, height - 30);
30:          currentFont = new Font("Dialog", Font.ITALIC, 12);
31:          comp2D.setFont(currentFont);
32:          comp2D.drawString("pitcher", width - 170, height - 10);
33:          currentFont = new Font("Dialog", Font.PLAIN, 12);
34:          comp2D.setFont(currentFont);
35:          comp2D.drawString("NEW YORK METS", width - 110, height - 10);
36:      }
37: }
```

After you compile the file with javac or another compiler, run the application. The program should resemble Figure 21.1.

FIGURE 21.1

Running the Player *application.*

The Player application is a frame that contains a panel where several strings will be drawn using different font objects. All of the work involving fonts takes place in the FontPanel class, which is defined in Lines 22–35.

The paintComponent(Graphics) method of a container functions the same as the paint(Graphics) method in an applet. This method is called automatically whenever the container needs to be redrawn.

The first thing that takes place in the method is the call to super.paintComponent(), which calls the method in the superclass to make sure that everything is set up correctly before you begin drawing in the panel.

Next, to make use of Java2D, the Graphics object is used to create a Graphics2D object called comp2D in Line 24. All subsequent font and drawing methods will be called on this object.

A Font object is created in Line 27 that represents a Dialog, bold 18-point font. The setFont() method of comp2D is called to make this the current font.

Next, the drawString(*String*) method of comp2D is called with the text of a string to display. The same thing happens with different fonts and strings in Lines 30–35.

The Player application uses the width and height of the panel to determine where the text should be drawn. The first text, the name of New York Mets closer Armando Benitez, is displayed 185 pixels to the left of the right edge and 30 pixels above the bottom edge. If you resize the application window, the text will move accordingly.

Using the Color Class

The simplest way to use a color in a Java program is to use one of the constant variables from the Color class. You can use the following constants: black, blue, cyan, darkGray, gray, green, lightGray, magenta, orange, pink, red, white, and yellow.

In an applet, you can set the background color of the applet window using these constants. The following is an example:

```
setBackground(Color.orange);
```

When you want to display text of a certain color or draw other graphics in different colors, you have to use a method that sets up the current color. You can do this from within the paintComponent() method of a container by using a setColor() method, as in the following:

```
public void paintComponent(Graphics comp) {
    Graphics2D comp2D = (Graphics2D)comp;
    comp2D.setColor(Color.orange);
    comp2D.drawString("Go, Buccaneers!", 5, 50);
}
```

Unlike the setBackground() method, which can be called directly on a container such as a panel or applet, the setColor() method must be used on an object that can handle a color change. The preceding example shows the setColor() method of the comp2D object being used to change the current color of the container window.

Other Ways to Choose Colors

21

To use a color not included in the 13 constant variables, you must specify the color's sRGB or HSB values. *sRGB*, which stands for Standard Red Green Blue, defines a color by the amount of red, green, and blue that is present in the color. Each value ranges from

0, which means there is none of that color, to 255, which means the maximum amount of that color is present. Most graphics editing and drawing programs will identify a color's sRGB values.

If you know a color's sRGB value, you can use it to create a Color object. For example, an sRGB value for dark red is 235 red, 50 green, and 50 blue, and an sRGB value for light orange is 230 red, 220 green, and 0 blue. The following is an example of a panel that displays light orange text on a dark red background:

```
import java.awt.*;
import javax.swing.*;

public class GoBucs extends JPanel {
    Color lightOrange = new Color(230, 220, 0);
    Color darkRed = new Color(235, 50, 50);

    public void paintComponent(Graphics comp) {
        Graphics2D comp2D = (Graphics2D)comp;
        comp2D.setColor(darkRed);
        comp2D.fillRect(0, 0, 200, 100);
        comp2D.setColor(lightOrange);
        comp2D.drawString("Go, Buccaneers!", 5, 50);
    }
}
```

This example calls the fillRect() method of Graphics2D to draw a filled-in rectangle using the current color. You will learn more about this method on Hour 23.

Light orange on a dark red background isn't much more attractive on a Java program than it was on the National Football League's Tampa Bay Buccaneers, which might be the reason they now wear brass-and-pewter uniforms. Using sRGB values enables you to select from more than 16.5 million possible combinations, although most computer monitors can only offer a close approximation for most of them. For guidance on whether burnt-semidark-midnight-blue goes well with medium-light-faded-baby-green, purchase a copy of the upcoming *Sams Teach Yourself Color Sense While Waiting in Line at This Bookstore*.

Another way to select a color in a Java program is the *HSB* system, which stands for Hue Saturation Brightness. Each of these values is represented by a floating-point number that ranges from 0.0 to 1.0. The HSB system isn't as commonly supported in graphics software, so you won't be using it as often in your programs as you use sRGB values.

However, one thing HSB values are convenient for is changing a color's brightness without changing anything else about the color. You'll see an example of this use and an example of using HSB values to choose a color in this hour's workshop.

Workshop: Displaying a Danger Message

You can use Java to present news headlines and other information in different ways. One special effect you might see on a Web page or graphical user interface is text that fades to black. You also might see the reverse—text that brightens from black to white. This hour's workshop uses the Font and Color classes to create text that cycles in brightness from dark to bright. The text looks like an alert about impending danger, so the panel will be called Danger.

To make the class more useful, the text of the warning will be set as an argument to a constructor. The text that will be used in this example warns of a "Core Breach in Sector 12," but you can substitute other threatening text of similar length.

If you're at a secure place in your life right now and can't think of anything suitably menacing, feel free to choose one of the following:

- "Mother-in-law wants to visit"
- "Boss approaching"
- "Dallas Cowboys scheduled to play here"
- "We have no bananas today"
- "No hamburger—cheeseburger"

Create a new file in your word processor called Danger.java. Each section of the class will be described as you enter it. Begin with the following statements:

```java
import java.awt.*;
import javax.swing.*;

public class Danger extends JPanel implements Runnable {
    String text = "No text has been specified";
    float hue = (float) 0.5;
    float saturation = (float) 0.8;
    float brightness = (float) 0.0;
    Font textFont = new Font("Dialog", Font.BOLD, 20);
    int textX;
    Thread runner;
```

21

The program begins like most Swing projects you create, by importing packages such as java.awt and javax.swing. The class statement defines Danger as a subclass of the JPanel class. It also uses the implements keyword to indicate that Danger implements the Runnable interface, which is required for all classes that function as threads.

The next several lines define variables and objects that will be used in the class. The string variable text is created with a default value, and it will be used to store the text that should be displayed onscreen. Three floating-point variables are used to store values for a color using its Hue Saturation Brightness ratings. The (float) portion of each line converts the value that follows it into a floating-point number. This conversion must be done because the hue, saturation, and brightness variables must be of type float.

The text of the panel will be displayed in 20-point Dialog bold. To do this, you need to create a Font object to store that font's values. The Font object, called textFont, is created for this purpose. Finally, the integer variable textX will be used when you're centering text from left-to-right on the panel, and a Thread object called runner is created to hold the thread that will run the Danger class.

After inserting a blank line, continue entering the Danger class by entering the constructor method of the class:

```
public Danger(String warning) {
    text = warning;
    FontMetrics fm = getFontMetrics(textFont);
    textX = 200 - fm.stringWidth(text) / 2;
    runner = new Thread(this);
    runner.start();
}
```

The constructor is called when objects of this class are created, and then it is never handled again. It's a good place to set up some things that weren't set up as instance or class variables. The first thing that happens is that the contents of warning, the string sent to the constructor, are copied to the text instance variable.

The FontMetrics class measures how wide a line of text will appear when it is displayed. Using the stringWidth() method of FontMetrics, you can place text at a different place in a container depending on how wide it is. The textX variable stores the horizontal position where the text should be displayed.

The last thing that happens in the constructor is the creation of a new Thread object and a call to its start() method, which causes the thread to begin running. The thread is associated with the Danger class because this was used as an argument to the Thread() constructor.

Now continue by entering the paintComponent() method of your class, which is called whenever the Danger panel needs to be updated. After leaving a blank line after the constructor method, enter the following:

```
public void paintComponent(Graphics comp) {
    super.paintComponent(comp);
    Graphics2D comp2D = (Graphics2D) comp;
    comp2D.setColor(Color.black);
    comp2D.fillRect(0, 0, 400, 200);
    Color textColor = Color.getHSBColor(hue, saturation,
        brightness);
    comp2D.setColor(textColor);
    comp2D.setFont(textFont);
    comp2D.drawString(text, textX, 30);
}
```

The paintComponent() method takes a Graphics object called comp as an argument, and then uses this object to cast a Graphics2D object called comp2D. The comp2D object holds all the information need to display something onscreen, and it has several methods you'll use.

The Color object called textColor is created using the HSB variables to select the color. The textColor object then becomes the current display color using the setColor() method of screen.

Using the drawString() method of screen2D, the variable text is displayed at the (x,y) position of textX and 30. The color of the text is the current display color.

The paintComponent() method handles most of the display work that takes place during the Danger application. All you have left to add is a method called pause(). Enter a blank line at the end of your program, and then continue with the following statements:

```
void pause(int duration) {
    try {
        Thread.sleep(duration);
    } catch (InterruptedException e) { }
}
```

The pause() method, which takes an argument called duration, pauses the thread by calling the Thread.sleep() method with an argument specifying the number of milliseconds to pause. When you are displaying changing graphics or text, you might need pauses of some kind to prevent things from changing too quickly. This pause() method shows one way to create these pauses.

21

To finish off the Danger class, you need to add a run() method that controls the threaded animation of the text. Add the following statements:

```
public void run() {
    Thread thisThread = Thread.currentThread();
    while (runner == thisThread) {
        pause(75);
        brightness += 0.05;
        if (brightness > 1) {
            brightness = (float) 0.0;
            pause(75);
        }
        repaint();
    }
}
```

The run() method begins with the same two statements used in other threaded programs. A Thread object is created that holds the currently running thread, and it is compared to the runner object in a while loop.

This while loop is what causes the animation of the text to take place. The pause(75) statement causes the animation to pause 75 milliseconds between each update of the panel. Without a pause of some kind, the text would flash different colors as quickly as a Java interpreter could handle it.

You have to change the value of the brightness variable for the text to change in brightness. The program increases the variable .05 (a 5% change), and if the variable has reached the maximum brightness of 1.0, it is reset to 0.0. Whenever brightness must be reset to 0.0, the program calls the pause() method.

The last thing that takes place in the run() method's while loop is a call to the repaint() statement. You use this statement any time you need to redraw the container because something has changed. Because the brightness variable changes each time through the while loop, you know there's a need to redisplay the text after every pause. The repaint() statement is a request for Java to call the paintComponent() method.

Save the Danger.java file, which should resemble Listing 21.3. The only difference might be in the way you have indented methods and other statements. That does not have to be changed for the program to run, but indentation and other spacing can make a program easier to understand.

LISTING 21.3   The Full Text of Danger.java

```
1: import java.awt.*;
2: import javax.swing.*;
3:
```

LISTING 21.3 continued

```
 4: public class Danger extends JPanel implements Runnable {
 5:     String text = "No text has been specified";
 6:     float hue = (float) 0.5;
 7:     float saturation = (float) 0.8;
 8:     float brightness = (float) 0.0;
 9:     Font textFont = new Font("Dialog", Font.BOLD, 20);
10:     int textX;
11:     Thread runner;
12:
13:     public Danger(String warning) {
14:         text = warning;
15:         FontMetrics fm = getFontMetrics(textFont);
16:         textX = 200 - fm.stringWidth(text) / 2;
17:         runner = new Thread(this);
18:         runner.start();
19:     }
20:
21:     public void paintComponent(Graphics comp) {
22:         Graphics2D comp2D = (Graphics2D) comp;
23:         comp2D.setColor(Color.black);
24:         comp2D.fillRect(0, 0, 400, 200);
25:         Color textColor = Color.getHSBColor(hue, saturation,
26:             brightness);
27:         comp2D.setColor(textColor);
28:         comp2D.setFont(textFont);
29:         comp2D.drawString(text, textX, 30);
30:     }
31:
32:     void pause(int duration) {
33:         try {
34:             Thread.sleep(duration);
35:         } catch (InterruptedException e) { }
36:     }
37:
38:     public void run() {
39:         Thread thisThread = Thread.currentThread();
40:         while (runner == thisThread) {
41:             pause(75);
42:             brightness += 0.05;
43:             if (brightness > 1) {
44:                 brightness = (float) 0.0;
45:                 pause(75);
46:             }
47:             repaint();
48:         }
49:     }
50: }
```

21

After compiling the file with the `javac` or another compiler, you need to create an application or applet that contains the `Danger` panel. Create a new file with your word processor called `DangerFrame.java`, and enter the text of Listing 21.4 into the file.

LISTING 21.4   The Full Text of `DangerFrame.html`

```
 1: import java.awt.*;
 2: import javax.swing.*;
 3:
 4: public class DangerFrame extends JFrame {
 5:     public DangerFrame () {
 6:         super("Warning!");
 7:         setSize(400, 70);
 8:         setDefaultCloseOperation(JFrame.EXIT_ON_CLOSE);
 9:         Danger gb = new Danger("Core Breach in Sector 12");
10:         Container pane = getContentPane();
11:         pane.add(gb);
12:         setContentPane(pane);
13:         setVisible(true);
14:     }
15:
16:     public static void main(String[] arguments) {
17:         DangerFrame frame = new DangerFrame();
18:     }
19: }
```

You can change the value in Line 9 to any other menacing sounding text, as long as it is similar in size to `Core Breach in Sector 12`. Compile and run the file to see the `Danger` panel in a frame (Figure 21.2).

FIGURE 21.2

Displaying the `Danger` *panel in an application.*

Summary

Now that you can use `Font` and `Color` objects in your programs to change the color scheme, you can no longer feign ignorance when it comes to designing an attractive program. By using fonts and color instead of sticking to the familiar black text on a light gray background, you can draw more attention to elements of your programs and make them more compelling for users.

By combining these features, you're now one step closer to writing programs that look MAH-ve-lous.

Q&A

Q **Is there a limit to the point size that can be used for text?**

A The limiting factor is the height and width of your component. Point sizes typically range from 9-point text for small lines that are readable to 48-point text for large headlines. Choosing the right size depends on the font typeface as well as the size, so it's largely a matter of trial and error.

Q **What happens if a color defined in a Java program can't be displayed on the monitor of someone displaying the program? For example, if my monitor is set to display only 256 colors, what will occur if I choose one of the 16.5 million colors that isn't in those 256?**

A When a monitor can't display a color selected with a `setColor()` or `setBackground()` method, it shows the closest existing color as a substitute. An example of this kind of substitution is the `Danger` application, which runs differently depending on the number of colors that can be shown as the text cycles from black to light blue to white.

Quiz

Test whether your font and color skills are MAH-ve-lous by answering the following questions.

Questions

1. Which one of the following is *not* a constant used to select a color?

    a. `Color.cyan`

    b. `Color.teal`

    c. `Color.magenta`

2. When you change the color of something and redraw it on a container, what must you do to make it visible?

    a. Use the `drawColor()` method.

    b. Use the `repaint()` statement.

    c. Do nothing.

3. What do the initials HSB stand for?

    a. Hue Saturation Brightness

    b. Hue Shadows Balance

    c. Lucy in the Sky with Diamonds

21

Answers

1. b.

2. b. The call to `repaint()` causes the `paintComponent()` method to be called manually.

3. a. If c. were the right answer, you could use colors that would only be visible years later during flashbacks.

Activities

To further explore the spectrum of possibilities when using fonts and color in your programs, do the following activities:

- Remove the `update()` method from the `Danger` application to see what effect it has on the quality of the display.

- Add a way to specify the background of the `Danger` application by sending an argument for the sRGB values of the desired background color.

To see Java programs that implement these activities, visit the book's Web site at `http://www.java24hours.com`.

Hour **22**

Playing Sound Files

If you're a science fiction fan, the concept of talking computers should be one that is familiar to you. For years, television shows such as *Star Trek* have featured computers with the gift of gab. These machines could talk, listen, and comprehend the quirks of spoken language better than many professional baseball players.

After watching the movie *2001: A Space Odyssey* as a teenager, I was deeply disappointed when my brand new Commodore 64 computer resisted all efforts to learn the English language. (On the plus side, it never tried to kill me, so there are some benefits to owning a less capable system.)

Today, sound is becoming more sophisticated in computer software, which brings us closer to the day when computers talk to us as comfortably as the HAL 9000 spoke to the astronauts in *2001*. Java offers the capability to play audio files in numerous formats, and you'll get a chance to make your machine sound off as you learn the following topics during this hour:

- The sound capabilities of the `JApplet` class
- Sound file formats that you can use
- Loading a sound into an `AudioClip` for playback

- Starting and stopping playback of sounds
- Creating a looping sound
- Mixing different sounds together
- Packaging an applet's files into a Java archive

Retrieving and Using Sounds

Until the introduction of JavaSound in Java 2, all sound capabilities of the Java language were handled through the JApplet class, the superclass of all Java 2 applets. Although this might make you think that sounds are strictly for use in applets, you can use methods of this class to load and play sound files in any of your Java programs.

> Grouping sound capabilities with applets is a quirk of the Java language's original design. When Java had many fewer classes as of version 1.0, audio features were included in the Applet class, perhaps because they were used most often with applets. JApplet inherits from the Applet class.

There are two ways that sounds can be played in a program: as a one-time occurrence or in a repeating loop.

Sounds are loaded from a file that must have a format supported by the JApplet class. Although past versions of the Java language could handle only one sound file format, Java 2 has been extended to handle each of the following formats:

- AU files
- AIFF files
- WAV files
- MIDI files

Each of these formats is a way to digitally represent actual sounds. To create a sound file in one of these formats, the actual sound is recorded by a computer and converted it into a form that can be saved to a file.

The name of these sound formats is used as their filename extensions, so WAV files are saved with the .WAV extension, AU with .AU, and AIFF with .AIFF

Java can also handle three different MIDI-based sound file formats: Type 0 MIDI, Type 1 MIDI, and RMF. These formats break down sound into the musical notes, instruments, and loudness used to create that sound. Each computer that can play MIDI files knows how to represent each of these things when they are encountered.

For example, if a MIDI file contains several musical notes played in a tuba-like sound, the software playing the file will encounter the notes and dutifully call upon its information on what a tuba sounds like and play the notes.

MIDI files are much smaller than their digital counterparts and are great for playing instrumental music and sound effects. What they can't do is represent more complex sounds, such as the spoken voice.

Simple Sound Playback

The simplest way to retrieve and play a sound is through the play() method of the JApplet class.

In an applet, the play() method can be called with two arguments:

- A URL object representing the folder on the World Wide Web that contains the sound file
- A string indicating the name of the file

If the URL object is a specific Web folder, such as http://www.java24hours.com/source, the sound file should be stored in this folder. However, if you move the applet to a new World Wide Web site later, you must change the source code of the program for it to continue working.

A more flexible solution is to use the applet's getCodeBase() method to provide a URL. This method returns the folder that contains the Java applet playing the sound file. As long as you store the applet and sound file in the same folder, the program will work without modification.

The following example retrieves and plays the sound kaboom.au, which is stored in the same place as the applet:

```
play(getCodeBase(), "kaboom.au");
```

The play() method retrieves and plays the given sound as soon as possible. You won't see an error message if the sound can't be found—silence is the only indicator that something might not be working as desired.

Loading Sounds into AudioClip Objects

If you want to do other things with a sound file, such as play it repeatedly or start and stop the sound, you must load the file into an AudioClip object. This is handled in an applet with the following two steps:

- Create an `AudioClip` object without calling a constructor method.
- Give this `AudioClip` object a value by calling the applet's `getAudioClip()` method.

The `getAudioClip()` method can be called with the same two arguments as the applet's `play()` method: a `URL` object (or `getCodeBase()`) and the name of the sound file.

The following statement loads a sound file into the `dance` object:

```
AudioClip dance = getAudioClip(getCodeBase(),
    "audio/chachacha.wav");
```

The filename includes a folder reference in this example, so the file `chachacha.wav` will be loaded from the subfolder `audio`.

The `getAudioClip()` method can be used only in an applet. If you want to load a sound file into an application, you must create an `AudioClip` object and give it a value by calling a class method of the `JApplet` class.

The class method `newAudioClip()` can be used to load audio files in an application. You must first create a `URL` object associated with the file, beginning the URL with the text `file:` to indicate that it is a local file rather than something accessed over the Internet. Once you have a `URL` object representing the audio file, you can load it using the `JApplet` method `newAudioClip(URL)`. The previous example could be modified for use in an application as follows:

```
URL dance = new URL("file:audio/chachacha.wav");
AudioClip danceClip = JApplet.newAudioClip(dance);
```

The reference to the `JApplet` class indicates that `newAudioClip()` is a class method. You don't need to create a `JApplet` object to call this method in an application.

When you work with `URL` objects, as you do to play audio files in an application, you must enclose the `URL` constructor in a `try-catch` block that deals with `MalformedURLException` exceptions. The `URL` class throws this exception whenever the URL does not follow the standard format for Internet addresses.

Playing and Looping `AudioClip` Objects

After you have created an `AudioClip` object and associated it with a sound file, you can use three of its methods to control how the sound is used.

- The `play()` method plays the sound once.
- The `loop()` method plays the sound repeatedly.
- The `stop()` method stops the sound from playing.

These methods are called without any arguments. Before you call them on an AudioClip object, you should make sure that the object does not have a value of null. This prevents you from trying to use the sound if the getAudioClip() or newAudioClip() methods did not find the sound file. Calling the methods of a null object will result in an error.

If you play more than one sound at a time, Java will automatically mix the sounds together, which enables some interesting effects. An example would be a MIDI file playing as background music while WAV files are used for sound effects in the foreground.

The LaughTrack application in Listing 22.1 consists of two classes: LaughButton, a new kind of clickable button that can laugh when it is clicked, and LaughTrack, a simple frame that contains one of these buttons.

This application uses Java's capability to mix several sound files together, creating a laugh track. If this term is new to you, you're probably one of the people responsible for the declining viewership of broadcast television. While you're off reading books, hiking, building ships-in-a-bottle, and engaging in other enriching pursuits, the rest of us are watching primetime television comedies. On these comedies, canned laughter often is played to make the shows seem more comic than might appear otherwise. This laughter is called a laugh track.

To create a laugh track in the LaughButton class, four different WAV files containing the sound of laughing people will be loaded into AudioClip objects. Each object will then be played in a loop, creating an impromptu laugh track. You'll have to decide if the end result approximates the sound of a television audience in fits of uncontrolled hysterics.

Enter the text of Listing 22.1 using your preferred word processor, and save the file as LaughTrack.java when you're done.

LISTING 22.1 The Full Source Code of LaughTrack.java

```
 1: import java.applet.*;
 2: import java.awt.*;
 3: import java.awt.event.*;
 4: import java.net.*;
 5: import javax.swing.*;
 6:
 7: public class LaughTrack extends JFrame {
 8:
 9:     public LaughTrack() {
10:         super("Laughtrack");
11:         setSize(190, 80);
12:         setDefaultCloseOperation(JFrame.EXIT_ON_CLOSE);
13:         Container content = getContentPane();
14:         FlowLayout flo = new FlowLayout();
```

LISTING 22.1 continued

```
15:            content.setLayout(flo);
16:            LaughButton haha = new LaughButton();
17:            content.add(haha);
18:            setContentPane(content);
19:            setVisible(true);
20:        }
21:
22:        public static void main(String[] arguments) {
23:            LaughTrack lt = new LaughTrack();
24:        }
25:
26: }
27:
28: class LaughButton extends JButton implements Runnable, ActionListener {
29:        AudioClip[] laugh = new AudioClip[4];
30:        Thread runner;
31:
32:        LaughButton() {
33:            super("Start Laughing");
34:            addActionListener(this);
35:            for (int i = 0; i < laugh.length; i++) {
36:                try {
37:                    URL laughIn = new URL("file:laugh" + i + ".wav");
38:                    laugh[i] = JApplet.newAudioClip(laughIn);
39:                } catch (MalformedURLException e) { }
40:            }
41:        }
42:
43:        public void actionPerformed(ActionEvent event) {
44:            String command = event.getActionCommand();
45:            if (command == "Start Laughing")
46:                startLaughing();
47:            if (command == "Stop Laughing")
48:                stopLaughing();
49:        }
50:
51:        void startLaughing() {
52:            if (runner == null) {
53:                runner = new Thread(this);
54:                runner.start();
55:                setText("Stop Laughing");
56:            }
57:        }
58:
59:        void stopLaughing() {
60:            if (runner != null) {
61:                for (int i = 0; i < laugh.length; i++)
62:                    if (laugh[i] != null)
63:                        laugh[i].stop();
```

LISTING 22.1   continued

```
64:                runner = null;
65:                setText("Start Laughing");
66:            }
67:      }
68:
69:      public void run() {
70:          for (int i = 0; i < laugh.length; i++)
71:              if (laugh[i] != null)
72:                  laugh[i].loop();
73:          Thread thisThread = Thread.currentThread();
74:          while (runner == thisThread) {
75:              try {
76:                  Thread.sleep(5000);
77:              } catch (InterruptedException e) { }
78:          }
79:      }
80: }
```

After you have saved LaughTrack.java, compile the application, but don't run it yet.

Before you can test this application, you must download the audio files being used in this project. Four files are required: laugh0.wav, laugh1.wav, laugh2.wav, and laugh3.wav. These are available from this book's Web site at http://www.java24hours.com on the Hour 22 page. Download these files and save them in the same folder as the LaughTrack applet's class file.

> This hour's workshop also requires its own files from the book's Web site: the WAV files plus.wav, equals.wav, and 11 numbered files beginning with number0.wav and ending with number10.wav. You can save some time by downloading these now.

When you have downloaded all the files used in the LaughTrack application, run the application.

Figure 22.1 shows the application running. You can click the button to start the laugh track, and click it again when you can't take any more of the racket.

FIGURE 22.1
Running the
LaughTrack
application.

If the result sounds anything like a real audience watching a television show being taped, it may explain why the stars of *Seinfeld* were ready to stop working on such a lucrative TV show. Bret Butler's stress-related departure from *Grace Under Fire* and similar troubles experienced by other stars also seem more understandable.

The sound playback features of the LaughButton class are running in a thread in Lines 69–79. The thread is started when the startPlaying() method is called and stopped when the stopPlaying() method is called. These calls take place in the event-handling method actionPerformed() in Lines 43–49.

Sound files, like animation, require a lot of processing time, so it's more efficient to place them into one or more threads.

Java Archives

Applets that use sound or graphics often require several different files to be loaded before the program can run successfully. The workshop you will undertake during this hour includes 12 sound files.

Because of the way the World Wide Web functions, each of these files requires its own connection between the Web server offering the applet and the user running the program during a Web surfing session. The same is true of World Wide Web pages—each graphic requires its own connection.

One way to reduce the time required to load an applet is to package all its files into a single archive file. The Software Development Kit includes a command-line tool called jar that enables Java archive files to be created, examined, and unpackaged.

Java archive files have the .JAR file extension. The jar tool is used to package a group of files into a single .JAR file. If you have created a SoundFX applet that includes 10 WAV files that have names beginning with fx, the following command could be entered at a command-line to package the applet and WAV files into a single JAR archive:

```
jar cf SoundFX.jar SoundFX.class fx*.wav
```

No file folders are included with the filenames in this example, so it must be used in the same folder that contains SoundFX.class and the WAV files used by the applet.

The jar tool takes the following arguments when it is run:

- Options determining what jar should do (cf in the previous example)
- The name of the archive (SoundFX.jar)
- The file (or files) to be archived, with each filename separated by a space (SoundFX.class and fx*.wav)

Wildcards can be used when specifying filenames, so fx*.wav refers to any file with a name that begins with fx and ends with .wav. You can also list each file separately.

> The jar tool includes its own built-in help feature. To see a brief rundown of the ways it can be used, enter jar at the command-line without any arguments.

After you have created a Java archive containing all files used in an applet, the ARCHIVE attribute of the <APPLET> tag is used to associate this archive with the applet.

Continuing the example of the SoundFX applet, you could include its JAR archive on a Web page with the following HTML code:

```
<applet code="SoundFX.class" archive="SoundFX.jar"
height=80 width=140>
</applet>
```

When the ARCHIVE attribute is used with an applet, the applet's main class file should be included in the specified archive file. The CODE attribute must still be used because the name of the main class file must still be identified, whether it's loaded directly or from an archive.

Java archives are a way to speed up the presentation of applets and to organize other multifile projects. All JavaBeans components are packaged into .JAR files, making them more self-contained and keeping them in a single file that's easier to make available for use in other Java programs.

Workshop: Making Your Computer Talk to You

At this point, you've seen how Java's audio capabilities can be used to either simulate hysterics or to promote them. Your workshop project this hour puts Java's aural features to more productive use by creating a simple math tutor.

The `MathMan` applet uses 12 sound files that are available from the book's Web site: `plus.wav`, `equals.wav`, and 10 numbered files from `number0.wav` to `number10.wav`. If you haven't retrieved these files yet, visit `http://www.java24hours.com`. All 12 files should be saved in the same folder you're going to use for this workshop's `.java`, `.class`, and `.html` files.

Each of these files contains a computer-synthesized voice speaking a specific word. See if you can guess what these words are as you enter the text of Listing 22.2 into your word processor.

LISTING 22.2   The Full Source Code of `MathMan.java`

```
 1: import java.awt.*;
 2: import java.applet.AudioClip;
 3:
 4: public class MathMan extends javax.swing.JApplet
 5:     implements Runnable {
 6:
 7:     AudioClip[] number = new AudioClip[11];
 8:     AudioClip plus;
 9:     AudioClip equals;
10:     int sum, num1, num2;
11:     Thread runner;
12:
13:     public void start() {
14:         if (runner == null) {
15:             runner = new Thread(this);
16:             runner.start();
17:         }
18:     }
19:
20:     public void stop() {
21:         if (runner != null)
22:             runner = null;
23:     }
24:
25:     public void init() {
26:         equals = getAudioClip(getCodeBase(), "equals.wav");
27:         plus = getAudioClip(getCodeBase(), "plus.wav");
28:         for (int i = 0; i < number.length; i++)
29:             number[i] = getAudioClip(getCodeBase(),
30:                 "number" + i + ".wav");
31:     }
32:
33:     public void run() {
34:         Thread thisThread = Thread.currentThread();
35:         while (runner == thisThread) {
36:             sum = (int) Math.floor(Math.random() * 10 + 1);
```

LISTING 22.2   continued

```
37:                num2 = (int) Math.floor(Math.random() * sum);
38:                num1 = sum - num2;
39:                repaint();
40:                number[num1].play();
41:                pause(600);
42:                plus.play();
43:                pause(600);
44:                number[num2].play();
45:                pause(600);
46:                equals.play();
47:                pause(600);
48:                number[sum].play();
49:                pause(5000);
50:            }
51:    }
52:
53:    public void paint(Graphics screen) {
54:        super.paint(screen);
55:        int width = getSize().width;
56:        int height = getSize().height;
57:        Graphics2D screen2D = (Graphics2D) screen;
58:        screen2D.setColor(Color.white);
59:        screen2D.fillRect(0, 0, width, height);
60:        screen2D.setColor(Color.black);
61:        Font dialog = new Font("Dialog", Font.BOLD, 48);
62:        screen2D.setFont(dialog);
63:        screen2D.drawString(num1 + " + " + num2 + " = " + sum,
64:            width / 2 - 100, height / 2 - 25);
65:    }
66:
67:    private void pause(int duration) {
68:        try {
69:            Thread.sleep(duration);
70:        } catch (InterruptedException e) { }
71:    }
72: }
```

When you're done, save the file as MathMan.java and create a new file. Enter the text of Listing 22.3 and save it as MathMan.html.

LISTING 22.3   The Full Text of MathMan.html

```
1: <applet code="MathMan.class" height=50 width=80>
2: </applet>
```

Compile the applet's class file and load the page `Mathman.html` in a Web browser. If you are using the SDK, you can compile and test this applet with the following command:

```
javac MathMan.java
MathMan.html
```

This applet will display a simple mathematical expression using addition, as shown in Figure 22.2.

FIGURE 22.2

Listening to the
`MathMan` *application.*

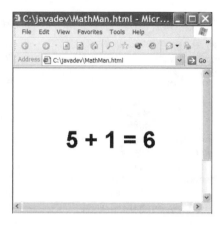

Each of the 12 WAV files required by this applet are loaded into their own `AudioClip` objects. These files will be played with calls to the `play()` method so that the mathematical expression is read aloud by the program.

Although this math tutor is a little basic for most people outside of the legislative branch of government, it's a good demonstration of how sound can enhance an educational presentation.

Summary

Now that you've had a chance to work with audio in your Java programs, you have a better perspective of the ever-present talking computers in science fiction movies, TV shows, and novels.

Your Java programs can now do something my Commodore 64 was either unwilling or unable to do back in the early '80s: speak. Applets and applications can also play music, sound effects, and other noises.

Using audio files in an applet is a way to bring some attention to a World Wide Web page, because pages you can hear are still a rarity. However, when choosing your own files, it's important to use sound judgment: The LaughTrack applet is not likely to encourage repeat visits to a Web site.

Q&A

Q Why is the Thread.sleep() method needed in the MathMan applet?

A The call to sleep() causes the thread controlling the program to pause for a set amount of time. The integer argument to the method indicates the number of milliseconds to delay before continuing the thread. This prevents the running together of different sounds when the mathematical expression is being read aloud. Experiment with different durations for the pause to see how it affects playback of the audio.

Q Is there a reason that JApplet should be used instead of the Applet class for audio playback?

A The JApplet class inherits all its sound capabilities from the Applet class, so it doesn't matter which class you use when working with sound. However, all Java 2 applets use the JApplet class, so there's no reason to use a different class when working with applet-related features.

Quiz

To see if this hour has been a resounding success, test your knowledge of Java's sound capabilities with the following questions.

Questions

1. Which of the following is not an audio format supported by Java?

    a. WAV

    b. AU

    c. DISCO

2. What's the benefit of using the getCodeBase() method to specify the location of a sound file in your applets?

    a. The sound file loads more quickly.

    b. You can move the applet to a new location on the World Wide Web without changing the program in any way.

    c. All your friends in the Java community already are doing it, so you won't be ostracized and ridiculed for being different.

3. What does URL stand for?

    a. Universal Resource Locator

    b. Uniform Resource Locator

    c. Unexpected Radio Link

Answers

1. c. DISCO is not a valid audio format in Java. Some people might argue that it isn't a valid audio format in life, either, but you won't hear that from this author. I'm still saving clothes for the day when gold chains, Gloria Gaynor, and wide collars open to the navel make their triumphant comeback.

2. b.

3. b. Actually, a. isn't too off the mark, because URLs are sometimes referred to as Universal Resource Locators.

Activities

If your ears aren't ringing from all the sound advice you've received, consider the following activities:

- Create a new version of the MathMan applet that uses subtraction instead of addition, making sure that the mathematical expression does not include any numbers higher than 10 or lower than 0.

- Create a JAR archive for the MathMan applet and all its audio files, then modify MathMan.html so it can load these files from the archive.

To see Java programs that implement these activities, visit the book's Web site at http://www.java24hours.com.

HOUR 23

Working with Graphics

Graphics can be represented on a computer in several ways. One way is to store the image using a file format that approximates what the graphic looks like. For example, if you took a photo of the Californian sasquatch swimming in your pool and scanned it into your computer, you could save it as a JPEG file. The JPEG format is ideal for storing photographic images in reasonably small file sizes.

You can also represent graphics as a series of drawing instructions used to create the image. These are called "vector graphics," and they are becoming popular on the World Wide Web in the form of Macromedia Flash programs. These graphics don't look like photographic images, but they are much smaller in file size and can be redrawn easily at different sizes, making them ideal for animation. If you created a cartoon about the sasquatch, you could save it in a vector format.

Java supports vector graphics through Java2D, the same classes that were used to draw text in different ways in Hour 21, "Using Fonts and Color." You'll get a chance to draw shapes of different colors in a program—everything from rectangles to ovals to lines.

The following subjects will be covered:

- The drawing methods of the `Graphics2D` class
- Drawing lines
- Drawing rectangles and rounded rectangles
- Drawing polygons
- Drawing ellipses
- Drawing with different colors
- Drawing filled and unfilled shapes

Using Graphics

This isn't meant as a knock to those of us who enjoy displaying arrays, incrementing variables, or using a constructor method, but let's face it—many subjects in a programming language such as Java tend to be dry. It's hard to impress your non-programming acquaintances with the way your `if-else` statement determines which method to use in a mathematical application. Dates don't get nearly as excited as you do when a `switch-case` block statement handles a variety of different circumstances correctly. Nobody ever made a movie about the ternary operator.

Graphics programming is the exception to this general rule. When you write a program that does something interesting with graphics, it's a way to have fun with a programming language and impress relatives, friends, strangers, and prospective employers.

Drawing things such as lines and polygons is as easy in a Java applet as displaying text. All you need are `Graphics` and `Graphics2D` objects to define the drawing surface and objects that represent the things to draw.

The `Graphics` class stores information required to display something onscreen. The most common use of the class is as an object that represents the area where something can be drawn in a container, such as a panel or an applet window.

In a container such as a `JPanel` component, a `Graphics` object is sent to the `paintComponent()` method as an argument:

```
public void paintComponent(Graphics comp) {
    // ...
}
```

The same thing happens in the `paint()` method of an applet:

```
public void paint(Graphics comp) {
    // ...
}
```

Both of these methods are called automatically whenever the container must be redrawn. For instance, if you have a Java frame open as an application is running and cover it up with another window, the frame's `paintComponent()` method will be called when the other window is closed.

Inside these paint methods, you should begin by calling the same method in the super-class, as in the following example:

```
public void paintComponent(Graphics comp) {
    super.paintComponent(comp);
}
```

Next, the `Graphics` object argument can be used to create a `Graphics2D` object, as in the following statement:

```
Graphics2D comp2D = (Graphics2D) comp;
```

Once you have a `Graphics2D` object, you draw by calling its methods. This `Graphics2D` object is called `comp2D` throughout this book, and its methods are used to draw text with a command such as the following:

```
comp2D.drawString("Draw, pardner!", 15, 40);
```

This statement causes the text `Draw, pardner!` to be displayed at the (x,y) coordinates of (15,40).

All of the shape- and line-drawing methods work using the same (x,y) coordinate system as text. The (0,0) coordinate is at the upper left corner of the container. The x values go up as you head to the right, and y values go up as you head downward. You can determine the maximum (x,y) value you can use in an applet with the following statements:

```
int maxXValue = getSize().width;
int maxYValue = getSize().height;
```

Drawing Lines and Shapes

Figure 23.1 shows a Java application that illustrates the different things you'll be learning to draw during this hour: lines, rectangles, ellipses, and polygons.

FIGURE 23.1

Displaying a sign using Java2D graphics.

With the exception of lines, all of the shapes you can draw can be filled or unfilled. A filled shape is drawn with the current color completely filling the space taken up by the shape. Unfilled shapes just draw a border with the current color.

Before you create an application to draw this sign, we'll describe each of the drawing methods. The comp2D object will be used as the Graphics2D object throughout this section.

The sign shown in Figure 23.1 is the international symbol that means "Use of Compressed Air Prohibited."

Drawing Lines

A 2D drawing operation in Java requires two steps:

- An object is created that represents the shape that is being drawn.
- A method of a Graphics2D object is called to actually draw that shape.

The objects that define shapes all are part of the java.awt.geom package of classes. There are two classes that can be used to create lines: Line2D.Float and Line2D.Double. These classes differ only in the way they are created: One is created using floating-point numbers to specify the beginning (x,y) point and ending (x,y) point of the line, and the other uses double values.

The following statement creates a line from the point (40,200) to the point (70,130):

```
Line2D.Float ln = new Line2D.Float(40F, 200F, 70F, 130F);
```

Each of the arguments to the `Line2D.Float` constructor is a number followed by an `F`, which indicates that the number is a floating-point value. This is necessary when creating a `Line2D.Float` object.

> `Line2D.Float` may look unusual because it includes a . character as part of the name. Normally, you'd expect this to mean that `Line2D.Float` refers to a variable called `Float` in the `Line2D` class. `Float` actually refers to an inner class that is defined inside the `Line2D` class. The capital letter that begins the name `Float` is an indicator that it's something other than a variable, because class and object variable names are either all lowercase or all uppercase. `Line2D.Float` is treated like any other class. The only difference is the . in the name.

After you create a drawing object of any kind, whether it's a line, ellipse, rectangle, or another shape, it is drawn by calling a method of the `Graphics2D` class. The `draw()` method draws the shape as an outline and the `fill()` method draws it as a filled shape.

The following statement will draw the `ln` object created in the previous example:

```
comp2D.draw(ln);
```

Drawing Rectangles

Rectangles can be filled or unfilled, and they can have rounded corners or square ones. They can be created using the `Rectangle2D.Float` class and specifying the following four arguments:

- The x coordinate at the upper left of the rectangle
- The y coordinate at upper left
- The width of the rectangle
- The height

The following statement draws an unfilled rectangle with square corners:

```
Rectangle2D.Float rr = new
    Rectangle2D.Float(245F, 65F, 20F, 10F);
```

This statement creates a rectangle with its upper-left corner at the (x,y) coordinate of (245,65). The width of the rectangle is 20 and the height is 10. These dimensions are expressed in pixels, the same unit of measure used for coordinates. To draw this rectangle as an outline, the following statement could be used:

```
comp2D.draw(rr);
```

If you want to make the rectangle filled in, use the `fill()` method instead of `draw()`, as in this statement:

```
comp.fill(rr);
```

You can create rectangles with rounded corners instead of square ones by using the `RoundRectangle2D.Float` class. The constructor to this class starts with the same four arguments as the `Rectangle2D.Float` class, and adds the following two arguments:

- A number of pixels in the x direction away from the corner of the rectangle
- A number of pixels in the y direction away from the corner

These distances are used to determine where the rounding of the rectangle's corner should begin.

The following statement creates a rounded rectangle:

```
RoundRectangle2D.Float ro = new RoundRectangle.Float(
    10F, 10F,
    100F, 80F,
    15F, 15F);
```

This rectangle has its upper-left corner at the (10,10) coordinate. The last two arguments to `drawRoundRect()` specify that the corner should begin rounding 15 pixels away from the corner at (10,10) and the other three corners, also.

As with other rectangle methods, the third and fourth arguments specify how wide and tall the rectangle should be. In this case, it should be 100 pixels wide and 80 pixels tall.

After the rounded rectangle is created, it is drawn using the `draw()` and `fill()` methods of a `Graphics2D` object.

Drawing Ellipses and Circles

Ellipses and circles can both be created with the same class: `Ellipse2D.Float`. This class takes four arguments: the (x,y) coordinates of the ellipse, and its width and height.

The (x,y) coordinates do not indicate a point at the center of the ellipse or circle, as you might expect. Instead, the (x,y) coordinates, width, and height describe an invisible rectangle that the ellipse fits into. The (x,y) coordinate is the upper-left corner of this rectangle. If it has the same width and height, the ellipse is a circle.

The following statement creates a circle at (245,45) with a height and width of 5 each:

```
Ellipse2D.Float cir = new Ellipse2D.Float(
    245F, 45F, 5F, 5F);
```

Drawing this object requires a call to `draw(cir)` or `fill(cir)`.

Drawing Arcs

Another circular shape you can draw in Java is an arc, a partial ellipse or circle. Arcs are created using the Arc2D.Float class, which has a constructor method with many of the same arguments. You draw the arc by specifying an ellipse, the portion of the ellipse that should be visible (in degrees), and the place the arc should begin on the ellipse.

To create an arc, specify the following integer arguments to the constructor:

- The x coordinate of the invisible rectangle that the ellipse fits into
- The y coordinate of the rectangle
- The width of the rectangle
- The height of the rectangle
- The point on the ellipse where the arc should begin (in degrees from 0 to 359)
- The size of the arc, also in degrees
- The type of arc it is

The arc's starting point and size range from 0 to 359 degrees in a counterclockwise direction, beginning with 0 degrees at the 3 o'clock position, as shown in Figure 23.2.

FIGURE 23.2
How arcs are defined in degrees.

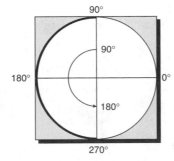

The type of arc is specified by using one of three class variables from the Arc2D.Float class: PIE if the arc should be drawn as a slice of a pie graph, CLOSED if the endpoints of the arc should be connected with a straight line, and OPEN if the endpoints should not be connected.

The following statement draws an open arc at (100,50) that is 120 degrees long, begins at the 30-degree mark, and has a height and width of 75 each:

```
Arc2D.Float smile = new Arc2D.Float(100F, 50F, 75F, 75F,
    30F, 120F, Arc2D.Float.OPEN);
```

You will work more with arcs later in this hour's workshop.

Drawing Polygons

Polygons are the most complicated shape to create because they have a varying number of points. The first step in creating a polygon is to create a `GeneralPath` object that will hold it. This object starts off without any points in the polygon being defined:

```
GeneralPath polly = new GeneralPath();
```

Once this object is created, its `moveTo()` method is used to define the first point in the polygon. For a closed polygon, such as an octagon, this can be any of the points. You can also define open polygons, and, in this case, your first point should be one of the end points of the polygon.

The `moveTo()` method takes two arguments: an x and a y coordinate. This (x,y) coordinate defines the point on the polygon. The following statement is an example:

```
polly.moveTo(100F, 20F);
```

After you have established the initial point in this manner, each successive point is added with the `lineTo()` method. This method also takes an x coordinate and y coordinate as arguments, as in the following statement:

```
polly.lineTo(80F, 45F);
```

You can call `lineTo()` as often as needed to create the sides of the polygon. When you have added the last point, you can close off the polygon by calling the `closePath()` method with no arguments:

```
polly.closePath();
```

If you don't call `closePath()`, the polygon will be open. When you have finished creating the shape, it can be drawn with the `draw()` and `fill()` methods like any other drawn object.

Drawing Lines of Different Widths

If you tried out all of the drawing operations you have learned about up to this point, you would see that they draw lines that are one pixel wide.

You can change the size of the line by using the `BasicStroke` class, part of the `java.awt` package. Objects of this class represent the width of the "drawing pen," and you can create one by calling the `BasicStroke(int)` constructor, as in the following example:

```
BasicStroke pen = new BasicStroke(12);
```

The integer specified in the constructor represents the width of the pen in pixels. Using `BasicStroke` objects is similar to working with fonts and colors. To draw with a pen you have created, call the setStroke() method of the Graphics2D class with the pen as an argument. The following example creates a 3-pixel wide stroke and assigns it to a Graphics2D object called comp2D:

```
BasicStroke brush = new BasicStroke(3);
comp2D.setStroke(brush);
```

Everything you draw will use the pen until you select a different one.

Creating the Sign

To put all of these shapes together, load your word processor and create a new file called Sign.java. Enter Listing 23.1 into the file and save it when you're done.

LISTING 23.1 The Full Text of Sign.java

```
 1: import java.awt.*;
 2: import javax.swing.*;
 3: import java.awt.geom.*;
 4:
 5: public class Sign extends JFrame {
 6:     public Sign() {
 7:         super("Use of Compressed Air Prohibited");
 8:         setSize(410, 435);
 9:         setDefaultCloseOperation(JFrame.EXIT_ON_CLOSE);
10:         SignPanel sp = new SignPanel();
11:         Container content = getContentPane();
12:         content.add(sp);
13:         setContentPane(content);
14:         setVisible(true);
15:     }
16:
17:     public static void main(String[] arguments) {
18:         Sign sign = new Sign();
19:     }
20: }
21:
22: class SignPanel extends JPanel {
23:     public void paintComponent(Graphics comp) {
24:         super.paintComponent(comp);
25:         Graphics2D comp2D = (Graphics2D) comp;
26:         comp2D.setColor(Color.white);
27:         comp2D.fillRect(0, 0, 400, 400);
28:
29:         // draw sign
30:         comp2D.setColor(Color.red);
31:         Ellipse2D.Float sign1 = new Ellipse2D.Float(0F, 0F, 400F, 400F);
32:         comp2D.fill(sign1);
33:         comp2D.setColor(Color.white);
```

23

LISTING 23.1 continued

```
34:          Ellipse2D.Float sign2 = new Ellipse2D.Float(55F, 55F, 290F, 290F);
35:          comp2D.fill(sign2);
36:
37:          // draw man
38:          comp2D.setColor(Color.black);
39:          Ellipse2D.Float head = new Ellipse2D.Float(160F, 96F, 32F, 32F);
40:          comp2D.fill(head);
41:          GeneralPath body = new GeneralPath();
42:          body.moveTo(159F, 162F);
43:          body.lineTo(119F, 303F);
44:          body.lineTo(139F, 303F);
45:          body.lineTo(168F, 231F);
46:          body.lineTo(190F, 303F);
47:          body.lineTo(213F, 303F);
48:          body.lineTo(189F, 205F);
49:          body.lineTo(203F, 162F);
50:          body.lineTo(247F, 151F);
51:          body.lineTo(236F, 115F);
52:          body.lineTo(222F, 118F);
53:          body.lineTo(231F, 140F);
54:          body.lineTo(141F, 140F);
55:          body.lineTo(101F, 190F);
56:          body.lineTo(112F, 197F);
57:          body.lineTo(144F, 162F);
58:          body.closePath();
59:          comp2D.fill(body);
60:
61:          // draw can
62:          comp2D.setColor(Color.black);
63:          comp2D.fillRect(251, 191, 33, 118);
64:          comp2D.fillRect(262, 160, 13, 31);
65:          GeneralPath nozzle = new GeneralPath();
66:          nozzle.moveTo(252F, 176F);
67:          nozzle.lineTo(262F, 160F);
68:          nozzle.lineTo(262F, 176F);
69:          nozzle.closePath();
70:          comp2D.fill(nozzle);
71:
72:          // draw lines
73:          comp2D.setColor(Color.black);
74:          BasicStroke pen = new BasicStroke(2F);
75:          comp2D.setStroke(pen);
76:          Line2D.Float ln1 = new Line2D.Float(203F, 121F, 255F, 102F);
77:          comp2D.draw(ln1);
78:          Line2D.Float ln2 = new Line2D.Float(255F, 102F, 272F, 116F);
79:          comp2D.draw(ln2);
80:          Line2D.Float ln3 = new Line2D.Float(272F, 134F, 252F, 158F);
81:          comp2D.draw(ln3);
82:
```

LISTING 23.1 continued

```
83:        // finish sign
84:        comp2D.setColor(Color.red);
85:        GeneralPath sign3 = new GeneralPath();
86:        sign3.moveTo(110F, 78F);
87:        sign3.lineTo(321F, 289F);
88:        sign3.lineTo(290F, 317F);
89:        sign3.lineTo(81F, 107F);
90:        sign3.closePath();
91:        comp2D.fill(sign3);
92:    }
93: }
```

After compiling the program successfully, run it at the command line. Your output should resemble Figure 23.1.

Workshop: Baking a Pie Graph

To draw this hour to a close, you will create PiePanel, a graphical user interface component that displays a pie graph. This component will be a subclass of JPanel, a simple Swing container that's useful as a place to draw something.

One way to begin creating a class is to define the way objects of the class will be created. Programs that use the PiePanel class must undertake the following steps:

- Create a PiePanel object by using the constructor method PiePanel(*int*). The integer specified as an argument is the number of slices the pie graph will contain.
- Call the object's addSlice(*Color, float*) method to give a slice the designated color and value.

The value of each slice in PiePanel is the quantity represented by that slice.

For example, Table 23.1 displays data about the status of student loan repayments in the U.S. from the start of the program in 1959 through November 1997, according to Congressional testimony by David A. Longanecker of the Office of Postsecondary Education.

TABLE 23.1 U.S. Student Loan Repayments

Amount repaid by students	$101 billion
Amount loaned to students still in school	$68 billion
Amount loaned to students making payments	$91 billion
Amount loaned to students who defaulted	$25 billion

You could use `PiePanel` to represent this data in a pie graph with the following statements:

```
PiePanel loans = new PiePanel(4);
loans.addSlice(Color.green, 101F);
loans.addSlice(Color.yellow, 68F);
loans.addSlice(Color.blue, 91F);
loans.addSlice(Color.red, 25F);
```

Figure 23.3 shows the result in an applet that contains one component: a `PiePanel` created with the student loan data.

FIGURE 23.3

Displaying student loan data on a pie graph.

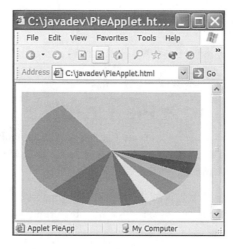

When a `PiePanel` object is created, the number of slices is specified in the constructor. You need to know three more things to be able to draw each slice:

- The color of the slice, represented by a `Color` object
- The value represented by each slice
- The total value represented by all slices

A new helper class, `PieSlice`, will be used to represent each slice in the pie graph:

```
class PieSlice {
    Color color = Color.lightGray;
    float size = 0;

    PieSlice(Color pColor, float pSize) {
        color = pColor;
        size = pSize;
    }
}
```

Each slice is constructed by calling PieSlice(*Color*, *float*). The combined value of all slices will be stored as a private instance variable of the PiePanel class, totalSize. There also will be instance variables for the panel's background color (background) and a counter used to keep track of slices (current):

```
private int current = 0;
private float totalSize = 0;
private Color background;
```

Now that you have a PieSlice class to work with, you can create an array of PieSlice objects with another instance variable:

```
private PieSlice[] slice;
```

When a PiePanel object is created, none of the slices have been assigned a color or size. The only things that must be done in the constructor are defining the size of the slice array and saving the background color of the panel:

```
public PiePanel(int sliceCount) {
    slice = new PieSlice[sliceCount];
    background = getBackground();
}
```

The addSlice(*Color*, *float*) method is used to add a slice of the pie to the panel:

```
public void addSlice(Color sColor, float sSize) {
    if (current <= slice.length) {
        slice[current] = new PieSlice(sColor, sSize);
        totalSize += sSize;
        current++;
    }
}
```

The current instance variable is used to put each slice into its own element of the slice array. The length variable of an array contains the number of elements the array has been defined to hold, so as long as current is not larger than slice.length, you can continue adding slices to the panel.

The PiePanel class handles all graphical operations in its paintComponent(*Graphics*) method, as you might expect. The trickiest thing about this task is drawing the arcs that represent each slice of the pie.

This is handled in the following statements:

```
float start = 0;
for (int i = 0; i < slice.length; i++) {
    float extent = slice[i].size * 360F / totalSize;
    comp2D.setColor(slice[i].color);
    Arc2D.Float drawSlice = new Arc2D.Float(
        xInset, yInset, width, height, start, extent,
```

```
        Arc2D.Float.PIE);
    start += extent;
    comp2D.fill(drawSlice);
}
```

The start variable keeps track of where to start drawing an arc, and extent keeps track of the size of an arc. If you know the total size of all pie slices and the size of a specific slice, you can figure out extent by multiplying the arc's size by 360 and dividing that by the total of all slices.

All of the arcs are drawn in a for loop: After each arc's extent is calculated, the arc is created and then extent is added to start. This causes each slice to begin right next to the last one. A call to the Graphics2D method fill() draws the arc.

To bring all of this together, load your word processor and create a new file called PiePanel.java. Enter the full text of Listing 23.2, and then save and compile the file when you're done.

LISTING 23.2   The Full Text of PiePanel.java

```
 1: import java.awt.*;
 2: import javax.swing.*;
 3: import java.awt.geom.*;
 4:
 5: public class PiePanel extends JPanel {
 6:     private PieSlice[] slice;
 7:     private int current = 0;
 8:     private float totalSize = 0;
 9:     private Color background;
10:
11:     public PiePanel(int sliceCount) {
12:         slice = new PieSlice[sliceCount];
13:         background = getBackground();
14:     }
15:
16:     public void addSlice(Color sColor, float sSize) {
17:         if (current <= slice.length) {
18:             slice[current] = new PieSlice(sColor, sSize);
19:             totalSize += sSize;
20:             current++;
21:         }
22:     }
23:
24:     public void paintComponent(Graphics comp) {
25:         super.paintComponent(comp);
26:         Graphics2D comp2D = (Graphics2D) comp;
27:         int width = getSize().width - 10;
28:         int height = getSize().height - 15;
```

LISTING 23.2 continued

```
29:            int xInset = 5;
30:            int yInset = 5;
31:            if (width < 5)
32:                xInset = width;
33:            if (height < 5)
34:                yInset = height;
35:            comp2D.setColor(background);
36:            comp2D.fillRect(0, 0, getSize().width, getSize().height);
37:            comp2D.setColor(Color.lightGray);
38:            Ellipse2D.Float pie = new Ellipse2D.Float(
39:                xInset, yInset, width, height);
40:            comp2D.fill(pie);
41:            float start = 0;
42:            for (int i = 0; i < slice.length; i++) {
43:                float extent = slice[i].size * 360F / totalSize;
44:                comp2D.setColor(slice[i].color);
45:                Arc2D.Float drawSlice = new Arc2D.Float(
46:                    xInset, yInset, width, height, start, extent,
47:                    Arc2D.Float.PIE);
48:                start += extent;
49:                comp2D.fill(drawSlice);
50:            }
51:        }
52: }
53:
54: class PieSlice {
55:     Color color = Color.lightGray;
56:     float size = 0;
57:
58:     PieSlice(Color pColor, float pSize) {
59:         color = pColor;
60:         size = pSize;
61:     }
62: }
```

After you save and compile the file, you will have a `PiePanel` class that can be added as a component to any Java program's graphical user interface. You can't run the class directly, so to test `PiePanel`, you need to create a class that uses it.

Listing 23.3 contains an applet that uses these panels, `PieApplet`.

LISTING 23.3 The Full Text of `PieApplet.java`

```
1: import java.awt.*;
2: import javax.swing.*;
3:
```

LISTING 23.3   continued

```
 4: public class PieApplet extends JApplet {
 5:     Color uneasyBeingGreen = new Color(0xCC, 0xCC, 0x99);
 6:     Color zuzusPetals = new Color(0xCC, 0x66, 0xFF);
 7:     Color zootSuit = new Color(0x66, 0x66, 0x99);
 8:     Color sweetHomeAvocado = new Color(0x66, 0x99, 0x66);
 9:     Color shrinkingViolet = new Color(0x66, 0x66, 0x99);
10:     Color miamiNice = new Color(0x33, 0xFF, 0xFF);
11:     Color inBetweenGreen = new Color(0x00, 0x99, 0x66);
12:     Color norwegianBlue = new Color(0x33, 0xCC, 0xCC);
13:     Color purpleRain = new Color(0x66, 0x33, 0x99);
14:     Color freckle = new Color (0x99, 0x66, 0x33);
15:
16:     public void init() {
17:         Container pane = getContentPane();
18:         PiePanel pie = new PiePanel(10);
19:         pie.addSlice(uneasyBeingGreen, 1284);
20:         pie.addSlice(zuzusPetals, 1046);
21:         pie.addSlice(zootSuit, 281);
22:         pie.addSlice(sweetHomeAvocado, 232);
23:         pie.addSlice(shrinkingViolet, 176);
24:         pie.addSlice(miamiNice, 148);
25:         pie.addSlice(inBetweenGreen, 143);
26:         pie.addSlice(norwegianBlue, 133);
27:         pie.addSlice(purpleRain,130);
28:         pie.addSlice(freckle, 127);
29:         pane.add(pie);
30:         setContentPane(pane);
31:     }
32: }
```

After compiling this applet, create a simple Web page that contains it by entering Listing 12.4 and saving it as `PieApplet.html`.

LISTING 23.4   The Full Text of `PieApplet.html`

```
1: <applet code="PieApplet.class" width="300" height="200">
2: </applet>
```

The `PieApplet` applet displays a pie graph showing the population of the 10 most populated countries (in millions), using figures from a August 2002 U.S. Census International Data Base report. In order, they are China (1.284 billion), India (1.046 billion), the United States (281 million), Indonesia (232 million), Brazil (176 million), Pakistan (148 million), Russia (145 million), Bangladesh (133 million), Nigeria (130 million), and Japan (127 million).

Since Java only has a few colors defined in the Color class, 10 new ones were created for use here and given descriptive names. The colors are expressed as hexadecimal values—in Java, hexadecimal numbers are preceded by 0x—but they could also have been specified as decimal values in each Color() constructor.

Figure 23.4 shows what this applet should look like in a browser such as Internet Explorer.

FIGURE 23.4

Displaying population figures in a pie graph.

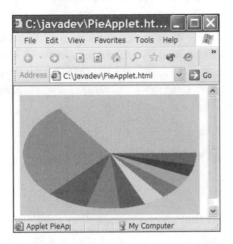

23

When you are viewing the PieApplet program, resize the applet window—the pie graph will be redrawn with dimensions that match the new size. This occurs because the (x,y), height, and width variables of the arcs use variables that are based on the size of the PiePanel. When the applet window is resized, Java resizes the panel also. These variables are defined in Lines 26–33 of Listing 23.2 by calling the component's getSize() method, which returns a Dimension object that has height and width instance variables describing how big the component is.

The names and hexadecimal values for the colors are from Hexadecimal Hues, a site devoted to assigning off-the-wall names to all the colors that can be used on the World Wide Web. To see more, visit the page http://tools.firmlist.com/hexagonalhues. At the time of this writing, you can see the U.S. Census world population figures by visiting the Web page http://www.census.gov/cgi-bin/ipc/idbrank.pl. If this page is unavailable, you can find similar information at the main Census page (http://www.census.gov) or the Population Research Bureau (http://www.prb.org).

Summary

Drawing something using the polygons and other shapes available with Java might seem like more trouble than it's worth, especially when you can load image files such as .GIF files and .JPG files, as you'll see in the next hour. However, graphics depicted with polygons have two advantages over graphics that are loaded from image files:

- Speed—Even a small graphic, such as an icon, would take longer to load and display than a series of polygons.

- Scaling—You can change the size of an entire image that uses polygons simply by changing the values to create it. For example, you could add a function to the Sign class that multiplies all (x,y) points in each shape by two before they are created, and it would result in an image twice as large. Polygon images scale much more quickly than image files and produce better results.

There are many instances where it makes more sense to use graphics files in your programs, and you will be trying some of them in the next hour.

Q&A

Q How can I draw arcs that go clockwise rather than counterclockwise?

A You can accomplish this by specifying the size of the arc as a negative number. The arc will begin at the same point, but go in the opposite direction in an elliptical path. For example, the following statement draws an open arc at (35,20) that is 90 degrees long, begins at the 0 degree mark, goes clockwise, and has a height of 20 and a width of 15:

```
Arc2D.Float smile = new Arc2D.Float(35F, 20F, 15F, 20F,
    0F, -90F, Arc2D.Float.OPEN);
```

Q Ellipses and circles don't have corners. What are the (x,y) coordinates specified with the Ellipses.Float constructor method?

A The (x,y) coordinates represent the smallest x value and smallest y value of the oval or circle. If you drew an invisible rectangle around it, the upper-left corner of the rectangle would be the x and y coordinates used as arguments to the method.

Quiz

Test whether your Java graphics skills are taking shape by answering the following questions.

Questions

1. What method is used to change the current color before you draw something in a program?

   a. `shiftColor()`

   b. `setColor()`

   c. Could you repeat the question?

2. If you want to use the height and width of a component to determine how big something should be drawn, what can you use?

   a. A ruler and a friend who's good at math

   b. `getHeight()` and `getWidth()`

   c. `getSize().height` and `getSize().width`

3. What societal problem did this hour's first example program call attention to?

   a. Overpopulation

   b. Defaulted student loans

   c. People who compress air in places with signs that clearly indicate it is prohibited, especially restaurants

Answers

1. b. You can use the `setBackground()` method to set the background color of an applet, and you can use the `setColor()` method of the `Graphics` class to select the current color.

2. c.

3. c. Though overpopulation is a pretty big deal, too.

Activities

To draw upon your vast storehouse of graphical skills, do the following activities:

- Create a version of the `PieApplet` class that takes color values and pie slice values as parameters instead of including them in the source code of the applet.

- Create a version of `Sign` that changes in shape to fit the available space in the panel (just like the `PiePanel` component does).

To see Java programs that implement these activities, visit the book's Web site at `http://www.java24hours.com`.

Hour **24**

Creating Animation

Whether you are reading this book in 24 one-hour sessions or in a single 24-hour-long-bring-me-more-coffee-can't-feel-my-hand-are-you-going-to-finish-that-donut marathon, you deserve something for making it all this way. Unfortunately, Sams Publishing declined my request to buy you a pony, so the best I can offer as a reward is the most entertaining subject in the book: animation.

At this point, you have learned how to use text, fonts, color, lines, polygons, and sound in your Java programs. For the last hour on Java's multimedia capabilities, and the last hour of the book, you will learn how to display image files in GIF and JPEG formats in your programs and present them in animated sequences. The following topics will be covered:

- Using `Image` objects to hold image files
- Putting a series of images into an array
- Cycling through an image array to produce animation
- Using the `update()` method to reduce flickering problems

- Using the `drawImage()` command
- Establishing rules for the movement of an image

Animating a Sequence of Images

Computer animation at its most basic consists of drawing an image at a specific place, moving the location of the image, and telling the computer to redraw the image at its new location. Many animations on Web pages are a series of image files, usually .GIF or .JPG files that are displayed in the same place in a certain order. You can do this to simulate motion or to create some other effect.

The first program you will be writing today uses a series of image files to create an animated picture of the Anastasia Island Lighthouse in St. Augustine, Florida. Several details about the animation will be customizable with parameters, so you can replace any images of your own for those provided for this example.

Create a new file in your word processor called `Animate.java`. Enter Listing 24.1 into the file, and remember to save the file when you're done entering the text.

LISTING 24.1   The Full Text of `Animate.java`

```
 1: import java.awt.*;
 2:
 3: public class Animate extends javax.swing.JApplet
 4:     implements Runnable {
 5:
 6:     Image[] picture = new Image[6];
 7:     int totalPictures = 0;
 8:     int current = 0;
 9:     Thread runner;
10:     int pause = 500;
11:
12:     public void init() {
13:         for (int i = 0; i < 6; i++) {
14:             String imageText = null;
15:             imageText = getParameter("image"+i);
16:             if (imageText != null) {
17:                 totalPictures++;
18:                 picture[i] = getImage(getCodeBase(), imageText);
19:             } else
20:                 break;
21:         }
22:         String pauseText = null;
23:         pauseText = getParameter("pause");
24:         if (pauseText != null) {
25:             pause = Integer.parseInt(pauseText);
```

LISTING 24.1 continued

```
26:          }
27:      }
28:
29:      public void paint(Graphics screen) {
30:          super.paint(screen);
31:          Graphics2D screen2D = (Graphics2D) screen;
32:          if (picture[current] != null)
33:              screen2D.drawImage(picture[current], 0, 0, this);
34:      }
35:
36:      public void start() {
37:          if (runner == null) {
38:              runner = new Thread(this);
39:              runner.start();
40:          }
41:      }
42:
43:      public void run() {
44:          Thread thisThread = Thread.currentThread();
45:          while (runner == thisThread) {
46:              repaint();
47:              current++;
48:              if (current >= totalPictures)
49:                  current = 0;
50:              try {
51:                  Thread.sleep(pause);
52:              } catch (InterruptedException e) { }
53:          }
54:      }
55:
56:      public void stop() {
57:          if (runner != null) {
58:              runner = null;
59:          }
60:      }
61: }
```

Because animation is usually a process that continues over a period of time, the portion of the program that manipulates and animates images should be designed to run in its own thread. This becomes especially important in a Swing program that must be able to respond to user input while an animation is taking place. Without threads, animation often takes up so much of the Java interpreter's time that the rest of a program's graphical user interface is sluggish to respond.

The `Animate` program uses the same threaded applet structure that you used during Hour 19, "Creating a Threaded Program." Threads are also useful in animation programming because they give you the ability to control the timing of the animation. The `Thread.sleep()` method is an effective way to determine how long each image should be displayed before the next image is shown.

The `Animate` applet retrieves images as parameters on a Web page. The parameters should have names starting at `"image0"` and ending at the last image of the animation, such as `"image3"` in this hour's example. The maximum number of images that can be displayed by this applet is six, but you could raise this number by making changes to Lines 6 and 13.

The `totalPicture` integer variable determines how many different images will be displayed in an animation. If less than six image files have been specified by parameters, the `Animate` applet will determine this during the `init()` method when `imageText` equals `null` after Line 15.

The speed of the animation is specified by a `"pause"` parameter. Because all parameters from a Web page are received as strings, the `Integer.parseInt()` method is needed to convert the text into an integer. The `pause` variable keeps track of the number of milliseconds to pause after displaying each image in an animation.

Loading and Displaying Images

As with most threaded programs, the `run()` method contains the main part of the program. A `while (runner == thisThread)` statement in Line 44 causes Lines 45–51 to loop until something causes these two `Thread` objects to have different values.

The first thing that happens in the `while` loop is a call to the applet's `repaint()` method. This statement requests that the applet's `paint()` method be called so that the screen can be updated. Use `repaint()` any time you know something has changed and the display needs to be changed to bring it up to date. In this case, every time the `Animate` loop goes around once, a different image should be shown.

In Java, you can never be sure that calling `repaint()` will result in the component or applet window being repainted. The interpreter will ignore calls to `repaint()` if it can't process them as quickly as they are being called, or if some other task is taking up most of its time.

The `paint()` method in Lines 29–34 contains the following statements:

```
Graphics2D screen2D = (Graphics2D) screen;
if (picture[current] != null)
    screen2D.drawImage(picture[current], 0, 0, this);
```

First, a `Graphics2D` object is cast so that it can be used when drawing to the applet window. Next, an `if` statement determines whether the `Image` object stored in `picture[current]` has a `null` value. When it does not equal `null`, this indicates that an image is ready to be displayed. The `drawImage()` method of the `screen2D` object displays the current `Image` object at the (x,y) position specified.

> The `paint()` method of this applet does not call the `paint()` method of its superclass, unlike some of the other graphical programs in the book, because it makes the animated sequence look terrible. The applet's `paint()` method clears the window each time it is called, which is OK when you're drawing a graphical user interface or some other graphics that don't change. However, clearing it again and again in a short time causes an animation to flicker.

24

The `this` statement sent as the fourth argument to `drawImage()` enables the program to use a class called `ImageObserver`. This class tracks when an image is being loaded and when it is finished. The `JApplet` class contains behavior that works behind the scenes to take care of this process, so all you have to do is specify `this` as an argument to `drawImage()` and some other methods related to image display. The rest is taken care of for you.

An `Image` object must be created and loaded with a valid image before you can use the `drawImage()` method. The way to load an image in an applet is to use the `getImage()` method. This method takes two arguments: the Web address or folder that contains the image file and the file name of the image.

The first argument is taken care of with the `getCodeBase()` method, which is part of the `JApplet` class. This method returns the location of the applet itself, so if you put your images in the same folder as the applet's class file, you can use `getCodeBase()`. The second argument should be a `.GIF` file or `.JPG` file to load. In the following example, a `turtlePicture` object is created and an image file called `Mertle.gif` is loaded into it:

```
Image turtlePicture = getImage(getCodeBase(), "Mertle.gif");
```

As you look over the source code to the Animate applet, you might wonder why the test for a null value in Line 31 is necessary. This check is required because the paint() method may be called before an image file has been fully loaded into a picture[] element. Calling getImage() begins the process of loading an image. To prevent a slowdown, the Java interpreter continues to run the rest of the program while images are being loaded.

Storing a Group of Related Images

In the Animate applet, images are loaded into an array of Image objects called pictures. The pictures array is set up to handle six elements in Line 6 of the program, so you can have Image objects ranging from picture[0] to picture[5]. The following statement in the applet's paint() method displays the current image:

```
screen.drawImage(picture[current], 0, 0, this);
```

The current variable is used in the applet to keep track of which image to display in the paint() method. It has an initial value of 0, so the first image to be displayed is the one stored in picture[0]. After each call to the repaint() statement in Line 45 of the run() method, the current variable is incremented by one in Line 46.

The totalPictures variable is an integer that keeps track of how many images should be displayed. It is set when images are loaded from parameters off the Web page. When current equals totalPictures, it is set back to 0. As a result, current cycles through each image of the animation, and then begins again at the first image.

Sending Parameters to the Applet

Because the Animate applet relies on parameters to specify the image files it should display, you need to create a Web page containing these file names before you can test the program. After saving and compiling the Animate.java file, open up a new file in your word processor and call it Animate.html. Enter Listing 24.2 into that file and save it when you're done.

LISTING 24.2   The Full Text of Animate.html

```
1: <applet code="Animate.class" width=215 height=298>
2: <param name="image0" value="lh0.gif">
3: <param name="image1" value="lh1.gif">
4: <param name="image2" value="lh2.gif">
```

LISTING 24.2 continued

```
5: <param name="image3" value="lh3.gif">
6: <param name="pause" value="800">
7: </applet>
```

This file specifies four image files: lh0.gif, lh1.gif, lh2.gif, and lh3.gif. These files are listed as the values for the parameters image0 through image3. You can find the files used in this example on the Hour 24 page of the book's Web site at http://www.java24hours.com.

You can also specify any of your own .GIF or .JPG files, if desired. Whichever files you choose should be placed in the same folder as the Animate.class and Animate.html files. With the "pause" parameter, you can specify how long the program should pause after each image is displayed.

You might be wondering why the files and the parameters are given names that start numbering with 0 instead of 1. This is done because the first element of an array in a Java program is numbered 0. Putting an image0 called lh0.gif into pictures[0] makes it easier to know where these images are being stored.

Once the files have been put in the right place, you're ready to try out the Animate applet. Type the following command to open the page in your Web browser and view the applet:

```
Animate.html
```

Figure 24.1 shows one of the four images being displayed as the applet runs.

Although this is a simple animation program, hundreds of applets on the Web use similar functionality to present a series of image files as an animation. Presenting a sequence of image files through Java is similar to the animated .GIF files that are becoming more commonplace on Web pages. Although Java applets are often slower to load than these .GIF files, they can provide more control of the animation and allow for more complicated effects.

Workshop: Follow the Bouncing Ball

This hour's workshop is an animation that definitely couldn't be replicated with an animated .GIF file or any other nonprogramming alternative. You'll write a program that bounces a tennis ball around the screen in lazy arcs, caroming off the sides of the panel that contains the animation. Though a few laws of physics will be broken along the way, you'll learn one way to move an image file around the screen.

Create a new file in your word processor called BouncePanel.java, and enter the text of Listing 24.3 into it. Save and compile the file when you're done.

LISTING 24.3   The Full Text of BouncePanel.java

```
 1: import java.awt.*;
 2: import javax.swing.*;
 3: import java.util.*;
 4:
 5: public class BouncePanel extends JPanel implements Runnable {
 6:     Image ball, court;
 7:     float current = 0F;
 8:     Thread runner;
 9:     int xPosition = 10;
10:     int xMove = 1;
11:     int yPosition = -1;
12:     int ballHeight = 185;
13:     int ballWidth = 190;
14:     int height;
15:
16:     public BouncePanel() {
```

LISTING 24.3   continued

```
17:            super();
18:            Toolkit kit = Toolkit.getDefaultToolkit();
19:            ball = kit.getImage("tennis.gif");
20:            court = kit.getImage("court.jpg");
21:            runner = new Thread(this);
22:            runner.start();
23:        }
24:
25:        public void paintComponent(Graphics comp) {
26:            Graphics2D comp2D = (Graphics2D) comp;
27:            height = getSize().height - ballHeight;
28:            if (yPosition == -1)
29:                yPosition = height - 20;
30:            if ((court != null) && (ball != null)) {
31:                comp2D.drawImage(court, 0, 0, this);
32:                comp2D.drawImage(ball,
33:                    (int) xPosition,
34:                    (int) yPosition,
35:                    this);
36:            }
37:        }
38:
39:        public void run() {
40:            Thread thisThread = Thread.currentThread();
41:            while (runner == thisThread) {
42:                current += (float) 0.1;
43:                if (current > 3)
44:                    current = (float) 0;
45:                xPosition += xMove;
46:                if (xPosition > (getSize().width - ballWidth))
47:                    xMove *= -1;
48:                if (xPosition < 1)
49:                    xMove *= -1;
50:                double bounce = Math.sin(current) * height;
51:                yPosition = (int) (height - bounce);
52:                repaint();
53:                try {
54:                    Thread.sleep(100);
55:                } catch (InterruptedException e) { }
56:            }
57:        }
58: }
```

24

Before you dive into the discussion of what's taking place in this class, you should see what it does. You need to create a program and add the BouncePanel component to the program's graphical user interface.

Create a new file in your word processor called `Bounce.java` and enter Listing 24.4 into it.

LISTING 24.4   The Full Text of `Bounce.java`

```
 1: import java.awt.*;
 2: import javax.swing.*;
 3:
 4: public class Bounce extends JFrame {
 5:     public Bounce() {
 6:         super("Tennis");
 7:         setSize(550, 450);
 8:         setDefaultCloseOperation(JFrame.EXIT_ON_CLOSE);
 9:         BouncePanel boing = new BouncePanel();
10:         Container pane = getContentPane();
11:         pane.add(boing);
12:         setContentPane(pane);
13:         setVisible(true);
14:     }
15:
16:     public static void main(String[] arguments) {
17:         Bounce frame = new Bounce();
18:     }
19: }
```

After saving this file, you need to get a copy of the `tennis.gif` and `court.gif` files and put them in the same folder as `Bounce.class` and `BouncePanel.class`. This file is available from the same place as the lighthouse image files: the book's Web site at `http://www.java24hours.com`.

Once you have copied the graphics files into the right place, run the `Bounce` application by typing this command:

`java Bounce`

Figure 24.2 shows the application running after both graphics have fully loaded.

This application displays the animation on the `BouncePanel` component: a `.GIF` file of a tennis ball bounces back and forth in front of a `.GIF` file depicting a net. When the ball hits a point at the bottom edge of the frame, it rebounds upward close to the top edge. When the ball hits the right or left edge, it bounces in the opposite direction.

FIGURE 24.2

Moving graphics files in an animation.

24

The animated sequence in the BouncePanel class illustrates how to animate an image file using Java. It consists of the following steps:

1. Draw the ball at its current location.
2. Move the ball according to the rules that have been established for how the ball should move.
3. Check whether the rules need to be changed based on the ball's new location.
4. Repeat.

Drawing the Image

The BouncePanel class is threaded, so all its image-manipulation code is placed in a run() method that will be called when the thread is started.

The paintComponent() method is where the court is drawn, followed by the ball at its current location.

If you display the tennis.gif file in a graphics viewer or editing program, you will see that it has a dark gray background around the ball. This background does not show up in the animated sequence because the tennis.gif file has been saved with that dark gray color designated as a transparent color. Java 2 supports transparency in graphics files, making it much easier to animate one image atop another.

The Image object called ball is loaded with the tennis.gif image in the init()
method. Several variables are used in the class to keep track of the ball's location and its
current rate of movement:

- xPosition—This variable is the x coordinate where the ball should be drawn. This
coordinate begins as 10.

- xMove—This variable is the amount the ball should move along the x axis after
every screen update. This amount starts out as 1, but it will change to -1 when the
ball hits the right edge of the applet window. It changes back and forth from -1 to
1 every time it hits an edge, and this change is handled by Lines 46–49.

- yPosition—This variable is the y coordinate where the ball should be drawn. This
coordinate is initially set to -1, which is a signal to the paint() method that the
yPosition needs to be set up before the ball can be drawn for the first time. The
yPosition value varies from a point near the bottom of the application frame to
the top edge.

- current—This floating-point number starts at 0 and increases by 0.1 each time the
ball is redrawn. When it reaches 3, it is set back to 0 again. The current variable is
used with a mathematical sine function to determine how high the ball bounces.
Sine waves are a good way to approximate the movements of a bouncing ball, and
the Math.sin()method enables a sine value to be used in conjunction with animation. The tennis ball is traveling half a sine wave each time it goes from the ground
to the top of the window and back.

The movement rules that you establish for an animated program will vary depending on
what you're trying to show. The Bounce application uses the Math.sin() method to create the slow arcs traveled by the ball.

Summary

The purpose of *Sams Teach Yourself Java 2 Programming in 24 Hours, Third Edition* is
to help you become comfortable with the concepts of programming and confident in your
ability to write your own applications and applets. Java has an approach that is somewhat
difficult to master. (Feel free to scratch out the word "somewhat" in the previous sentence if it's a gross misstatement of the truth.)

As you build experience in Java, you're building experience that will be increasingly rele-
vant in the coming years, because concepts such as object-oriented programming, virtual
machines, and secure environments are on the leading edge of software development.

If you haven't already, you should read the appendixes to find out about this book's Web
site, additional Java books from Sams Publishing, and other useful information.

At the conclusion of this hour, you can explore Java in several different places. Programmers are discussing the language in `comp.lang.java.programmer` and other Usenet discussion groups. Several hundred Java User Groups meet regularly, according to the list published at Sun's Java site (`http://servlet.java.sun.com/jugs`). Numerous Java job openings are displayed in the database of employment World Wide Web sites such as `http://www.careerbuilder.com`. There's also a Web site for this book at `http://www.java24hours.com` where you can send electronic mail to the author and read answers to reader questions, clarifications to the book, and (gulp) corrections.

Of course, my favorite way for you to continue building your skills as a Java programmer is to read *Sams Teach Yourself Java 2 in 21 Days, Third Edition*. I coauthored the book with Laura Lemay, and it expands on the subjects covered here and introduces new ones, such as JavaSound, JavaBeans, and network programming.

My apologies for this brazen attempt to hawk another book…if I sell enough copies, my name is entered into a drawing with other top Sams authors to win special prizes.

My heart's set on a Kool Orange Schwinn Sting-Ray bicycle with a banana seat.

—Rogers Cadenhead

Q&A

Q Does a threaded animation program have to use `Thread.sleep()` to pause, or can you omit it to produce the fastest possible animation?

A You have to put some kind of pause in place in an animation program, or the program will crash or behave erratically. Without pauses, Java won't be able to keep up with constant `repaint()` requests and may be unable to respond to mouse-clicks on its interface and other user input. Part of the process of animation design in Java is finding the right display speed that all environments can handle.

Q What happens if you draw something, such as an image, to coordinates that aren't within the window?

A Methods that draw something to a coordinate will continue to draw it even if none of it is visible within the area shown by the applet window or application frame. This is a good way to have something move into view, because the portion of the image that falls into the visible area will be displayed.

Quiz

Animate yourself as much as you can muster and answer the following questions to test your skills.

Questions

1. Where is the (0,0) coordinate on a container?

    a. In an offscreen double-buffering area

    b. The exact center of the window

    c. The upper-left corner of the container

2. What thing did you *not* learn during this hour?

    a. How to load images in an application

    b. How to make sure an image is not displayed until it loads

    c. Why the tennis ball is bouncing off thin air instead of the ground in the `BouncePanel` application.

3. In a threaded animation applet, where should you handle most of the movement of an image?

    a. The `run()` method

    b. The `init()` method

    c. The `paint()` method

Answers

1. c. The x value increases as you head to the right, and the y value increases as you head downward.

2. c. Would you believe clear-air turbulence?

3. a. Some movement might be handled by statements in the `paint()` method, but most of it will take place in `run()` or a method called from within `run()`.

Activities

Before you're stranded and the subject of graphics is abandoned, picture yourself doing the following activities:

- Create an applet that contains a `BouncePanel` component and a slider or text field in which the animation speed can be changed from 100 to another value.

- Create a version of the `Animate` project that runs as an application instead of an applet.

To see Java programs that implement these activities, visit the book's Web site at `http://www.java24hours.com`.

PART VII
Appendixes

APPENDIX A

Tackling New Features of Java 2 Version 1.4

Every new edition of Java 2 includes dozens of new features, so it's always a challenge to cover them in 24 hours.

Many new features are tailored toward advanced programming, putting them a bit beyond the scope of a book such as this one. However, there are always some new classes, methods, and techniques that new and intermediate-skilled Java programmers should know about, such as the addition of assertions in version 1.4, which was covered during Hour 18, "Handling Errors in a Program."

Another is the addition of Java Web Start, which enables you to install and run applications by clicking a link in a Web browser. It's an amazing new feature of the language that will change the way programmers distribute applications, but it couldn't be shoehorned into the first 24 hours. So, I'm going into at least 40 minutes of overtime by covering the following topics:

- How Java programs can be distributed
- How to download and install the Java Runtime Environment

- How to install and run Java applications in a Web browser
- How to set up an application to be run over the Web
- How to publish your application's files and run them

Java Web Start

One of the issues you must deal with as a Java programmer is how to make your software available to the people who will be using your work.

Applications require a Java interpreter, so one must either be included with the application, or users must install an interpreter themselves. The easiest solution (for you) is to require that users download and install the Java Runtime Environment from Sun's Web site at http://java.sun.com/getjava/.

Regardless of how you deal with the requirement for an interpreter, you distribute an application like any other program, making it available on a CD or Web site, or by some other means. A user must run an installation program to set it up, if one is available, or copy the files and folders manually.

Applets are easier to make available, because they can be run by Web browsers such as Microsoft Internet Explorer, Netscape Navigator, and Mozilla. However, if your program is a Java 2 applet, users must be running browsers that are equipped with the Java Plug-in. This too can be downloaded from Sun as part of the Java Runtime Environment.

There are several drawbacks to offering applets instead of applications, as detailed during Hour 17, "Creating Interactive Web Programs." The biggest is the default security policy for applets, which makes it impossible for them to read and write data on a user's computer, among other restrictions.

In Java 2 version 1.4, Sun offers support for an alternative means of distribution: Java Web Start, a method of downloading and running applications by clicking links on Web pages.

Java Web Start, which requires the Java Runtime Environment, offers a way to install and run applications as if they were applets. Here's how it works:

- A programmer packages an application into a JAR file along with a file that uses the Java Network Launching Protocol (JNLP), part of Java Web Start.
- The file is published on a Web server along with a Web page that links to that file.
- A user loads the page with a browser and clicks the link.

- If the user does not have the Java Runtime Environment, a dialog box opens asking if it should be downloaded and installed. The full installation is currently 5.7MB in size, which might take 30-45 minutes to download on a 56k Internet connection.

- The Java Runtime Environment installs and runs the program, opening new frames and other interface components like any other application. The program is saved in a cache, so it can be run again later without requiring another installation.

To see it in action, visit Sun's Java Web Start site at `http://java.sun.com/products/javawebstart` and click the Demos link. The Web Start Demos page contains pictures of several Java applications, each with a Launch button you can use to run the application, as shown in Figure A.1.

FIGURE A.1

Presenting Web Start applications on a Web page.

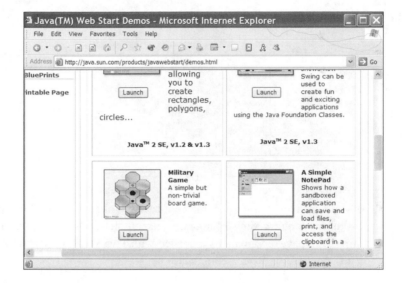

Click the Launch button of one of the applications. If you don't have the Java Runtime Environment yet, a dialog box opens asking whether you'd like to download and install it.

The runtime environment includes the Java Plug-in, a Java interpreter that adds support for the current version of the language to browsers such as Internet Explorer and Mozilla. The environment can also be used to run applications, whether or not they make use of Java Web Start.

When you run an application using Java Web Start, a title screen will be displayed on your computer briefly and the application's graphical user interface will appear.

A

If you installed the Java 2 Software Development Kit or tested Java 2 applets during Hour 17, you are likely to have the Java Runtime Environment on your computer already.

Figure A.2 shows one of the demo applications offered by Sun, a military strategy game in which three black dots gang up on a red dot and attempt to keep it from moving into their territory.

FIGURE A.2

Running a Java Web Start application.

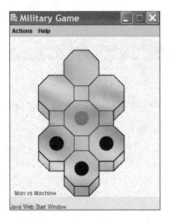

As you can see in Figure A.2, the application looks similar to the applications you created during the preceding 24 hours. Unlike applets, which are presented in conjunction with a Web page, applications launched with Java Web Start run in their own windows, as if they were run from a command line.

 If you try out the dot game, be advised that the red dot is a lot tougher than he looks, even when outnumbered. I tried it out numerous times during the preparation of this part of the book, and in every single game my black dots were trounced. They did so badly I wanted to call in reinforcements.

One thing that's different about a Java Web Start application is the security that it offers to users. When an application attempts to do some things such as reading and writing files, Java Web Start can ask the user for permission.

For example, another one of the demo programs is a text editor. When you try to save a file with this application for the first time, the Security Advisory dialog box opens (Figure A.3).

FIGURE A.3

Choosing an application's security privileges.

If the user does not permit something, the application will be unable to function fully. The kinds of things that would trigger a security dialog are the same things that are not allowed by default in applets: reading and writing files, loading network resources, and the like.

Once Java Web Start runs an application, it is stored in a cache, enabling you to run it again later without having to install it. The only exception is when a new version of the application has become available. In this circumstance, the new version will be automatically downloaded and installed in place of the existing one.

Although you run a Java Web Start application for the first time using a Web browser, you don't have to use a browser every time you run it. To see this, run one of the demo programs such as the dot strategy game several times. A dialog box will appear asking if you want to create shortcuts to run it without a browser (Figure A.4).

A

FIGURE A.4
Adding Java Web Start shortcuts.

Using Java Web Start

Any Java application can be run using Java Web Start, as long as the Web server that will offer the application is configured to work with the technology.

To prepare an application to use Java Web Start, you must save the application's files in a Java Archive (JAR) file, create a special Java Web Start file for the application, and upload the files to the Web server.

The special file that you must create uses Java Network Launching Protocol (JNLP), an XML file format that specifies the application's main class file, its JAR archive, and other things about the program.

> XML, which stands for Extensible Markup Language, is a way of describing data that's similar in some ways to HTML, the language used to create Web pages. You don't need to know anything about XML to create a JNLP file, because the format of JNLP files is relatively self-explanatory.

The next project you will undertake is to use Java Web Start to launch and run the LottoMadness application from Hour 15, "Responding to User Input." To get ready, put a copy of that project's files in your main Java programming folder (which is J24work if you followed one of the suggestions in the book). The files you need are LottoEvent.class and LottoMadness.class, though you might also want LottoEvent.java and LottoMadness.java, in case you decide to make any changes to the application.

The first thing you must do is package all of an application's class files into a Java Archive (JAR) file along with any other files it needs. If you are using the Software Development Kit, you can create the JAR file with the following command:

```
jar -cf LottoMadness.jar LottoEvent.class LottoMadness.class
```

A JAR file called `LottoMadness.jar` is created that holds both of the class files.

Next you should create an icon graphic for the application, which will be displayed when it is loaded and used as its icon in menus and desktops. The icon can be in either GIF or JPEG format, and should be 64 pixels wide and 64 pixels tall.

For this project, if you don't want to create a new icon, you can download `lottobigicon.gif` from the book's Web site. Go to `http://www.java24hours.com` and open the Appendix A page. Right-click the `lottobigicon.gif` link and save the file to the same folder as your `LottoMadness.jar` file.

The final thing you must do is to create the JNLP file that describes the application. Listing A.1 contains a JNLP file used to distribute the LottoMadness application. Open your word processor and enter the text of this listing, then save the file as `LottoMadness.jnlp`.

LISTING A.1 The Full Text of `LottoMadness.jnlp`

```
 1: <?xml version="1.0" encoding="utf-8"?>
 2: <!-- JNLP File for LottoMadness Application -->
 3: <jnlp
 4:   codebase="http://www.cadenhead.org/book/java24hours/java"
 5:   href="LottoMadness.jnlp">
 6:   <information>
 7:     <title>LottoMadness Application</title>
 8:     <vendor>Rogers Cadenhead</vendor>
 9:     <homepage href="http://www.java24hours.com"/>
10:     <icon href="lottobigicon.gif"/>
11:     <offline-allowed/>
12:   </information>
13:   <resources>
14:     <j2se version="1.4"/>
15:     <jar href="LottoMadness.jar"/>
16:   </resources>
17:   <application-desc main-class="LottoMadness"/>
18: </jnlp>
```

The structure of a JNLP file is similar to the HTML markup that was required in Hour 17 to put a Java applet on a Web page. Everything within < and > marks is a tag, and tags are placed around the information the tag describes. There's an opening tag before the information and a closing tag after it.

For example, Line 7 of Listing A.1 contains the following text:

```
<title>LottoMadness Application</title>
```

A

In order from left to right, this line contains the opening tag `<title>`, the text `LottoMadness Application`, and the closing tag `</title>`. The text between the tags—`LottoMadness Application`—is the title of the application, which will be displayed when it is loaded and used in menus and shortcuts.

The difference between opening tags and closing tags is that closing tags begin with a slash (`/`) character and opening tags do not. In Line 8, `<vendor>` is the opening tag, `</vendor>` is the closing tag, and these tags surround the name of the vendor who created the application. I've used my name here. Delete it and replace it with your own name, taking care not to alter the `<vendor>` or `</vendor>` tags around it.

Some tags have an opening tag only, such as Line 11:

```
<offline-allowed/>
```

The `<offline-allowed/>` tag indicates that the application can be run even if the user is not connected to the Internet. If it were omitted from the JNLP file, the opposite would be true, and the user would be forced to go online before running this application.

In XML, all tags that do not have a closing tag end with `/>` instead of `>`.

Tags can also have attributes, which provide another way to define information in an XML file. An attribute is a word inside a tag that is followed by an equals sign and some text within quotes.

For example, consider Line 9 of Listing A.1:

```
<homepage href="http://www.java24hours.com"/>
```

This is the `<homepage>` tag, and it has one attribute, `href`. The text between the quote marks is used to set the value of this attribute to `http://www.java24hours.com`. This defines the home page of the application—the Web page that users should visit if they want to read more information about the program and how it works.

The LottoMadness JNLP file defines a simple Java Web Start application that does not make use of any Java features that require special permission.

In addition to the tags that have already been described, Listing A.1 defines other information required by Java Web Start.

Line 1 indicates that the file uses XML and the UTF-8 character set. This same line can be used on any of the JNLP files you create for applications.

Line 2 is a comment. Like other comments in Java, it's placed in the file solely for the benefit of humans. Java Web Start will ignore it.

Lines 3–5 indicate where the JNLP file for this application can be found. The `codebase` attribute in Line 4 is the URL of the folder that contains the JNLP file. The `href` attribute in Line 5 is the name of the file. These lines indicate that the file is at the Web address `http://www.cadenhead.org/book/java24hours/java/LottoMadness.jnlp`.

Lines 6 and 12 use the `<information>` and `</information>` tags to surround information about the application. Tags can contain other tags in XML: This tag contains `<title>`, `<vendor>`, `<homepage>`, `<icon/>`, and `<offline-allowed/>` tags.

Line 10 indicates the location of the program's icon, which uses the `codebase` attribute described previously. In this example, the file is at the Web address `http://www.cadenhead.org/book/java24hours/java/lottobigicon.gif`.

Lines 13 and 16 use the `<resources>` and `</resources>` tags to surround information about resources used by the application.

Line 14 indicates the version of the Java interpreter that should run the application: Java 2 version 1.4.

Line 15 indicates the application's JAR file. This also uses `codebase`, so this file is in `http://www.cadenhead.org/book/java24hours/java/LottoMadness.jar`.

Line 17 indicates which class file should be run to start the application: `LottoMadness`. Note that the `.class` file extension is not specified—only the name of the class itself.

Line 18 ends the definition of this JNLP file. All JNLP files must be contained within an opening `<jnlp>` tag and a closing `</jnlp>` tag.

After you have created this file, change Line 4 of Listing A.1 so that it refers to the folder on a Web server where your application's JAR file, icon file, and JNLP file will be stored.

Upload all three of the files to this folder, then run your browser and load the JNLP file using its full Web address. If your Web server is configured to support Java Web Start, the application will be loaded and will begin running, as in Figure A.5.

FIGURE A.5

Running LottoMadness using Java Web Start.

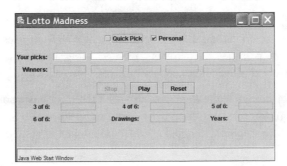

If your server does not support Java Web Start, which is more likely than not given the fact that it is a relatively new technology, you may see the text of your JNLP file loaded in a page and the application will not open.

A Web server must be configured to recognize that JNLP files are a new type of data that should be run as an application, not delivered to the user as text in a browser window. On an Apache Web server, the server administrator can support JNLP by adding the following line to the server's mime-types (or .mime-types) file:

```
application/x-java-jnlp-file JNLP
```

If you can't get Java Web Start working on your server, you can test this project on the book's official site. Load the Web page http://www.cadenhead.org/books/java24hours/java/LottoMadness.jnlp, or save your carpal tunnel nerves and visit the Web address http://www.java24hours.com and open the Appendix A page.

Java Web Start applications should run exactly as they do when run by other means. However, there appear to be a few bugs in how much space is allocated to components on a graphical user interface. On a Windows system, you might need to add 50 pixels to the height of the LottoMadness application before employing it in Java Web Start. Otherwise, the text fields are not tall enough to display numbers.

Summary

At the end of Hour 24, we said farewell to each other, exchanging poignant goodbyes like a couple of friends at their high school graduation who are going to different colleges.

You probably didn't expect to hear from me again so soon. The name of the book isn't *Teach Yourself Java 2 in 24 Hours and 40 Minutes*, after all.

However, Java Web Start is such an exciting way to distribute Java applications that I felt that it was worth bending the rules a little. Java Web Start itself bends the rules, running applications as if they were applets, then escaping the browser entirely, running applications using shortcuts that keep themselves up-to-date using the World Wide Web.

The project you completed in this appendix used the most basic configuration options in JNLP: the XML file format used to define and set up Java Web Start. It can also be used to change the title graphic that appears when the application is launched, run signed applications that have different security privileges, run an application using different versions of the Java interpreter, and other options.

For more information on making use of the technology with your own applications, visit Sun's Java Web Start site at the address `http://java.sun.com/products/javawebstart/1.2/docs/developersguide.html`.

A

APPENDIX B

Using the Java 2 Software Development Kit

When the Java programming language was introduced to the public in 1995, Sun Microsystems also made available a free tool to develop Java programs: the Java 2 Software Development Kit.

The Software Development Kit is a set of command-line programs that are used to create, compile, and run Java programs. Every new release of Java is accompanied by a new release of the development kit—the current version is Java 2 SDK version 1.4.

Although more sophisticated Java programming tools are now available, such as Borland JBuilder, IntelliJ IDEA, and Sun ONE Studio, many programmers continue to use the Software Development Kit. I've been using it as my primary Java programming tool for years.

This appendix covers how to download and install the Software Development Kit, set it up on your computer, and use it to create, compile, and run a simple Java program. It also describes how to correct the most common cause of problems for a beginning Java programmer—a misconfigured Software Development Kit. The material that follows is primarily focused on Windows, because each Windows operating system can be ornery in regard to the kit.

Choosing a Java Development Tool

If you're using a Microsoft Windows or Apple MacOS system, you probably have a Java interpreter installed that can run Java programs. For several years, an interpreter was included with the Microsoft Internet Explorer and Netscape Navigator Web browsers. To develop Java programs, you need more than an interpreter.

The Software Development Kit includes a compiler, interpreter, debugger, file archival program, and several other programs. The kit is simpler than other development tools. It does not offer a graphical user interface, text editor, or other features that many programmers rely on. To use the kit, you type commands at a text prompt. MS-DOS, Linux, and Unix users will be familiar with this prompt, which is also called a command line.

Here's an example of a command you might type while using the Software Development Kit:

```
javac RetrieveMail.java
```

This command tells the `javac` program—the Java compiler included with Java 2 SDK 1.4—to read a source code file called `RetrieveMail.java` and create one or more class files. These files contain compiled bytecode that can be executed by a Java interpreter. When `RetrieveMail.java` is compiled, one of the files will be named `RetrieveMail.class`. If the class file was set up to function as an application, a Java interpreter can run it.

People who are comfortable with command-line environments will be at home using the Software Development Kit. Everyone else must become accustomed to the lack of a graphical point-and-click environment as they develop programs.

If you have another Java development tool and you're certain it is completely compatible with version 1.4 of the Java language, you don't need to use the Software Development Kit. Many different development tools can be used to create the tutorial programs in this book.

> If you have any doubts regarding compatibility, or this book is your first experience with the Java language, you should probably use SDK 1.4 or a tool described in Appendix D, "Using Sun ONE Studio."

Installing the Software Development Kit

You can download version 1.4 of the Java 2 Software Development Kit from Sun's Java Web site at http://java.sun.com.

The Web site's Downloads section offers links to several different versions of the Java Software Development Kit, and it also offers Sun ONE Studio and other products related to the language. The product you should download is called the Java 2 Platform Standard Edition 1.4, Software Development Kit.

SDK 1.4 is currently available for the following platforms:

- Windows 95, 98, Me, NT (with Service Pack 4), 2000, and XP
- Solaris SPARC and Intel
- Linux

The kit requires a computer with a Pentium processor that is 166 MHz or faster, 32MB of memory, and 70MB of free disk space. Sun recommends at least 48MB of memory if you're going to work with Java 2 applets (which you will do on Hour 17, "Creating Interactive Web Programs").

> A version of the Software Development Kit for the Macintosh is available directly from Apple. At the time of this writing it supports version 1.3 rather than 1.4, but a new version of MacOS with Java 1.4 tools should be available by the time you read this. To find out more about Apple's kit and download the tool, visit the Web site http://devworld.apple.com/java/.

> If you're using another platform, you can check to see whether it has a tool that supports Java 1.4 by visiting Sun's site at `http://java.sun.com/cgi-bin/java-ports.cgi/`.

When you're looking for this product, you might find that the Software Development Kit's version number has a third number after 1.4, such as "SDK 1.4.1." To fix bugs and address security problems, Sun periodically issues new releases of the kit and numbers them with an extra period and digit after the main version number. Choose the most current version of SDK 1.4 that's offered, whether it's numbered 1.4.0, 1.4.1, 1.4.2, or higher.

> Take care not to download two similarly named products from Sun by mistake: the Java 2 Runtime Environment, Standard Edition, version 1.4 or the Java 2 Software Development Kit, Standard Edition, Source Release.

To go directly to the kit's download page, the current address is `http://java.sun.com/j2se/1.4/`.

To set up the kit, you must download and run an installation program (or install it from a CD). On Sun's Web site, after you choose the version of the kit that's designed for your operating system, you can download it as a single file that's around 35-40MB in size. After you have downloaded the file, you're ready to set up the development kit.

Windows Installation

Before installing SDK 1.4, you should make sure that no other Java development tools are installed on your system (assuming, of course, that you don't need any other tool at the moment). Having more than one Java programming tool installed on your computer can often cause configuration problems with the Software Development Kit.

To set up the kit on a Windows system, double-click the installation file or click Start, Run from the Windows taskbar to find and run the file.

The InstallShield Wizard will guide you through the process of installing the software. If you accept Sun's terms and conditions for using the kit, you'll be asked where to install the program, as shown in Figure B.1.

FIGURE B.1

Choose a destination folder for SDK 1.4.

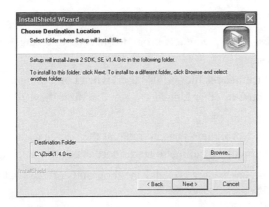

The wizard will suggest a folder where the kit should be installed. In Figure 1.1, the wizard is suggesting the folder C:\j2sdk1.4.0-rc. When you install the kit, the suggested name might be different.

> Before continuing, write down the name of the folder you have chosen. You'll need it later to configure the kit and fix any configuration problems that may occur.

Click the Next button to use the suggested folder. If you want to pick a different folder, click Browse and use the Windows file open dialog box to select a location.

Next, you are asked what parts of the Software Development Kit to install. This dialog box is shown in Figure B.2.

FIGURE B.2

Selecting components of SDK 1.4 to install.

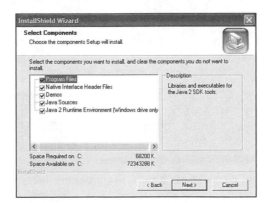

By default, the wizard will install all components of the SDK:

- Program files—The executable programs needed to create, compile, and test your Java projects.
- Native interface header files—Files used when combining Java programs with programs written in other languages. You can omit these for the tutorials in this book.
- Demos—Java 2 programs you can run and the source code files used to create them, which you can examine to learn more about the language.
- Java sources—The source code for the thousands of classes that make up the Java 2 class library.
- Java 2 runtime environment—A Java interpreter you can distribute with the programs you create.

If you accept the default installation, you need around 72MB of free hard disk space. You can save space by omitting everything but the program files. However, the demo programs and Java 2 runtime environment are extremely useful, so if you have the room, it's a good idea to install them. Neither the native header files nor Java source files are needed for any of the material in this book—both are primarily of interest to experienced Java programmers.

After you choose the components to install, click the Next button to continue. You'll be asked to set up the Java Plug-in to work with the Web browsers on your system (see Figure B.3).

FIGURE B.3

Setting up the Java Plug-in with Web browsers.

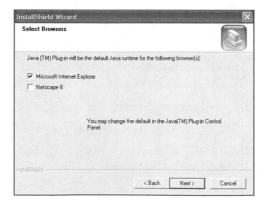

The Java Plug-in is an interpreter that runs Java programs incorporated into Web pages. These programs, which are called applets, can work with different interpreters. Sun offers the plug-in, which has the advantage of supporting the current version of the Java language. An alternative is the Microsoft virtual machine, which works with Internet Explorer but can only run Java 1.0 and 1.1 applets.

 Java 1.0 is the original version of the language, which was released by Sun Microsystems in 1995. Java 1.1 is its successor, which came out a year later.

B

Choose the browsers that will use the Java Plug-in and click Next, then click Finish on the last dialog box. The InstallShield Wizard will install SDK 1.4 on your system.

Configuring the Software Development Kit

After the InstallShield Wizard installs SDK 1.4, you must edit your computer's environment variables to include references to the kit.

Experienced MS-DOS users can finish setting up the SDK by adjusting two variables and then rebooting the computer:

- Edit the computer's PATH variable and add a reference to the Software Development Kit's bin folder (which is C:\j2sdk1.4.0-rc\bin if you installed the kit into the C:\j2sdk1.4.0-rc folder).
- Edit or create a CLASSPATH variable , so that it contains a reference to the current folder—a period character and semi-colon (".;" without the quotation marks)—followed by a reference to the tools.jar file in the kit's lib folder. (which is C:\j2sdk1.4.0-rc\lib\tools.jar if the kit was installed into C:\j2sdk1.4.0-rc).

For inexperienced MS-DOS users, the following section covers in detail how to set the PATH and CLASSPATH variables on a Windows system.

Users of other operating systems should follow the instructions provided by Sun on its Software Development Kit download page.

Using a Command-Line Interface

The Java Software Development Kit requires the use of a command line to compile Java programs, run them, and handle other tasks. A command line is a way to operate a computer entirely by typing commands at your keyboard, rather than by using a mouse. Very few programs designed for Windows users require the command line today.

To get to a command line in Windows:

- On Windows 95, 98, or Me, click the Start button, choose Programs, and then click MS-DOS Prompt (as shown in Figure B.4).

- On Windows NT or 2000, click the Start button, choose Programs, choose Accessories, and then click Command Prompt.

- On Windows XP, click the Start button, choose All Programs, choose Accessories, and then click Command Prompt.

FIGURE B.4

Finding a command line from the Windows 95, 98, or Me taskbar.

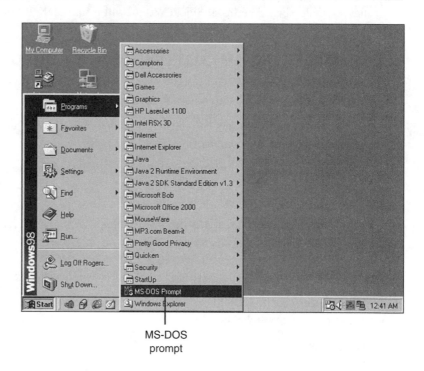

MS-DOS
prompt

When you open a command line in Windows, a new window opens where you can type commands. The command line in Windows uses commands borrowed from MS-DOS, the Microsoft operating system that preceded Windows. MS-DOS supports the same functions as Windows—copying, moving, and deleting files and folders; running programs; scanning and repairing a hard drive; formatting a floppy disk; and so on. A command-line window is shown in Figure B.5.

FIGURE B.5

Using a newly opened command-line window.

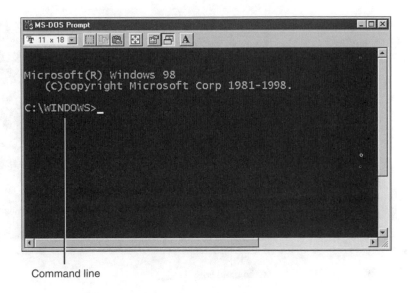

Command line

In the window, a cursor will blink on the command line whenever you can type in a new command with your keyboard. In Figure B.5, `C:\WINDOWS>` is the command line.

Because MS-DOS can be used to delete files and even format your hard drive, you should learn something about the operating system before experimenting with its commands. If you'd like to learn a lot about MS-DOS, a good book is *Special Edition Using MS-DOS 6.22, Third Edition*, published in 2001 by Que (and I do mean "a lot"—the book is 1,056 pages long).

You only need to know a few things about MS-DOS to use the Software Development Kit: how to create a folder, how to open a folder, and how to run a program.

Opening Folders in MS-DOS

When you are using MS-DOS on a Windows system, you will have access to all the folders you normally use in Windows. For example, if you have a `Windows` folder on your `C:` hard drive, the same folder is accessible as `C:\Windows` from a command line.

To open a folder in MS-DOS, type the command **CD** followed by the name of the folder and press Enter. Here's an example:

```
CD C:\TEMP
```

When you enter this command, the `TEMP` folder on your system's `C:` drive will be opened, if it exists. After you open a folder, your command line will be updated with the name of that folder, as shown in Figure B.6.

FIGURE B.6

Opening a folder in a command-line window.

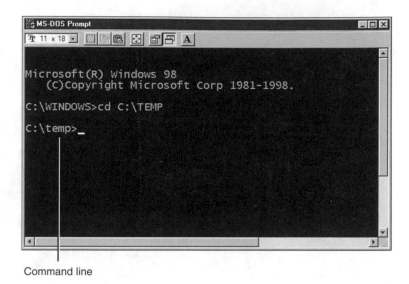

Command line

You also can use the CD command in other ways:

- Type **CD** \ to open the root folder on the current hard drive.
- Type **CD** *foldername* to open a subfolder matching the name you've used in place of *foldername*, if that subfolder exists.
- Type **CD** .. to open the folder that contains the current folder. For example, if you are in C:\Windows\Fonts and you use the CD .. command, C:\Windows will be opened.

One of the book's suggestions is to create a folder called J24work where you can create the tutorial programs described in the book. If you have already done this, you can switch to that folder by using the following commands:

1. CD \
2. CD J24work

If you haven't created that folder yet, you can accomplish the task within MS-DOS.

Creating Folders in MS-DOS

To create a folder from a command line, type the command MD followed by the name of the folder and press Enter, as in the following example:

MD C:\STUFF

The STUFF folder will be created in the root folder of the system's C: drive. To open a newly created folder, use the CD command followed by that folder's name, as shown in Figure B.7.

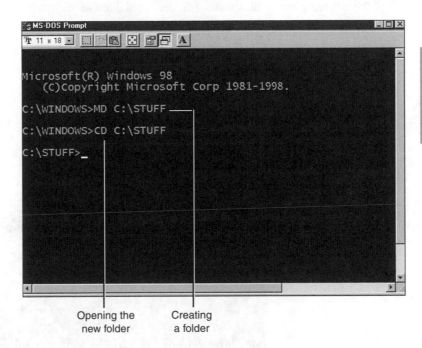

Opening the   Creating
new folder   a folder

If you haven't already created a J24work folder, you can do it from a command line:

- Change to the root folder (using the CD \ command).
- Type the command MD J24work and press Enter.

After J24work has been created, you can go to it at any time from a command-line by using this command:

```
CD \J24work
```

The last thing you need to learn about MS-DOS to use the Software Development Kit is how to run programs.

Running Programs in MS-DOS

The simplest way to run a program at the command line is to type its name and press Enter. For example, type **DIR** and press Enter to see a list of files and subfolders in the current folder.

You also can run a program by typing its name followed by a space and some options that control how the program runs. These options are called *arguments*. To see an example of this, change to the root folder (using CD \) and type **DIR J24work**. You'll see a list of files and subfolders contained in the J24work folder, whether it contains any.

After you have installed the Software Development Kit, you should run the Java interpreter to see that it works. Type the following command at a command line:

```
java -version
```

In the preceding example, java is the name of the Java interpreter program and -version is an argument that tells the interpreter to display its version number. You can see an example of this in Figure B.8, but your version number might be a little different depending on what version of the SDK you have installed.

FIGURE B.8

Running the Java interpreter in a command line window.

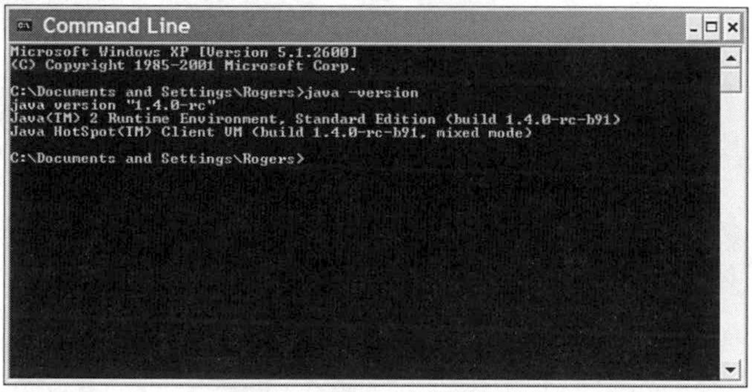

If java -version works and you see a version number, it should begin with 1.4 because you are using SDK 1.4. Sun sometimes tacks on a third number, but as long as it begins with 1.4 you are using the correct version of the Software Development Kit.

If you see an incorrect version number or a Bad command or filename error after running java -version, you need to make some changes to how the Software Development Kit is configured on your system.

Correcting Configuration Errors

When you are writing Java programs for the first time, the most likely source for problems is not typos, syntax errors, or other programming mistakes. Most errors result from a misconfigured Software Development Kit.

If you type java -version at a command line and your system can't find the folder that contains java.exe, you will see one of the following error messages or something similar (depending on your operating system):

- Bad command or filename
- 'java' is not recognized as an internal or external command, operable program, or batch file

To correct this, you must configure your system's PATH variable.

Setting the PATH on Windows 95, 98, or Me

On a Windows 95, 98, or Me system, you configure the PATH variable by editing the AUTOEXEC.BAT file in the root folder of the your main hard drive. This file is used by MS-DOS to set environment variables and configure how some command-line programs function.

AUTOEXEC.BAT is a text file you can edit with Windows Notepad. Start Notepad by clicking Start, Programs, Accessories, Notepad from the Windows taskbar. The Notepad text editor will open. Choose File, Open from Notepad's menu bar, go to the root folder on your main hard drive, and then open the file AUTOEXEC.BAT. When you open the file, you'll see a series of MS-DOS commands, each on its own line, as shown in Figure B.9.

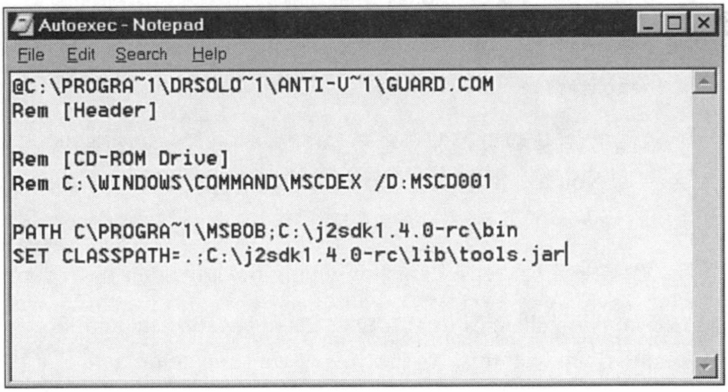

FIGURE B.9

Editing the AUTOEXEC.BAT *file with Notepad.*

```
Autoexec - Notepad
File  Edit  Search  Help
@C:\PROGRA~1\DRSOLO~1\ANTI-U~1\GUARD.COM
Rem [Header]

Rem [CD-ROM Drive]
Rem C:\WINDOWS\COMMAND\MSCDEX /D:MSCD001

PATH C\PROGRA~1\MSBOB;C:\j2sdk1.4.0-rc\bin
SET CLASSPATH=.;C:\j2sdk1.4.0-rc\lib\tools.jar
```

The only commands you need to look for are any that begin with PATH. The PATH command is followed by a space and a series of folder names separated by semicolons. It sets up the PATH variable, a list of folders that contain command-line programs you use.

PATH is used to help MS-DOS find programs when you run them at a command line. In the preceding example, the PATH command in Figure B.9 includes two folders:

- C:\PROGRA~1\MSBOB
- C:\j2sdk1.4.0-rc\bin

You can see what PATH has been set to by typing the following command at a command line:

PATH

To set up the Software Development Kit correctly, the folder that contains the Java interpreter must be included in the PATH command in AUTOEXEC.BAT.

The interpreter has the filename java.exe. If you installed SDK 1.4 in the C:\j2sdk1.4.0-rc folder on your system, java.exe is in C:\jdk1.4.0-rc\bin.

If you can't remember where you installed the kit, you can look for java.exe: Choose Start, Find, Files or Folders. You might find several copies in different folders. To see which one is correct, open a command-line window and do the following for each copy you have found:

1. Use the CD command to open a folder that contains java.exe.
2. Run the command java -version in that folder.

When you know the correct folder, create a blank line at the bottom of the AUTOEXEC.BAT file and add the following:

PATH rightfoldername;%PATH%

For example, if c:\j2sdk1.4.0\bin is the correct folder, the following line should be added at the bottom of AUTOEXEC.BAT:

PATH c:\j2sdk1.4.0\bin;%PATH%

The %PATH% text keeps you from wiping out any other PATH commands in AUTOEXEC.BAT.

After making changes to AUTOEXEC.BAT, save the file and reboot your computer. When you are done with this, try the java -version command. If it displays the correct version of the Software Development Kit, your system is probably configured correctly. You'll find out for sure when you try to create a sample program later in this appendix.

Setting the Path on Windows NT, 2000, or XP

On a Windows NT, 2000, or XP system, you configure the Path variable using the Environment Variables dialog, one of the features of the system's Control Panel.

To open this dialog:

1. Right-click the My Computer icon on your desktop or Start menu and choose Properties. The System Properties dialog box opens.

2. Click the Advanced tab to bring it to the front.

3. Click the Environment Variables button. The Environment Variables dialog box opens (Figure B.10).

B

FIGURE B.10

Setting environment variables in Windows NT, 2000, or XP.

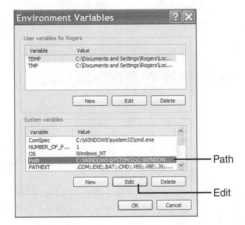

There are two kinds of environment variables you can edit: System variables, which apply to all users on your computer, and user variables that only apply to you.

Path is a system variable that helps MS-DOS find programs when you run them at a command line. It contains a list of folders separated by semicolons.

To set up the Software Development Kit correctly, the folder that contains the Java interpreter must be included in the Path. The interpreter has the filename java.exe. If you installed SDK 1.4 in the C:\j2sdk1.4.0-rc folder on your system, java.exe is in C:\jdk1.4.0-rc\bin.

If you can't remember where you installed the kit, you can look for `java.exe`: Choose Start, Search. You might find several copies in different folders. To see what one is correct, open a command-line window and do the following for each copy you have found:

1. Use the `CD` command to open a folder that contains `java.exe`.
2. Run the command `java -version` in that folder.

When you know the correct folder, return to the Environment Variables dialog, select `Path` in the System variables list, and then click `Edit`. The Edit System Variable dialog opens with `Path` in the Variable name field, and a list of folders in the Variable value field (Figure B.11).

FIGURE **B.11**

Changing your system's Path *variable.*

To add a folder to the `Path`, click the Variable value field and move your cursor to the end without changing anything. At the end, add a semicolon followed by the name of the folder that contains the Java interpreter.

For example, if `c:\j2sdk1.4.0\bin` is the correct folder, the following text should be added to the end of the `Path` variable:

```
c:\j2sdk1.4.0\bin
```

After making the change, click OK twice: Once to close the Edit System Variable dialog, and another time to close the Environment Variables dialog.

Try it: Open a command-line window and type the command **java -version**. If it displays the right version of the software development kit, your system is probably configured correctly, though you won't know for sure until you try to use the kit later in this appendix.

Using a Text Editor

Unlike more sophisticated Java development tools, the Software Development Kit does not include a text editor to use when you create source files. For an editor or word processor to work with the kit, it must be able to save text files with no formatting. This feature has different names in different editors. Look for a format option such as one of the following when you save a document or set the properties for a document:

- Plain text
- ASCII text
- DOS text
- Text-only

If you're using Windows, there are several editors included with the operating system.

Windows Notepad is a no-frills text editor that only works with plain text files. It can handle only one document at a time. Click Start, All Programs, Accessories, Notepad to run it on Windows XP or Start, Programs, Accessories, Notepad on other Windows systems.

Windows WordPad is a step above Notepad. It can handle more than one document at a time and can handle both plain text and Microsoft Word formats. It also remembers the last several documents it has worked on and makes them available from the File pull-down menu. It's also on the Accessories menu along with Notepad.

Windows users can also use Microsoft Word, but must save files as text rather than in Word's proprietary format. Unix and Linux users can author programs with emacs, pico, and vi; Macintosh users have SimpleText or any of the above mentioned Unix tools available for Java source file creation.

One disadvantage of using simple text editors such as Notepad or WordPad is that they do not display line numbers as you edit. Seeing the line number helps in Java programming because many compilers indicate the line number at where an error occurred. Take a look at the following error generated by the SDK compiler:

```
Palindrome.java:8: Class Font not found in type declaration.
```

The number 8 after the name of the Java source file indicates the line that triggered the compiler error. With a text editor that supports numbering, you can go directly to that line and start looking for the error.

B

Usually there are better ways to debug a program with a commercial Java programming package, but kit users must search for compiler-generated errors using the line number indicated by the javac tool. This is one of the best reasons to move on to an advanced Java development program after learning the language with the Software Development Kit.

> Another alternative is to use the kit with a programmer's text editor that offers line numbering and other features. One of the most popular for Java is jEdit, a free editor available for Windows, Linux, and other systems at http://www.jedit.org/. Another popular programmer's editor for Windows is the shareware program Zeus available from http://www.zeusedit.com/.

Creating a Sample Program

Now that you have installed and set up the Software Development Kit, you're ready to create a sample Java program to make sure it works.

Java programs begin as source code—a series of statements created using a text editor and saved as a text file. You can use any program you like to create these files, as long as it can save the file as plain, unformatted text. The Software Development Kit does not include a text editor, but most other Java development tools include a built-in editor for creating source code files.

Run your editor of choice and enter the Java program in Listing B.1. Make sure all the parentheses, braces, and quotation marks in the listing are entered correctly and capitalize everything in the program exactly as shown. If your editor requires a filename before you start entering anything, call it HelloSailor.java.

LISTING B.1   Source Code of HelloSailor.java

```
1: public class HelloSailor {
2:     public static void main(String[] arguments) {
3:         System.out.println("Hello, Sailor!");
4:     }
5: }
```

The line numbers and colons along the left side of Listing B.1 are not part of the program—they're included so that I can refer to specific lines by number in each program.

If you're ever unsure about the source code of a program in this book, you can compare it to a copy on the book's official World Wide Web site at the following address:

`http://www.java24hours.com`

After you finish typing in the program, save the file somewhere on your hard drive with the name `HelloSailor.java`. Java source files must be saved with the extension `.java`.

> If you have created a folder called J24work, save `HelloSailor.java` and all other Java source files from this book in that folder. This makes it easier to find them while using a command-line window.

If you're using Windows, a text editor such as Notepad might add an extra `.txt` file extension to the filename of any Java source files you save. For example, `HelloSailor.java` is saved as `HelloSailor.java.txt`. As a work-around to avoid this problem, place quotation marks around the filename when saving a source file. Figure B.12 shows this technique being used to save the source file `HelloSailor.java` from Windows Notepad.

FIGURE B.12

Saving a source file from Windows Notepad.

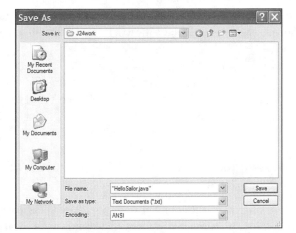

> A better solution is to permanently associate .java files with the text editor you'll be using: In Windows, open the folder that contains `HelloSailor.java` and double-click the file. If you have never opened a file with the .java

> extension, you'll be asked what program to use when opening files of this
> type. Choose your preferred editor and select the option to make your
> choice permanent. From this point on, you can open a source file for editing
> by double-clicking the file.

The purpose of this project is to test the Software Development Kit—none of the Java programming concepts used in the five-line `HelloSailor` program are described in this appendix.

You'll learn the basics of the language during the four hours of Part 1, "Getting Started!" If you have figured out anything about Java simply by typing in the source code of Listing B.1, it's entirely your fault. I didn't teach you anything yet.

Compiling and Running the Program in Windows

Now you're ready to compile the source file with the Software Development Kit's Java compiler, a program called `javac`. The compiler reads a `.java` source file and creates one or more `.class` files that can be run by a Java interpreter.

Open a command-line window, and then open the folder where you saved `HelloSailor.java`. If you saved the file in the `J24work` folder inside the root folder on your main hard drive, the following MS-DOS command will open the folder:

```
cd \J24work
```

When you are in the correct folder, you can compile `HelloSailor.java` by entering the following at a command prompt:

```
javac HelloSailor.java
```

Figure B.13 shows the MS-DOS commands used to switch to the `\J24work` folder and compile `HelloSailor.java`.

The Software Development Kit compiler does not display any message if the program compiles successfully. If there are problems, the compiler lets you know by displaying each error along with a line that triggered the error.

If the program compiled without any errors, a file called `HelloSailor.class` is created in the same folder that contains `HelloSailor.java`.

FIGURE B.13

Compiling a Java program in a command-line window.

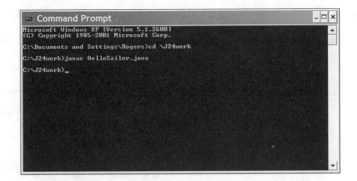

The class file contains the Java bytecode that will be executed by a Java interpreter. If you get any errors, go back to your original source file and make sure that you typed it exactly as it appears in Listing B.1. After you have a class file, you can run that file using a Java interpreter. The SDK's interpreter is called java, and it also is run from the command line.

Run the HelloSailor program by switching to the folder containing HelloSailor.class and entering the following:

java HelloSailor

You will see the text "Hello, Sailor!"

> When running a Java class with the kit's Java interpreter, don't specify the .class file extension after the name of the class. If you do, you'll see an error such as the following:
>
> Exception in thread "main" java.lang.NoClassDefFoundError:
> HelloSailor/class

Figure B.14 shows the successful output of the HelloSailor application along with the commands used to get to that point.

If you can compile the program and run it successfully, your Software Development Kit is working and you are ready to start Hour 1 of this book. If you cannot get the program to compile successfully even though you have typed it exactly at it appears in the book, there may be one last problem with how the Software Development Kit is configured on your system: the CLASSPATH environment variable might need to be configured.

FIGURE B.14

Running a Java application.

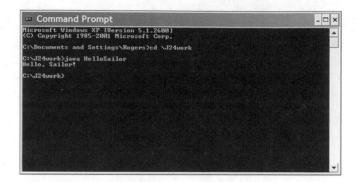

Setting Up the CLASSPATH Variable

All the Java programs that you write rely on two kinds of class files: The classes you create and the Java class library, a set of hundreds of classes that represent the functionality of the Java language.

The Software Development Kit needs to know where to find Java class files on your system. In many cases, the kit can figure this out on its own by looking in the folder where it was installed. You also can set it up yourself by creating or modifying another environment variable: CLASSPATH.

Setting the CLASSPATH on Windows 95, 98, or Me

If you have compiled and run the HelloSailor program successfully, the Software Development Kit has been configured successfully. You don't need to make any more changes to your system. On the other hand, if you see a Class not found error or NoClassDefFound error whenever you try to run a program, you need to make sure your CLASSPATH variable is set up correctly.

To do this, run Windows Notepad, choose File, Open and go to the root folder on your system, and then open the file AUTOEXEC.BAT. A file containing several different MS-DOS commands is opened in the editor, as shown in Figure B.15.

Look for a line in the file that contains the text SET CLASSPATH= command followed by a series of folder and filenames separated by semicolons.

FIGURE B.15

Editing your system's environment variables.

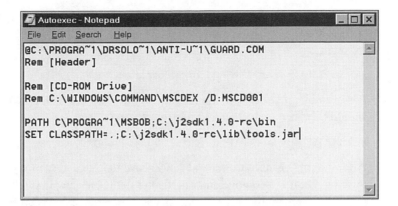

CLASSPATH is used to help the Java compiler find the class files that it needs. The SET CLASSPATH= command in Figure B.15 includes two things with a semicolon between them:

- .

- c:\j2sdk1.4.0-rc\lib\tools.jar

A CLASSPATH can contain folders or files. It also can contain a period character (" . "), which is another way to refer to the current folder in MS-DOS.

You can see your system's CLASSPATH variable by typing the following command at a command line:

ECHO %CLASSPATH%

If your CLASSPATH includes folders or files that you know are no longer on your computer, you should remove the references to them on the SET CLASSPATH= line in AUTOEXEC.BAT. Make sure to remove any extra semicolons also.

To set up the Software Development Kit correctly, the file containing the Java class library must be included in the SET CLASSPATH= command. This file has the filename tools.jar. If you installed the kit in the C:\jdk1.4.0 folder on your system, tools.jar is probably in the folder C:\jdk1.4.0\lib.

If you can't remember where you installed the kit, you can look for tools.jar by clicking Start, Find, Files or Folders from the Windows taskbar. If you find several copies, you should be able to find the correct one using this method:

1. Use CD to open the folder that contains the Java interpreter (java.exe)

2. Enter the command CD ..

3. Enter the command CD lib

The `lib` folder normally contains the right copy of `tools.jar`. When you know the correct location, create a blank line at the bottom of the `AUTOEXEC.BAT` file and add the following:

```
SET CLASSPATH=%CLASSPATH%;.;rightlocation
```

For example, if `tools.jar` file is in the `c:\j2sdk1.4.0\lib` folder, the following line should be added at the bottom of `AUTOEXEC.BAT`:

```
SET CLASSPATH=%CLASSPATH%;.;c:\j2sdk1.4.0\lib\tools.jar
```

After making changes to `AUTOEXEC.BAT`, save the file and reboot your computer. After this is done, try to compile and run the `HelloSailor` sample program again. You should be able to accomplish this after the `CLASSPATH` variable has been set up correctly.

Setting the `Classpath` on Windows NT, 2000 or XP

On a Windows NT, 2000, or XP system, you also configure the `Classpath` variable using the Environment Variables dialog.

To open it:

1. Right-click the My Computer icon on your desktop or Start menu and choose Properties. The System Properties dialog box opens.
2. Click the Advanced tab to bring it to the front.
3. Click the Environment Variables button. The Environment Variables dialog box opens (Figure B.16).

FIGURE B.16

Setting environment variables in Windows NT, 2000, or XP.

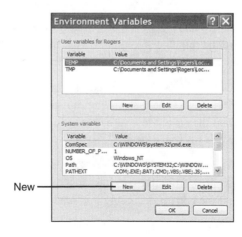

New —

If your system has a `Classpath` variable, it will probably be one of the system variables. Your system might not have a `Classpath`—the Software Development Kit can normally find class files without the variable.

However, if your system has a `Classpath`, it must be set up with at least two things: a reference to the current folder (a period) and a reference to a file that contains the Java class library: `tools.jar`.

If you installed the kit in the `C:\jdk1.4.0` folder, `tools.jar` is in the folder `C:\jdk1.4.0\lib`. If you can't remember where you installed the kit, you can look for `tools.jar` by clicking Start, Search from the Windows taskbar. If you find several copies, you should be able to find the correct one using this method:

1. Use `CD` to open the folder that contains the Java interpreter (`java.exe`)

2. Enter the command `CD ..`

3. Enter the command `CD lib`

The `lib` folder normally contains the right copy of `tools.jar`. When you know the correct folder, return to the Environment Variables dialog shown in Figure B.16.

If your system does not have a `Classpath`, click the `New` button under the System variables list. The New System Variable dialog box opens. If your system has a `Classpath`, choose it and click the `Edit` button. The Edit System Variable dialog box opens. Both boxes contain the same thing: A Variable Name field, and a Variable Value field.

Enter `Classpath` in the Variable Name field and the correct value for your `Classpath` in the Variable Value field. For example, if you installed the Software Development Kit in `c:\j2sdk1.4.0`, your `Classpath` should contain the following:

`.;C:\j2sdk1.4.0\lib\tools.jar`

Figure B.17 shows how I set up `Classpath` for my system, which has the Software Development Kit installed in `C:\j2sdk1.4.0-rc`.

FIGURE B.17

Setting up a `Classpath` *in Windows XP.*

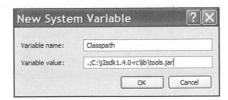

After setting up your Classpath, click OK twice: Once to close the Edit or New System Variable dialog box, and another time to close the Environment Variables dialog. Unlike Windows 95, 98, and Me users, you don't have to reboot the system before you can try it out. Open a command-line window and type the command java -version. If it displays the right version of the software development kit, your system might be configured correctly and require no more adjustments. Try creating the sample HelloSailor program again—it should work after the CLASSPATH variable has been set up correctly.

Troubleshooting Your Kit Installation

This book has a Web site where you can find solutions to problems, corrections, answers to reader questions, and other useful material.

There's an online version of this appendix on the site and a way to contact author Rogers Cadenhead if you are still having problems with the Software Development Kit. The site is available at http://www.java24hours.com/.

APPENDIX C

Programming with the Java 2 Software Development Kit

The Java 2 Software Development Kit (SDK) can be used throughout this book to create, compile, and run Java programs.

The tools that make up the kit contain numerous features that many programmers don't explore at all, and some of the tools themselves might be new to you.

This appendix covers features of the SDK that you can use to create more reliable, better-tested, and faster-running Java programs.

The following topics will be covered:

- Running Java applications with the interpreter
- Compiling programs with the compiler
- Running Java applets with the applet viewer

- Creating documentation with the documentation tool
- Finding bugs in your program and learning more about its performance with the debugger
- Setting system properties with the interpreter and applet viewer

An Overview of the SDK

Although there are several dozen development environments you can use to create Java programs, the most widely used is the Software Development Kit (SDK) from Sun Microsystems. The kit is the set of command-line tools that are used to develop software with the Java language.

There are two main reasons for the popularity of the kit:

- It's free. You can download a copy at no cost from Sun's official Java World Wide Web site at http://java.sun.com.
- It's first. Whenever Sun releases a new version of the language, the first tools that support the new version are in the SDK.

The SDK uses the command line—also called the MS-DOS prompt, command prompt, or console under Windows, or the shell prompt under Unix. Commands are entered using the keyboard, as in the following example:

```
javac VideoBook.java
```

This command compiles a Java program called VideoBook.java using the SDK compiler. There are two elements to the command: the name of the SDK compiler, javac, followed by the name of the program to compile, VideoBook.java. A space character separates the two elements.

Each SDK command follows the same format: the name of the tool to use, followed by one or more elements indicating what the tool should do. These elements are called *arguments*.

The following illustrates the use of command-line arguments:

```
java VideoBook add VHS "Invasion of the Bee Girls"
```

This command tells the Java interpreter to run a class file called VideoBook with three command-line arguments: the strings add, VHS, and Invasion of the Bee Girls.

You might think there are more than three command-line arguments because of the spaces in the string Invasion of the Bee Girls. The quotation marks around that string cause it to be considered one command-line argument, which makes it possible to include spaces in an argument.

Some arguments used with the SDK modify how a tool will function. These arguments are preceded by a hyphen character and are called *options*.

The following command shows the use of an option:

```
java -version
```

This command tells the Java interpreter to display its version number rather than trying to run a class file. It's a good way to find out whether the SDK is correctly configured to run Java programs on your system. Here's an example of the output run on a system equipped with SDK 1.4.0:

```
java version "1.4.0"
Java(TM) 2 Runtime Environment, Standard Edition (build1.4.0)
Java HotSpot(TM) Client VM (build 1.4.0, mixed mode)
```

In some instances, you can combine options with other arguments. For example, if you compile a Java class that uses deprecated methods, you can see more information on these methods by compiling the class with a -deprecation option, as in the following:

```
javac -deprecation OldVideoBook.java
```

The java Interpreter

java, the Java interpreter, is used to run Java applications from the command line. It takes as an argument the name of a class file to run, as in the following example:

```
java BidMonitor
```

Although Java class files end with the .class extension, this extension will not be specified when using the interpreter.

The class loaded by the Java interpreter must contain a class method called main() that takes the following form:

```
public static void main(String[] arguments) {
    // Method here
}
```

Some simple Java programs might consist of only one class—the one containing the main() method. In more complex programs that make use of other classes, the interpreter automatically loads any other classes that are needed.

The Java interpreter runs bytecode—the compiled instructions that are executed by a Java virtual machine. After a Java program is saved in bytecode as a .class file, it can be run by different interpreters without modification. If you have compiled a Java 2 program, it will be compatible with any interpreter that fully supports Java 2.

> Interestingly enough, Java is not the only language that you can use to create Java bytecode. NetRexx, JPython, JRuby, JudoScript, and several dozen other languages will compile into .class files of executable bytecode through the use of compilers specific to those languages. Robert Tolksdorf maintains a comprehensive list of these languages at http://grunge.cs.tu-berlin.de/~tolk/vmlanguages.html.

There are two different ways to specify the class file that will be run by the Java interpreter. If the class is not part of any package, you can run it by specifying the name of the class, as in the preceding java BidMonitor example. If the class is part of a package, you must specify the class by using its full package and class name.

For example, consider a SellItem class that is part of the com.prefect.auction package. To run this application, the following command would be used:

java com.prefect.auction.SellItem

Each element of the package name corresponds to its own subfolder The Java interpreter will look for the SellItem.class file in several different places:

- The com\prefect\auction subfolder of the folder where the java command was entered (if the command was made from the C:\J24work folder, for example, the SellItem.class file can be run successfully if it was in the C:\J24work\com\prefect\auction folder)

- The com\prefect\auction subfolder of any folder in your CLASSPATH setting

If you're creating your own packages, an easy way to manage them is to add a folder to your CLASSPATH that's the root folder for any packages you create, such as C:\javapackages or something similar. After creating subfolders that correspond to the name of a package, place the package's class files in the correct subfolder.

Java 2 version 1.4 includes support for assertions, a new feature to improve the reliability of programs. To run a program using the Java interpreter and make use of any assertions that it contains, use the command line -ea, as in the following example:

```
java -ea Outline
```

The Java interpreter will execute all assert statements in the application's class and all other class files that it uses, with the exception of classes from the Java class library.

To remove that exception and make use of all assertions, run a class with the -esa option.

If you don't specify one of the options that turns on the assertions feature, all assert statements will be ignored by the interpreter.

The javac Compiler

javac, the Java compiler, converts Java source code into one or more class files of byte-code that can be run by a Java interpreter.

Java source code is stored in a file with the .java file extension. This file can be created with any text editor or word processor that can save a document without any special formatting codes. The terminology varies depending on the text-editing software being used, but these files are often called plain text, ASCII text, DOS text, or something similar.

A Java source code file can contain more than one class, but only one of the classes can be declared to be public. A class can contain no public classes at all if desired, although this isn't possible with applets because of the rules of inheritance.

If a source code file contains a class that has been declared to be public, the name of the file must match the name of that class. For example, the source code for a public class called BuyItem must be stored in a file called BuyItem.java.

To compile a file, the javac tool is run with the name of the source code file as an argument, as in the following:

```
javac BidMonitor.java
```

You can compile more than one source file by including each separate filename as a command-line argument, such as this command:

```
javac BidMonitor.java SellItem.java
```

You also can use wildcard characters such as * and ?. Use the following command to compile all .java files in a folder:

```
javac *.java
```

When you compile one or more Java source code files, a separate .class file will be created for each Java class that compiles successfully.

If you are compiling a program that makes use of assertions, you must use the -source 1.4 option, as in this command:

```
javac -source 1.4 Outline.java
```

The 1.4 argument refers to Java 2 version 1.4, the first version of the language that supports the assert statement. If the -source option is not used and you try to compile a program that contains assertions, javac displays an error message and won't compile the file.

Another useful option when running the compiler is -deprecation, which causes the compiler to describe any deprecated methods that are being employed in a Java program. Normally, the compiler will issue a single warning if it finds any deprecated methods in a program. The -deprecation option causes the compiler to list each method that has been deprecated, as in the following command:

```
javac -deprecation SellItem.java
```

If you're more concerned with the speed of a Java program than the size of its class files, you can compile its source code with the -0 option. This creates class files that have been optimized for faster performance. Methods that are static, final, or private might be compiled *inline*, a technique that makes the class file larger but causes the methods to be executed more quickly.

If you are going to use a debugger to look for bugs in a Java class, compile the source with the -g option to put all debugging information in the class file, including references to line numbers, local variables, and source code. (To keep all this out of a class, compile with the -g:none option.)

Normally, the Java compiler doesn't provide a lot of information as it creates class files. In fact, if the source code compiles successfully and no deprecated methods are employed, you won't see any output from the compiler at all. No news is good news in this case.

If you'd like to see more information on what the javac tool is doing as it compiles source code, use the -verbose option. The more verbose compiler will describe the time it takes to complete different functions, the classes that are being loaded, and the overall time required.

The appletviewer Browser

`appletviewer`, the Java applet viewer, is used to run Java programs that require a Web browser and are presented as part of an HTML document.

The applet viewer takes an HTML document as a command-line argument, as in the following example:

```
appletviewer NewAuctions.html
```

If the argument is a Web address instead of a reference to a file, `appletviewer` will load the HTML document at that address. For example:

```
appletviewer http://www.javaonthebrain.com
```

When an HTML document is loaded by `appletviewer`, every applet on that document will begin running in its own window. The size of these windows depends on the `HEIGHT` and `WIDTH` attributes that were set in the applet's HTML tag.

Unlike a Web browser, `appletviewer` cannot be used to view the HTML document itself. If you want to see how the applet is laid out in relation to the other contents of the document, you must use a Java-capable Web browser.

> The current versions of Netscape Navigator and Microsoft Internet Explorer do not offer built-in support for Java applets, but support for the language is available as a browser plug-in from Sun Microsystems. The Java Plug-in from Sun can be used to run a Java 2 applet in a browser in place of the browser's Java interpreter. The Plug-in can be installed along with the Software Development Kit, so it may already be present on your system. You also can download it from Sun's Web site at http://java.sun.com/products/plugin/.

Using `appletviewer` is reasonably straightforward, but you may not be familiar with some of the menu options that are available as the viewer runs an applet. Figure C.1 shows the options on the `appletviewer` tool's Applet pull-down menu.

The following menu options are available:

- The Restart and Reload options are used to restart the execution of the applet. The difference between these two options is that Restart does not unload the applet before restarting it, whereas Reload does. The Reload option is equivalent to closing the applet viewer and opening it up again on the same Web page.

- The Start and Stop options are used to call the start() and stop() methods of the applet directly.
- The Clone option creates a second copy of the same applet running in its own window.
- The Tag option displays the program's <APPLET> or <OBJECT> tag, along with the HTML for any <PARAM> tags that configure the applet.

FIGURE C.1

The Applet pull-down menu of appletviewer.

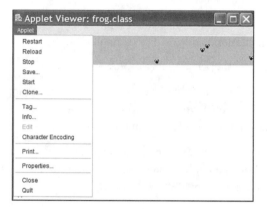

Another option on the Applet pull-down menu is Info, which calls the getAppletInfo() and getParameterInfo() methods of the applet. A programmer can implement these methods to provide more information about the applet and the parameters that it can handle. The getAppletInfo() method will return a string that describes the applet. The getParameterInfo() method will return an array of string arrays that specify the name, type, and description of each parameter.

Listing C.1 contains a Java 2 applet that demonstrates the use of these methods.

LISTING C.1   The Full Text of AppInfo.java

```
 1: import java.awt.*;
 2:
 3: public class AppInfo extends javax.swing.JApplet {
 4:     String name, date;
 5:     int version;
 6:
 7:     public String getAppletInfo() {
 8:         String response = "This applet demonstrates the "
 9:             + "use of the Applet's Info feature.";
10:         return response;
11:     }
```

LISTING C.1   continued

```
12:
13:     public String[][] getParameterInfo() {
14:         String[] p1 = { "Name", "String", "Programmer's name" };
15:         String[] p2 = { "Date", "String", "Today's date" };
16:         String[] p3 = { "Version", "int", "Version number" };
17:         String[][] response = { p1, p2, p3 };
18:         return response;
19:     }
20:
21:     public void init() {
22:         name = getParameter("Name");
23:         date = getParameter("Date");
24:         String versText = getParameter("Version");
25:         if (versText != null)
26:             version = Integer.parseInt(versText);
27:     }
28:
29:     public void paint(Graphics screen) {
30:         Graphics2D screen2D = (Graphics2D) screen;
31:         screen2D.drawString("Name: " + name, 5, 50);
32:         screen2D.drawString("Date: " + date, 5, 100);
33:         screen2D.drawString("Version: " + version, 5, 150);
34:     }
35: }
```

The main function of this applet is to display the value of three parameters: Name, Date, and Version. The getAppletInfo() method returns the following string:

This applet demonstrates the use of the Applet's Info feature.

The getParameterInfo() method is a bit more complicated if you haven't worked with multidimensional arrays. The following things are taking place:

- Line 13 defines the return type of the method as a two-dimensional array of String objects.

- Line 14 creates an array of String objects with three elements: "Name", "String", and "Programmer's Name". These elements describe one of the parameters that can be defined for the AppInfo applet. They describe the name of the parameter (Name in this case), the type of data that the parameter will hold (a string), and a description of the parameter ("Programmer's Name"). The three-element array is stored in the p1 object.

- Lines 15–16 define two more `String` arrays for the `Date` and `Version` parameters.
- Line 17 uses the `response` object to store an array that contains three string arrays: p1, p2, and p3.
- Line 18 uses the `response` object as the method's return value.

Listing C.2 contains a Web page that can be used to load the `AppInfo` applet.

LISTING C.2   The Full Text of `AppInfo.html`

```
1: <applet code="AppInfo.class" height=200 width=170>
2: <param name="Name" value="Rogers Cadenhead">
3: <param name="Date" value="12/01/02">
4: <param name="Version" value="3">
5: </applet>
```

Figure C.2 shows the applet running with the applet viewer, and Figure C.3 is a screen capture of the dialog box that opens when the viewer's Info menu option is selected.

FIGURE C.2

The `AppInfo` *applet running in* `appletviewer`*.*

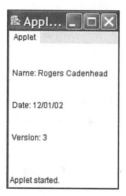

FIGURE C.3

The Info dialog box of the `AppInfo` *applet.*

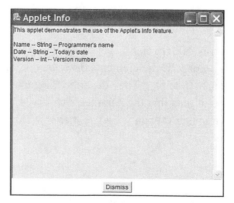

These features require a browser that makes this information available to users. The SDK's `appletviewer` handles this through the Info menu option, but the Java Plug-in and Internet Explorer's Java virtual machine do not offer anything like it at this time.

The `javadoc` Documentation Tool

`javadoc`, the Java documentation creator, takes a `.java` source code file or package name as input and generates detailed documentation in HTML format.

For `javadoc` to create full documentation for a program, a special type of comment statement must be used in the program's source code. Tutorial programs in this book use `//`, `/*`, and `*/` in source code to create *comments*—information for people who are trying to make sense of the program.

Java also has a more structured type of comment that can be read by the `javadoc` tool. This comment is used to describe program elements such as classes, variables, objects, and methods. It takes the following format:

```
/** A descriptive sentence or paragraph.
 * @tag1 Description of this tag.
 * @tag2 Description of this tag.
 */
```

A Java documentation comment should be placed immediately above the program element it is documenting and should succinctly explain what the program element is. For example, if the comment precedes a `class` statement, it will describe the purpose of the class.

In addition to the descriptive text, different items can be used to document the program element further. These items, called *tags,* are preceded by an @ sign and are followed by a space and a descriptive sentence or paragraph.

Listing C.3 contains a thoroughly documented version of the `AppInfo` applet called `AppInfo2`. The following tags are used in this program:

- `@author`—The program's author. This tag can be used only when documenting a class, and it will be ignored unless the `-author` option is used when `javadoc` is run.
- `@version` *text*—The program's version number. This also is restricted to class documentation, and it requires the `-version` option when you're running `javadoc` or the tag will be ignored.
- `@return` *text*—The variable or object returned by the method being documented.

- @serial *text*—A description of the data type and possible values for a variable or object that can be *serialized*, saved to disk along with the values of its variables and retrieved later.

LISTING C.3   The Full Text of AppInfo2.java

```
 1: import java.awt.*;
 2:
 3: /** This class displays the values of three parameters:
 4:    * Name, Date and Version.
 5:    * @author <a href="http://java24hours.com">Rogers Cadenhead</a>
 6:    * @version 3.0
 7:    */
 8: public class AppInfo2 extends javax.swing.JApplet {
 9:     /**
10:        * @serial The programmer's name.
11:        */
12:     String name;
13:     /**
14:        * @serial The current date.
15:        */
16:     String date;
17:     /**
18:        * @serial The program's version number.
19:        */
20:     int version;
21:
22:     /**
23:        * This method describes the applet for any browsing tool that
24:        * requests information from the program.
25:        * @return A String describing the applet.
26:        */
27:     public String getAppletInfo() {
28:         String response = "This applet demonstrates the "
29:             + "use of the Applet's Info feature.";
30:         return response;
31:     }
32:
33:     /**
34:        * This method describes the parameters that the applet can take
35:        * for any browsing tool that requests this information.
36:        * @return An array of String[] objects for each parameter.
37:        */
38:     public String[][] getParameterInfo() {
39:         String[] p1 = { "Name", "String", "Programmer's name" };
40:         String[] p2 = { "Date", "String", "Today's date" };
41:         String[] p3 = { "Version", "int", "Version number" };
42:         String[][] response = { p1, p2, p3 };
43:         return response;
```

LISTING C.3   continued

```
44:    }
45:
46:    /**
47:     * This method is called when the applet is first initialized.
48:     */
49:    public void init() {
50:        name = getParameter("Name");
51:        date = getParameter("Date");
52:        String versText = getParameter("Version");
53:        if (versText != null)
54:            version = Integer.parseInt(versText);
55:    }
56:
57:    /**
58:     * This method is called when the applet's display window is
59:     * being repainted.
60:     */
61:    public void paint(Graphics screen) {
62:        Graphics2D screen2D = (Graphics2D)screen;
63:        screen.drawString("Name: " + name, 5, 50);
64:        screen.drawString("Date: " + date, 5, 100);
65:        screen.drawString("Version: " + version, 5, 150);
66:    }
67: }
```

The following command will create HTML documentation from the source code file
AppInfo2.java:

```
javadoc -author -version AppInfo2.java
```

The Java documentation tool will create several different Web pages in the same folder
as AppInfo2.java. These pages will document the program in the same manner as Sun's
official documentation for the Java 2 class library.

> To see the official documentation for Java 2 SDK 1.4 and the Java class
> libraries, visit http://java.sun.com/j2se/1.4/docs/api/.

To see the documentation that javadoc has created for AppInfo2, load the newly created
Web page index.html on your Web browser. Figure C.4 shows this page loaded with
Internet Explorer 6.0.

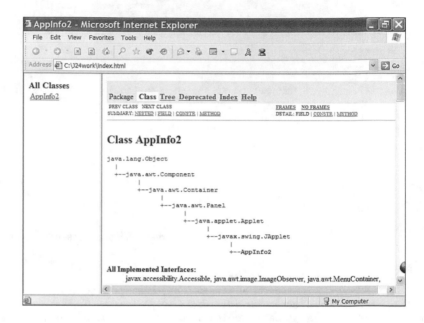

The javadoc tool produces extensively hyperlinked Web pages. Navigate through the pages to see where the information in your documentation comments and tags shows up.

If you're familiar with HTML markup, you can use HTML tags such as <A>, <TT>, and <B> within your documentation comments. Line 5 of the AppInfo2 program uses an <A> tag to turn the text "Rogers Cadenhead" into a hyperlink to this book's Web site.

The javadoc tool also can be used to document an entire package by specifying the package name as a command-line argument. HTML files will be created for each .java file in the package, along with an HTML file indexing the package.

If you would like the Java documentation to be produced in a different folder than the default, use the -d option followed by a space and the folder name.

The following command creates Java documentation for AppInfo2 in a folder called C:\JavaDocs\:

```
javadoc -author -version -d C:\JavaDocs\ AppInfo2.java
```

The following list details the other tags you can use in Java documentation comments:

- @deprecated *text*—A note that this class, method, object, or variable has been deprecated. This causes the javac compiler to issue a deprecation warning when the feature is used in a program that's being compiled.

- `@exception class description`—Used with methods that throw exceptions, this tag documents the exception's class name and its description.

- `@param name description`—Used with methods, this tag documents the name of an argument and a description of the values the argument can hold.

- `@see class`—This tag indicates the name of another class, which will be turned into a hyperlink to the Java documentation of that class. This can be used without restriction in comments.

- `@see class#method`—This tag indicates the name of a method of another class, which will be used for a hyperlink directly to the documentation of that method. This is usable without restriction.

- `@since text`—This tag indicates a note describing when a method or feature was added to its class library.

The `jar` Java File Archival Tool

When you deploy a Java program, keeping track of all the class files and other files required by the program can be cumbersome.

To make this easier, the kit includes a tool called `jar` that can pack all a program's files into a Java archive—also called a JAR file. The `jar` tool also can be used to unpack the files in one of these archives.

JAR files can be compressed using the Zip format or packed without using compression.

To use the tool, type the command **jar** followed by command-line options and a series of filenames, folder names, or wildcards.

The following command packs all a folder's class and GIF image files into a single Java archive called `Animate.jar`:

```
jar cf Animate.jar *.class *.gif
```

The argument `cf` specifies two command-line options that can be used when running the `jar` program. The `c` option indicates that a Java archive file should be created, and `f` indicates that the name of the archive file will follow as one of the next arguments.

You also can add specific files to a Java archive with a command such as the following:

```
jar cf MusicLoop.jar MusicLoop.class muskratLove.mp3 shopAround.mp3
```

This creates a `MusicLoop.jar` archive containing three files: `MusicLoop.class`, `muskratLove.mp3`, and `shopAround.mp3`.

Run `jar` without any arguments to see a list of options that can be used with the tool.

One use for `jar` is to put all files necessary to run a Java applet in a single JAR file. This makes it much easier to deploy the applet on the Web.

The standard way of placing a Java applet on a Web page is to use `<APPLET>` or `<OBJECT>` to indicate the primary class file of the applet. A Java-enabled browser then downloads and runs the applet. Any other classes and any other files needed by the applet are downloaded from the Web server.

The problem with running applets in this way is that every single file an applet requires—helper classes, images, audio files, text files, or anything else—requires a separate connection from a Web browser to the server containing the file. This can significantly increase the amount of time it takes to download an applet and everything it needs to run.

If you can reduce the number of files the browser has to load from the server by putting many files into one Java archive, your applet can be downloaded and run by a Web browser more quickly. If the files in a Java archive are compressed, it loads even more quickly.

Versions 4.0 and higher of the Microsoft Internet Explorer and Netscape Navigator Web browsers support JAR files.

After you create a Java archive, the `ARCHIVE` attribute is used with the `<APPLET>` tag to show where the archive can be found. You can use Java archives with an applet with tags such as the following:

```
<applet code="MusicLoop.class" archive="MusicLoop.jar" width=45 height=42>
</applet>
```

This tag specifies that an archive called `MusicLoop.jar` contains files used by the applet. Browsers and browsing tools that support JAR files will look inside the archive for files that are needed as the applet runs.

> Although a Java archive can contain class files, the `ARCHIVE` attribute does not remove the need for the `CODE` attribute. A browser still needs to know the name of the applet's main class file to load it.

When using an `<OBJECT>` tag to display an applet that uses a JAR file, the applet's archive file is specified as a parameter using the `<PARAM>` tag. The tag should have the name attribute "archive" and a value attribute with the name of the archive file.

The following example is a rewrite of the preceding example to use `<OBJECT>` instead of `<APPLET>`:

```
<object code="MusicLoop.class" width=45 height=42>
    <param name="archive" value="MusicLoop.jar">
</object>
```

The jdb Debugger

jdb, the Java debugger, is a sophisticated tool that helps you find and fix bugs in Java programs. You can also use it to understand better what is taking place behind the scenes in the Java interpreter as a program is running. It has a large number of features, including some that might be beyond the expertise of a Java programmer who is new to the language.

You don't need to use the debugger to debug Java programs. This is fairly obvious, especially if you've been creating your own Java programs as you read this book. After the Java compiler generates an error, the most common response is to load the source code into an editor, find the line cited in the error message, and try to spot the problem. This dreaded compile-curse-find-fix cycle is repeated until the program compiles without complaint.

After using this debugging method for a while, you might think that the debugger isn't necessary to the programming process because it's such a complicated tool to master. This reasoning makes sense when you're fixing problems that cause compiler errors. Many of these problems are simple things such as a misplaced semicolon, unmatched { and } brackets, or the use of the wrong type of data as a method argument. However, when you start looking for logic errors—more subtle bugs that don't stop the program from compiling and running—a debugger is an invaluable tool.

The Java debugger has two features that are extremely useful when you're searching for a bug that can't be found by other means: single-step execution and breakpoints. *Single-step execution* pauses a Java program after every line of code is executed. *Breakpoints* are points where execution of the program will pause. Using the Java debugger, these breakpoints can be triggered by specific lines of code, method calls, or caught exceptions.

The Java debugger works by running a program using a version of the Java interpreter that it has complete control over.

Before you use the Java debugger with a program, you will compile the program with the -g option, which causes extra information to be included in the class file. This information greatly aids in debugging. Also, you shouldn't use the -O option because its optimization techniques might produce a class file that does not directly correspond with the program's source code.

Debugging Applications

If you're debugging an application, the jdb tool can be run with a Java class as an argument. This is shown in the following:

```
jdb WriteBytes
```

This example runs the debugger with WriteBytes.class, an application that's available from the book's Web site at http://www.java24hours.com. Visit the site, select the Appendix C page, and then save the files WriteBytes.class and WriteBytes.java in the same folder that you run the debugger from.

The WriteBytes application writes a series of bytes to disk to produce the file pic.gif.

The debugger loads this program but does not begin running it, displaying the following output:

```
Initializing jdb...
>
```

The debugger is controlled by typing commands at the > prompt.

To set a breakpoint in a program, the stop in or stop at commands are used. The stop in command sets a breakpoint at the first line of a specific method in a class. You specify the class and method name as an argument to the command, as in the following hypothetical example:

```
stop in SellItem.SetPrice
```

This command sets a breakpoint at the first line of the SetPrice method. Note that no arguments or parentheses are needed after the method name.

The stop at command sets a breakpoint at a specific line number within a class. You specify the class and number as an argument to the command, as in the following example:

```
stop at WriteBytes:14
```

If you're trying this with the WriteBytes class, you'll see the following output after entering this command:

```
Deferring breakpoint WriteBytes:14
It will be set after the class is loaded.
```

You can set as many breakpoints as desired within a class. To see the breakpoints that are currently set, use the clear command without any arguments. The clear command lists all current breakpoints by line number rather than method name, even if they were set using the stop in command.

By using clear with a class name and line number as an argument, you can remove a breakpoint. If the hypothetical SellItem.SetPrice method was located at line 215 of SellItem, you can clear this breakpoint with the following command:

```
clear SellItem:215
```

Within the debugger, you can begin executing a program with the run command. The following output shows what the debugger displays after you begin running the WriteBytes class:

```
run WriteBytes
VM Started: Set deferred breakpoint WriteBytes:14

Breakpoint hit: "thread=main", WriteBytes.main(), line=14 bci=413
14                    for (int i = 0; i < data.length; i++)
```

After you have reached a breakpoint in the WriteBytes class, experiment with the following commands:

- list—At the point where execution stopped, this command displays the source code of the line and several lines around it. This requires access to the .java file of the class where the breakpoint has been hit, so that you must have WriteBytes.java in either the current folder or one of the folders in your CLASS-PATH.
- locals—This command lists the values for local variables that are currently in use or will soon be defined.
- print text—This command displays the value of the variable, object, or array element specified by text.
- step—This command executes the next line and stops again.
- cont—This command continues running the program at the point it was halted.
- !!—This command repeats the previous debugger command.

After trying out these commands within the application, you can resume running the program by clearing the breakpoint and using the cont command. Use the exit command to end the debugging session.

The WriteBytes application creates a file called pic.gif. You can verify that this file ran successfully by loading it with a Web browser or image-editing software. You'll see a small letter J in black and white.

After you have finished debugging a program and you're satisfied that it works correctly, recompile it without the -g option.

Debugging Applets

You can't debug an applet by loading it using the jdb tool. Instead, use the -debug option of the appletviewer, as in the following example:

```
appletviewer -debug AppInfo.html
```

This will load the Java debugger, and when you use a command such as run, the appletviewer will begin running also. Try out this example to see how these tools interact with each other.

Before you use the run command to execute the applet, set a breakpoint in the program at the first line of the getAppletInfo method. Use the following command:

```
stop in AppInfo.getAppletInfo
```

After you begin running the applet, the breakpoint won't be hit until you cause the getAppletInfo() method to be called. This is accomplished by selecting Applet, Info from the appletviewer's menu.

Advanced Debugging Commands

With the features you have learned about so far, you can use the debugger to stop execution of a program and learn more about what's taking place. This might be sufficient for many of your debugging tasks, but the debugger also offers many other commands. These include the following:

- up—This command moves up the stack frame, so that you can use locals and print to examine the program at the point before the current method was called.
- down—This command moves down the stack frame to examine the program after the method call.

In a Java program, often there are places where a chain of methods is called. One method calls another method, which calls another method, and so on. At each point where a method is being called, Java keeps track of all the objects and variables within that scope by grouping them together. This grouping is called a *stack*, as if you were stacking these objects such as a deck of cards. The various stacks in existence as a program runs are called the *stack frame*.

By using up and down along with commands such as locals, you can better understand how the code that calls a method interacts with that method.

You can also use the following commands within a debugging session:

- classes—This command lists the classes currently loaded into memory.
- methods—This command lists the methods of a class.
- memory—This command shows the total amount of memory and the amount that isn't currently in use.
- threads—This command lists the threads that are executing.

The threads command numbers all the threads, which enables you to use the suspend command followed by that number to pause the thread, as in suspend 1. You can resume a thread by using the resume command followed by its number.

Another convenient way to set a breakpoint in a Java program is to use the catch *text* command, which pauses execution when the Exception class named by *text* is caught.

You can also cause an exception to be ignored by using the ignore *text* command with the Exception class named by *text*.

Using System Properties

One obscure feature of the SDK is that the command-line option -D can modify the performance of the Java class library.

If you have used other programming languages prior to learning Java, you might be familiar with environment variables, which provide information about the operating system in which a program is running. An example is the CLASSPATH setting, which indicates the folders in which the Java interpreter should look for a class file.

Because different operating systems have different names for their environment variables, they cannot be read directly by a Java program. Instead, Java includes a number of different system properties that are available on any platform with a Java implementation.

Some properties are used only to get information. The following system properties are among those that should be available on any Java implementation:

- java.version—The version number of the Java interpreter
- java.vendor—A string identifying the vendor associated with the Java interpreter
- os.name—The operating system in use
- os.version—The version number of that operating system

Other properties can affect how the Java class library performs when being used inside a Java program. An example of this is the `java.io.tmpdir` property, which defines the folder that Java's input and output classes use as a temporary workspace.

A property can be set at the command line by using the –D option followed by the property name, an equal sign, and the new value of the property, as in this command:

```
java -Djava.io.tmpdir="C:\javatemp" Auctioneer
```

The use of the system property in this example will cause the `Auctioneer` application to use the `C:\javatemp` folder as the temporary folder for files created during file input and output.

You also can create your own properties and read them using the `getProperty()` method of the `System` class, which is part of the `java.lang` package.

Listing C.4 contains the source code of a simple program that displays the value of a user-created property.

LISTING C.4   The Full Text of `ItemProp.java`

```
1: class ItemProp {
2:     public static void main(String[] arguments) {
3:         String n = System.getProperty("item.name");
4:         System.out.println("The item is named " + n);
5:     }
6: }
```

If this program is run without setting the `item.name` property on the command line, the output is the following:

```
The item is named null
```

The `item.name` property can be set using the –D option, as in this command:

```
java -Ditem.name="Microsoft Bob" ItemProp
```

The output is the following:

```
The item is named Microsoft Bob
```

The –D option is used with the Java interpreter. To use it with the `appletviewer` as well, all you have to do differently is precede the –D with -J. The following command shows how this can be done:

```
appletviewer -J-Djava.io.tmpdir="C:\javatemp" AuctionSite.html
```

This example causes `appletviewer` to use the `C:\javatemp` folder as the temporary file input/output folder.

Summary

This appendix explores several features of the SDK that are increasingly helpful as you develop more experience with Java:

- Using the Java debugger with applets and applications
- Creating an optimized version of a compiled class
- Writing applet methods that provide information to a browser upon request
- Using the Java documentation creation tool to describe a class, its methods, and other aspects of the program fully

C

These SDK features weren't required during the 24 hours of this book because of the relative simplicity of the tutorial programs. Although it can be complicated to develop a Swing application or to work with threads and streams for the first time, your biggest challenge lies ahead: integrating concepts such as these into more sophisticated Java programs.

Tools such as `javadoc` and the debugger really come into their own on complex projects. When a bug occurs because of how two classes interact with each other, or similar subtle logic errors creep into your code, a debugger is the best way to identify and repair the problems. As you create an entire library of classes, `javadoc` can easily document these classes and show how they are interrelated.

Q&A

Q The official Java documentation is filled with long paragraphs that describe classes and methods. How can these be produced using `javadoc`?

A In the Java documentation creator, there's no limit to the length of a description. Although they're often as brief as a sentence or two, they can be longer if necessary. End the description with a period, immediately followed by a new line with a tag of some kind or the end of the comment.

Q **Do I have to document everything in my Java classes if I'm planning to use the `javadoc` tool?**

A The Java documentation creator will work fine no matter how many or how few comments you use. Deciding what elements of the program need to be documented is up to you. You probably should describe the class and all methods, variables, and objects that aren't hidden from other classes.

The `javadoc` tool will display a warning each time a serializable object or variable is defined in a program without a corresponding Java documentation comment.

APPENDIX D

Using Sun ONE Studio

For most of Java's existence, programmers have learned the language using the Software Development Kit (SDK) from Sun Microsystems, a set of command-line tools used to create Java programs, described in Appendices B and C.

The kit is highly popular, but it lacks some features most professional programmers take for granted—such as a built-in text editor, graphical user interface, and project management tools. These features, which are essential for everyday programming, are typically supplied in an integrated development environment (IDE).

One IDE you can choose for creating Java software is Sun ONE Studio, also offered by Sun Microsystems.

This appendix covers how to download and install Sun ONE Studio and use it to create, compile, and run a simple Java program.

Choosing a Java Development Tool

Several different integrated development environments are available for Java programming.

Sun ONE Studio includes tools you will use all the time: A text editor, graphical user interface designer, Web page editor, file archival tool, and project manager.

The IDE also includes tools that aren't essential now, as you're getting started with the language, but could become indispensable later, including a debugger, Java servlet and JavaServer Pages editing and testing tool, and JDBC database connection developer.

There are three versions of Sun ONE Studio:

- The Community Edition, available for free from Sun's Web site.
- The Mobile Edition, a free version that supports the Java 2 Platform Micro Edition (J2ME), a different version for personal digital assistants, smart cards, mobile phones, and other off-the-desktop technology.
- The Enterprise Edition, which currently sells for $1,995 (or $995 if you bought a past edition of Forte for Java or recent versions of Borland JBuilder, IBM VisualAge for Java, Microsoft Visual Basic, or WebGain Visual Café).

As you might expect from the price, the Enterprise Edition is targeted at professional Java programmers doing large-scale development for corporate and government enterprises.

The Community Edition contains most of the functionality of the Enterprise Edition—including everything you'll need to complete the tutorials in this book.

Sun ONE Studio supports Java 2 version 1.4 (and can be configured to support other versions), so you can continue using it as Sun releases new versions of Java.

Installing Sun ONE Studio

Sun ONE Studio, formerly known as Forte for Java, is available at several different places on Sun's Web site. To see what versions are available for download, visit the Web page http://forte.sun.com/ffj/downloads/.

The Downloads page includes the Community, Micro, and Enterprise editions of Sun ONE Studio along with dozens of add-on programs that enhance the functionality of the software.

To use Sun ONE Studio, you must also install a compatible version of the Java 2 Software Development Kit. The easiest way to do this is to download and install a version of Sun ONE Studio Community Edition that includes the SDK.

On the Sun ONE Studio downloads page, this product is currently being called the Community Edition, release 4—J2SE 1.4 Cobundle.

> By the time you visit the page, the name of this product may be different because of Sun's penchant for giving things laboriously complicated names and changing them around from time to time (something the author of this book has no business mocking). Anything that's called a Community Edition "Cobundle" is probably what you need.

The Sun ONE Studio cobundle is currently available for the following platforms:

- Windows XP, 98, NT, 2000 (with Service Pack 2)
- Solaris SPARC and Intel
- Linux

The Windows and Linux versions of Sun ONE Studio require a computer with a Pentium III processor that is 500 MHz or faster, 125MB of free disk space, and 256MB of memory.

> There is no Macintosh version of Sun ONE Studio, but the Solaris version runs on Mac OS X. Apple offers a free version of the SDK and a Project Builder integrated development environment. To find out more about Apple's Java programming tools, visit the Web site http://devworld.apple.com/java/.
>
> If you're using another platform, you can check to see whether it has a tool that supports Java 1.4 by visiting Sun's site at http://java.sun.com/cgi-bin/java-ports.cgi/.

To set up Sun ONE Studio, you must download and run an installation program (or install it from a CD). After you have downloaded the file, you're ready to set it up on your system.

Running the Installation Wizard

Before installing the Studio/SDK cobundle, you must remove any version of the kit that's presently installed on your system. Otherwise, Sun ONE Studio may have trouble finding the kit and using it to perform some of its tasks.

To set up the software on a Windows system, double-click the installation file icon or click Start, Run from the Windows taskbar to find and run the file.

An installation wizard will guide you through the process of setting up the software. If you accept Sun's terms and conditions for using Sun ONE Studio and a second set of terms and conditions for the SDK, you'll be asked where to install the program, as shown in Figure D.1.

FIGURE **D.1**

Choosing a destination folder for Sun ONE Studio and the SDK.

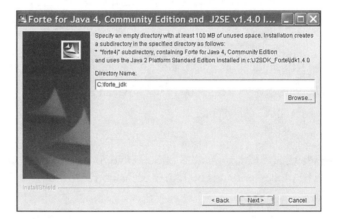

The wizard will suggest a folder where the cobundle should be installed. In Figure D.1, the wizard is suggesting the folder C:\forte_jdk.

If you want to pick a different folder, click Browse and use the Windows file open dialog box to select a location.

Click the Next button to review the folder where Sun ONE Studio and the kit will be installed. If it's acceptable, click Next to install the software and add Sun ONE Studio to your Start menu.

Configuring Sun ONE Studio

The first time you run Sun ONE Studio, you'll be asked several questions about how to configure the software.

Although the name of the software has been changed to Sun ONE Studio on Sun's Web site, at the time of this writing the version of the software available on the site hasn't been updated to reflect the name change. It still is titled Forte for Java.

To run the program:

- On Windows XP, choose Start, All Programs, Forte for Java 4.0 CE, Forte for Java CE.

- On other Windows systems, choose Start, Programs, Forte for Java 4.0 CE, Forte for Java CE.

The first question you're asked is where to store your programming projects (Figure D.2).

FIGURE D.2

Choosing a work folder for your Sun ONE Studio projects.

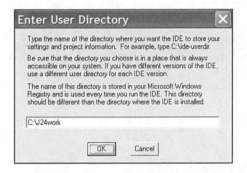

The folder you choose should not be the folder where Sun ONE Studio was installed. In Figure D.2, I've chosen `C:\J24work`.

Next, you are asked whether you want to import settings from a previous installation of Forte or NetBeans 3.0 or 3.1. Choose an option using the Yes or No radio button and click Next to import settings, or Finish if you have no settings to import.

> After deciding whether to import settings, you may see an error message about a disk drive. During installation on a Windows XP system, an error dialog opened with this message: "There is no disk in the drive. Please insert a disk into drive `\Device\Harddisk1\DR1`."
>
> This appears to be a bug in the installation program rather than a problem that prevents the software from installing correctly. Click Continue to close the dialog and continue setting up Sun ONE Studio.

A setup wizard opens so that you can finish configuring the software (Figure D.3).

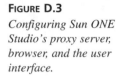

FIGURE D.3

Configuring Sun ONE Studio's proxy server, browser, and the user interface.

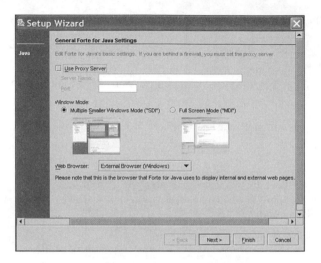

The default settings are as follows, shown in Figure D.3:

- Don't use a proxy server.
- Open different Sun ONE Studio projects in the same window—a feature also known as a *single document interface (SDI).*
- Use the system's default Web browser to test Java applets.

These settings will be fine for most new users getting started with Sun ONE Studio, unless you're in a corporate or academic environment where you must use a firewall to connect to the Internet. In that case, enable the Use Proxy Server checkbox and provide the server name and port of your Internet firewall. Click Next to continue.

The wizard will tell you to click Next for advanced setup options or click Finish. Using the advanced options, you can choose what Sun ONE Studio modules to install (rather than accepting the default set of modules) and set up automatic software updates. If you're using Sun ONE Studio primarily to learn Java, you probably should skip the advanced setup at this point.

After you complete installation and click Finish, you'll be asked to register the software over the Internet.

Creating a Sample Program

Now that you have installed Sun ONE Studio and set up the software, you're ready to use it in the creation of a sample Java program.

If you have never used an integrated development environment before, you're likely to be a little shell-shocked when you close the software's Welcome window and see Sun ONE Studio for the first time. There are more than a hundred menu commands, toolbar buttons, and other interface components at your disposal.

Most IDEs are designed to make experienced programmers more productive rather than to help new programmers learn a language. Sun ONE Studio is no exception.

It can be difficult to learn how to use an IDE at the same time you are learning Java. This is probably the biggest selling point for the Java 2 Software Development Kit—you can start using it quickly by learning a few simple text commands.

However, if you'd like to make use of the power and convenience of Sun ONE Studio while learning Java, this section and some supplementary reading will be enough to get started.

In this section, you'll create a short Java application and run it, displaying the output of the program.

To start, create a new project in Sun ONE Studio by selecting the menu command File, New. The New Template Wizard opens (Figure D.4).

FIGURE D.4

Selecting the template for a new project in Sun ONE Studio.

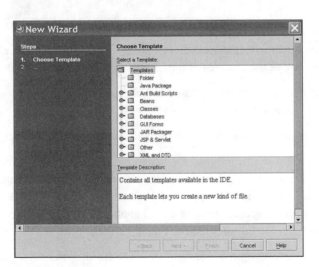

Sun ONE Studio offers templates for the most common programming projects you will undertake. Your first project is to create an application, which can be done with the Main template. In the Select a Template window, double-click the Classes folder to open it and choose the Main template.

In the Template Description text area, the wizard describes the template you have chosen. Click the Next button to confirm your choice.

The next step is to choose a name for the application and a place where its files will be stored (Figure D.5).

FIGURE D.5

Entering the name for a new project in Sun ONE Studio.

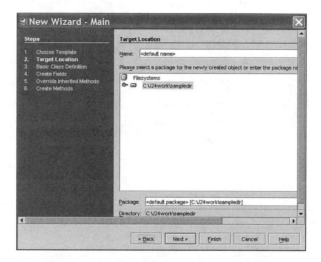

When you create a Java class, you can make it part of a group of classes by putting it in a package—one of the features of the language you learned about during Part III.

The wizard suggests a default name and package for your new project, using the work folder you specified the first time you ran the software.

Enter the text HelloUser in the Name field and accept the package suggested by the wizard.

At this point, you can click Next to set up more aspects of the program. However, because this project is so simple, you don't need to do that—click Finish. Sun ONE Studio creates the source code for a Java application called HelloUser and opens it for editing in a Source Editor window (Figure D.6).

All Java programs begin as source code—a series of statements created using a text editor and saved as a text file.

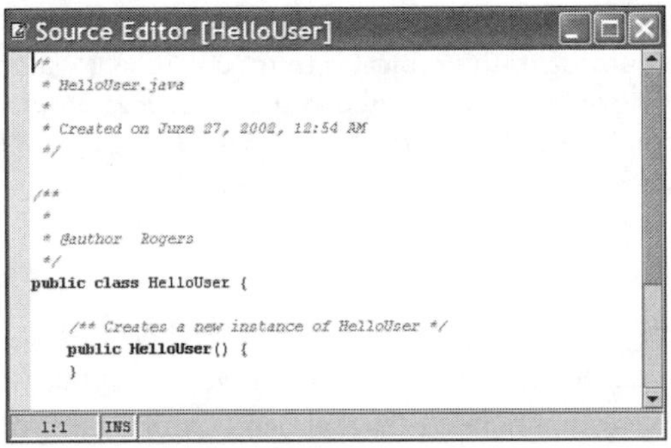

FIGURE D.6

The Source Editor window in Sun ONE Studio.

The Sun ONE Studio Source Editor window numbers lines along the left edge of the window. When you create the HelloUser project, it contains the following Java statements as Lines 20–21:

```
public static void main (String[] args) {
}
```

Insert a blank line between these two lines and enter the following statements at that place in the file:

```
String username = System.getProperty("user.name");
System.out.println("Hello, " + username);
```

When you're done, Lines 20–23 should be the same as Listing D.1. Make sure all the parentheses, braces, and quotation marks in the listing are entered correctly and capitalize everything in the program exactly as shown.

LISTING D.1 Partial Source Code of the HelloUser Program

```
20:    public static void main (String[] args) {
21:        String username = System.getProperty("user.name");
22:        System.out.println("Hello, " + username);
23:    }
```

The line numbers and colons along the left side of Listing D.1 are not part of the program—they're included, so that I can refer to specific lines by number in this book. If you're ever unsure about the source code of a program in this book, you can compare it to a copy on the book's official World Wide Web site at the following address:

```
http://www.java24hours.com
```

After you finish typing in the program, save the project by choosing the menu command File, Save.

The purpose of this project is to try out Sun ONE Studio—none of the Java programming concepts used in the HelloUser program are described in this appendix. You'll learn the basics of the language on Hour 2, "Writing Your First Program."

Running the Program

When you save source code, Sun ONE Studio saves it in your work folder and then compiles it, creating one or more class files that can be run by a Java interpreter.

To run the program, right-click the HelloUser icon in the Explorer window (Figure D.7) and choose Execute.

FIGURE D.7

Running a Java application in Sun ONE Studio.

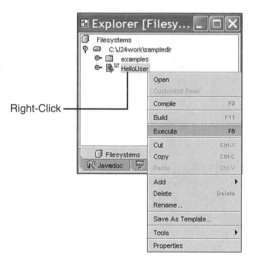

Right-Click

Figure D.8 shows the successful output of the HelloUser application: the text "Hello," followed by your name—or at least what your system believes it to be.

Additional Help for Beginners

Sun Microsystems offers a two resources for beginning Sun ONE Studio users in the developer resources section of the Studio Web site: the *Community Edition Getting Started Guide* and the *Community Edition Tutorial*.

FIGURE D.8

Viewing the output of the HelloUser *application.*

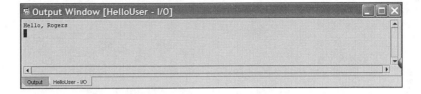

To find this tutorial and other online help, visit `http://forte.sun.com/ffj/documentation/`. It's a good idea to read these before starting this book—assuming you read this appendix first, of course.

This book has a Web site where you can find solutions to problems, corrections, answers to reader questions, and other useful material.

The site is available at `http://www.java24hours.com/`.

D

APPENDIX E

Where to Go from Here: Java Resources

After you have finished this book, you might be wondering where you can go to improve your Java programming skills. This appendix lists some books, World Wide Web sites, Internet discussion groups, and other resources that you can use to expand your Java knowledge.

Other Books to Consider

Sams publishes several books on Java programming topics, including many that follow up on the material covered in this book. The following list includes ISBN numbers, which will be needed at bookstores if they don't currently carry the book that you're looking for:

- *Sams Teach Yourself Java 2 in 21 Days, Third Edition*, by Rogers Cadenhead (me! me! me!) and Laura Lemay. ISBN: 0-67232-370-2. Though some of the material in the first two weeks of this book will be redundant, it's covered in more depth and adds a lot of advanced topics. If you're ready to make another 504-hour commitment to learning Java, this may be a suitable book.

- *Sams Teach Yourself J2EE in 21 Days* by Martin Bond and others. ISBN: 0-67232-384-2. A tutorial for Java developers who want to use the Java 2 Enterprise Edition (J2EE).

- *JXTA: Java P2P Programming* by Daniel Brookshier and others. ISBN: 0-67232-366-4. An introduction to Sun Microsystem's JXTA classes, which support peer-to-peer networked programming.

- *MySQL and JSP Web Applications: Data-Driven Programming Using Tomcat and MySQL* by James Turner. ISBN: 0-67232-309-5. Advice and programming tutorials for JavaServer Pages programmers using the MySQL database with their Web applications.

- *Developing Java Servlets, Second Edition,* by James Goodwill and Samir Mehta. ISBN: 0-67232-107-6. A tutorial on Java servlet and JavaServer Pages programming and how to use them with XML, Enterprise Java Beans, and the Java 2 Enterprise Edition.

- *Jini and JavaSpaces Application Development* by Robert Flenner. ISBN: 0-67232-258-7. A guide to wireless networked programming using Jini, Sun's technology for connecting different disconnected devices using Java.

Chapters and other material from many Sams Java books have been made available for free on the World Wide Web at InformIT, a Web site for information technology professionals produced in collaboration with Sams at `http://www.informit.com`.

InformIT also includes chapters from upcoming books, a Linux resource called InfoBase, and new articles by computer book authors and IT professionals.

The Sams Publishing Web site, `http://www.samspublishing.com`, includes an online catalog, a list of upcoming releases, and links to author Web sites. It's a good place to see what's coming up from Sams and other parts of the Pearson Technology Group.

Sun's Official Java Site

The Java software division of Sun Microsystems Inc. maintains an active Web site at `http://java.sun.com`.

This site is the first place to visit when looking for Java-related information. New versions of the Java 2 Software Development Kit and other programming resources are available for downloading, along with documentation for the entire Java class library (and lots and lots of enthusiastic Sun press releases).

The site offers the following features:

- Products and APIs—Development tools, Java class libraries, and new Java technologies can be downloaded from the Java division, including the Software Development Kit, language documentation, and more than 50 other products and new Java class libraries. (API is an acronym for Application Programming Interface, which in Java is simply another term for a class library.)

- Developer services—Technical information of interest to Java programmers, including complete documentation for the Java class library in HTML format. After you register for a free developer account, you can find information on language conferences, a searchable database of Java bug reports, and a discussion forum for Java developers and people learning the language.

- Documentation and training—Thousands of pages of free documentation and tutorials covering the Software Development Kit, the Java class library for Java 2 version 1.4 and all previous versions, and information on Sun's official Java books.

- Online support—Technical support, customer service, and sales assistance for purchasers of Java products and users of Java development tools.

- Community discussion—The site offers a large number of Web-based discussion areas on topics for beginners and experienced pros alike. Sun gives out prizes for participants who earn the most "Duke Dollars," which are given out by members of the discussion community when someone provides helpful information.

- Industry news—Announcements related to upcoming product releases and Java-related events such as JavaOne, the yearly conferences for Java programmers held in San Francisco and Japan. There are also press releases from Sun's Java software division and "success stories," examples of how the language is being used professionally.

- Solutions marketplace—A database of information about products and services of interest to Java developers. If you're shopping for JavaBeans components, development tools, consultants, or new class libraries, you can find them here.

The site is continually updated with free resources useful to Java programmers.

E

Java 2 Version 1.4 Class Documentation

Perhaps the most useful part of Sun's Java site is the documentation for every class, variable, and method in Java 2's class library. Thousands of pages are online at no cost to show you how to use the classes in your programs.

To visit the class documentation for Java 2 version 1.4, visit the Web page at `http://java.sun.com/j2se/1.4/docs/api/`.

Other Java Web Sites

Because so much of the Java phenomenon was originally inspired by its use on Web pages, a large number of Web sites focus on Java and Java programming.

This Book's Official Site

This book has an official Web site at `http://www.java24hours.com` that is described fully in Appendix F, "This Book's Web Site."

Café au Lait

Elliotte Rusty Harold, the author of several excellent books on Java programming, offers Café au Lait, a frequently updated weblog covering Java news, product releases, and other sites of interest to programmers. The site is an invaluable resource for people interested in Java and is published at `http://www.ibiblio.org/javafaq/`. Harold also offers a list of frequently asked questions related to Java, as well as some unofficial documentation compiled by programmers over the past several years.

Workbench

I also publish a weblog named Workbench that covers Java, Internet technology, computer books, and similar topics. Though I won't go as far as calling it an "invaluable resource," I'm pretty sure that my mother would. It's published at `http://workbench.cadenhead.info`.

Java Review Service

The Java Review Service reviews new programs, components, and tools that are published on the Web, recognizing some as "Top 1%," "Top 5%," or "Top 25%." Resources are also categorized by topic, with a description of each resource and links to download the source code, if it is available. To access the Java Review Service (JARS) Web site, which is another directory that rates Java applets, direct your Web browser to `http://www.jars.com`.

JavaWorld Magazine

One of the best magazines that serves the Java programming community is also the cheapest. *JavaWorld* is available for free on the World Wide Web at http://www. javaworld.com. *JavaWorld* publishes frequent tutorial articles along with Java development news and other features, which are updated monthly.

Gamelan: Earthweb's Java Directory

Because Java is an object-oriented language that offers JavaBeans as a means to create self-contained programming components, it's easy to use resources created by other developers in your own programs. Before you start a Java project of any significance, you should scan the World Wide Web for resources that you might be able to use in your program.

A good place to start is Gamelan, Earthweb's Java directory. This site catalogs Java programs, programming resources, and other information at http://softwaredev. earthweb.com/java.

Lists of Java Books

Those of us who write Java books like to think that you're forsaking all others by choosing our work. However, anecdotal studies (and the number of Java books on our shelves) indicate that you might benefit from other books devoted to the language.

The previously mentioned Elliotte Rusty Harold maintains a list of Java- and JavaScript-related books at http://www.ibiblio.org/javafaq/books.html.

E

Java Newsgroups

One of the best resources for both novice and experienced Java programmers is Usenet, the international network of discussion groups that is available to most Internet users through either an Internet service provider or a news service, such as Google Groups (http://groups.google.com/) or NewsGuy (http://www.newsguy.com). The following are descriptions of some of the Java discussion groups that are available on Usenet:

- comp.lang.java.programmer—Because this group is devoted to questions and answers related to Java programming, it is the place for all subjects that don't belong in one of the other groups. Any Java-related topic is suitable for discussion here.

- `comp.lang.java.advocacy`—This group is devoted to any Java discussions that are likely to inspire heated or comparative debate. If you want to argue the merits of Java against another language, this is the place for it. This group can be a good place to consult if you want to see whether Java is the right choice for a project that you're working on.

- `comp.lang.java.announce`—This group, which has been inactive in recent years, is a place to read announcements, advertisements, and press releases of interest to the Java development community. It is moderated, so all postings must be submitted for approval before they are posted to the group.

- `comp.lang.java.beans`—This group is devoted to discussions related to JavaBeans programming, announcements of Beans that have been made available, and similar topics concerning component software development.

- `comp.lang.java.corba`—This advanced discussion group is devoted to Java-language implementations of CORBA, the Common Object Request Broker Architecture.

- `comp.lang.java.databases`—This group is used for talk related to JDBC, the Java Database Connectivity Libraries, and other solutions for connecting Java programs to databases.

- `comp.lang.java.gui`—This group is devoted to the Abstract Windowing Toolkit, Swing, and other graphical user interface class libraries and development tools.

- `comp.lang.java.help`—This group provides a place to discuss installation problems related to Java programming tools and similar issues that bedevil beginners.

- `comp.lang.java.machine`—The most advanced of the Java discussion groups, this group is devoted to discussing the implementation of the language, issues with porting it to new machines, the specifics of the Java virtual machine, and similar subjects.

- `comp.lang.java.programmer`—This group contains questions and answers related to Java programming, which makes it another good place for new programmers to frequent.

- `comp.lang.java.security`—This discussion group is devoted to security issues related to Java, especially in regard to running Java programs and other executable content on the World Wide Web.

Job Opportunities

If you're one of those folks who is learning Java as a part of your plan to become a captain of industry, several of the resources listed in this appendix have a section devoted to job opportunities. Check out some of the Java-related job openings that may be available.

If you are interested in joining Sun's Java division itself, visit `http://java.sun.com/jobs`.

Although it isn't specifically a Java employment resource, the World Wide Web site Careerbuilder.com enables you to search the job classifieds of more than two dozen job databases, including newspaper classifieds and many other sources. You have to register to use the site, but it's free, and there are more than 100,000 job postings that you can search using keywords such as *Java* or *Internet* or *snake charmer*. Go to `http://www.careerbuilder.com`.

E

APPENDIX F

This Book's Web Site

As much as I would like to think otherwise, there are undoubtedly some things you're not clear about after completing the 24 hours of this book.

Programming is a specialized technical field that throws strange concepts and jargon at you, such as "instantiation," "ternary operators," and "big- and little-endian byte order." Some of these concepts are pretty big, and when they hit you, it hurts.

If you're unclear about any of the topics covered in the book, or if I was unclear about a topic (shrug), visit the book's Web site at `http://www.java24hours.com` for assistance.

I use the book's Web site to offer each of the following:

- Error corrections and clarifications: When errors are brought to my attention, they will be described on the site with the corrected text and any other material that will help.

- Answers to reader questions: If readers have questions that aren't covered in this book's Q&A sections, many will be presented on the site.

- The source code, class files, and working applets for all programs you create during the 24 hours of this book.
- Sample Java programs: Working versions of some programs featured in this book are available on the site.
- Solutions, including source code, for activities suggested at the end of each hour.
- Updated links to the sites mentioned in this book: If sites mentioned in the book have changed addresses and I know about the new URL, I'll offer it here.

You also can send email to me by visiting the book's site. Click the Feedback link and you'll be taken to a page where you can send email directly from the Web.

This doesn't have to be said, as I learned from past editions of this book, but I'll say it anyway: Feel free to voice all opinions, positive, negative, indifferent, or undecided.

I have been a user of the Internet and online services long enough to have my parentage questioned in seven spoken languages and one particularly memorable nonverbal one. Any criticism you send will be interpreted as "tough love," and nothing you say could be rougher than what my music teacher said after my audition for the lead in the Yale Elementary School production of *Jesus Christ Superstar*.

Rogers Cadenhead

INDEX

H

I

Hey, you've got enough worries.

Don't let IT training be one of them.

Get on the fast track to IT training at InformIT,
your total Information Technology training network.

 | **www.informit.com** | **SAMS**

■ Hundreds of timely articles on dozens of topics ■ Discounts on IT books from all our publishing partners, including Sams Publishing ■ Free, unabridged books from the InformIT Free Library ■ "Expert Q&A"—our live, online chat with IT experts ■ Faster, easier certification and training from our Web- or classroom-based training programs ■ Current IT news ■ Software downloads ■ Career-enhancing resources